The Jews in Christian Art

The Jews
in Christian Art

An Illustrated History

Heinz Schreckenberg

CONTINUUM · NEW YORK

1996
The Continuum Publishing Company
370 Lexington Avenue
New York, NY 10017

Translated from the German *Die Juden in der Kunst Europas. Ein Bildatlas,*
published 1996 by Vandenhoeck & Ruprecht, Göttingen.

Copyright © Vandenhoeck & Ruprecht 1996

Translation © John Bowden 1996

Printed in Great Britain

Library of Congress Cataloging-in-Publication Data
Schreckenberg, Heinz.
  [Juden in der Kunst Europas.   English]
  The Jews in Christian art: an illustrated history/Heinz
Schreckenberg.
    p.   cm.
  Includes bibliographical references and index.
  ISBN 0–8264–0936–9
    1. Jews in art.   2. Christian art and symbolism——Europe.   3. Art.
European.   I. Title.
N7942.S3713   1996
704.9'4990904924——dc20   96–42107
                                                                  CIP

Contents

Preface

The collection of pictures presented here has been made gradually over the course of around twenty years. To begin, with the pictures were used at lectures in the Institutum Judaicum Delitzschianum at the University of Münster, since it became evident that while important features and motivating factors of the history of Christian-Jewish relations could be discovered from textual sources, they could often be understood better by the introduction of relevant pictures. Not only did the pictures have a direct use, but in the long run they also became a strong personal interest. So I was concerned to complete collections once they had begun.

My efforts in this direction were encouraged in particular by D.-A.Koch and H.Lichtenberger, the directors of the Institute. I also received stimulation and suggestions from students, colleagues and friends: here special mention should be made of D.Aschoff, G.Jászai, R.Kampling, H.Lichtenberger and S.Waldhoff. Henrik Hansen contributed most to the completion of the work by his advice and activity. I also had some help from the staff of the manuscript room of the University Library of Münster and the central photographic laboratory of the university. I am deeply grateful to all concerned.

It is above thanks to the strong interest of H.Lichtenberger that the collection, something of a side–interest over a long period, has finally become a book. On the publishing side, Dr A. Ruprecht and Frau R. Hartog advised me on the preparation of the manuscript and gave the work the form in which it now appears.

An undertaking of this kind is impossible without interregional and international co-operation, so I must thank many people in libraries, museums, archives and publishing houses for making the illustrated matter available, giving permission for the inclusion of the pictures, and helping with information and suggestions of one kind or another. In particular, mention must be made at this point of the institutions in:

Aachen: Suermondt–Ludwig Museum (Dr U.Schneider)
Amiens: Bibliothèque municipale (C.Carrier)
Augsburg: Universitätsbibliothek (Dr P.B.Rupp); Staats- und Stadtbibliothek (Finkl); Maximilianmuseum and Diözesanbauamt (Amt für Bauwesen und sakrale Kunst) (Dr N.Leudemann)
Bamberg: Staatsbibliothek, Historisches Museum (L.Hennig)
Basel: Öffentliche Bibliothek der Universität Basel (Dr M.Steinmann); Öffentliche Kunstsammlung Basel, Kunstmuseum and Kupferstichkabinett (F.Heuss); Birkhäuser Verlag (H.Sieber)
Berlin: Staatsbibliothek zu Berlin Preussischer Kulturbesitz: manuscripts (C.Dickmann); engravings (E.Küster); sculpture (Dr Lindemann, R.Schenck); art historical archive (K.Holland); Koehler & Amelang Buchverlag Union (G.Stoerk); Aufbau Verlag Ruetten & Loening (P.Dempewolf)
Bern: Burgerbibliothek
Besançon: Bibliothèque municipale
Beuron: Beuroner Kunstverlag (L.Kruthoff)
Bonn: Rheinisches Landesmuseum (Dr. I Krueger)
Brandenburg/Havel: Domstiftsarchif (Schössler)
Bruges: Grootseminarie (J.Bonny); Stedelijke Musea (Dr V.Vermeersch)
Brussels: Bibliothèque Royale Albert Ier. Cabinet des manuscrits (E.Defrene)
Cambridge: Corpus Christi College. The Parker Library
Chantilly: Musée Condé (A.Lefébure)
Cividale del Friuli (Udine): Museo Archeologico Nazionale (Dr P.Lopreato)
Cologne: Universitäts- und Stadtbibliothek (John); Museen der Stadt Köln, Rheinisches Bildarchiv (Dr R.Neu-Kock)
Constance: Rosgartenmuseum (U.Benkö)
Copenhagen: Det Kongelige Bibliotek, Handskriftenafdelingen (P.Ringsted); Nationalmuseet (A.H.Nielsen, P.Grinder-Hansen)
Darmstadt: Hessisches Landesmuseum (Dr T.Jülich); Hessische Landes- und Hochschulbibliothek, Handschriften- und Inkunabelabteilung (I.Bröning); Wissen-

schaftliche Buchgesellschaft (F.Ludolph)

Deggendorf: Stadtmuseum (B.Petschek–Sommer)

Donaueschingen: Ehemaliger Fürstlich-Fürstenbergischer Besitz (court library)

Dorsten: Jüdisches Museum Westfalen (W.Stegemann); Prof Dr G.Kreytenberg

Dortmund: Museum für Kunst- und Kulturgeschichte (W.E.Weick)

Douai: Bibliothèque municipale

Dresden: Sächsische Landesbibliothek. Abteilung Deutsche Fotothek

Eisenstadt: Edition Roetzer

Erfurt: Angermuseum (K.Anglet)

Florence: Museo Nazionale del Bargello; Fratelli Alinari (Archivi Alinari S.p A.)

Frankfurt: Historisches Museum (Dr R.Koch); Insel Verlag (M.Reiner)

Freckenhorst: Katholische Kirchengemeinde St Bonifatius (Pfarrdechant Schüller)

Freiburg im Breisgau: Universitätsbibliothek (Dr W.Hagenmaier); Stadtarchiv (Hefele, Dr Schadek); Verlag Herder (S.Dalmühle)

Fribourg (Switzerland): Museum für Kunst und Geschichte (R.Blanchard)

Fulda: Hessische Landesbibliothek

Ghent: Rijksuniversiteit. Centraale Bibliotheek, Afdeling der Handschriften en kostbare werken (Prof. Dr A.Derolez)

Graz: Universitätsbibliothek. Abteilung für Sondersammlungen (Dr H.Zotter); Akademische Druck und Verlagsanstalt (Dr M.Kramer)

Halberstadt: Evangelische Stadt- und Domgemeinde, Domschatzverwaltung (Domkustos Leuschner)

Halle a.d.Saale: Prof. Dr H.L.Nickel

Hamburg: Staats- und Universitätsbibliothek Hamburg Carl von Ossietzky (E.Horváth); Hamburger Kunsthalle (Dr G.Syamken, Beckmann, E.Walford); Verlag Rogner & Bernard

Hanover: Niedersächsisches Landesmuseum (C.Tintemann); Kestner Museum (Dr H.Hilschenz-Mlynek)

Heidelberg: Universitätsbibliothek (Stanske)

Jerusalem: The Israel Museum (A.Keshet)

Karlsruhe: Badische Landesbibliothek (R.Buchta); Staatliche Kunsthalle (Dr S.Holsten)

Kassel: Gesamthochschul-Bibliothek Kassel. Handschriftenabteilung (S.von Hilchen, K.Wiedemann)

Klosterneuburg: Chorherrenstift. Stiftsmuseum (W.Huber); I. Kitlitschka

Koblenz: Landeshauptarchiv Koblenz (Dr M.Schoebel);

Görres-Gymnasium (Studiendirektor R.Dahm)

Krems an der Donau: Historisches Museum (Dr F.Schönfellner)

Kremsmünster: Stiftsbibliothek (Dr H.Fill)

Landau: Pfälzische Verlagsanstalt (P.Dressing)

Landshut: Stadtarchiv (Dr G.Spitzlberger); H.Zdera

Laon: Bibliothèque municipale (J.Lefebvre)

Leiden: Universiteitsbibliotheek. Western manuscripts division (Dr A.T.Bouwman)

Leipzig: Edition Leipzig GmbH; Verlag für Kunst und Wissenschaft (K.Meister); Kunstverlag GmbH E.A.Seemann

Liverpool: National Museums and Galleries on Merseyside (Central Services)

London: The British Library (C.Mescall); Victoria and Albert Museum; New Holland Publishers Ltd; University of London, The Warburg Institute (Dr P.Taylor)

Lucerne: Zentralbibliothek and Zentralverwaltung der Stadt Luzern (L.Fischer)

Lugano-Castagnola: Fondazione Thyssen-Bornemisza (D.Morax)

Madrid: Fundación Colleción Thyssen-Bornemisza (E.Alonso, Mar Borobia)

Mainz: Landesmuseum (Dr H.Reber, B.Jänsch)

Manchester: The John Rylands University Library (J.Tuck)

Marburg: Bildarchiv Foto Marburg im Kunstgeschichtlichen Institut des Philipps–Universität

Metz: Bibliothèque–Mediathèque (P.Hoch)

Moritzburg: Schloss Moritzburg, Verwaltung (R.Giermann)

Munich: Bayerische Staatsbibliothek (Dr H.Hauke); Bayerische Staatsgemäldesammlungen, Neue Pinakothek (Dr C.Syre); Hirmer Verlag

Münster: Universitätsbibliothek; Westfälisches Landesmuseum für Kunst und Kulturgeschichte (Dr G.Jászai, H.Musik); Westfälisches Amt für Denkmalspflege (Wiesmann); Aschendorffsche Verlagsbuchhandlung (G.Backhaus)

Neustift: Augustiner Chorherrenstift (T.I.Innerhofer)

New York: The Pierpont Morgan Library (Schmugge, C.E.Pierce); Hacker Art Books

Nuremberg: Germanisches Nationalmuseum (H.Maué)

Oslo: University Museum of National Antiquities (V.Hov)

Osnabrück: Diözesanbibliothek/Diözesanmuseum (Bischöfliches Generalvikariat, Heitmeyer)

Oxford: Bodleian Library, Department of Western Manuscripts

Paris: Bibliothèque Nationale (S.Raybaud); Centre national de la recherche scientifique, Institut de recherche et d'historie des textes, section latine (G.Renaud); CNTS Editions

Pleasantville, NY: Abaris Books (E.A.Pratt)

Poznan: Muzeum Narodowe w Poznaniu

Prague: Národní Museum (Dr H.Turková)

Regensburg: Verlag Schnell & Steiner (Dr J.Restorff)

Remscheid: Dr W.Bunte

Rome: Città del Vaticano. Biblioteca Apostolica Vaticana

Rotterdam: Museum Boymans-van Beuningen (F.de Jong)

Saarbrücken: Kunsthistorisches Seminar der Universität des Saarlandes. Archiv zur Buchmalerei (Dr H.-C.Graf von Bothmer)

Schaffhausen: Stadtbibliothek (Dr R.Specht)

Speyer: Stadtarchiv (Hopstock)

St Gallen: Kantonsbibliothek (Vadiana) (H.Thurnheer)

Stockholm: Riksantikvarieämbetet Staten historiska museer (D.Waern); Kungl. Vitterhets Historie och Antikvitets Akademien (S.Helmfrid)

Stuttgart: Württembergische Landesbibliothek, Handschriftenabteilung; Württembergisches Landesmuseum Stuttgart (Dr H.Meurer); Staatsgalerie; Belser Verlag (S.Stephan)

Tel Aviv: Beth Hatefutsoth. The Nahum Goldmann Museum of the Jewish Diaspora (H.Gilead)

Trier: Stadtbibliothek/Stadtarchiv (Dr Nolden); Bischöfliches Generalvikariat. Amt für Denkmalsplege (R.Heyen)

Ulm: Stadtbibliothek (I.Kirsch); Ulmer Museum (B.Kühn)

Utrecht: Rijksmuseum Het Catharijnenconvent

Verdun: Bibliothèque de Verdun (Mme Ben Lakhdar–Kreuwen)

Vienna: Österreichische Nationalbibliothek, Bild–Archiv und Porträt–Sammlung (E.Hofbauer); Kunsthistorisches Museum (E.Rasper); Österreichische Galerie im Belvedere (H.Steindl); Verlag der Österreichischen Akademie der Wissenschaften (Prof. Dr W.Selb)

Warsaw: Muzeum Narodowe w Warszawie (J.Galas); Museum Wojska Polskiego (Z.Świecicki)

Weimar: Stiftung Weimarer Klassik, Herzogin Anna Amalia Bibliothek (P.Ellermann–Minda); C.Beyer

Wolfenbüttel: Herzog August Bibliothek (Prof.Dr W.Milde; Dr H.Haase; C.Hogrefe)

Würzburg: Universitätsbibliothek, Handschriften-Abteilung (A.Pabel); Prof. Dr Dr K.Wittstadt; Verlag Schöningh

Zurich: Schweizerisches Landesmuseum (J.Frey); Kunsthaus Zürich (C.Brunner)

Zwettl: Zisterzienserstift Zwettl, Library (P.Georg König).

The customary information about sources (permissions from individuals or institutions, photographs, classifications, inventory numbers and the like) are given at the foot of each picture printed. I have tried to make contact with all those holding rights in the pictures. If I have neglected anything in this respect I offer my apologies and ask those concerned to get in touch with the publishers. In a few exceptional instances, where there was no usable illustrated material or where attempts to get permission came up against excessive difficulties, I have dispensed with an illustration. In that case, however, descriptions of the picture (along with an indication of where it has been published) are some substitute.

I. Introduction

Given the large number of pictures which have been collected here, a few preliminary comments may make it easier for readers to find their way around the book. These comments are intended to indicate the general framework, draw attention to some of the main perspectives, and help in orientation; they are not intended to direct or constrict the reader's interpretation of the pictures.

1. Pictures as a historical source

It is well known that, in their own way, pictures also afford valuable historical information when artists are illuminating, say, contemporary cultural and social–historical conditions or reflecting the mood of their own time. However, insufficient use is still being made of pictures. Ursula Stiff, *Das Kunstwerk als historische Quelle*, Westfalen im Bild, Kunst und Kulturgeschichte in westfälischen Museen 4, Münster 1985, is an arresting example of such an approach. The present volume is intended to be used along with already existing collections of texts on Christian–Jewish controversies and the history of the Jews in Christian Europe, as a work which explicitly seeks to inform solely through pictures. Initially one is hardly aware that even the Christian iconography which makes use of anti-Jewish apologetic subject-matter also continually conveys insights into social history. But this iconography does also provide deep insights into the existence of the Jews as a group on the periphery of a unified Christian society, because when medieval artists depict figures from the Old and New Testaments, the garments, head-dress, style of beards, overall appearance and so on is that of the Jews of their own time. The hostile attitude towards Christ and everything Christian which is sweepingly attributed to the Jews is also such a projection.

2. The relationship between texts and pictures

The Christian controversy with Judaism in literature began in the second century, after the parting of the ways. But it was only after the Council of Nicaea in 325 that the two ways irrevocably divided; for now the messiahship of Jesus of Nazareth was no longer the main theme of the controversy. The Council decided that Jesus is God of God, of the same substance (*homoousios*) as God the Father, begotten not made, and so the trinitarian confession was irrevocably fixed. To Jews it could seem that the Christians regarded the founder of their religion as a supernatural heavenly being, and no longer as a real human being (*purus homo*). At all events, now the link with strict Jewish monotheism had been completely broken, and what had begun as a Jewish sect was a world religion *sui generis*. In the long run this religion predominantly felt that the Jews were members of an alien religion, and even regarded them as peculiar relics of the former Old Testament people of God and the old covenant, long obsolete and doomed to hell.

Only around five hundred years later, in the Carolingian renaissance, was literary apologetic against the Jews combined with an extended pictorial depiction of the controversy (for details of this development see *Bijdragen. Tijdschrift voor filosofie en theologie* 49, 1988, 119–38). From then on, however, it continued into modern times. This is true of Europe and the Latin West. The development in Byzantium and the cultural sphere under its influence was different: here pictorial art avoided theological dispute and all forms of anti–Jewish caricature (details in E.Revel-Neher, *The Image of the Jew in Byzantine Art*, Oxford 1992). While for some time after the ninth century the theological statements of Western pictorial art centred above all on the allegorical pair Ecclesia and Synagoga and the typological proofs from the Old Testament, from the high and – more intensively – the late Middle Ages Christian art became more aggressive, for example with pictures of the 'Judensau' and the 'Living Cross'. Indeed the label 'Christian' art is almost out of place for the numerous caricatures which accompanied the economic and civic rise of the Jews between the sixteenth and nineteenth centuries. After the Middle Ages there was no longer any significant religious dialogue between Christians and Jews; in the course of modern times the controversy between Christian and Jewish scholars ebbed away, since theologically everything seemed to have been said; and a debate on emancipation driven by polemics forced learned theological treatises into the background. It was at this time that the anti–Jewishness in pictorial art increased sharply. In 'Christian' Europe, the thought of which was nationalistic and 'racist' in many places, many caricatures were aimed against the Jews as an undesirable hostile, alien group. Whereas most examples of medieval iconography had still accorded them (and Synagoga as an allegorical personification) some dignity as the former people of God, from the early modern period, often sheer hatred displaced respect for the descendants of the old covenant.

This volume is arranged in such a way that the pictures can often be combined with relevant literary and poetic texts and illuminate their statements; in turn, the texts can be interpreted in the light of the pictures. This is clearest in the case of pictures on title pages, because the frontispiece is usually related to the content of the writing which it prefaces. However, the pictures always also speak for themselves: they often illustrate particular aspects of the social situation of the Jews in Christian Europe and make the motives for historical developments immediately clear. Some pictures perhaps also contribute towards answering a question which is much discussed today, namely whether there are 'Christian roots to the hostility to the Jews, from the New Testament to the present day' (thus the title of an article by E.Stegemann, *Reformatio* 37, 1988, 366–80). Here I believe that the pictures suggest that the root of hostility to Jews is not the New Testament, but depravities in Christianity after the New Testament period. In this connection there is no mistaking the fact that it is only when there is an increasing chronological distance from the New Testament, and theological judgments are replaced by para-theological, non-Christian and social evaluations, that the tone gets shriller. Certainly the anti-Jewish thought-patterns behind Christian pictorial art are also inspired by Christian authors (and texts), but as a rule these are authors who could no longer see the Jews as 'older brothers' and who even suppressed the Jewishness of Jesus of Nazareth and his mother.

3. The pictures and their public

The influence of pictures on forming opinion cannot be overestimated. Throughout the Middle Ages and until deep into modern times, people were aware that religious pictures were for the mass of illiterate simple people what books were for theologians and priests. Thus Hermann von Scheda writes in the twelfth century: 'Pictures are for the simple uneducated people what books are for us' (*quod ergo nobis codices, hoc rudi vulgo representant imagines,* [*Opusculum de conversione sua,* ed. G.Niemeyer, Weimar 1963, 80]). Albertus Magnus (thirteenth century) speaks of 'pictures' as the 'books of the laity' (*picturae, quae sunt libri laicorum*); others speak here of 'dumb preaching' (*muta praedicatio,* cf. W.O.Hassall, *The Holkham Bible Picture Book,* London 1954, 43f.; cf. I.Willli-Plein and T.Willli, *Glaubensdolch und Messiasbeweis,* Neukirchen 1980, 57, on Raimundus Martini [thirteenth century] who described pictures in the churches as the Bible of simple people). That pictures were the reading-matter of the illiterate has been wrongly doubted by R.Schenda (*Internationales Archiv für Sozialgeschichte der deutschen Literatur* 12, 1987, 82–106), for while for a long time non-clerics certainly had no access to miniatures in liturgical books, they could see stained-glass windows, frescoes, reliefs and altar pictures in all the churches. This whole art, which was created specifically for instructing and edifying all Christians, including the laity, often took the form of 'posters' – a term introduced by the art historian A.M.Warburg (1866–1929) – in that it made it possible to feel directly what the picture was saying. This includes, for example, Synagoga standing hardened under the cross, stubbornly turning away from the crucifix and being then rejected; the depiction of the New Testament Jewish opponents of Jesus as medieval Jews; and the 'descent into hell' of the Jews seized by the devil and the punishment there which they have to suffer as Jews without even having committed any special misdeeds. The 'posters' also include scenes in which Jews are strikingly characterized as aliens by their special form of dress (especially the pointed hat, *pileus cornutus*). Quite a few such pictures show numerically far more Jewish hats than faces. In this remarkable perspective the Jews to some degree lose their personality, and individuals are replaced by the new collective identity of a social group defined by its traditional characteristics. The present volume presents numerous examples of this.

4. The special form of Jewish dress in the Middle Ages and the early modern period

Among other things the Fourth Lateran Council (1215) ordained: 'In some provinces, the dress (*habitus*) of Jews and Saracens (i.e. Muslims) distinguishes them from Christians, but in others a degree of confusion has arisen, so that they cannot be recognized by any distinguishing marks. As a result, in error Christians have sexual intercourse with Jewish or Saracen women, and Jews or Saracens have sexual intercourse with Christian women. In order that the crime of such an accursed mingling shall not in future have an excuse and an evasion under the pretext of error, we resolve that (Jews and Saracens) of both sexes in all Christian lands shall distinguish themselves publicly from other people by their dress (*qualitate habitus*). According to the testimony of scripture, such a precept was already made by Moses (Lev.19.19; Deut.22.5,11)' (*Conciliorum oecumenicorum decreta*, Bologna 1973, 266).

The effect of this Canon 68, which in 1234 was incorporated into canon law (*Liber extra*) by Gregory IX, lasted for centuries. The Council required that in Christian Europe, Jews and Muslims should retain their traditional oriental form of dress and not assimilate in clothing to the Christian population. Those who thought differently should look different. In that way it was thought possible to counter the danger to the salvation of the Christian soul which was supposed to emanate from people of other faiths. Some of the pictures in this book which date from before 1215 still show clearly Jews wearing the form of dress meant by the Lateran Council (conical hat, full-length garments). All the forms of medieval Jewish hat that we know developed from the basic form of this pointed hat (or the Phrygian cap akin to it). The cone could be bent slightly forward or could be pointed; it could be more or less rounded on top (so as to become bell- or dome-shaped), or it could taper to a more or less funnel shape on top, with or without a bobble on the end. This tapering upwards could also be terraced, with a shaft on top, which could be thin and pointed, but could also be rounded on top like the finger of a glove. Certain forms of this Jewish hat (*pileus cornutus*) can be associated with particular regions and times so that – presupposing that the collection of relevant sources is approximately complete – one could attempt a kind of European land register of special forms of Jewish dress.

At all events, it should be noted that in the Middle Ages a new cultural situation developed, since in antiquity clothing was not usually the distinguishing feature of a group, and 'the Diaspora Jews of antiquity were not easily recognizable, if indeed they were recognizable at all. Jews looked like everyone else, dressed like everyone else, and in general closely resembled their Gentile neighbours' (Cohen 1993, 39). Whether the preference for white as the colour of the Jewish hat, which is striking in the twelfth and thirteenth centuries, is of oriental origin is a matter of conjecture; there is no firm evidence. At any rate the *tabulae*, the two tables of the law (cf. Ex.31.18), which were prescribed for the Jews as a sign after 1215, are said to be 'white' in the sources, and the wheel *(rota)* which, similarly after 1215, became customary as a distinguishing mark on the European continent, was by preference yellow or white; this was still the case in the late Middle Ages (T. and M.Metzger, *Jüdisches Leben im Mittelalter*, Würzburg 1983, e.g. figs.195, 199; and for example the Jews in the depiction of an alleged profanation of the host by Paolo Ucello, altar painting in Urbino from 1467-9, also wear white rings). From a present-day perspective, among other things it seems strange that the Decalogue in the form of two tables – which Christians still venerate today – was used to isolate the Jews socially.

The prescription of special dress was originally intended by the church as a defensive measure, arising out of pastoral concern for the salvation and protection of Christian souls. But in the long run the Jewish hat and the Jewish ring – the latter to a much greater degree – became defamatory marks of identification. This often becomes particularly clear with pictorial representations of anti-Jewish legends (profanation of images, profanation of the host, poisoning of wells, ritual murder), and also in corresponding Old and New Testament scenes (e.g. the dance round the Golden Calf, the Pharisees as the enemies of Jesus). Thus in their own way, almost like key fossils, the Jewish hat and the Jewish ring make it easier to define precisely the forms and motives of Christian thought-patterns on the theme of the Jews. Here new discoveries are still possible.

5. The themes of the pictures

The themes of this collection are usually also the subjects of texts of different kinds: theological treatises, poems, chronicles, forms of oaths, political and social writings. This concrete relationship to texts helps in the interpretation of the pictures; however, in addition, a short glance at the basic presuppositions and perspectives which are relevant to the various groups of themes may prove helpful:

(a) Traditional theological views

The Old Testament is a Christian book and a book of the church, in so far as it points forward typologically and allegorically to Christ and the Christian saving event. After Golgotha the old covenant and the Torah are outdated or abolished.

The Jews do not understand their own scriptures: they are blind (to Christ and the prophecies of Christ in the Old Testament) and hardened. Their unbelief or their perverse belief (*perfidia*) leads them to read the Bible in a fleshly, literal way instead of figuratively (in respect of the *figurae* [*typoi*]) and spiritually.

With their rejection of the Messiah Jesus, the Jews are continuing their misdeeds of the biblical period (worship of the Golden Calf, persecution and murder of the prophets, etc.). The killing of the Son of God burdens the whole Jewish people with collective guilt for ever.

The Jews are hateful to God: they are enemies of God and of Christians; they are instigated by the devil to evil deeds or they are in alliance with the devil.

Election and covenant have passed over to the Christians, who are now the true Israel and the new people of God; the Jews who do not believe in Christ are apostates from their own honourable biblical tradition which issues in Christ; they have replaced the Bible (which in this sense is already Christian) with the Talmud.

The destruction of the Temple in Jerusalem (in 70 CE) and the dispersion of the Jews among all nations are God's punishment for their crucifixion of Christ and a historical proof of the truth of Christianity (the chief witness here is the Jewish historian Flavius Josephus).

The wretched existence of the Jews in the Diaspora all over the earth is their due fate. Their once exalted religion has degenerated into unbelief (*perfidia*) and superstition; while it must be tolerated, they themselves must be homeless and itinerant, live as slaves (*servi*) under oppressive laws, and serve Christians as Esau served Jacob (Gen.25.23: *maior minori serviet*). The homelessness of the Jews is irreversible, and the Jerusalem Temple will never be rebuilt.

The only way of salvation open to Jews is conversion to Jesus Christ; at the end of the world, on the return of Christ, the redemption of all Jews or at least a remnant of them is guaranteed; the Jewish people must continue to exist for the sake of this eschatological event: an extermination of the Jews would set God's plan of salvation at nought.

(b) Ecclesia and Synagoga

The Christian iconography of the allegorical pair Ecclesia and Synagoga appears at a very early stage. Here we have what initially is a relatively objective controversy in which the subjected opponent usually continues to have a remnant of dignity even in defeat (it is visible symbolically: her crown falls from her head; the tables of the law are lowered or held upside-down, i.e. with the rounded end lowermost, or falling from her hand, and her military standard is shattered; Synagoga's gaze is lowered, or she is already lying on the ground or mounted on a failing steed). In the course of the Middle Ages this type of depiction was increasingly loaded with aggressive polemic, especially in the form of the 'Living Cross'. Here we no longer have the pictorial articulation of theological standpoints, but the inexorable annihilation of an enemy.

In view of the great importance of Ecclesia–Synagoga in Christian iconography, it may be useful to investigate the spiritual roots of this configuration briefly. They can be found in biblical exegesis from the time of the church fathers. Here Lamentations 1.1 ('How lonely sits the city that was full of people! How like a widow has she become, she that was great among the nations! She that was a princess among the cities has become a vassal') and 5.16–17 ('The crown has fallen from our head; woe to us, for we have sinned! For this our heart has become sick, for these things our eyes have grown dim' [*cecidit corona capitis nostri... contenebrati sunt oculi nostri*]) were applied to Judaism. Thus many pictures from the ninth century onwards depict conquered Judaism allegorically in the form of a woman, sitting or standing, with a crown falling from her head and a blindfold over her eyes. The Roman custom of depicting a conquered land or a captured city in personified allegorical form as a seated woman (e.g. on the so-called *Judaea capta* coins) also had a strong influence on such representations. Similarly, from the time of the church fathers, Genesis 29.17 ('Leah's eyes were weak, but Rachel was beautiful and lovely') was also understood in terms of Judaism and Christianity, and later pictorial art made a connection between Leah's weak eyes and the blindness of Synagoga to Christ. The 'mother' of Song of Songs

1.6 (and 3.4; 8.2,5) become the type of Judaism or Synagoga, while the 'bride' was interpreted in terms of Ecclesia.

Some New Testament texts are also spiritual antecedents of the later female figure of Synagoga. First comes Matt.23.37 ('O Jerusalem, Jerusalem, killing the prophets and stoning those who are sent against you'), then Matt.25.33, 41 (right hand and left hand as symbols of good and evil and the last words at Christ's final judgment, 'Depart from me, you cursed, into eternal fire'); this influences many pictures in which either Synagoga or the Jews on the left (heraldically) of Christ are approaching the entrance to hell. II Corinthians 3.14–15 (the hardening of the Jews: a veil lies on the reading of the Old Testament which is removed only by conversion to Christ) underlies some pictures from the high Middle Ages which show Christ himself removing the blindfold from Synagoga's eyes, cf. Rom.11.26 ('then all Israel will be saved'). In II Cor.11.2; Eph.5.23–27; Rev.19.7; 21.9) Ecclesia appears as the bride of Christ, i.e. in the role which she later occupies in Ecclesia–Synagoga iconography. From the high Middle Ages onwards an iconographic affinity develops between Judaism–Death–Night–Old Testament–Law, as a contrast to Church–Life–New Testament–Grace. Starting points for such constructions include John 1.17 (*Lex per Moysen data est, gratia et veritas per Jesum Christum facta est*); II Cor.3.6 (*littera [sc.legis] enim occidit, Spiritus autem vivificat*; cf. II Cor.3.3), and Gal.4.21–31 (the two Testaments, Hagar and Sarah).

From the time of the church fathers the lines emanating from here are drawn more boldly and widely: Justin Martyr (second century), *Dialogue with the Jew Trypho* 134.3, 5 ('Leah is your people and the synagogue, while Rachel is our church...; Leah has weak eyes, and the eyes of your spirit are also weak'). Prudentius (died after 405), *Patrologia Latina* 60, 319 on Ex.34.30 (*Talem [sc.fulgorem] revertens legifer/de monte vultum detulit,/ Judaea quem plebs, aureo/bove inquinata et decolor/ expavit, et faciem retro/detorsit impatiens Dei*), makes 'the Jewish people' turn away from the divine splendour and thus perhaps in a way prepares for Synagoga turning away from the crucifix, as she does so frequently in iconography, or provides a possible explanation for this. Another Christian poet, Sedulius (after the middle of the fifth century, *Corpus Scriptorum Ecclesiasticorum Latinorum* 10, 140, vv.357–8), is even clearer: Synagoga is to go away... Christ has united himself with Ecclesia in fair love (*discedat Synagoga...Ecclesiam Christus pul-*

chro sibi iunxit amore). Here *discedere* seems an anticipatory comment on the departure of Synagoga from the scene on Golgotha which is so often depicted later. Cyril of Alexandria's work *The Defection of the Synagogue* (*De Synagogae defectu*, first half of the fifth century, now lost) also seems to have played a role. However, what is quite manifest is the great effect of the pseudo-Augustinian writing *The Dispute of the Church and the Synagogue* (*Altercatio Ecclesiae et Synagogae, Patrologia Latina* 41, 1131–40), which was probably written in the second half of the fifth century. In it two women argue in the form of a legal dispute before the censors about a claim to property and about domination generally. Synagoga – a widow – claims that the prophets came to her and that her failings could not have resulted in any loss of her earlier rights. Ecclesia accuses her opponent among other things of shameful behaviour towards the prophets and proves the messiahship of Jesus with testimonies from the Old Testament. But her main argument is a proof from history, namely the low social status of the Jews towards the end of the West Roman empire (476). At the end of the argument Synagoga declares herself beaten, and Ecclesia can triumph (*Synagoga: Ego sceptro et legionibus fulta apud Jerosolymam regnabam... Ecclesia: Audi, Synagoga, audi... ego sum regina, quae te de regno deposui*). In the ninth century Agobard of Lyons speaks of Synagoga as an outcast ugly old woman (MG, *Epistolae* 5, p.199,29: *maculosa, ruosa et repudiata synagoga*). At the end of a poetic prayer we read in Ps.Bernard of Clairvaux (Bernard died in 1153): *Isaias cecinit, /synagoga meminit,/ nunquam tamen desinit/ esse caeca./ Si non suis vatibus, /credat vel gentilibus, /Sibyllinis versibus/ haec praedicta./ Infelix propera, /crede vel vetera; cur damnaberis,/ gens misera?/ Quem docet littera,/ natum considera; ipsum en genuit/ puerpera. Amen.* If the Jewish people (*synagoga*; here we are probably also to think of the allegorical female figure Synagoga) does not believe in the promises of Christ in the biblical prophets, they should at least believe the pagan Sibyl, who similarly prophesied the coming of Christ. The synagogue should still arrive at the true faith and thus avoid damnation, even if it is late in doing so. Here we have the expression of an inward, almost imprecatory, hope of conversion, that the blind Synagoga may one day still recognize that Isaiah's promises of Christ (e.g. Isa.7.14; 9.5; 11.1; 52.13–53.12) have been fulfilled in Jesus of Nazareth. This wish for the conversion of the 'unfortunate' perhaps has a parallel in the sensitive statues of Synagoga in Gothic cathedrals, which still give the allegorical personification of Judaism a certain dignity, indeed tragic greatness (the best known example is in Strasbourg Cathedral).

(c) Typology

Another favourite theme of Christian iconography on Judaism is that of the links between Old Testament types (*figurae*, prefigurements of the future saving event) and the corresponding New Testament 'real types', the details of the reality of salvation given with Christ's incarnation, life and passion. In this sense, for example, the saving brazen serpent of Num.21.6–9 fixed on a staff points to Christ nailed to the cross; the widow of Zarephta with her wood points to the beams of the cross (I Kings 17); the closed gates through which only the Messiah can go (Ezek.44.12) represents the virginity of Mary the Mother of God. Such typological relations were often so misunderstood in the Christian tradition that after the realization of salvation in the form of Jesus Christ the relevant 'types' and 'shadows' of the Jewish Bible became basically superfluous and dispensable along with the writings of the Jews. By contrast, today it is generally emphasized that the holy scriptures of the Jews have not lost value as a result of the later interpretation of the New Testament (see e.g. J.Willebrands, *Münchener Theologische Zeitschrift* 38, 1987, 295–310).

(d) The passion of Christ

The passion of Christ is often disproportionately a theme of pictorial art, and this encouraged the rise and consolidation of hostile attitudes to the Jews in Christian Europe; for countless pictures portrayed Christ's tormentors in the dress of medieval Jews and thus imposed the stigma of collective guilt on them. In the late Middle Ages a particular group developed from the depictions of the passion in the form of the *arma Christi* devotional pictures. They show Jesus as the Man of Sorrows, surrounded by the agents and instruments (*arma*) of his passion: crown of thorns, scourge, reed (or bundle of reeds), hammer, nails, pincers, robe and dice; a hand which is striking or mocking, a spitting head (cf. Matt.26.67), along with Judas, Herod, Pilate, Peter and Old Testament prophets (predicting Christ's passion). Often the head (or bust) of a Jew with his typical medieval hat appears among the tormentors, so that the compassionate viewers of such pictures were constantly made aware of the collective involvement (complicity) of

the Jews of his own time. Such depictions in particular also belong among the 'posters', since those looking at them would almost automatically associate the New Testament opponents of Jesus with the persons wearing pointed hats whom they met every day on the streets of medieval cities.

(e) The mission to the Jews, the hardening and damnation of the Jews

The ongoing existence of the Jewish people even after the event on Golgotha was a problem and a persistent challenge for Christianity, indeed a thorn in the flesh. No less a figure than John Chrysostom thought that 'if Jewish worship is honourable and meaningful, then ours can only be lies and deception' (*Patrologia Graeca* 48, 852). It seemed possible to solve the problem by the conversion of all Jews, so the efforts of the Christian mission to the Jews – based above all on the universal mission command in Matt.28.19–20 – went on indefatigably for many centuries down to most recent times. In church history, relaxed toleration of the other religion was more the exception.

Two lines of tradition in particular run through the history of the mission to the Jews. The first is the one which begins from the interpretation of Luke 14.23 in Augustine, *Contra Gaud*.1.25, 28 (*Corpus Scriptorum Ecclesiasticorum* 53, 226–7, 'The invitation to the banquet': 'Compel them to come in, that my house may be full'). This was often used as an argument for compelling heretics and those of other faiths to become Christians. The second, a relatively tolerant line, was formulated in the twelfth century in the 'Decree' of the canon lawyer Gratian: 'The Jews are not to be compelled to (Christian) faith; but once they have accepted it, even involuntarily, they must abide by it' (*Decretum Gratiani, Dist.* XLV,4: *Judaei non sunt cogendi ad fidem, quam tamen, si inviti susceperint, cogendi sunt retinere*). While this opposed forcible conversion, in fact it did turn Jews who had been forcibly baptized and wanted to revert to their religion into heretics, with the threat of the stake. Thus toleration was relative and limited.

It was the general conviction that hardened Jews, Jews who did not want to become Christians in any circumstances, were damned. They belong to the 'host of the damned' (*massa perditionis*, e.g. in the canon lawyer Stephen of Tournai [died 1203], *Patrologia Latina* 211, 333). On 4 February 1442, the seventeenth Universal (Ecumenical) Council of Basel–Ferrara–Florence

(1431ff.) resolved, among other things, that 'Neither Jews nor heretics nor schismatics can partake of eternal life, but they will go "into the eternal fire" (Matt.25.41)' (*nec Iudeos aut hereticos atque scismaticos eterne vite fieri posse participes, sed in ignem eternum ituros* [*Conciliorum oecumenicorum decreta*, Bologna 1973, 578]). Bishop Fulgentius of Ruspe (died 532) might be mentioned as an example from the period of the church fathers: 'Not only all pagans, but also all Jews and heretics who die outside the present Catholic church, will go into the eternal fire which has been prepared for the devil and his angels' (*Patrologia Latina* 65, 704 on Matt.25.41).

(f) Jewish professions

Here Christian pictorial art depicts almost exclusively two groups: doctors and money-lenders. Whereas the activity of Jews as doctors is depicted only rarely, but not in an unfriendly way, in this part of the iconographic spectrum pawnbroking and lending on credit appear quite often, and are usually depicted polemically.

According to Ex.22.24; Lev.25.36–37; Deut.23.20–21, Jews were forbidden to receive interest on loans to fellow-believers (cf. also Ps.15.5; Ezek.22.12), but were allowed to receive interest from non-Jews (according to Deut.23.20: 'to a foreigner you may lend upon interest'). By comparison, the Christian attitude was inconsistent: for the most part the levying of interest was taken to be forbidden (according to Luke 6.34–35), but Matt.25.27 (with the parallel Luke 19.23) could also justify it. The *Summa Parisiensis*, an anonymous commentary on the Decree of Gratian composed around 1160 (ed. T.P.McLaughlin, Toronto 1952, 170), says that canon law forbids the laity and the priesthood to lend money against interest, but that in secular law it is permissible to lend money against interest (*iure fori licet usuras exigere, sed iure canonum tam clericis quam laicis est prohibitum*). One way of avoiding the unworldly prohibition against levying interest among Christians was to conceal the interest in the sum of money lent (an appropriate amount was stuck on at the start). Thus for example a vineyard could be sold, and at the same time a later buy-back could be agreed at a higher price; this was a 'disguised loan' (see e.g. R.Flade, *Die Würzburger Juden*, Würzburg 1987, 33–4).

Jews also encountered the more or less energetic Christian prohibition against levying interest by disguising the interest in the form of 'indemnification against arrears' or the like. In the sixteenth century, Josel von Rosheim attacked the practice of adding interest to the capital quarterly: this caused the debt to rise rapidly and quite often made it impossible to repay. Granted, for such cases on occasion there was a kind of guarantee against default from the Jewish community, but Jewish creditors probably claimed this only in emergencies. Because of the enormous social uncertainties and high risks in the Middle Ages, rates of interest were also comparatively high, and the frequent impoverishment of Christian debtors and their inability to pay often gave Jewish money-lenders a bad reputation. However, the same was also true of the Christian 'usurers' who were frequent in some areas of Europe: for example Bernard of Clairvaux (twelfth century) complains about the *Christiani feneratores* (*Patrologia Latina* 182, 567; ed. Leqerc VIII, 316), and Innocent III made similar comments about the Christian usurers in Artois in the Pas de Calais (*Patrologia Latina* 215, 1380): if these were all punished (say by excommunication), the churches would have to be shut because there were so many of them. See G.Liebe, *Das Judentum in der deutschen Vergangenheit*, Leipzig 1903, 38; H.-J.Gilomen, *Historische Zeitschrift* 250, 1990, 265-303; W.P.Eckert, in *Antisemitismus*, ed. G.B.Ginzel, Cologne 1991, 84-6; K.R.Stow, *Alienated Minority. The Jews of Medieval Latin Europe*, Cambridge, Mass. 1992, 213-30.

(g) The Jewish oath

One of the focal themes of this collection of pictures is the 'Jewish oath' (oath *more judaico*), since the relevant depictions give a good explanation of a key point in the web of Christian-Jewish relations, in the context of legal history. From the early Middle Ages up to the nineteenth century, Jews involved in a legal dispute with non-Jews had, if need be, to give an oath 'according to Jewish custom'. Initially and for a long time such texts were almost always an accommodation, since it was not possible for non-Christians to pronounce the religious formulae of Christian oaths; they were therefore given elements of the Talmudic law on oaths with comprehensive references to appropriate passages in the Old Testament, the 'Jewish Bible', to add more credibility to the punishment they drew upon themselves in case of perjury. On occasion, however, in the course of the Middle Ages, the procedure also took on anti-Jewish features. For example, the Jew taking the oath was required to stand on the dugs of a bloody sow's skin. The reason for such discriminatory elements is not completely clear. Was such an object required to exploit the Jewish abhorrence of pigs as unclean animals (Lev.11.7), in order to make the oath more stringent? Since business and social contacts with Christians were indispensable for Jews, they had to accept these ignominious special oaths whether they wanted to or not (see further V.Zimmermann, *Die Entwicklung des Judeneides*, Bern 1973; F.Lotter, in *Lexikon des Mittelalters* V, Munich 1991, 789).

(h) The 'Judensau' motif

The thematic affinity of the 'Judensau' ('Jew sow') motive to the use of a sow's skin could also indicate that certain discriminatory practices in the Jewish oath were deliberately meant as a defamation; for at approximately the same time as the regulation was made that the Jew taking the oath had to stand on the skin of a sow, the 'Judensau' appears as a stone relief or in some other form in and on numerous churches of Europe. This is a sow, or more precisely a mother pig, at whose dugs Jews are sucking either alone or with piglets, or with which they are having other dealings, usually obscene (scatological, coprophagistic). First of all it should be noted that concepts like sin, impurity and dissipation were associated with the pig in the Middle Ages. But the configuration of pig and Jew probably also denotes that the Jew is different in nature from the Christian. The Jew is not a human being 'like us'; the Jew is not a human being at all. In this connection the great mother pig is probably an allegory of Judaism or the Jewish religion, so to speak the nurturing mother of all Jews, and to some degree also a later vulgar variant of that other allegorical personification, Synagoga, who had at least been allowed a remnant of personal dignity. However, it is only late medieval literary evidence which points in the direction of such a view, though it does so all the more clearly, for the inscription which accompanies a relevant picture – included in this book – dated around 1470 describes the sow as mother of the Jews, and in a Shrove Tuesday play the poet Hans Folz (c.1515) speaks of the pig as mother of the Jews, under whom they snuggle and suck (*Fastnachtsspiele*, ed A.von Keller, Stuttgart 1853ff., no.20, 184). Yet other concrete affinities to the 'Judensau' motif are evident in the wider context and at an earlier date. The church father Ephraem (fourth century) remarks that 'the people which does not eat of the pig is a pig which sprinkles with much blood. Flee and distance yourselves from it; it is shaking

itself – so that you are not stained by spots of blood' (*Corpus Scriptorum Christianorum Orientalium* 249, 29–30). John Chrysostom (died 407) thinks that the Jews are people 'who live by their belly, gape at what they have before their eyes, and in their indiscipline are no better than pigs and goats'. The church teacher Jerome (died 420) says that the praying and psalm-reciting of the Jews and the praises of the heretics are like the grunting of pigs and the whinnying of asses before God (*Corpus Christianorum, Series Latina* 76, 295 on Amos 5.23). Hrabanus Maurus (died 856) interprets s*ynagoga* etymologically as *congregatio*, gathering of beasts, and *ecclesia* as *convocatio*, convention (or assembly) of human beings (*Patrologia Latina* 111, 89–90; cf. Hrabanus 111, 206 on the pig as a symbol of impurity, dissipation and sin, who in this connection also speaks of the Jews). For Peter the Venerable (died 1158), the Jews are 'mindless, shameless dogs and flatulent swine' (*Patrologia Latina* 189, 622). For Alanus ab Insulis (died 1203), the pig is a symbol of 'lust and impurity' (*Patrologia Latina* 210, 409). Peter of Blois (died 1204) dismisses the apologetic objections of Jews to Christianity as the 'grunting' of swine, in other words, the sound of animals which is incomprehensible to ordinary people, and in any case is not to be taken seriously. An ancient forerunner of this development is Petronius (Fr.37): the Jews worship a 'pig deity' (*porcinum numen*), a taunt derived from their abstinence from pork.

Jews can be seen in some 'Judensau' pictures riding on the sow, facing backwards and looking towards its rear end. To ride the wrong way round on an animal which is not made for riding on symbolizes the perverse, incomprehensible, deviant thought of the Jews. At all events this riding is meant to be defamatory, as is shown by the parallel of the early modern pictures designed to shame defaulting debtors – within Christianity – or guarantors (there is a good example in *Brunswieck 1131, Braunschweig 1981, Festschrift zur Ausstellung*, Brunswick 1981, 373 pl.1: picture with letter to Sander of Oberg and other guarantors, dated 1542 [shown riding the wrong way round on a pig]). For this see *Handwörterbuch zur deutschen Rechtsgeschichte* IV, Berlin 1990, 1349–51: 'Schandbilder'. For the theme generally see I.Shachar, *The 'Judensau'. A Medieval Anti-Jewish Motive and its History*, London 1974.

(i) Modern caricatures directed against equal civil rights and the emancipation of the Jews

The last of the themes which needs to be mentioned in this introduction relates to the period between the seventeenth and the twentieth centuries. Here many pictures illustrate the widespread antipathy to emancipation. These pictures are no longer 'Christian' in the narrower sense of the word, since the unified Christian society of the European Middle Ages with its sacral orientation secularizes and develops values and images few, if any, of which are provided by Christian theology. Such pictures are now rooted in the social problems of a secularized, bourgeois European society. Against the Enlightenment and against attempts to make the Jews integrated citizens instead of disruptive aliens through equal civil rights and assimilation – and also in the form of the mission to the Jews and Christianization – caricaturists in their illustrations make the statement: Jews cannot and will not become reliable citizens. Their oaths are not to be trusted (in business or as soldiers under allegiance to the flag); by character they are unsuited to military discipline, the life of the soldier and bravery in battle; their interest in the culture of their host country is only superficial or even seems comical, and they are not in a position to play a creative part in its culture. A recalcitrant business sense would inevitably break through, and in the end their Jewishness and their egotism would prevent them from being completely loyal citizens. Thus above all in the nineteenth and earlier twentieth centuries the Jews are often presented as people who neither can nor will put off their Jewish characteristics (special form of dress; a 'Yiddish' which seems comical in the German-speaking world; and un-German, undignified behaviour): at best they are capable of mimicry (which can easily be seen through).

6. Iconographic preferences and tendencies

This volume can offer only an abbreviated, pointed selection. This shows that iconographic interpretations of the Old and New Testaments – differentiated depending on the level of interest – portray the Jews sometimes in a friendly way, sometimes polemically, and sometimes neutrally. Thus as a rule for example the Jewish ambience of Jesus' birth in Bethlehem or the depiction of Jesus in the Temple is unpolemical, friendly or even loving (Joseph often wears the medieval Jewish hat, even on the

flight into Egypt); and the same is true of the action of Moses and the prophets, who often have haloes like Christian saints, but also quite often wear the Jewish medieval hat as a matter of course. However, the same Jewish hat can also be a polemical characterization of the Israelites dancing round the Golden Calf or the New Testament opponents of Jesus (the Pharisees, the scourgers at the passion and others), and thus include the Jews in Christian Europe collectively in the (assumed) guilt of their forefathers in a defamatory manner. Among the numerous pictorial themes, that of the circumcision of Jesus is particularly striking (Luke 2.21). Initially it is still presented without polemic, as a detail of the childhood of Jesus which is registered in a friendly way along the lines of the Gospel of Luke; however, in the late Middle Ages ugly depictions mount up which present the event as repulsive, as an act of evil Jews and as a prelude to the later passion.

Unusually, for example Luke 2.41–50 (the twelve-year-old Jesus among the Jewish teachers) is also often a theme, and the appearance of some examples in this volume indicates the extraordinary popularity of this material in Christian pictorial art generally. Why was this topic thought to be so attractive? An 1879 painting by Max Liebermann still bears witness to the fascination caused by Luke 2.41–50 as the subject; it provoked a long controversy (most recently see *Hamburger Kunsthalle. Der zwölfjährige Jesus im Tempel*, von Max Liebermann, ed. H.R.Peppien, Hamburg [1989?]). We now see that Luke 2.41–50 probably has a historical nucleus; for here we have a 'brief depiction of a form of Jewish religious teaching which already existed at that time and still exists to the present day. Jesus apparently crept into the portico of the Temple – where access was open to others. His questioning of the scholars also corresponds to the form of instruction in rabbinic gatherings. But only the scholars debated among themselves; the disciples merely asked questions. Moreover that also happened later in the circle around Jesus: there too the disciples only asked questions' (D.Flusser, *Das Christentum – eine jüdische Religion*, Munich 1990, 73f.). However, the artists hardly ever enquired into the actual role of the boy Jesus. Already in the fifth century we have the beginning of a marked line of tradition in the course of which the young Jew is singled out from among the teachers, is enthroned above them or gives them a lecture: the pupil instructs the 'teachers'; he is no longer a Jewish child among adult Jews, a boy who 'listens and asks questions', but anticipates his future role as teacher of Israel. Jesus is already so to speak the first 'missionary to the Jews'. And consistently in such depictions the Jewish teachers are very often distinguished by their 'Jewish' appearance (Jewish hat, ring and sometimes also physiognomy) from Jesus, whose Jewishness seems almost completely to have been eliminated. This is a tendency which can also be noted elsewhere. It belongs in the wider context of the de–Judaizing of the New Testament: Jesus and the apostles think differently from the Jews and therefore also look different from them! With ultimate consistency, this tendency leads in the first half of the twentieth century to attempts to prove that the founder of Christianity was Aryan.

It is a further tendency of Christian pictorial art in certain scenes from the Old and New Testaments often to depict the agents out of proportion as medieval Jews (with Jewish hat and/or Jewish ring). This is the case, for example, with the account of the brazen serpent in Num.21.6–9, which was evidently regarded as a strange and exotic event (albeit, under the protection of the understanding of it in John 3.14, without any negative connotation); consequently here the Israelites usually wear the Jewish hat – which seems oriental and exotic in Western Europe. The same is also true, *mutatis mutandis*, for the dance round the Golden Calf (Ex.32.19); here, however, the special medieval Jewish form of dress is generally exploited polemically. In the Christian tradition this is regarded as a kind of prototype of Jewish apostasy, superstition and perfidy.

The Jewishness of figures is generally emphasized where this is thought desirable for particular reasons. Thus in many portrayals the Jewish historian Flavius Josephus wears the Jewish hat as a witness to the truth of Christianity (he comes from the enemy camp and is therefore especially prized, see in detail H.Schreckenberg and K.Schubert, *Jewish Historiography and Iconography in Early and Medieval Christianity. With an Introduction by D.Flusser*, Compendia Rerum Iudaicarum ad Novum Testamentum III, 2, Assen, Maastricht and Minneapolis 1992, 87–130); so too, often, is the Levite Judas at the discovery of the cross of Christ (the legend of Helena). Perhaps the most striking example of a deliberate preference for the 'Jewish' head–dress is the iconography of the Emmaus narrative (Luke 24.13–35), in so far as occasionally, by way of exception, even Jesus himself wears the Phrygian cap, a variant of the conical Jewish hat (as a disguise!), in order to look like an ordinary Jew.

In the course of the Middle Ages the Jewish hat –

initially and for some time still serving as a neutral group characteristic – becomes a negative symbol. Thus the well–known signs of Jewishness appear: alongside the pointed hat above all the ring, massively in pictorial depictions of anti–Jewish legends (ritual murder, profanation of the host, profanation of images); they are also trivial in the highly polemical 'Judensau' scenes. What is most striking is perhaps the way in which anti–Jewish polemic increases by leaps and bounds in the graphic art of the late Middle Ages and in the early modern period, and particularly also at the time of the Reformation – here a connection with the social problems of the time is clear. Not only are the Jews associated with death and hell, as Synagoga formerly had been in the context of the opposition between Old and New Testament, but there are also monstrous abominations. Often the pictures no longer seek to bring out theological contrasts, but simply to defame.

7. The structure of the book

Numerous connecting links associate the spectrum of pictures selected here with the Christian *Adversus Judaeos* texts. Indeed, over wide stretches they provide a parallel to the content of these texts. That is why at the end of this volume there is a 'List of Titles of Christian Texts on Judaism' as an appendix.

Many illustrations in turn tell a story the details of which fit in with lines of development and thematic patterns, some of which I have attempted to indicate by a systematic contents page.

Given the focal point of this volume, I have refrained from including miniatures in medieval Hebrew manuscripts and have also almost completely left out of account other Jewish illustrative material, since this is already comparatively well known and has been published, e.g. by Thérèse and Mendel Metzger, *Jüdisches Leben im Mittelalter*, Würzburg 1983, or in *Jüdische Lebenswelten* (exhibition catalogue and 'essays' volume), Berlin 1991. To save space, the details on individual pictures (location, secondary literature, details of illustration, remarks on the subject of the picture) have been limited to essentials and presented in the briefest form possible. Readers are invited where need be, and as they wish, to consult the list of literature cited in abbreviated form at the end of the volume. This was the only way of reproducing as many pictures as possible and not separating them from the relevant text. Even so, those looking at these pictures have been given great freedom to make their own discoveries: the journey leads through large areas of little–known cultural landscapes.

Quite a trivial circumstance led to comparatively few paintings being included in this volume: it was too expensive to reproduce them in colour, and in black and white there was often an intolerable loss of picture quality. So for the most part I have dispensed with colour illustrations and have been concerned above all to select miniatures, wood-cuts and other book illustrations which can be reproduced clearly. However, occasionally some less good examples, damaged over the course of time, have had to be used, because they either provide valuable information or round off the overall picture in a significant way.

In particular in the case of stone reliefs and sculptures, which now are often heavily weathered, it seemed useful to refer back to good old drawings which are comparatively nearer to the originals or which show the details better. I was aware that there was a danger of uncertainty here, but this seemed tolerable because of the manifest advantages, and because as a rule it is still possible for the reader to compare the drawings critically with photographs of the objects in their present state of preservation. In any case, sometimes no other way is possible, as in the case of the miniatures in the *Hortus deliciarum* of Herrad of Landsberg, the only codex of which was destroyed in 1870 in the bombardment of Strasbourg by German troops. The mural on the Brückenturm in Frankfurt am Main discussed by Goethe in *Dichtung und Wahrheit* (Book 4) is a similar case. It was destroyed in 1801 but has been preserved in numerous, albeit free, drawings. Taken together, though, these make us deeply regret the loss of the original (see the chapter on the 'Judensau' theme).

A number of overarching thematic connections cannot be demonstrated by the division of this volume into specific chapters. Here, too, readers are invited to make their own discoveries. For example the pictorial affinity between 'Jews, the devil and hell' (and their theological roots) is not limited to one chapter. One solution would have been to include many pictures in more than one section of the book, or to introduce a large number of cross-references. However, I wanted to avoid anything which might have given the impression that I was taking charge of the reader. This would not have been appropriate for the subject-matter of the work – which so far has not been explored adequately. My intention is not to form opinions but to provide comprehensive information with a view to well-founded discussion.

One last comment needs to be made on the illustrations on the topic of profanation of images, the host and charges relating to blood. Here, where appropriate, I have put the pictures in chronological order of subject-matter; in other words, the pictures are in order of the years of the events they depict, not the years in which they were made (which were different, and often considerably later).

II. Rome versus Judaea (66–70 CE) and the Christian Appropriation of This Theme

1. The relief on the Arch of Titus in Rome and the *Judaea capta* coins

1. Triumphal procession in Rome (71 CE) with plunder from the Jerusalem temple after the victory over the Jews in the war of 66–70. Relief of the Triumphal Arch of Titus, erected after his death (81 CE). Literature: Eltester 1960; Yarden 1991; *Jahrbuch der Berliner Museen* 29–30, 1987–88, 87; *Qadmoniot* 25, 1992, 116–22; Edwards 1992; Schreckenberg II, 447–9. Illustration after Reber 1877, 398 (copy).

2. . Triumphal procession in Rome (as 1). Illustration after Reinach 1890 (photograph of the original).

3. *Judaea capta* coins. An example of the coins minted after 71/72 CE in various forms to commemorate Rome's victory in the war of 66–70. The allegorical personification of the conquered land is sitting in front of a palm tree (symbol of the East); behind her stands a Roman soldier as a representative of the victor. SC indicates that the minting was authorized by a resolution of the Senate *(senatus consultum)*. The year 70 is a significant subject for Christian theology and art. Literature: Brin 1984; Edwards 1992; Schreckenberg II, 450–3. Illustration after *JüdLex* III, 1929, 547.

2. The capture and destruction of Jerusalem as a theme of Christian pictorial art. Effects of the Christian appropriation of Josephus' *Bellum Judaicum*

1. The Jewish historian Flavius Josephus, author of the *Bellum Judaicum*, and Vespasian. As in the medieval Christian legend, Josephus appears as the leader of the Jews and Vespasian is portrayed as a Christian emperor for whom the Jew is writing his work, which was regarded as usefully pro–Christian. Miniature in a Josephus manuscript made between 1181 and 1188 in the Benedictine abbey of Weingarten (Baden–Württemberg). Fulda, Hessische LB, HS.C 1, folio 1 verso. Literature: Schreckenberg II, 614. Illustration after Köllner 1976, no.441.

▶ 2. The Jewish historian Flavius Josephus hands over to Vespasian and Titus his history, in which the downfall of Jerusalem is described. In Christian poetry and legend Titus and Vespasian are often portrayed as Christian rulers of the West who as instruments of heaven destroy Jerusalem and kill the surviving Jews or sell them as slaves. Miniature in a manuscript of the *Bellum Judaicum* written in Toulouse. Paris, BN, Lat.5058, folio 2 verso–3 recto. Literature: Schreckenberg II, 520f. Illustration after Robb 1973, fig.112.

STEMATE VESTITVS PREFVLGET
CVM PATRE TITVS

QVOD VATES BELLVM CREVIT NON ESSE DVELLVM
CODIT & MVLTIS VOBIS QVI CERNERE VVLTI
EST IOSEPHVS DICTVS FERT LIBRVM CORPORE PICTVS

3. Christ weeps over the imminent destruction of Jerusalem (Luke 19.41–44). This is presented in visionary anticipation along with a particularly impressive detail from the *Bellum Judaicum* of the Jewish historian Flavius Josephus (6, 201ff.). The Jewish woman Mary, starving in the siege of Jerusalem, kills her own child in order to eat it. From the time of the church fathers onwards, the fall of Jerusalem was regarded as a compelling anti–Jewish historical proof.

Miniature in the Evangeliary of Otto III, produced about 1000 in the school of Reichenau. Munich, SB, Clm 5453, folio 188 verso. Literature: Mütherich 1979; Mayr–Harting 1991, fig.133; Schreckenberg II, 497f. Illustration after Duby I, 1984, 33.

4. The capture of Jerusalem by Titus. Painting by Nicolas Poussin, 1638–9. Vienna, Kunsthistorisches Museum. Literature: Blunt 1967, pl.117; Deutsch 1982, fig.1.

5. Commemoration (engraving) of a decree of Napoleon (1806), with which he gave decisive encouragement to the emancipation of the Jews of France and their integration into French society. Here the Emperor appears as a kind of new Moses who is inaugurating a new era for the Jews. The link with Jewish tradition in this picture is provided by Mount Sinai (in the background) and the cultic vessels of the temple in Jerusalem which was destroyed in 70 CE. As an allegorical personification of the Jewish people, in the foreground there is the iconographical descendant of Judaea–Jerusalem–Synagoga, seated in defeat, but here in the process of rising up again. On the left of the picture is Rabbi Sinzheim, the President of the Great Sanhedrin. Literature: *Napoleon e gli Ebrei*, ed D.Gallingani, Bologna 1991; Battenberg 1990, I, 110ff.; cf. the illustrations in *EJ* 1971, XVI, 474 (Medal in honour of the Napoleonic emancipation of the Jews of Westphalia, 1808): Judaea with the two tables of the law and a broken chain before her is giving thanks for her freedom. The final stage of the iconographic tradition which ultimately derives from the image on the *Judaea capta* coins in the first century is reached in the *Israel Liberata* coins of 1958 (see *EJ* 1971, XI, 1169 fig.2). Illustration after *JüdLex* II, 761.

6. Destruction of Jerusalem, by Wilhelm von Kaulbach, 1846. Munich, Neue Pinakothek (Inv–no.WAF 403). This colossal painting (589 x 703 cm) combines various elements of theological and profane anti–Jewish thought (below left e.g. the fleeing Ahasuerus). Literature: Nagler 1835ff., VIII, 398f. (a detailed description of the picture); Becker 1964, pl.1; *Bilder sind nicht verboten* 1982, fig. p.56; Dittmar 1987, fig.9 (cf. Dittmar in *IDEA. Jahrbuch der Hamburger Kunsthalle* 6, 1987, 81–96, pl.11); Steingräber 1980, pl.III.

8. The Jews are killed by two kings. In a moralizing interpretation, Ps.17.1 is understood as a petition of Christ to his father that 'he may have retribution on the Jews for their wickedness, so that they lose the land and city which they killed Christ to preserve'. The two kings suggest Titus and Vespasian. One of the Jews – who seems still to be asking for mercy – is wearing a conical Jewish hat. Miniature in a *Bible moralisée*, c.1240. Paris BN, Lat.11560, folio 6 recto (section). Illustration after Blumenkranz 1965, no.52.

7. Destruction of Jerusalem by the Romans in 70. Conquered Judaism is represented in an allegorical personification which is shaped by the tradition of her predecessors *Judaea capta,* Hierusalem and Synagoga: the mistress and ruler is robbed of her power and suffers the fate of subjection and imprisonment. Above: Noah's ark, heaven, the tabernacle. Frontispiece to *Alle de Werken van Flavius Josephus*, etc. (Low German translation by W.Sewel), Amsterdam 1722, from which the illustration is taken.

III. Ecclesia versus Synagoga. The Dispute between the Two Allegorical Personifications and their Reconciliation

1. The dispute between two queens. The defeat of Synagoga, her fight against the 'lamb of God', her departure from the cross, her way to into hell, her death

(a) Early Middle Ages (to the end of the eleventh century)

◀ 1. Crucifixion with Ecclesia, stripping Synagoga (still enthroned) of her power. The latter has a circumcising knife as an attribute and is wearing a mural crown, which also identifies her as an allegorical personification of Jerusalem or Judaea. As such she stands in iconographic succession to the seated Judaea of the *Judaea capta* coins. Ivory relief from the cover of an evangeliary, Metz school, c. third quarter of the ninth century. Paris, BN, Lat.9383. Literature: Jochum 1993, fig.8; Schreckenberg II, 476–80. Illustration after Goldschmidt I, 1914, no.83.

▶ 2. Crucifixion with Ecclesia and Synagoga, the latter left (heraldically) of the crucifix, in process of departing but still looking back (as though banished or defiant?). She is still holding her battle standard high, and so probably has yet to take in her defeat. Ivory relief of the later Metz school, end of the ninth century. London, Victoria and Albert Museum, no.250.67. Literature: Schreckenberg II, 484–96. Illustration after Goldschmidt I, 1914, no.85.

◀ 3. Crucifixion with Ecclesia, who is calling for the abdication of Synagoga. Synagoga, to that point still ruling (her symbol of domination is the globe, *gyrus terrae*), is sitting in front of a background which probably denotes Jerusalem. Ivory relief from a liturgical book, third quarter of the ninth century. Munich, SB, Clm 4452. Literature: Kashnitz 1988; Jochum 1993, fig.7; Schreckenberg II, 470–6. Illustration after *Mon.Jud.Handb.* 1963, no.60.

▼ 4. Crucifixion with Ecclesia and Synagoga, the latter (heraldically) on the extreme left, defiantly leaving the scene of the saving event. Ivory relief from the later Metz school, c.900. Florence, Museo nazionale del Bargello: avorio Carrand inv.32. Literature: Kashnitz 1988, pl.62; Jochum 1993, fig.5; Schreckenberg II, 487f. Illustration after Goldschmidt I, 1914, no.114.

▲ 5. Crucifix with Ecclesia and Synagoga: the former with chalice and crown, the latter blindfolded with a scroll of scripture, a sign that the Jews do not recognize the Christ promised in their own scriptures (i.e. in the Old Testament). Miniature in a sacramentary which was presumably made during the second third of the eleventh century in the Benedictine abbey of Niederaltaich, Bavaria. Rome, BAV, Ross.204. folio 10 recto. Illustration after Plotzek and Surmann 1982, 101.

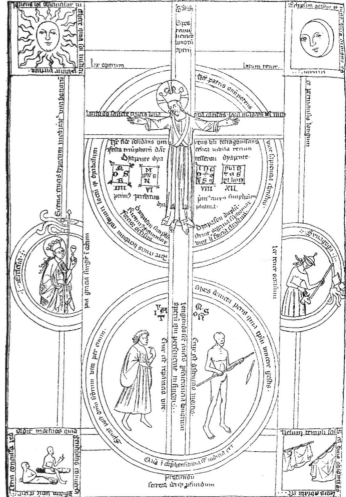

6. Crucifix with (Gratia–)Ecclesia and (Lex–)Synagoga and the parallel allegorical personifications Vita and Mors; here Vita–Ecclesia and Mors–Synagoga are to be linked. Miniature in an evangelistary commissioned by Uota von Moosberg, abbess of the Benedictine convent of Niedermünster in Regensburg (1002–1025). Munich, SB, Lat. 13601, folio 3 verso. Literature: Mayr–Harting 1991; Schreckenberg II, 502–6. Illustration after Goldschmidt II, 1918, pl.77.

7. Copy of the previous illustration. Miniature in a composite manuscript from Metten monastery made in 1415. Munich, SB, Clm 8201, folio 97 verso. Literature: Weis 1958, fig.9; Seiferth 1964, 25f.; Rademacher 1975, fig.120, Illustration after Weber 1894, 66.

8. Crucifix with Ecclesia and Synagoga on right and left respectively. Synagoga is holding a (stylized) palm frond (a symbol of the East) as an attribute and is in process of leaving the scene of the saving event. A new feature here by comparison with earlier reliefs with a soteriological theme (the victory of Christ over death and sin, the resurrection of the dead) is the inclusion of the birth of Christ (lower area) and his ascension (upper area). Maas region, ivory relief from Liège, first half of the eleventh century. Brussels, Musées Royaux d'art et d'histoire. Literature: Schreckenberg II, 500f. Illustration after Goldschmidt II, 1918, no.55.

10. Crucifixion with Ecclesia and Synagoga in the customary iconographic position under the cross. Synagoga is given a (stylized) palm frond. She is turning away from Christ, who is turning towards Ecclesia. Ivory relief on the cover of an evangeliary. Middle of the eleventh century. Tongres, cathedral treasury. Literature: Schreckenberg II, 510–12. For a roughly contemporaneous example of Synagoga departing from the cross in the Byzantine sphere (very rare) see Schiller IV, 1, 1976, fig.101, and Jochum 1993, fig.6. This illustration after Goldschmidt II, 1918, no.47.

9. Ecclesia and Synagoga, the latter without the protection and dignity of clothing, so that her upper body is bare (a sign of shame). She is sitting bowed in grief with closed eyes: the book has slipped from her grasp. In the iconographic context ('Gunhild Cross'),

Vita and Mors are among those appearing. Walrus tusk relief, around the third quarter of the eleventh century. Copenhagen, Nationalmuseet. Literature: Jochum 1993, fig.39; Schreckenberg II, 514–16. Illustration after Seiferth 1964, nos.8–9.

(b) High Middle Ages (twelfth to thirteenth centuries)

11. Crucifixion with Ecclesia and Synagoga, together with the man piercing Christ with a spear and the man holding a sponge, whose names (Longinus and Stefaton) only appear in legends after the New Testament. Ecclesia is being embraced by an angel and led to Christ (as bride). Synagoga, an old woman in shabby clothing, is being driven from the scene of the sacred event by a second angel. Ivory relief from southern Italy, c.1070–1080. Berlin–Dahlem, Staatliche Museen Preussischer Kulturbesitz, sculpture section, Inv. no.589. Literature: Jochum 1993, fig.9; Schreckenberg II, 516f. Illustration after Seiferth 1964, no.11.

1. Christ casts out Synagoga, who is leaving the scene of salvation towards the left (heraldically) and going to the jaws of hell, which are wide open. By contrast, Ecclesia is elected and crowned or blessed. Synagoga's defeat is made plain by the way her crown has fallen and her standard has been broken. Miniature in the *Liber floridus* of Lambert of St Omer, c.1100–1120. Ghent, Rijksuniversiteit, Centraale Bibliotheek, Ms 92, folio 253 recto. Literature: V.G.Tuttle, *An Analysis of the Structure of the* Liber Floridus, Ohio State University dissertation 1979; Büchsel 1987, fig.7; Williams 1992; Jochum 1993, fig.12; Schreckenberg II, 523–5. Illustration after Derolez 1968, folio 253.

2. Crucifix with Ecclesia and Synagoga: the latter is wearing the conical hat (truncated to the point of being domed) which often appears in the twelfth century as a group characteristic of Jews. She is turning away from Christ, gazing at the ground and putting her left foot forward to depart. She has lowered her standard – a sign of her defeat – but retains a certain dignity, though her dress is rather simpler than that of the ruler Ecclesia. Miniature in the Essen Missal, a work which was produced in the Rhineland c.1100. Düsseldorf, Heinrich-Heine-Institut (formerly Landes-bibliothek), Cod.D 4, folio 8 verso. Literature: Schreckenberg II, 522f. Illustration after Schiller IV 1, 1976, 109.

3. Crucifix with Ecclesia and Synagoga. Wisdom is above the cross (cf. Prov.8.1ff.), and below is the treader of the grapes (Isa.63.1ff.), an Old Testament prefiguration of Christ; bottom left is Isaiah with a halo, and top right a group of Jews is standing beside Synagoga, three of them with the funnel-shaped Jewish hat (as a group characteristic). Because of overpaint-ing in the restoration of the picture it is no longer possible to read the inscriptions: presumably Deut.21.23 was quoted in connection with the Jews or Synagoga. Mural in the monastic church of Kleinkomburg near Schwäbisch-Hall, c.1108. Literature: Schreckenberg II, 526f. Illustration after Marrow 1979, fig.58.

4. Christ, Ecclesia and the rejected Synagoga. Initial O*(sculetur)* (Song of Songs 1.1) in the twelfth-century 'Giant Bible' in Montalcino. Montalcino, Biblioteca communale, Cod s.s. Vol.II, folio 56 recto. Literature: Schiller IV.1, 1976, fig.123; Jochum 1993, fig.11. Illustration after a photograph in the Bildarchiv zur Buchmalerei, Kunsthistorisches Institut der Universität Saarbrücken.

5. Crucifix with Ecclesia and Synagoga. Here for the first time the latter is carrying an ox-yoke as a symbol of the 'yoke of the law'. Above all after the Letter of Barnabas, the servitude of the Jews under the law is one of the accusations of anti-Jewish polemic. Miniature in the antiphonary of the Benedictine abbey of St Peter, Salzburg, c.1160. Vienna, ÖN, Cod.ser.nova 2700, 300. Literature: Schreckenberg II, 564. Illustration after Lind 1870, pl.XI.

▶ 6. Crucifix with Ecclesia, Synagoga and scenes from the Old and New Testaments. Surface of a portable altar from Stavelot, Belgium, c.1160. Brussels, Musées royaux, Inv. no.1580. Literature: Kemp 1987, fig. p.64; Prache 1992, pl.XXIII; Schreckenberg II, 557f. Illustration after Braun I, 1924, pl.93.

◀ 7. Crucifix with Ecclesia and Synagoga. Enamel surface of a portable altar from the Maas region, c.1160. Augsburg, Maximilian Museum. Literature: Schreckenberg II, 556f. Illustration after *Suevia sacra* 1973, no.118.

◀ 8. Crucifix with Ecclesia and Synagoga. The latter has a cloth over her eyes which makes her blind (to Christ); she is also holding instruments of the passion (the staff with a sponge and the lance) as her attributes. Thus she is defined iconographically as an adversary, but is not yet stripped of her power and humiliated. Mönchengladbach, former Benedictine abbey of St Vitus. Literature: Schreckenberg II, 560f. Illustration after *Mon.Jud.Handb.*1963, no.63.

9. Enlarged detail of the previous illlustration. Illustration after Blumenkranz 1965,
no.66.

10. Crucifix with Ecclesia and Synagoga.
The inscription around it reads: *Hec parit,
hec credit, obit hic, fugit hec, hic obedit* (i.e.
Mary gives birth, Ecclesia believes, Christ
dies, Synagoga flees, John obeys). Gilded
enamelled copper disc, originally the front
of a reliquary, c.1170. Paris, Musée Cluny.
Literature: de Winter 1985, fig.90; Brandt
1988, fig.10; Schreckenberg II, 578f. Illustration after Barral i Altet 1983, no.234.

11. Crucifix with Ecclesia and Synagoga. The pictures round the edge show christological 'types' of the Old Testament. Engraving on a paten of the former abbey of Tremessen (Poland) c.1170. Gniezno, cathedral treasury. Literature: Schreckenberg II, 575–7. Illustration after Skubiszewski 1980, no.3.

▲ 12. Deposition from the cross, with Ecclesia and Synagoga. An angel (Raphael) is flying down from above – acting on a commission from heaven – and pressing down Synagoga's helmeted head (inscription: *Synagoga deponitur*, i.e. she is robbed of her power as ruler and warrior). The inscription next to Raphael gives the reason for this: *vere is filius fierat* (i.e. Synagoga did not recognize that Jesus was Son of God). On the other side of the cross stands Ecclesia, her standard raised high in her left hand, and the chalice with the blood of Christ in her right hand (the ascription is *Ecclesia exaltatur*, i.e. Ecclesia is exalted, becomes the new ruler in place of Synagoga). Synagoga's final defeat also becomes evident from the fact that her trident standard is broken and its banner is trailing on the floor. Parma, cathedral, marble relief by Benedetto Antelami, dated 1178. Literature: Zimmermann 1897, 106–9; Hauttmann 1929, fig. p.527; Christoffel 1940; Schiller II, 1968, fig.555; IV, 1976, 49; von Simson 1972, fig.344; Hurkey 1983, fig.221; *Lexikon der Kunst* I, Freiburg 1987, 210f.; Schreckenberg II, 592f. Illustration after Durliat 1983, no.289.

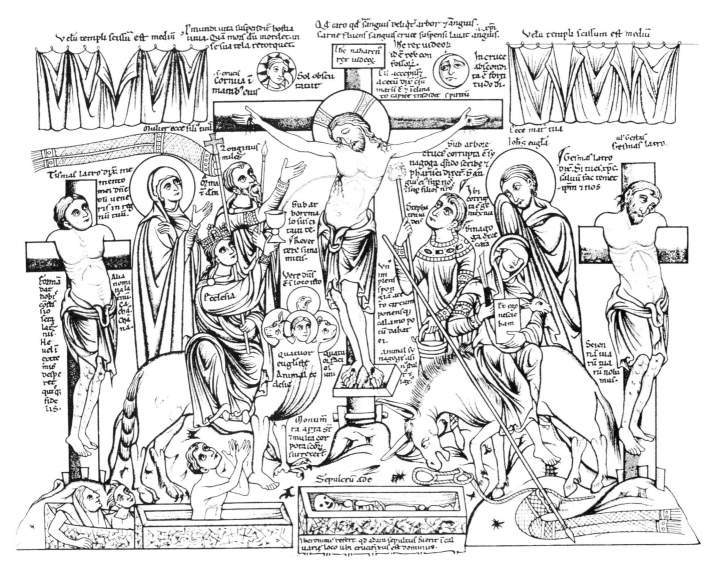

◀ 13. Ecclesia and Synagoga. Here a provisional final stage in the iconographic history of 'Ecclesia versus Synagoga' seems to have been reached. The latter, although humiliated and in a desperate situation, still shows a remnant of stubborn defiance in the position of her head and right hand. Miniature in the inital Q of a homily for the dedication festival of a church in a collection of sermons from the last quarter of the twelfth century (arranged according to the church year). Verdun, Bibliothèque municipale, Ms.121. Literature: Jochum 1993, fig.45 (cf. Jochum fig.11: Rejected Synagoga, lying on the ground, looks up sorrowfully towards Christ and Ecclesia, but is still holding a kid – the symbol of her past cult – firmly in her arms: see Schiller IV, 1976, 54, on fig.123 = Montalcino, Bibl.Comunale, Cod.s.s.Vol.II, folio 56 recto ['Giant Bible of the twelfth century']; see above III, 1b, middle of the twelfth century); Schreckenberg II, 601–4. Illustration after Schubert 1979, no.11.

14. Crucifixion with Ecclesia and Synagoga, the latter with circumcising knife and kid (symbol of Old Testament sacrifice) as attributes. Her eyes are lowered, a sign of her blindness to Christ, and in defeat her banner is trailing on the ground. Her mount is an ass (regarded as stubborn or stupid). Miniature in the *Hortus deliciarum* of Herrad of Landsberg, around 1185, folio 150 recto (old copy from the time before the loss of the only manuscript, i.e. before 1870 [Paris, BN]). Literature: Jochum 1993, fig.40; Schreckenberg II, 601–4. Illustration after Green II, 1979, fig.234.

15. Crucifix with Ecclesia and Synagoga. The latter has almost been forced out of the scene of salvation: the crown is falling from the head of the former ruler, which is bent in sorrow; her standard (in the reproduction only part of the staff can be seen) is turned downwards, as are the tables of the law. Miniature of the so-called Ingeborg Psalter, made in Paris c.1195. Chantilly, Bibliothèque du Musée Condé, Ms.9, folio 27 recto (upper half). Literature: Schreckenberg II, 611f., 657; Engelhart 1987 (II, pl.262). Illustration after Deuchler 1985 (commentary volume), no.31.

16. Ecclesia and Synagoga, the latter blinded by a snake winding itself around her head (i.e. the devil), as by a blindfold elsewhere. Above the miniature is a thematically related text (Ps.Bernard of Clairvaux, *Patrologia Latina* 184, 1327–8): *Ysaias cecinit, Sinagoga meminit, numquam tamen desinit esse caeca.* Miniature in the illustrated Bible of Petris de Funes, made in 1197. Amiens, Bibliothèque municipale, Cod.108, folio 43 verso. Literature: Jochum 1993, fig.31; Schreckenberg II, 610. Illustration after Seiferth 1964, no.22.

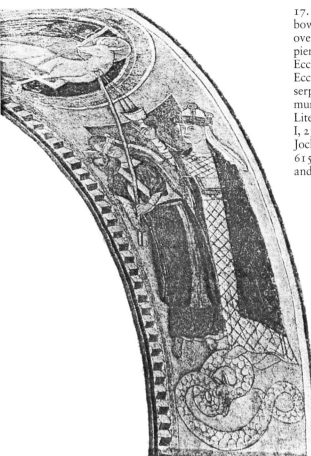

17. Ecclesia and Synagoga. The latter, bowed, blinded (to Christ) by a blindfold over her eyes, with a falling crown, is piercing the lamb of God with a lance, and Ecclesia is receiving his blood in a chalice. Ecclesia is putting her right foot on the serpent. Spenstrup (Denmark), church, mural in the arch of the apse, c.1200. Literature: Weis 1958, 1197; Zafran 1973, I, 239f.; Schiller IV.1, 1976, figs. 116–17; Jochum 1993, fig.35; Schreckenberg II, 615f. Illustration after de Boor 1934, no.4, and Schubert 1978, no.48.

18. Ecclesia and Synagoga, the latter permanently blinded by a devil in the form of a beast. Here hope for her regaining sight (by lifting the blindfold) seems to be totally eliminated. Stained glass in Chartres Cathedral (Passion Window). First half of the thirteenth century. Literature: Revel–Neher 1992, fig.85; Jochum 1993, fig.32. Illustration after Weber, 1894, 88 (copy).

19. Cross with lamb, Ecclesia and Synagoga. The broken spear of the blind Synagoga is pointed at the lamb of God (i.e. Christ) in the medallion at the centre of the cross. Ecclesia is catching the blood flowing down in her chalice. The miniature is painted in an initial T*(e igitur)*, i.e. in a letter which has a formal affinity to the cross (cf. also Ezek.9.4, *signa thau*, etc.). Synagoga's face has been deliberately destroyed in the manuscript. The stabbing of the lamb by Synagoga imputes to the Jews the desire to repeat Christ's passion; it also suggests the later anti-Jewish legends about the profanation of the host (stabbing the host, etc.). Miniature in a liturgical book, beginning of the thirteenth century. Metz, Bibliothèque muncipale, Ms.1169, folio 146. Literature: Schreckenberg II, 622. Illustration after Leroquais 1937, pl.XX.

20. Crucifix with Ecclesia and Synagoga. Miniature in the Psalter of Blanche of Castile, made around 1230. Paris, BA, Ms 1186, folio 24. Literature: *Lexikon der Kunst* V, Freiburg 1988, 176. Illustration after Erlande–Brandenburg 1984, no.132.

21. Deposition from the cross with Ecclesia and Synagoga. Here there are also typological representations of the saving and redeeming sacrifice of the cross (Moses with the brazen serpent; Isaac's sacrifice by Abraham; the pelican which brings its dead young to life with drops of blood from its breast [*per sanguinem redempturus*]; cf. Luke 24.21). Cover of a manuscript made in the first half of the thirteenth century in northern Germany. Wolfenbüttel, HAB Cod.Helmst. 522. Literature: Engelhart 1987, II, no.317.

22. Ecclesia and Synagoga. Stone sculptures, Strasbourg cathedral, c.1230. Literature: Seiferth 1964, figs.35–7; von Simson 1984, 104–25. Illustration after *Mon.Jud.Handb.*1963, pl.67.

Die Christi blüt vberwind ich dich.

Disse zwey Alte bilder schön   Am Münster/in dem hindern thor   Darauff man sicht der alten kunst
Find man zu Straßburg also sechs   Wan man geht auff die Fronhof vor: Vnd was sie han geglaubet sunst

Dasselbige Blüt das blendet mich.

Vom Euangelio vnd Gesatz/   Vnd wie derselbig vberwind   Derhalb vmb lieb vnd künstligkeyt
Wie allein halt der Glaub den platz/   Beid welt vn gsatz/die macht der sünd: Erhalt man solche bilder heut.

23. Free woodcuts by Tobias Stimeer of the Strasbourg Ecclesia and Synagoga, made around 1572. Basel Public Art Collection, Engravings. Literature: Strauss 1973, 136–9; *Spätrenaissance* 1984, nos.14–15.

24. (Ecclesia and) Synagoga. Ecclesia and Synagoga introduce apostles and prophets or are grouped with these in terms of the *Concordia Veteris et Novi Testament*i. In the case of Synagoga the interpreters speak of the 'helpless stubbornness of the conquered enemy' (Moriz–Eichborn 1899,18) or see her lips 'painfully distorted' (Seiferth 1964, 166). At all events, here the dramatic moment of the falling of the crown is depicted and thus the intrinsic connection between blindness (to Christ) and loss of rule. Reims, Notre Dame Cathedral, c.1225–1240. Literature: Michel 1906, fig.131; von Simson 1972, fig.71; Kurmann 1984, fig.52. Illustration after Moriz–Eichborn 1899, pl.XV.

◀ 25. Ecclesia and Synagoga. Bamberg Cathedral, Prince's Portal, 1230–1240. Literature: Verheyen 1962; Seiferth 1964, figs.32–34; *EJ* III, 1971, 91–2; von Simson, 1972, fig.216: Haag 1985, figs.187–8; Suckale 1987, fig.38; Deneke 1988, fig.171. Illustration after Jantzen 1925, nos.74, 77.

▼ 26. (Ecclesia and) Synagoga. Her hair is falling free; she has the usual blindfold, and is still firmly holding the Old Testament law in her left hand (in the form of tables, like the Bamberg Synagoga). In her right hand she was probably holding a spear with a banner (which has been lost). Magdeburg, cathedral, porch, c.1245 (photograph C.Beyer, Weimar). Literature: Giesau 1924, fig. p.72; Seiferth 1964, 168; Sachs, nd., pl.13.

27. Ecclesia and Synagoga, the latter stabbing the lamb of God. Miniature on the leaf of a missal which was made in northern France before 1250 (Noyon Missal). Baltimore, The Walters Art Gallery, Collection Mr and Mrs P.Hofer. Literature: Seiferth 1964, fig. 18; Schiller IV.1, 1976, fig.119; Jochum 1993, fig.33. Illustration after *Mon.Jud.Handb.*1963, no.65.

28. Ecclesia and Synagoga. Trier, Liebfrauenkirche (west portal), c. 1250. Literature: Bunjes 1938, fig.131; Erler 1954, 7; Ben–Sasson II, 1979, fig. after p.118. Illustration after *Mon.Jud.Handb.* 1963, no.70 (cf. ibid., Catalogue A 47).

29. Crucifixion (through the four virtues) with Ecclesia and Synagoga. Miniature in the psalter of a Cistercian monastery (Psalter from Bonmont), in upper Rhineland (diocese of Basel or Constance), c.1260. Besançon, Bibliothèque municipale, Ms.54, folio 15 verso. Literature: Michel II 1, 1906, fig.270; Schiller II, 1968, fig.450; von Simson 1972, fig.70; *Zeit der Staufer* 1977, II, fig.514. Illustration after Leroquais 1940, II, pl. XCI.

30. Crucifix with Ecclesia and Synagoga, the latter being driven away from the scene of salvation by an angel (above right). She is depicted as an old woman holding a container for unguents (?); Ecclesia, above left (i.e. heraldic right) being led to Christ by another angel, is holding a model of the church in both hands. Siena, cathedral, pulpit relief by Nicola Pisano, c.1265–1268. Literature: Weber 1894, 85; de Francovich 1928, fig.18; Middeldorf-Kosegarten 1969, fig.14; Schiller IV.1, 1976, fig.507; Kreytenberg 1984, no.433. Illustration after Foto Fratelli Alinari, Florence. Cf. *Regensburger Buchmalerei* 1987, pl.133: Synagoga being driven away by an angel (Oxford, Keble College, Ms.49, folio 7 recto [lectionary from Regensburg, c.1275]).

32. (Ecclesia and) Synagoga. Silver figure on a reliquary shrine (Eleutherius shrine), completed 1247. Tournai, cathedral treasury. Literature: Schiller IV.1, 1976, figs.126–7; Schubert 1978, figs.55–6; Eckert 1991, 362. Illustration after Seiferth 1964, no.38.

31. Ecclesia and Synagoga. Stained glass in the east end of the choir of the Elisabethkirche in Marburg, c.1240. Literature: Seiferth 1964, fig.29; Schiller IV 1, 1976, figs.133–4; *Zeit der Staufer* V, 1977, fig.42; Kötzsche and von der Osten-Sacken 1984, fig.40; Jochum 1993, fig.28. Illustration after *Mon.Jüd. Handb.*1963, no.68.

◄ 33. Ecclesia and the dead Synagoga, whose scroll of the law (torn by Christ?) is lying on the dead (or dying) wrinkled old woman. Alongside is her broken banner (the heraldic beast is the scorpion). The book of Christ, the New Testament, has conquered the Torah. Ecclesia is bowing in concern over the old woman. Miniature in a *Bible moralisée*, thirteenth century. Paris, BN Ms fr. 9561, folio 74 verso. Literature: Erler 1954, 7f.; Seiferth 1964, 185. Illustration after Weber 1894, 109.

► 34. (Ecclesia and) Synagoga. Relief on a misericord, former monastery of Pöhlde (Osterode district, Harz), c.1284. Hanover, Niedersächsisches Landesmuseum. Literature: Seiferth 1964, fig.42; Schubert 1978, fig.57; Ben-Sasson II, 1979, fig. after 118; Bremer 1986, fig.32; Jochum 1993, fig.27; illustration after *Mon.Jud. Kat.*1963, A 48, no.21.

► 35. (Ecclesia and) Synagoga. Synagoga is depicted as a seductive woman wearing an almost transparent dress (with a hem at the top) and with her long hair loose. The crown slipping from her head seems almost displaced. However, the goat's head is also traditional (as a symbol of the past Old Testament sacrificial cult), as is the veil – which can only be faintly be seen in the picture. As always, blindness and the falling of the crown stand in a causal relationship.

Here the theme is an (assumed) affinity between Jews and excess and sin; this is also the case *mutatis mutandis* with the treatment of the 'Judensau' theme. Painting on the wooden sanctuary ceiling of a church in Al, Hallingdalen (north-west of Oslo), second half of the thirteenth century. Oslo, Museum of National Antiquities: Ål Stave Church (C no.11707). Illustration after Blumenkranz 1965, no.70.

(c) Late Middle Ages (fourteenth to fifteenth centuries)

1. (Ecclesia and) Synagoga. Worms, cathedral, stone figure on the right pillar of the south portal, Rhenish work c.1300. Literature: Weber 1894, 141; de Coo 1965, fig.28; Schiller IV.1, 1976, fig.115. Illustration after Wolfius II, 1600, 869 (copy).

2. Crucifix with Ecclesia and Synagoga, the latter with a yellow robe. The adversaries (left and right below the crucifixion scene, each in her own field) are riding against each other as in a joust, both with their usual attributes. Synagoga's defeat is already anticipated iconographically: her standard is broken and she seems to be sinking on her mount, but is holding on to her biblical tradition (the goat's head as symbol of the old covenant and its sacrificial cult). Freiburg Cathedral, stained glass ('Cloth Window') c.1300. Literature: Seiferth 1964, 141; Schiller IV.1, 1976, 52. Illustration after Geiges 1931, nos.244–6.

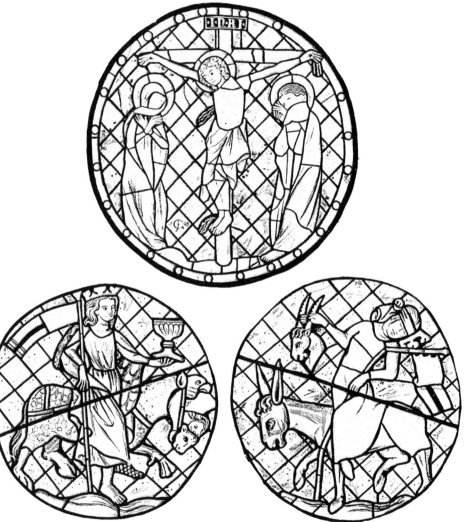

▲ 3. Ecclesia and Synagoga, with the wise and foolish virgins (Matt.25.1–3), a sign of election and repudiation. Freiburg, Minster, sculptures in the porch c.1290 to 1310. Literature: Weber 1894, 95f.; Schmitt 1922, fig.33; Schmitt II, 1926, figs.143, 144, 147; Künstle I, 1928, figs.22–23; *RDK* IV, 1957, 1203 fig.8; Münzel 1959, figs. pp. 196, 199, 236; Seiferth 1964, 166–9; Schiller I, 1966, fig.283; IV.1, 1976, 58. Illustration after *Mon.Jud.Handb.*1963, no.69.

▶ 4. Crucifix with Ecclesia and Synagoga. Miniature in a missal from the St Peter Stift in Fritzlar, c. 1320. Kassel, Gesamthochschul-Bibliothek, Ms.theol.2°162, folio 95 verso. Literature: *Biblia* 1977, fig.p.60. Illustration after Deckert 1928, pl.168.

Without illustration. Ecclesia and Synagoga ('Crucifixion through the Virtues'). Mary is piercing her breast with a sword, and Synagoga (or, with Schiller, Sponsa), standing in front of the church, is piercing Christ's side with a lance – as Longinus does elsewhere. A later viewer of the picture tried to obliterate the sword and the lance. Here Synagoga's behaviour is akin to her stabbing the lamb of God. Miniature in a collection of sermons by Bernard of Clairvaux, lower Rhineland, c.1300. Cologne, historical archive W 255, folio 117 verso. Literature: Swarenski II, 1936, fig.162; Schiller II, 1968, fig. 448; Oliver 1978, fig.15; *Zisterzienser* 1980, fig. p.373; Verdier 1982, fig.37; Jochum 1993, fig.36; illustration in *Mon.Jud. Kat.*1963, A 49. no.22.

5. Crucifix with Ecclesia and Synagoga, the latter above right as an old woman being forced away from the scene of salvation by an angel: by contrast Ecclesia (with the chalice as an attribute) is being led to Christ. Pistoia, S.Andrea, pulpit relief by Giovanni Pisano, 1298–1301. Literature: de Francovich 1938, fig.203; White 1966, pl.32; Kreytenberg 1984, no.434. Illustration Foto Fratelli Alinari, Florence.

6. (Ecclesia and) Synagoga. The serpent of the evil one is making her blind. Bordeaux, St Seurin, c. 1300. Literature: *EJ* 1971, III, 93–4, fig.1c.; Schiller IV.1, 1976, no.114. Illustration after Viollet–le–Duc V, 1875, 156.

7. The crucifixion is depicted in the middle of the so–called Parament of Narbonne (c.1375): connected to it from the outside, on the level of the cross-beam of the cross, are Ecclesia (being guided by Isaiah to the cross; he is holding the inscription Isa.53.4, *vere languores nostros ipse tulit*) and Synagoga (still resisting, she is being led by David to Christ; he is holding the inscription Ps.84.10: *respice in faciem Christi tui*). Paris, Louvre. Literature: Troescher 1966, pl.2; von Wilken 1977, figs.18–19; *DMA* V, 1985, fig. p.679; Erlande-Brandenburg 1988, figs.330–1; Sterling 1987, figs.127–8; illustration after Weber 1894, 111.

8. The dead Synagoga being laid in a sarcophagus. Ecclesia is at her head and Christ at her feet, pointing to Ecclesia (or blessing the dead woman?). Synagoga is left her dignity; she keeps the crown and the tables of the law even in the sarcophagus. Four figures with haloes stand by (probably the evangelists, not the prophets), joining in the mourning. The context is the typological interpretation of the death of Miriam, Moses' sister ('The death of Mary in the wilderness and the fact that Aaron and Moses also died there means that the old law cannot lead believers out of the wilderness of this life, but only the new law'). Miniature in a *Bible moralisée*, c.1410. Paris, BN, Ms fr. 166, folio 40 verso. Literature: Weber 1894, fig. p.110; Oepke 1950, 337f.; Blumenkranz 1965, fig. 47; Schubert 1978, fig.26; Schiller IV.1, 1976, fig.139; Eckert 1991, 365; Jochum 1993, fig.46. Illustration after Seiferth 1964, no.52.

10. Crucifix with Ecclesia and Synagoga. Miniature in a *Biblia pauperum* made between 1320 and 1330 in upper Austria. Budapest, Museum of Fine Arts, folio 18 recto. Literature: *Hommage à Alexis Petrovics*, Budapest 1934, fig.96: Berve 1989. Illustration after Schmidt 1959, pl.14b.

11. Ecclesia and Synagoga. Miniature in a manuscript of the French translation of the *Rationale divinorum officiorum* (i.e. handbook of liturgy) of William Durandus the Elder (died 1296), made in the fourteenth century. Paris, BA, Ms 2002, folio 2. Literature: Martin 1924, fig CVIII; cf. Rabel 1992, fig.3. Illustration after Martin-Lauer 1929, pl.XXXV.

9. Crucifix with Ecclesia and Synagoga (within a depiction of the tree of Jesse [Isa.11.11]). Ecclesia's inscription reads *Potus* [sic] *Cypri dilectus meus in vineis Engaddi* (*potus* is an error for *botrus*, cf. Song of Songs 1.13). Synagoga's inscription reads *maledictus qui pendet in ligno* (cf. Deut.21.23). Miniature in a *Speculum salvationis* ('Mirror of salvation') manuscript, made in 1324 in upper Rhineland or German-speaking Switzerland. Kremsmünster (Austria), Stiftsbibliothek, Codex Cremifanensis 243, folio 55 recto. Literature: Mayer 1962, fig.28; Mazal 1975, fig.55; Ohly 1985, fig.23; Unger 1986, 64f.; *DMA* XII, 1989, fig. p.182. Illustration after Neumüller 1972 (facsimile volume).

12. Man of Sorrows with Ecclesia and Synagoga: Synagoga (with a Jewish ring!) is not looking at Christ, but turning away from her; her standard is broken and her crown falling (upside down). With her right hand she is pouring the wine from her chalice (an affinity to the five foolish virgins who have no oil for their lamps?). Scriptural scroll: *et ego nesciobam*, after Gen.28.16: *vere Dominus est in loco isto et ego nesciebam*; she is holding a goat in her left hand (sacrificial animal as a symbol of the old covenant which she is unwilling to give up). Miniature in a manuscript of the Dominican house in Eichstätt, Bavaria, beginning of the fifteenth century. Literature: Mayer 1962, no.25. Illustration from Bildarchiv Foto Marburg.

13. Synagoga. Stone statue at the entrance to the refectory in the monastery of Pamplona, fourteenth century. Illustration after Marsy 1888, 189.

14. Ecclesia and Synagoga. Ecclesia (depicted as a young knight with a fish as heraldic emblem) is engaged in a joust with her lance set against Synagoga, a figure characterized by a Jewish hat. The latter is riding on a sow in the hopeless battle, without weapons, holding the bridle in her right hand and seeking support with her left. The whole picture is a polemical allegory of the battle between Christianity and Judaism. Relief on a misericord in Erfurt Cathedral c.1400–1410. Literature: Bergner 1905, fig.484; Becker 1929, fig.180; Weis 1958, 1208; Hootz 1968, fig.75; Zafran 1973, I, 12; Shachar 1974, pl.28; Schubert 1978, fig. 58; Schubert II, 1979, fig.27; *Germ.Jud*.III,1, 1987, 312; Eckert 1991, fig. p.365; Schille IV.1, 1976, no.140; Jochum 1993, fig.38. Illustration Bildarchiv Foto Marburg.

15. Ecclesia and Synagoga; the latter lying senseless on the ground, while Jews and Christians anxiously take note of the event. Miniature in a *Bible moralisée*, c.1410. Paris, BN, Fr.166. Literature: Oepke 1950, 337; Schiller IV.1, 1976, 59. Illustration after Weber 1894, 92f. pl.V.

16. Ecclesia and Synagoga. Miniature in a *Bible moralisée*, c.1410. Paris, BN, Fr.166. Illustration after Weber 1894, 42f. pl.V.

◀ 17. The allegorical pair are here put in a bourgeois room: Synagoga, dressed in yellow, as usual with head bent, is on her way out: the thin veil before her eyes cannot be made out in most reproductions. Her standard (apparently with two Jewish hats as heraldic emblems) is broken, but she is holding the tables of the law – inscribed with the pseudo-Hebrew characters frequent in the late Middle Ages – firmly on her arm. *Speculum salvationis* altar of Konrad Witz, c.1440. Basel, Öffentliche Kunstsammlung, Kunstmuseum. Literature: Ganz 1947, figs.1, 2, 4; Meng-Koehler 1947, 21f., 47; Stange IV, 1951, pls.194–5; Pinder II, 1956, fig.431; Eckert 1961, 70f.; Röttgen 1961, 48 fig.58: *Mon.Jud.Handb.*1963, fig.71; Seiferth 1964, fig.58; *KLM* V, 1968, fig. p.795; Schiller IV.1, 1976, 58f.; Mellinkoff 1984, fig.8; Eckert 1991, 363f.; Gantner 1943, pls. 14–15; Jochum 1993, fig.26.

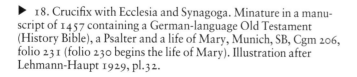

▶ 18. Crucifix with Ecclesia and Synagoga. Minature in a manuscript of 1457 containing a German-language Old Testament (History Bible), a Psalter and a life of Mary, Munich, SB, Cgm 206, folio 231 (folio 230 begins the life of Mary). Illustration after Lehmann-Haupt 1929, pl.32.

▲ 19. The old and new covenants. Woodcuts at the end of the OT or beginning of the NT in the German Bible of the printer Anton Sorg (Augsburg 1477), folios 429–30. The portrayal of Synagoga is associated with the martyrdom of a saint. Literature: Schulz 1927, pl. after p.29; *RDK* V, 1967, 1501, fig.15. Illustration after Schramm 1920, IV, nos. 317–18.

◄ 20. Christ (with tiara) as ruler of the world, surrounded by Ecclesia and Moses, with prophets, angels and the symbols of the four evangelists. Here Moses has so utterly assumed Synagoga's place that he has even taken over her attributes (broken standard, tables of the law turned downwards, which threaten to slip from her fingers) and attitude (gaze lowered and averted from Christ, in the process of departing). Miniature in the Missal of Poitiers, end of the fifteenth century. Poitiers, cathedral treasury, folio 38 recto. Literature: Mellinkoff 1970, fig.118. Illustration after Leroquais 1937, pl.CIII.

(d) The culmination of the polemic: the 'Living Cross'

1. Woodcut from 1600 (relatively rough copy) after a fresco of the parish church of St Andreas in Göss (near Leoben, Steiermark), painted in the last quarter of the fifteenth century. A picture with a traditional soteriological programme. The heavenly Jerusalem is above, and the jaws of hell are below. Literature: Weber 1894, 139; Füglister 1964, fig.XXIV; Seiferth 1964, 200–2. Illustration after Wolfius 1600, II, p.586.

ISTA FLET HEC SVRG̅ OB HIC CAD̅ HEC DOLET ISTE

ANGELVS EXILARAT D̅N̅I QVOS MORS CRVCIARAT

◄ Plate 1 (on III, 1b). Crucifix with Ecclesia and Synagoga. Ecclesia and Synagoga appear below the cross and once again outside the central picture, on the left and the right. Cover of an evangeliary: the inside is an enamel panel, the outside a walrus tusk relief on gilded sheet copper. From St Godehard in Hildesheim, c.1170. Trier, cathedral treasure, Codex 141/126; Amt für kirchliche Denkmalpflege, Trier (photograph: A. Münchow). Literature: Legner 1982, fig.383; *Schatzkunst Trier* 1984, fig. p.128; Meckseper II, 1985, fig. p.198; Jochum 1993, fig. 37; Schreckenberg II, 584–7.

► Plate 2 (on III, 1c). Crucifix with Ecclesia and Synagoga. The crown of Synagoga, who is dressed in yellow, is falling off (upside-down), and her standard is broken in several places. A small devil is riding on her and putting his right arm over her eyes, so that she could not see Christ even if she wanted to. Here again the iconography suggests a certain affinity between Jews and the devil. Miniature in a German History Bible from Zittau, first half of the fifteenth century. Dresden, Sächsische Landesbibliothek, MS.A 49, folio 189 recto. Literature: Weis 1958, 1199f.; Bruck 1906, no.184. Illustration after Jochum 1993, fig.30.

Plate 3 (on III, 1c). Crucifix with Ecclesia and Synagoga. Miniature in *Biblia pauperum. Apocalypsis*, Weimar Ms, c.1340–50. Weimar, Stiftung Weimarer Klassik, Herzogin Amalia Bibliothek, Fol.max., folio 22. Illustration after Behrends 1977 (facsimile volume), folio 22.

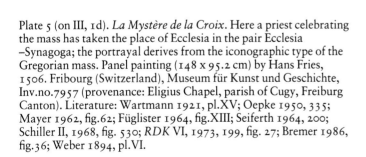

Plate 5 (on III, 1d). *La Mystère de la Croix*. Here a priest celebrating the mass has taken the place of Ecclesia in the pair Ecclesia –Synagoga; the portrayal derives from the iconographic type of the Gregorian mass. Panel painting (148 x 95.2 cm) by Hans Fries, 1506. Fribourg (Switzerland), Museum für Kunst und Geschichte, Inv.no.7957 (provenance: Eligius Chapel, parish of Cugy, Freiburg Canton). Literature: Wartmann 1921, pl.XV; Oepke 1950, 335; Mayer 1962, fig.62; Füglister 1964, fig.XIII; Seiferth 1964, 200; Schiller II, 1968, fig. 530; *RDK* VI, 1973, 199, fig. 27; Bremer 1986, fig.36; Weber 1894, pl.VI.

Plate 4 (on III, 1c). Painting by the 'Master of the Ursula Legend', fourth quarter of the fifteenth century. Synagoga's turban follows the increasing tendency in the late Middle Ages for Christian art to depict Jews as Orientals. This in any case emphasizes what – from a Western perspective – was the foreign appearance of the Jews in their special dress. Bruges, Groeningemuseum (photograph: Van Mieghem A., Ostend). Literature: Vos 1982, 151–4; Jochum 1993, fig.20.

Plate 6 (on III, 1 d). Living Cross (section), the work of Thomas von Villach. Ecclesia is at Christ's right hand (riding on her tetramorph, holding a model of the church in her hands and crowned by a hand growing out of the beam of the cross); there is also Mary, picking hosts from the tree of life. On the heraldic left is blind Synagoga, whose crown is falling off and whose standard is shattered. She is riding on a mortally wounded ass and being pierced by the hand growing out of the cross beam, but is nevertheless holding in her left hand the head of a he-goat, the symbol of the long-past Old Testament sacrificial cult. On her side there is also Eve with an apple and a skull. This produces a contrast between Mary–Ecclesia–life–new covenant (the host as a bloodless sacrifice) and Eve–Synagogue–death–old covenant (the he-goat as a bloody sacrifice). Fresco in the village church of Thörl (near Arnoldstein, Carinthia) c.1475–1480. Literature: Lohrmann 1982, 313; Schuder and Hirsch 1991, pl. pp.210f. Illustration after Stegemann and Eichmann 1991, 37.

3. (Ecclesia and) Synagoga. Detail of a 'Living Cross'. A hand with a sword growing out of the cross–beam is striking Synagoga (with a scorpion as a heraldic beast on her banner, the shaft of which has already been broken). As usual her eyes are bound. Painting by an anonymous artist of the sixteenth cenutry. Beaune, Musée des Beaux Arts. Literature: Füglister 1964, 82. Illustration after Bulard 1935, pl.IX.

2. Synagoga riding on a failing he-goat is killed by a hand reaching out from the cross-beam on the left (heraldically). The inscription attached to her (written in abbreviated form and at times barely legible) runs: *hircorum sanguis me decipit velut anguis, heum sum cecata (et) a regno dei separata*; Ecclesia: *sanguine doctata sum Christi sponsa vocata ad coelum scandit qui mihi selera pandit* [sic]. A second hand from the cross is crowning Ecclesia; the one below is knocking with a hammer on the gateway of (the forecourt of) hell, and a fourth is opening the gate of heaven. Wall painting by Giovanni da Modena, dated 1421. Bologna, Basilica S.Petronio. Literature: Füglister 1962, pl.IVB; Goetz 1965, fig.89; Schiller II, 1968, fig.527; Kirschbaum II, 1970, 597f.; Eckert 1989, 78f.; Eckert 1991, fig.p.366; *Bolletino d'arte* 76, 1991, 22; Jochum 1993, fig.44 (cf. ibid., figs.41–43, further examples). Illustration after Schubert 1978, no.59.

4. Miniature in a gradual for the Clarissa Convent in Munich 'On the Anger', made in southern Germany between 1494 and 1497. Munich, SB Clm 23041, folio 181r verso (initial K of the *Kyrie*) and identically folio 31 verso in the initial A (on the Introit, *Ad te levavi animam meam*). Literature: Weber 1894, fig. p.120; *Bayerns Kirche* 1960, fig.61; Füglister 1964, fig.XII; Seiferth 1964, fig.59; Schiller II, 1968, 171ff.; *Martin Luther* 1983, fig.467. Illustration after Blumenkranz 1965, no.71.

2. Reconciliation of the adversaries. Conversion of (Jerusalem-) Synagoga, the unity of the Old and New Testaments (*Concordia Veteris et Novi Testamenti*)

1. Christ between Ecclesia and Synagoga, who has had the veil taken from her eyes (II Cor.3.13–16; cf. Ex.34.34f.; Lam.5.17). Here the hope of an eschatological convergence of Christianity and Judaism is realized in anticipation. This corresponds to the theological notions of Abbot Suger, during whose term of office (1122–1151) the church of the Benedictine abbey of Saint-Denis was erected. Stained glass in the abbey church of Saint-Denis (in Paris) c.1145. Literature: Rudolph 1990; Bur 1991; Jochum 1993, fig.24; Schreckenberg II, 535–9. Illustration after Twining 1852, pl.XXVII, no.3.

2. Crucifix with Ecclesia and Jerusalem; the former is standing in front of a romanesque church and catching the blood of Christ in her chalice in the way customary in iconography; she is thus legitimated as the administrator of the sacrament and representative of the new covenant. Jerusalem is standing before a city wall with pointed towers (presumably an indication of the city of Jerusalem or the temple there) and is looking up at Christ in worship (or in terrified helplessness); he, however, is turning from her and towards Ecclesia. Late Carolingian ivory relief of a book cover, c.900. Tournai, Notre Dame, treasury. Literature: Kirschbaum I, 565; Jochum 1993, fig.2; Schreckenberg II, 489f. Illustration after *Mon.Jud.Handb.* 1963, no.108.

3. The twelve apostles on the shoulders of the prophets. Sandstone font (badly weathered) in the cathedral at Merseburg, around the second quarter of the twelfth century. This is an early example of a view of the relationship beween the old and the new covenants, the former regarded so to speak as the supportive substructure of New Testament salvation. The Old Testament is not the preparation which has to disappear when the task has been fulfilled, nor does it just consist of (fleeting) shadowy prefigurations of future salvation: rather, it is an indispensable holy book of the church, and the testimony of the prophets to Christ also supports the claim of Christianity to the truth in the face of all unbelievers, including the Jews. Literature: Schiller IV.1, 1976, fig.96; Legner 1982, fig.216. Illustration after Twining 1852, 88, pl.XLIII, no.13 (copy) and *Mon.Jud.Handb.*1963, no.55 (total view).

5. Synagoga with Moses, Abraham and the prophets. As an allegorical personification of Old Testament Judaism, Synagoga is bearing the prophets and Moses (who promise Christ): the latter with the two tables of the law and the twelfth-century Jewish hat. Miniature in Hildegard of Bingen's (died 1179) *Liber Scivias*. Wiesbaden, LB, Cod.I (lost after 1945). Literature: Fox 1985; Feldmann, 1991; Craine 1992; Schreckenberg II, 225–31, 587f. Illustration after *Mon.Jud.Handb.*1963, no.62.

4. Crucifix with Ecclesia and Synagoga. Ecclesia (behind Mary) and Synagoga (behind John) are looking in harmony and in reconciliation towards Christ. Ivory relief of the cover of an evangeliary. Cologne (St George), middle of the eleventh century. Darmstadt, Landesmuseum, Inv.no. KG 54,210b. Literature: Jochum 1993, fig.3; Schreckenberg II, 508f. Illustration after *Mon.Jud.Kat.*1963, A 19, no.9.

6. Moses and Christ as a two-headed being: Christ with the chalice of the sacrament, Moses with the sprinkling stick of Jewish worship (cf. Num.19.1–22); in addition there are the inscriptions *Moyses emundandum populum aspergit saguine et cinere vitule rufe*, 'Moses sprinkles the people with the blood and ashes of the red cow for purification', and *Christus sanctificat fidelem populum sanguine suo et* *cinere corporis sui*, 'Christ sanctifies believers through his blood and the ashes of his body'; also *Lex per Moysen data est, gracia et veritas per Jhesum Christum facta est* (John 1.17). The seven-branched candlestick indicates the Holy Spirit (in the sense of Isa.11.2: the seven gifts of the Holy Spirt): *Septiformis spiritus est candelabrum. Candelabrum signum septiformem spiritum qui illuminans prophetas,* *apostolos et evangelistas, per illos composuit utrumque testamentum*, 'the sevenfold Spirit illuminated the prophets, apostles and evangelists and through them he created both testaments'. Miniature in the *Hortus deliciarum* of Herrad of Landsberg (Paris, BN), c.1185. Literature: Schreckenberg II, 602. Illustration after Green I, 1979, folio 67 recto, fig.98, p.112.

8. Matthew on the shoulders of Isaiah. A further example of a theme frequent in medieval iconography (the Old Testament prophets carrying the apostles – which enables them to look further); the pair thus created symbolizes the concord of Old and New Testaments. Stained glass in Chartres Cathedral, first half of the thirteenth century (c.1220–1230). Literature: Mâle 1986, fig.107. Illustration after Michel II, 1, 1906, fig.227.

7. Genealogy of Christ (Matt.1.1–16) and *Ecclesia universalis*. God the Father is planting (or holding) the genealogical tree on a mountain; above it is Abraham, to whom an angel is showing the stars of heaven (in the sense of Gen.15.5); immediately above Abraham are Christ's ancestors in seven rows, including fourteen kings; on the left are patriarchs, kings and high priests; on the right prophets, kings and five Jews with their characteristic group hallmark in the form of the hat; above is Joseph of Nazareth, and above him are Mary, Christ and the dove of the Holy Spirit; on the left and right alongside Christ on each side there are six apostles (Peter right at the front [with tonsure] and Paul facing him), a pope, bishops, martyrs (holding stylized palm branches) and others. Miniature in *Hortus deliciarum* (folio 80 verso) of Herrad of Landsberg. Literature: Schreckenberg II, 602. Illustration after Gillen 1979, 73.

9. The veil over Synagoga's face is removed by God's hand. She is sitting on a throne, with the scrolls of the law in her right hand and in her left a jar of unguent (i.e. oil for anointing, which was used for various cultic purposes in biblical times and so could be regarded as a symbol for the Jewish cult). Moses is standing on the heraldic right, alongside the Torah scroll; on the left, alongside the anointing oil, is Aaron as representative of the Jewish cult. The inscription around this reads: *Hactenus obscuris velata figuris, adveniente fide rem Synagoga vide*, 'Synagoga, you who were previously blinded by the veil of the shadows of the (Old Testament) law, look on the reality (of salvation, i.e. the real types of the New Testament), now faith (in Christ) has come to you'; cf. Schreckenberg II, 467ff. ('Unveiling of Moses by the evangelists' in Carolingian Bibles in connection with Rev.4.2ff. or Rev.6–8). Miniature in a manscript of the Apocalypse of John, made in England in the thirteenth century. Eton, Eton College Library, Ms.177, folio 7 recto. Literature: Schiller IV.1, 1976, fig.120; Schubert 1978, fig.54. Illustration after Blumenkranz 1965, no.73.

10. Crucifix (on a Tau sign) with Mary and Moses, a secondary variant of the traditional group with Ecclesia and Synagoga and a further development along the lines of the medieval *Concordia Veteris et Novi Testamenti* – woodcut by Hans Burgkmair for a sermon of Luther on the theme of the cross (*Ain Sermôn von dem Hayligen Creutz*, Augsburg: M.Ramminger 1522). Literature: Hollstein, 1954, V,39; *Martin Luther* 1983, fig.492. Illustration after Geisberg I, 1930, no.306.

11. The Shunamite woman (=Synagoga) and the Jews. In the exegesis of the Song of Songs in the high Middle Ages the Shunamite woman can symbolize the Jews who are converted before the end of the world; five of them appear here as her escort (superscript: *Judei*). Miniature in a manuscript of the exegesis of the Song of Songs by Honorius Augustodunensis, second half of the twelfth century (Bavaria/Austria). Augsburg, University Library, Cod.I.2.2° 13, folio 48 verso. Literature: Schreckenberg II, 546–6, 723; Franckenberger and Rupp 1987, pl. p.46.

12. Apostles on the shoulders of the prophets. Here, too, this stands symbolically both for the *Concordia Veteris et Novi Testamenti* (in the sense of continuity in the history of salvation) and for the greater vision and fundamental superiority of the new covenant. Bamberg Cathedral, Prince's Portal 1230–1240. Literature: *RDK* I, 1937, 822, fig.10; Pinder 1952, fig.373; Feulner–Müller 1953, fig.67; *Mon.Jud. Handb.*1963, fig.56; Ohly 1966, 50ff.; Jochum 1993, fig.48. Illustration after Jantzen 1925, no.53.

13. Ecclesia and Synagoga. As in II Cor.3.13–16, Synagoga one day, at the latest at the end of days, has the veil lifted from her eyes. Now finally she understands the law (in a christological sense), the symbol of which she holds in her hands in the form of the two tables, offering them to Christ (in the mandorla alongside her). The hand of God comes down from above, removing the veil from her face so that she can see Christ. On the other side is Ecclesia, who is offering the chalice and the host (with hands veiled out of reverence). Miniature in the initial *W(ere dignum et iustum est, equum et salutare)* of the preface to the order of the mass in a sacramentary from Tours, twelfth century. Paris, BN, Lat.193, folio 71 recto. Literature: Jochum 1993, fig.25; Schreckenberg II, 550f. Illustration after Blumenkranz 1965, no.72.

14. Isaiah presents the Messiah (cf. e.g. Isa.7.14; 9.5; 11.1). Some of the Jews (who wear pointed or Phrygian hats in thirteenth-century style) accept Christ in faith, while others throw stones at him. Miniature in a *Bible moralisée*, c.1240. Paris, Lat.11560, folio 124. Literature: Schawe 1988, fig.5. Illustration after Weber 1894, 99.

3. Mary (–Ecclesia) and the Jews

1. Jews and Gentiles subject themselves to Mary (–Ecclesia). From the Middle Ages onwards, the Mother of God increasingly replaces Ecclesia in iconography, and in modern times displaces her almost completely. In view of the iconographic affinity of Synagoga–Jews–serpent–devil, one could also think of the influence of Gen.3.15 (*ipsa conteret caput tuum*), but in the foreground of the imagery there is probably wishful Christian missionary thinking, that even the Jews and pagans (who are still unconverted) will voluntarily subject themselves to the church, and the whole of humankind will become an *ecclesia ex circumcisione et ex gentibus*. Münster, cathedral, stone relief in the porch, 1250–1265. Literature: Budde 1982; Pieper-Müller 1993, pls.48-9; cf. Shachar 1974, pl.9 (Xanten, cathedral choir): an (unconverted) Jew under the corbel of the pillar on which Mary is standing (last third of the thirteenth century). In a psalter illustration from the beginning of the thirteenth century, Jews (and pagans?) serve the enthroned Trinity as a kind of footstool (*Das Münster* 35, 1982, 241). Illustration after Aschoff 1993, 582 (photograph T.Samek).

2. Mary with the child Jesus and a Jew (with a beard and a red and white cruciform sign of his Jewishness on his upper garment); a Christian seems to be teaching the Jews, who are listening openly, about the mystery of faith in the incarnation of God. Miniature in a fourteenth-century French manuscript. Paris, BN, MS. fr.820, folio 192. Literature: Robert 1891, pl.1 (with further examples of the cruciform mark of the Jews). Illustration after Rubens 1967, fig.119.

IV. Interpretation of the Old Testament in terms of the Contemporary Situation: The Israelites of Biblical Times Depicted as Medieval Jews

1. The special form of medieval Jewish dress as a group characteristic: Abraham, Moses, Aaron, prophets and others

(a) High Middle Ages (twelfth to thirteenth centuries)

1. Moses with a Jewish hat. With his left, weaker arm he is holding the tables of the law (cf. Ex.31.18); in his stronger right hand he is holding a book which is the Pentateuch or perhaps the New Testament; if it were the latter, the theme would be the concord of the Old and New Testament, the harmonious unity of law and gospel. The fact that the eye on the side of the law seems troubled could fit this. Miniature in a historical composite manuscript from the Benedictine abbey of Zweifalten (Kreis Reutlingen), c.1160–1170. Stuttgart, LB, Cod.hist. 2° 411, folio 5 verso. Literature: Borries–Schulten 1987, fig. 265. Illustration after Löffler, pl.36.

▶ 3. Moses (with Jewish hat) and the brazen serpent, typologies of the cross. Moses is wearing the Jewish hat of the twelfth century; the crucifix is hanging on a stylized vine with two stems. The traditional soteriological programme also includes the widow of Zarephath (I Kings 17.12), where the Latin Bible changed the 'two sticks of wood' of the Hebrew text into *duo ligna*, in order to make the affinity to the cross of Christ more evident. Miniature for the initial *I(n principio)* at the beginning of the *Antiquitates Judaicae* of Flavius Josephus in a manuscript from Zweifalten monastery (Reutlingen district, c. 1180). Stuttgart, LB, Cod.hist.fol.428, folio 3 recto. Literature: Schreckenberg II, 597f. Illustration after Legner 1982, no.477.

◀ 2. Abraham and the three angels; the expulsion of Hagar (Gen.18.1ff.; 21.8ff). Verona, San Zeno, door with bronze reliefs, c.1100–1130 (partly later, c.1200). Literature: Lasko 1972, pl.233; Grimme 1985, fig.33; Schwartz 1988, fig.7; Schreckenberg II, 530–2. Illustration after Mende 1983, pl.83.

▲ 4. Brazen serpent (Num.12.4–9) as a type of the crucifix *(mysterium crucis)*. In contrast to Moses, who has a halo as a holy figure of the prehistory of Christianity, one of the Israelites is wearing a form of the Jewish hat of the high Middle Ages (skull-cap with bobble or stud). Sunk enamel plate from the Maas region, c. 1170. Lucerne, Kofler-Truniger collection. Illustration after *Mon.Jud.Handb.*1963, no.39.

5. Moses (with Jewish hat) departs for Egypt (Ex.4.20). The Jewish hat as a group characteristic has no negative connotations here. Enamel plate on the altar of Nicolas of Verdun, completed 1181. Klosterneuburg (Austria), Stiftskirche, photograph I.Kitlitschka. Literature: Buschhausen 1980; Fillitz and Pippal 1987; Buschhausen 1987: *LMA* VI, 1993, 1188f.; Schreckenberg II, 598–600; Griessmaier 1972, no.24.

6. Circumcision of Isaac (Gen.21.4). Abraham (with a Jewish hat) and Sarah look anxiously on: the baby is weeping. Inscription: *flet circumcisus Ysaac tuus o Sara risus* (Isaac, about whom you laughed, Sarah, weeps at his circumcision). By contrast, the circumcision of Christ which similarly appears in the programme of the pictures on the Klosterneuburg altar depicts the circumcision of Christ in a more friendly way along the lines of Luke 2.21 (Joseph himself does the circumcising). Photograph I.Kitlitschka. Literature: Griessmaier 1972, no.17; *Das Münster* 45, 1992, 230.

7. Miracle of the sprouting rod (Num.17.16–26). Moses and the twelve rulers of Israel. The picture (which is in a bad state of preservation) is a good example of the depiction of the Jews as a group – often robbing them of their individuality. Moses, who has a kind of bishop's mitre, has a halo (so to speak as a pre–Christian). Fresco in the parish church of Berghausen, Westphalia. Beginning of the thirteenth century. Literature: Schreckenberg II, 621. Illustration after *Year 1200*, III, 1975, 118, fig.24.

8. Samson's circumcision. Inscription: *Vulnere digna reis notatis tum iussio legis* (the commandment of the law punishes with a wound as for an offender who has had a dishonourable punishment imposed). As already in the case of the circumcision of Isaac, here we have a negative Christian assessment of circumcision, which is regarded as something specifcially Jewish. At this time the Jewish hat is not yet defined as a negative symbol, but it is striking that it appears disproportionately often in the theme of circumcision. Provenance as in nos. 5 and 6 above. Photograph I.Kitlitschka. Literature: Griess-maier 1972, no.18.

9. Esther's feast (Esther 7): the Persian king Ahasuerus–Xerxes (485–465), Esther, Mordecai (with a Jewish hat) and Haman on the gallows. On the table are knives – which also served as spoons – fish, bread (and a pretzel), and a container. By the table is a kind of steward with a staff as a sign of his office. Miniature in the *Hortus deliciarum* of Herrad of Landsberg (folio 60 verso), c.1185. Literature: Schreckenberg II, 602. Illustration after Gillen 1979, 53.

11. Moses(?) with a large Jewish hat. This enigmatic figure is interpreted as the 'Eternal Jew' (Ahasuerus), but it seems more likely that he is Moses, because the same figure appears in the same manuscript enthroned on the earth, as Synagoga does elsewhere (see on the Mönchen Gladbach portable altar, c. 1160). Iconographically, such a powerful sign of Jewishness as this tall funnel hat fits the architect of Judaism better. Miniature (coloured pen drawing) in a manuscript of Augustine written before 1165, but only illustrated (incompletely) in the last third of the twelfth century. Munich, SB, Clm 13085, part II, folio 89 recto. Literature: van Run 1987; Schreckenberg II, 600f. Illustration after Klemm I, 1980, no.122.

10. Brazen serpent. The large T makes clear the typological relationship to the cross of Christ. Stained glass (disc) in a private collection in Aachen (Dr Peter and Irene Ludwig), first half of thirteenth century. Literature: Grimme 1960–61, fig.31. Illustration after *Mon.Jud.Kat.* 1963, no. A 25.

12. The Israelites are given silver and gold at the exodus from Egypt (Ps.105.37; cf. Ex.3.21–22). Miniature in the 'Elizabeth Psalter'; this was made shortly after 1200 in a scriptorium in lower Saxony and was given by St Eilzabeth of Thuringia to the cathedral of Aquileia in 1229. Cividale del Friuli, Mus.Arch.Naz (Palazzo Nordis), Cod.Ms.CXXXVII, folio 120 verso. Literature: Büchler 1991, 158 fig.8. Illustration after Pausch 1986, 69.

13. Journey of the Israelites through the Sea of Reeds (Ex.14.15–31). Relief on a bronze font in Hildesheim Cathedral, c.1230. Literature: Zeller 1979, figs.51–55; Legner 1982, figs. 308–12; Eckert 1991, 367. Illustration after Hamann 1934, no.19.

◄ 14. Brazen serpent. Miniature in a psalter of English origin, made in Gloucester in the first quarter of the thirteenth century, probably before 1220. Munich, SB, Cod.lat.835. Literature: Mellinkoff 1978, fig.59; Green II, 1979, fig.80. Illustration after Ehrenstein 1923, 384 fig.34.

15. Moses gives the law to the Israelites. Miniature in a manuscript of the Chronicle of the World by Rudolf of Ems, made in Bavaria or Austria c.1270–1300. Munich, SB, Cgm 6406, folio 68 recto. Literature: Mellinkoff 1970, fig.90: Bremer 1986, fig.11; *Verfasserlexikon* VIII.2, 1991, 332–45. Illustration after Ehrenstein 1923, 396, no.61.

16. Abraham instructs Eliezer; Rebecca receives Eliezer and gives water to his camels (Gen.24). Miniature in the Psalter of Louis IX of France, c. 1260–1270. Paris, BN, Lat.10525. Literature: Thomas 1970. Illustration after Ehrenstein 1923, 207 no.5.

17. The spies with the giant bunch of grapes (Num.13.23). In the tradition of biblical exegesis the bunch of grapes was regarded as a type of bearing the cross or the crucifixion: here the grapes point to Christ hanging on the cross. Miniature (provenance as in 16). Literature: Heimann 1956, fig.122. Illustration after Ehrenstein 1923, 449 no.101.

18. Brazen serpent. Pulpit relief of the former collegiate church (of the Augustinian canons) in Wechselburg (north-west of Chemnitz), made c.1230–1240 as part of a rood screen. Literature: Steche 1890, fig.79 (with supplement XIV); Hootz 1970, fig.114. Illlustration after Ehrenstein 1923, 429, no.114.

19. Moses with a shining face (Ex.34.29–35). Ceiling painting in the parish church of St Maria Lyskirchen, Cologne. Middle of the thirteenth century. Literature: *Juden in Köln* 1984, fig. p.101; Eckert 1989, 76. Illustration after Goldkuhle 1954, no.30.

◀ 20. The first nine plagues (Ex.7–10). Miniature in the Psalter of Louis IX of France, c.1260–1270. Paris, BN, Lat.10525, folio 31 verso. Literature: Ehrenstein 1923, 350 fig.6. Illustration after Sterling I, 1987, 33 fig.5.

21. Moses prays on Mount Nebo (Deut.32.49). Miniature in a manuscript of the Chronicle of the World by Rudolf of Ems, made in Bavaria or Austria, c.1270–1300. Munich, Cgm 6406, folio 99 verso. Literature: Jerchel 1933, pl.8. Illustration after *Zeit der Staufer* 1977, II, no.168.

(b) Late Middle Ages (fourteenth to fifteenth centuries) and early modern period

◀ 1. The spies with the giant bunch of grapes (Num.13.23). Miniature in a manuscript of the *Biblia pauperum* from the Benedictine abbey of Tegernsee, middle of the fourteenth century. Munich, SB, Clm 1941, folio 157 verso (see Kirschbaum I, 295, 555). Illustration after Cornell 1925, 264 fig.29.

2. Brazen serpent. Stained glass, probably from the former Premonstratensian abbey of Arnstein (above the Lahn valley, Rheinland-Pfalz), c.1360. Frankfurt am Main, Städelsches Kunstinstitut. Literature: *RDK* IV, 1958, 827, fig.7; *Das Münster* 34, 1981, fig. p.150; Jászai 1986, fig. p.65. Illustration after Ehrenstein 1923, 429 no.117.

3. Jacob (with a yellow Jewish hat) goes to Egypt with his family: Joseph receives his father and brothers (Ex.46.1–7, 28–30). Miniature in a manuscript of the Chronicle of the World by Rudolf of Ems, made in the region of Lake Constance, c.1300. St Gallen, Kantonsbibliothek (Vadiana), HS.302, folio 39 recto. Illustration after Beer 1982 (facsimile volume).

4. Moses sees God from behind; Moses brings new tables of the law (Ex.33.18–23; 34.29–35). As the previous illustration, folio 65 recto. Illustration after Beer 1982 (facsimile volume).

5. Moses speaks to the leaders of Israel: Aaron's staff blossoms (Num. 17.16–23). As the previous illustration, folio 76 recto. Illustration after Beer 1982 (facsimile volume).

6. Moses asks for God's help; the brazen serpent (Num. 21.4–9). As the previous illustration, folio 78 recto. Illustration after Beer 1982 (facsimile volume).

7. Moses bids farewell to his people and chooses Joshua as his successor; he looks over the land of Canaan and is buried in the valley of Moab (Num.27.12–13; Deut.34.6). As the previous illustration, folio 88 recto. Illustration after Beer 1982 (facsimile volume).

8. Joshua pours water upon the earth; he speaks with the people of Israel at Shechem (not reported in the book of Joshua, but depicted after Rudolf's Chronicle of the World, vv.17211–17217). As the previous illustration, folio 97 recto. Illustration after Beer 1982 (facsimile volume).

9. Samuel's sacrifice at Mizpah; a storm puts the Philistines to flight; Samuel erects a memorial stone (not according to I Kings but according to the Chronicle of the World [folio 135]). As the previous illustration, folio 135 recto. Illustration after Beer 1982 (facsimile volume).

10. The Last Supper, with an Old Testament type (the gathering of manna, Ex.16). Inscriptions: *Christus manducat pascha cum discipulis suis: Manna datur filiis israhel. Iste est panis, quem dedit vobis Dominus ad vescendum.* Miniature (provenance as previous illustration), Kremsmünster, Stiftsbibliothek, Cod.Crem.243, folio 21 verso. Literature: Burger I, 1913, fig.247; Ehrenstein 1923, 373, fig.6; Mellinkoff 1970, fig.80. Illustration after Neumüller 1972 (facsimile volume).

11. The law is given to Moses on Mount Sinai (inscription: *Lex data est Moysi in monte Synay*). Miniature in a *Speculum salvationis* manuscript, made in 1324 in the upper Rhineland/German-speaking Switzerland. Kremsmünster (Austria), Stiftsbibliothek, Cod. Crem.243, folio 40 recto. Illustration after Neumüller 1972 (facsimile volume).

12. Old Testament prefigurations of the baptism of Christ in the Jordan: Ex.14 (passage of the Israelites through the sea); Num.13 (the grapes on the staff); Isa.12.3: *haurietis aquas in gaudio de fontibus salvatoris*; Ps.68.27: *in ecclesiis benedicite (Deo Domino de) fontibus Israel*. Miniature in a *Biblia pauperum* from Klosterneuberg, c. 1310–1330. Vienna, ÖN, Cod.1198. Illustration after Camesina 1863, pl.IX.

13. The Israelites with the ark of the covenant. Miniature in a Middle German manuscript of the Chronicle of the World by Rudolf of Ems. Second quarter of the fourteenth century. Berlin, Staatsbibliothek zu Berlin – Preussischer Kulturbesitz. Ms.germ.fol.623, folio 17 recto. Illustration after Wegener 1928, no.7.

14. Brazen serpent. Vienna, St Stephen's Cathedral, stained glass, fourteenth century. Illustration after Ehrenstein 1923, 429 fig.116.

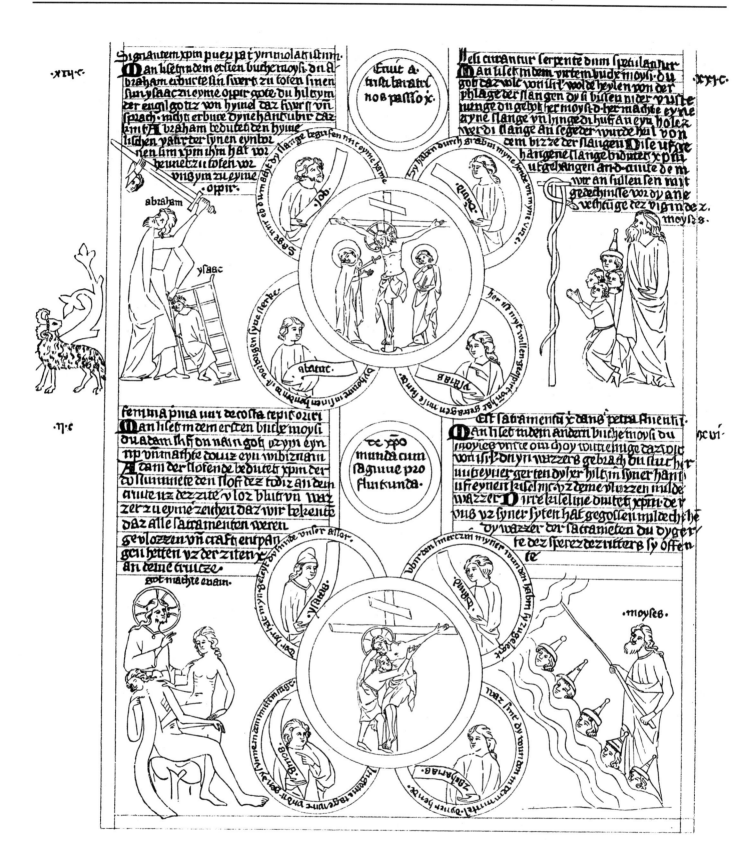

◀ 15. The crucifixion of Christ and Old Testament prefigurations (brazen serpent; Moses strikes water from the rock [Ex.17.1–7]). The inscriptions emphasize the soteriological aspect, e.g. *eruit a tristi baratri nos passio Christi*, and *lesi curantur serpentem dum speculantur*. Miniature in a *Biblia pauperum* made in the area of Lake Constance in the fourteenth century. Constance: Rosgartenmuseum, Ms.31. Illustration after Laib and Schwarz 1867, pl.12; cf. *Liturgy* 8, 1989, 29ff.

▲ 16. Brazen serpent and crucifixion in a typological relationship. Miniature in a *Biblia pauperum*, c.1358. Vienna, ÖN, Cod.370, folio 20 recto. Illustration after Schmidt and Unterkircher 1967 (facsimile volume).

17. Jews of the biblical period in the special dress of medieval Jews (with the Jewish ring and conical hats). Miniatures in a popular French historical Bible (an edition of the *Historia scholastica* of Petrus Comestor [died c.1179]), fourteenth century. Literature: *The Jewish Encyclopedia* II, New York 1902, 425; Ausubel 1964, 498. Illustration after Robert 1891, pl.III.

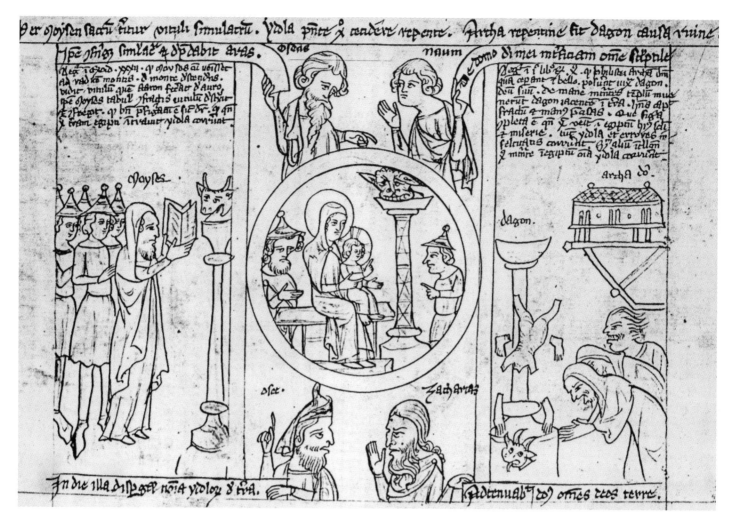

18. New Testament real types and Old Testament prefigurations. This illustrates the typological relationship between the apocryphal infancy Gospel (the fall of the idols in Egypt) and Old Testament types (Moses and the Golden Calf; the fall of the idol Dagon [I Sam.5.1–5]). Miniature in a *Biblia pauperum* from the third quarter of the fourteenth century. Stuttgart, LB, Cod.theol. et phil.2° 279. Literature: Schneemelcher, *NT Apocrypha* I, 1991, 464. Illustration after Irtenkauf 1985, 25.

▶ 19. Numbers 28.1ff. (God gives Moses the regulations for sacrifice). Miniature in the *Wenzelbibel*, c.1390. Vienna, ÖN, Cod.2759–2764, II, folio 164 recto. Illustration after *Wenzelsbibel* (facsimile edition) II, 1982, 164 recto.

20. Numbers 26 (mustering of the Israelites). Miniature in the German illustrated Bible which Wenzel (1378–1400, a German king) had made for himself in Prague c.1390. Vienna, ÖN, Cod.2759–2764, II, folio 162 verso. Literature: Unterkircher 1983; Thomas and Schmidt 1989; Appuhn 1990. Illustration after *Wenzelsbibel* (facsimile edition) II, 1982, 162 verso.

21. Deuteronomy 1.13ff. (Moses hands on God's instructions to the Israelites). Miniature in the *Wenzelsbibel*, c.1390. Vienna, ÖN, Cod.2759–2764, II, folio 175 recto. Illustration after *Wenzelsbibel* (facsimile edition) II, 1982, 175 recto.

22. Deuteronomy 1.19ff. (Moses speaks to the Israelites). Miniature in the *Wenzelsbibel*, c.1390. Vienna, ÖN, Cod.2759–2764, II, folio 175 recto. Illustration after *Wenzelsbibel* (facsimile edition) II, 1982, 175 recto.

23. Deueteronomy 10.1ff. (ark of the covenant). Miniature in the *Wenzelsbibel*, c.1390. Vienna, ÖN, Cod.2759–2764, III, folio 186 verso. Illustration after *Wenzelsbibel* (facsimile edition) III, 1982, 186 verso.

24. Deuteronomy 17.18ff. (the king of Israel is always to have a copy of the law in his hand and read in it). Miniature in the *Wenzelsbibel*, c.1390. Vienna, ÖN, Cod.2759–2764, III, folio 194 verso. Illustration after *Wenzelsbibel* (facsimile edition) III, 1982, 194 verso.

25. Deuteronomy 21.10–14 (regulations about marriage to a woman prisoner of war). Miniature in the *Wenzelsbibel*, c.1390. Vienna, ÖN, Cod.2759–2764, III, folio 198 recto. Illustration after *Wenzelsbibel* (facsimile edition) III, 1982, 198 recto.

26. II Chronicles 7.1–10 (the consecration of the temple by king Solomon). Miniature in the *Wenzelsbibel*, c.1390. Vienna, ÖN, Cod.2759–2764, VII, folio 43 recto. Illustration after *Wenzelsbibel* (facsimile edition) VII, 1982, 43 recto.

27. Abraham and Sarah before Pharaoh. Miniature in a manuscript of the *Postilla* of Nicholas of Lyra (died 1340) on Genesis and Exodus, made in 1396 by Rüdiger Schopf (pastor at Freiburg Cathedral). Basel, UB, Cod.A II 1, folio 36. Illustration after Stamm 1981, no.184.

28. II Chronicles 31.1 (abolition of idolatry and reform of the cult). Miniature in the *Wenzelsbibel*, c.1390. Vienna, ÖN, Cod.2759–2764, VII, folio 71 verso. Illustration after *Wenzelsbibel* (facsimile edition) VII, 1982, 71 verso.

29. The Last Supper and its Old Testament prefigurations (Jewish Passover, gathering the manna, Abraham and Melchizedek). Miniature in a *Speculum salvationis* manuscript, Cologne, c.1360. Darmstadt, LB, Hs.2505. Literature: *Köln Westfalen* 1980, II, 77 (no.258). Illustration after Appuhn 1981, 34f.

30. Gathering the manna (Ex.16.1ff.). It is raining rolls and pretzels. Stained glass, c.1390–1400. Rothenburg ob der Tauber, Jakobskirche, choir window (the so–called 'Baker's Window'). Literature: Geiger 1931, pl.487; Wentzel 1951, pl.166; Ress 1959, pl.70; *Zeitschrift für Kunstgeschichte* 56, 1993, 89. Illustration after Ehrenstein 1923, 373 no.7.

31. Balaam's vision (Num.23.9). Miniature in a manuscript of the *Postilla* of Nicholas of Lyra on Leviticus, Numbers and Deuteronomy, written in 1397. Basel, UB, Cod.A II 2, folio 91. Illustration after Stamm 1989, no.207.

▲ 32. The spies and the grapes. Miniature in a manuscript of the *Postilla* of Nicholas of Lyra on Leviticus, Numbers and Deuteronomy, written in 1397. Basel, UB, Cod.A II 2, folio 67. Literature: Stamm 1981. Illustration after Gollek–Gretzer 1966, no.86.

33. Raining manna and catching quails. Miniature in a manuscript of the *Postilla* of Nicholas of Lyra, made in 1397. Basel, UB, Cod.A II 1, folio 131 verso. Illustration after Stamm 1981, no.55.

34. Joseph is sold by his brothers; the brothers bring Jacob the bloody coat (Gen.37.23–36). Miniature in a copy of parts of the Chronicle of the World by Rudolf of Ems ('Toggenburg Bible'), made in the region of Lake Constance in 1411. Berlin, Kupferstichkabinett, no.78 E 1, folio 54 recto. Literature: Jerchel 1932. Illustration after Anzelewsky 1972, pl.6.

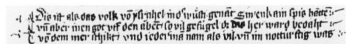

◀ 35. The Israelites are fed in the wilderness with quails and manna (Ex.16). Miniature in a copy of parts of the Chronicle of the World by Rudolf of Ems ('Toggenburg Bible'), made in the region of Lake Constance in 1411. Berlin, Kupferstichkabinett, no.78 E 1, folio 89 verso. Literature: Jerchel 1932. Illustration after Anzelewsky 1972, pl.15.

▶ 36. The crucifixion of Christ and its Old Testament prefigurations (the sacrifice of Isaac by Abraham; the brazen serpent). Miniature in a *Biblia pauperum* from the Benedictine foundation of Metten (near Deggendorf, Lower Bavaria), made in 1414. Munich, SB, Clm 8201, folio 86 verso. Illustration after Cornell 1925, pl.39.

37. Eucharist: with Old Testament pre-figurations alongside it (raining manna, Abraham and Melchizedek). Miniature in a German *Biblia pauperum* (block book), c.1430. Heidelberg, UB, Cod.pal.germ.438, folio 18. Illustration after Schreiber 1926, IX, no.115.

38. New Testament real type and Old Testament types. This illustrates the typological relationship between the apocryphal infancy Gospel (fall of the idols in Egypt) and Old Testament prefigurations (Moses destroys the Golden Calf; fall of the idol Dagon). Miniature in a *Biblia pauperum* of the second quarter of the fifteenth century, made in north Hessen or Thuringia. Rome, BAV, Cod.Pal.Lat. 871, folio 6 recto. Literature: Unger 1986, 65–6. Illustration after Wirth 1982, I, folio 6 recto.

39. Birth of Christ; alongside it Old Testament prefigurations of the immaculate nature of Mary (the thornbush which burns but is not consumed [Gen.3.1ff.]; Aaron's staff [Num.17.16–26]). Aaron is wearing a terraced Jewish hat (perhaps in the shape of a pyramid). Miniature in a German *Biblia pauperum* (block book), c.1430. Heidelberg, UB, Cod.pal.germ. 438. Illustration after Bock 1930, 141.

40. Crucifixion of Christ and Old Testament prefigurations (sacrifice of Isaac by Abraham [Gen.22.1–19]; brazen serpent (Num.21,6–9]). Miniature in a *Biblia pauperum* from the second quarter of the fifteenth century, made in north Hessen or Thuringia. Rome, BA, Cod.Pal.Lat. 871, folio 13 verso. Literature: Unger 1986, 65–6. Illustration after Wirth 1982, I, folio 13 verso.

41. Brazen serpent. Miniature in a Bavarian–Austrian manuscript ('Chronicle of Christ the Lord') made around 1410 with a total of 220 illustrations on the Old and New Testaments. Berlin, SB, Ms germ.fol.1416, folio 87 recto. Illustration after Wegener 1928, no.15.

42. Joshua wants to cross the Jordan with the people. One of the Israelites is wearing his medieval Jewish hat drawn down deeply over his eyes, a sign of the Jewish blindness (to Christ). Miniature in a history Bible (workshop of Diebolt Lauber), made in Hagenau (Alsace) around 1430. Darmstadt, LB, Hs 1, on the book of Joshua. Illustration after Zimmermann 1980, 46.

43. The passage through the sea (Ex.14.15–31). Woodcut in the 'Cologne Bible' of the printer and publisher Heinrich Quentell (Cologne, c.1479). Literature: Kunze 1975, fig.224; Kunze 1979, I, 286. Illustration after Schramm 1920, VIII, no.389.

44. The punishment of Korah and his followers (Num.16.25–35). Woodcut in the 'Cologne Bible' of the printer and publisher Heinrich Quentell (Cologne, c.1479). Illustration after Schramm 1920, VIII, no.405.

45. The spies and the grapes (Num.13.23) as an Old Testament christological type. Merseburg Cathedral, bas-relief on choir stall, 1446. Illustration after Baier 1982, no.250.

46. Exodus of the children of Israel from Egypt; Abraham raised up out of the fire of the Chaldaeans by God; Lot leaves Sodom. The Jewish hat covering the eyes symbolizes

the blindness of the Jews to the Christian truth which already appears in the Old Testament. Woodcuts in a German-language *Speculum salvationis* book

printed by Bernhard Richel, Basel 1476. Illustration after Schramm 1920, XXI, nos.165–7.

47. Aaron's staff sends out shoots (Num.17.16–28). Woodcut in the 'Cologne Bible' of Heinrich Quentell (Cologne, c.1479). Illustration after Hamp 1966, 223.

48. Appointment of Joshua (Deut.31.1–8).
Woodcut in the 'Cologne Bible' of Heinrich
Quentell (Cologne, c.1479). Illustration
after Schramm 1920, VIII, no.410.

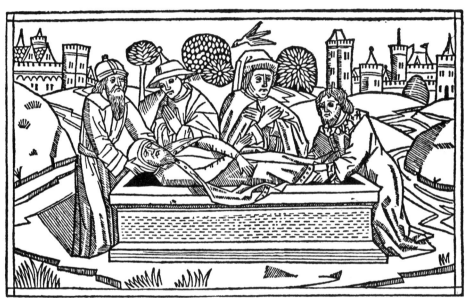

49. Burial of Josiah (II Kings 23.30; II
Chron.35.24). Woodcut in the 'Cologne
Bible' of Heinrich Quentell (Cologne,
c.1479). Illustration after Schramm 1920,
VIII, no.440.

50. The lawgiving on Sinai. Woodcut in a
German-language *Speculum salvationis*
book printed by Bernhard Richel, Basel
1476. Illustration after Schramm 1920,
XXI, no.186.

51. The spies Joshua and Caleb with the grapes (Num.13.1–33). The head-covering of the man in front again has a shape which is closest to the type of the Phrygian cap, but here as often in the late Middle Ages it has a broad brim turned upwards. Woodcut in the 'Cologne Bible' of Heinrich Quentell (Cologne, c.1479). Literature: *Gutenberg* 1968, fig. p.61; Eichenberger and Wendland 1977, fig.113; Wendland 1987, fig.p.55. Illustration after Hamp 1966, 310.

52. God dictates the law to Moses. Woodcut at the beginning of the book of Deuteronomy in the German Bible of Anton Koberger (Nuremberg 1483). Literature: Eichenberger and Wendland 1982, 91ff.; Leonhard 1982, fig.77; Kastner 1985, II, fig.435. Illustration after Schmidt 1977, no.75.

53. The spies with the grapes. Choir stall relief in the church of the monastery of Karthaus in Weddern (south-east of Coesfeld in Westphalia). Illustration after Ludorff 1913, 124.

54. David brings the ark of the covenant into Jerusalem (II Sam.6.4f.). Woodcut in the German Schönsperger Bible of 1490. Illustration after Eichenberger and Wendland 1977, no.175.

55. Moses before God. Woodcut in the 'Otmar Bible' of 1507. The itinerant printer Johann Otmar (Othar, Oltmar), who was active in Reutlingen, Tübingen and Augsburg, printed the thirteenth German Bible, decorated with fine woodcuts, in Augsburg in 1507. Illustration after Eichenberger and Wendland 1977, no.211.

2. The special form of dress as a means of criticism or polemic: the Golden Calf, circumcision scenes and the like

1. Worship of the Golden Calf. Miniature in a psalter of English origin, made in Gloucester in the first quarter of the thirteenth century, probably before 1222. Munich, SB, Cod.Lat. 835. Illustration after Ehrenstein 1923, 408 no.82.

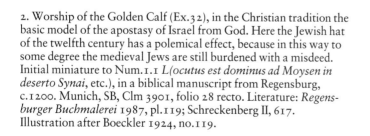

2. Worship of the Golden Calf (Ex.32), in the Christian tradition the basic model of the apostasy of Israel from God. Here the Jewish hat of the twelfth century has a polemical effect, because in this way to some degree the medieval Jews are still burdened with a misdeed. Initial miniature to Num.1.1 L(ocutus est dominus ad Moysen in deserto Synai, etc.), in a biblical manuscript from Regensburg, c.1200. Munich, SB, Clm 3901, folio 28 recto. Literature: *Regensburger Buchmalerei* 1987, pl.119; Schreckenberg II, 617. Illustration after Boeckler 1924, no.119.

3. Worship of the Golden Calf. Miniature in the psalter of Blanche of Castile, made c.1230. Paris, BA, Ms 1186, folio 14 recto (lower half). Literature: Mellinkoff 1970, fig.65. Illustration after Ehrenstein 1923, 408 no.81.

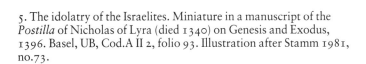

4. Worship of the Golden Calf. Miniature in a manuscript of the *Postilla* of Nicholas of Lyra (died 1340) on Genesis and Exodus, 1396. Basel, UB, Cod.A II a, folio 176 verso. Illustration after Stamm 1981, no.68.

5. The idolatry of the Israelites. Miniature in a manuscript of the *Postilla* of Nicholas of Lyra (died 1340) on Genesis and Exodus, 1396. Basel, UB, Cod.A II 2, folio 93. Illustration after Stamm 1981, no.73.

6. Worship of the Golden Calf (Ex.32). The Israelites are wearing the Jewish hats of the twelfth century (pointed or with a truncated cone). Exodus 32.1–6 often serves traditionally in Christian theology as an anti-Jewish apologetic proof-text, and so here the Jewish hat is used polemically. Miniature in a Bible from the Benedictine monastery of Admont (diocese of Salzburg), c. 1140. Vienna, ÖN, Series nova 2701, folio 44. Literature: Schreckenberg II, 535. Illustration after Ehrenstein 1923, 407 no.79.

◄ 7. Dance around the Golden Calf; Moses shatters the tables of the law (Ex.32.1–9). Miniature in the 'Toggenburg Bible' (a copy of parts of the Chronicle of the World by Rudolf of Ems), made in the region of Lake Constance in 1411. Berlin, Kupferstichkabinett, no.78 E 1, folio 78 verso. Literature: Jerchel 1932, pl.24. Illustration after Anzelewsky 1970, pl.16.

▶ 8. The betrayal by Judas and its Old Testament prefigurations (his brothers sell Joseph; Absalom betrays his father [II Sam.15]). Miniature in a *Biblia pauperum* from the Benedictine house at Metten (near Deggendorf, lower Bavaria), made in 1414. Munich, SB, Clm 8201, folio 85 recto. Illustration after Cornell 1925, pl.36.

Legitur in Gñ xxxvij quod fres Joseph viderunt adsaulsi prem sui
a fris pessima denerauit fillum suum Joseph ij eum fecerunt dolose
se conspirantes in mortem suo sed Joseph astribus suis dolose
venditus cum fi qui Judas dolose venditus sunt vnde ti
Turba maligñat fratru prcet ut pimat

Legitur in Gñ q fres Joseph eum ysmahelitis vendiderunt xxx
argenteis Joseph iste suis astribus dolose venditus caui
qui Judeis a Juda est venditus xxx argenteis vnde x
De signat ipse juuenis vendidarus iste

In s' bb x legñ xv quod absolon filius dauid venit a diuini
pre ciuitaris iste, et ipso ingrediente loquebatur dicens Quis me
constituat judicem Et sic loquens inclinauit odua vnnu qui
secum conspirantes contra dauid prem suo qui regem constituerunt
et postea prem pfectus in mortem intendebat Absolon iste hi
dauid traditorem sige qui morte xpi cu impissim judeis z phdis
constituit vn x. Finirur infata patris proles scelenta

Legitur in Gñ xxxix q aum ysmahelite Joseph insua induxe
runt tuum vendiderunt tuum in egyptum prgpe pñstide te
qis egyptu noie pstutifer Joseph iste venditus psta ligñ qui
abipo Juda traditore venditus est, vnde x
Conuenit hoc xpo qdq pius sit misto

9. Old Testament scenes including worship of the Golden Calf. Miniature in a manuscript of the *Breviari d'amor* of Matfre Ermengaud (died after 1322), made in the fourteenth century. Illustration after Laske-Fix 1973, 154, nos. 35–40 (= Codex N).

10. In an illustration for the *Goldener Spiel* by Ingold, which appeared in Augsburg (from Günther Zainer) in 1472, a scene is depicted as an example of the dance which is very reminiscent of the Jews dancing around the Golden Calf. The emphatically Jewish dress of a man standing by also points in this direction. Literature: Kunze 1979, fig.77. Illustration after Schramm 1920, II, no.277.

11. The Golden Calf. Woodcut in a Bible printed by Johann Grüninger (Strasbourg 1485). Illustration after Schramm 1920, XX, no.40.

12. Susanna and the Jewish elders whom she puts to shame for falsely accusing her of adultery. Here the Jewish ring – unusual on Old Testament figures – which is clearly visible signifies censure. Woodcut by Hans Schäufelein (died 1538/1540). Literature: Zafran 1973, I, 17. Illustration after Hirth 1923, I, pl.68.

13. Samson smites a thousand Philistines (Judges 16.15). It is very rare for Jews of the biblical period – like Samson here – to wear the Jewish ring (*rota*). Perhaps Samson is meant to be portrayed here as a kind of ruffian, in contrast to the peacefulness of Jesus. Woodcut in a *Speculum salvationis* book from the workshop of the printer Lucas Brandis of Lübeck, c.1475. Literature: Zafran 1973, I, 163. Illustration after Schramm 1920, X, no.379.

V. Emphasis on the Opposition between the Old and New Testaments and the Old and New Covenants

1. Before the Reformation (thirteenth to fifteenth centuries)

1. Tree of paradise (tree of life and corruption; symbolic representation of redemption and death, of the New and the Old Testament). Despite the bad state of preservation, the soteriological statement of the picture can clearly be recognized: 'Above the girlish face of the temptress clearly inclined to the left, the haloed figure of God the Father is enthroned amidst the foliage of the twofold tree, raising his right hand in blessing and holding an apple in the other. On both sides of the intertwined trunk stand Mary and Eve. On the left the mother of humanity, whose nakedness is covered by a hovering bunch of leaves, is holding a skull out to six Jews and with her outstretched right hand is plucking the forbidden apple from the tree. Opposite her, in a mirror position, Mary is holding high a crucifix in one hand and with the other offering to a pope and four other representatives of the church (a cardinal, a bishop and two monks) a small bright round object which we may quite certainly recognize as a host, although on both sides the tree is bearing only apples' (Füglister, 140). Miniature in a Latin Bible, c.1420. Breslau, Stadtbibliothek, MS 1006, folio 3 verso. Literature: Kloss 1942, fig.176. Illustration after Füglister 1964, no.1.

2. 'Living Cross' with Ecclesia and Judaism, the latter depicted as a dying old man who is associated with the old covenant (sacrificial animal), death and Eve (? above right). Small panel painting (28.5 x 18.5) of a diptych from Westphalia, c.1400. Madrid, Fundación Colección Thyssen–Bornemisza. Literature: Schiller II, 1968, fig.528; Mellinkoff, 1984, fig.5; I.Lübbeke, *The Thyssen-Bornemisza Collection. Early German Painting 1350–1550*, London 1991, 110–15; Thyssen 1969, pl.4.

3. Old covenant and new covenant. Eve–Moses–Jews (with Jewish hats)–skulls–apples are standing over against Mary–the pope–bishops–hosts. Pen drawing in a German Life of Mary which was made in Lucerne in 1465. Bern, Bürgerbibliothek. Cod.hist. helv.X, 50, folio 127. Literature: Füglister 1964, no.2.

4. Law and baptism. The creation of Eve and the birth of Ecclesia. The relationship of the Old Testament to the New is interpreted as a unity with the help of Ezek.1.12–16 (*rota in medio rotae*). Miniature in a *Bible moralisée*, c.1240. Paris, BN, Lat.11560, folio 186 recto. Literature: Weber 1894, 112; Neuss 1912, 246 fig.53; Laborde III, 1913, pl.140; Sauer 1924, fig. p.305; Gurewich 1957, pl.26b; Schiller IV.1, 1976, fig.220. Illustration after Seiferth 1964, no.49.

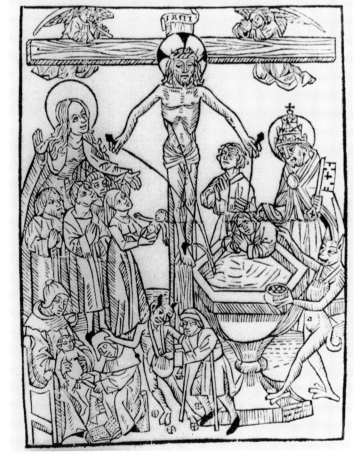

5. Baptism and circumcision (i.e. NT and OT or new and old covenants), the devil and Jews. The picture is based on an affinity between old covenant, circumcision, Jews and the devil. Frontispiece to *Speculum adhortationis Judice ad Christum* (Mirror to admonish Jews to turn to Christ), Cologne 1507. Literature: *Das Münster* 20, 1967, 230; Zafran 1973, I, 261f.; Bienert 1982, fig.5; *Juden in Köln* 1984, fig. p.142; Nolden 1988, fig. p.52; Bohatcová 1991, fig.20; Eckert 1991, 383f. Illustration after *Mon.Jud.Kat.* 1963, no.25 (copy from Cologne, UB, no. AD pl.150).

2. After the beginning of the Reformation (sixteenth century)

1. Title–page woodcut by Lucas Cranach the Younger (composition of evangelical dogmas: sin and redemption, old covenant and new covenant). The same woodcut is used for the Luther Bible 'of the last hand', Wittenberg 1545. Literature: Jahn 1972, fig. p.698; Leonhard 1982, fig.10; Hofmann 1983, fig.85; Reinitzer 1983, figs.pp.182,287; Ohly 1985, fig. p.22. Illustration after Volz 1978, no.271.

▶ 2. Fall and redemption (or old covenant and new covenant, law and grace, justification). Broadsheet (22 x 32 cm) by Lukas Cranach the Elder (1472–1553), a close friend of Luther and Melancthon, who became the creator of an art active on Luther's behalf. The depiction is to some degree a lesson in Protestant dogmatics. Beginning with the fall of Adam and Eve it leads through the law and the prophets (with their promise of Jesus Christ) to the birth, passion, resurrection and victory of the Redeemer, all in a synchronous series of scenes taken over from the Middle Ages. Death and the devil are driving a damned

man into hellfire; Moses (with the two tables of the law), accompanied by the prophets, cannot help the sinner, for the law is useless. John the Baptist leads over to the right-hand half of the picture. The tree of life in the middle is withered on the side of the law and God's wrath, but is becoming green on the side of God's grace through Christ's act of redemption. Unusually the brazen serpent (Num.21.6–9) appears on the side of grace because (as an Old Testament prefiguration of the crucifixion of Christ) for Luther it became an important proof of justification through faith alone. On the right, alongside it, is the

proclamation to the shepherds in the fields and above left on the mountain, the virgin Mary. A stream of blood is issuing from Christ – beside him stands his symbol of the lamb of God that takes away the sins of the world (cf. John 1.29) – towards the person standing alongside John (pointing to Christ as a source of redemption). It brings him the gift of the Holy Spirit which renews life. On the right, below, Christ is emerging from his coffin and the cave of hell and as victor is trampling on death (in the form of a skeleton) and the devil (in the form of a dragon). On the left, above, is Christ (together with Mary and the disciple John) as

ruler of the world and strict judge. The texts given as legends or as help in interpreting the woodcut are: Rom.1.18; Isa.7.14; Rom.3.23; I Cor.15.56; Rom.4.15; Rom.3.20; Matt.11.13; Rom.1.7; Rom.3.28; John 1.29; I Peter 1.2; I Cor.15.55. Literature: Hollstein 1954, VI, 124 fig.14; Harbison 1976, fig.1; Neumeister 1976, fig.4; *Bilder* 1982, fig.12; *Buch* 1982, fig.10; Hofmann 1983, fig.84; Ohly 1985, fig.p.17. Illustration after *Martin Luther* 1983, 399, no.538 (= London, BM Department of Prints and Drawings 1895–1–22–285).

3. Fall and redemption (or old covenant and new covenant, law and grace, justification). Erhard Altdorfer's title page for the Luther Bible (translated into Low German by Johannes Bugenhagen), Lübeck: Dietz 1553. The tree of life, which separates the old covenant from the new, is withered on the side of the old covenant. Above left God the Father is giving Moses the tables of the law; below is the fall of the first human beings; alongside below is the erection of the brazen serpent (Num.21.6–9), the most significant prefiguration of Christ's saving act on the cross; on the level ground a dead man (unredeemed) lies on a sarcophagus. All this contrasts with the right half: above, an angel is proclaiming Christ's birth to Mary (cf. Luke 1.26ff.); below is the crucifix with the lamb of God conquering sin and death and the proclamation to the shepherds in the fields; at the very bottom the victory of Christ over death documented by the resurrection is depicted allegorically by a skeleton. At the foot of the tree sits sinful man, as it were at the cross–roads. A prophet (with his book prophesying Christ as an attribute) and probably John the Baptist (or Paul?) both point to the New Testament Christ event as the only way of redemption. For Altdorfer, as for Lucas Cranach and other artists, the leading idea was the human situation of decision between the old and the new covenants; between death and redemption by the crucified Christ, to whom it was necessary to look up in faith as the Israelites looked up to the brazen serpent. Literature: Schoeller 1915, pl.62; Schiller II, 1968, fig.538; *Dokumente* 1978, fig.p.45; Volz 1978, fig.396; Hasse 1982, fig.28; Hofmann 1983, figs.11 and 86a; Reintzer 1983, fig. p.167; Ohly 1985, fig.23; *Nederland* 1986, fig.12; Meinardus 1991. Illustration after Geisberg I, 1930, pl.1.

VI. Interpretation of the New Testament in Terms of the Contemporary Situation

1. A friendly perspective on New Testament Judaism through the use of the special medieval form of Jewish dress as a group characteristic of Jewishness

(a) Mary's husband Joseph, apostles, Nicodemus, Joseph of Arimathea and others

1. The birth of Christ. Joseph is wearing the conical Jewish hat of the twelfth century, which is meant to emphasize his Jewishness and the Jewish background to the birth of Jesus. Here, as in some other pictures of this kind, he does not have a halo, probably because this did not seem to fit in well with a Jewish hat. Relief on the font at Freckenhorst (Westphalia), 1129. Literature: Schreckenberg II, 530.

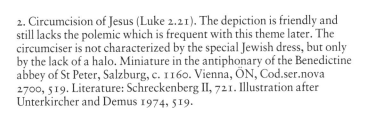

2. Circumcision of Jesus (Luke 2.21). The depiction is friendly and still lacks the polemic which is frequent with this theme later. The circumciser is not characterized by the special Jewish dress, but only by the lack of a halo. Miniature in the antiphonary of the Benedictine abbey of St Peter, Salzburg, c. 1160. Vienna, ÖN, Cod.ser.nova 2700, 519. Literature: Schreckenberg II, 721. Illustration after Unterkircher and Demus 1974, 519.

3. Ascension of Christ (Acts 1.11), before the devout gazes of a group of Christians and Jews. The otherness of the latter and their character as a group is brought out by the funnel–shaped Jewish hats (more hats than faces?). Miniature in the evangeliary from the Cistercian monastery of Hardehausen, c.1160. Kassel, Landesbibliothek, Ms. Theol.59, folio 17 verso. Literature: Schreckenberg II, 721; Deckert 1928, pl.155. Illustration Bildarchiv Foto Marburg.

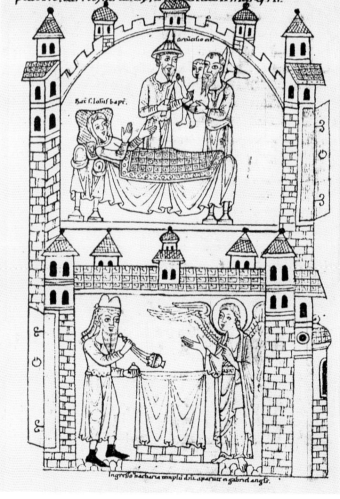

4. Birth and circumcision of John the Baptist (Luke 1.57–66): Elizabeth is on the maternity bed; Zachariah's Jewish hat is falling from his head (Börries–Schulten, 'this means putting off the old faith'); the circumciser is wearing the same hat. The lower half of the picture depicts Zachariah and the angel (Luke 1.8ff.). Inscriptions: *Nativitas S.Johannis Baptiste. Circumcisio eius.* Miniature in a composite manuscript from the Zwiefalten monastery, c.1162. Stuttgart LB, Cod.hist. 2° 415, folio 44 verso (martyrology on 24 June). Illustration after Borries-Schulten 1987, no.250.

5. Messianic entry of Christ into Jerusalem (Matt.21.1–11; cf. Luke 19.1–10, Zacchaeus). Here is one of the rare examples of Jesus' disciples wearing Jewish hats, i.e. they are still seen as Jews among Jews. Miniature in the Liutold Evangeliary, which was made in the third quarter of the twelfth century in the Benedictine abbey of Mondsee. Vienna, ÖN, Cod.1244, folio 140 verso. Literature: Schreckenberg II, 568f. Illustration after Mazal 1988, 86.

6. The birth of Christ. Joseph, with a Jewish hat, is sitting rather to the side, as is frequent in pictures of this kind, as though the event did not immediately concern him: the hat and the lack of a halo are meant to characterize an otherness, but without any negative connotations. Miniature in a composite manuscript from Zwiefalten monastery, c. 1161. Stuttgart, LB, Cod.hist.2° 415, folio 83 verso (on 25 December). Literature: Schreckenberg II, 541f. Illustration after Löffler 1928, pl.32.

7. Jesus as guest in the house of Simon the Pharisee (Luke 7.36–50). The inscription round the edge reads: *Pascit doctorem Symon; oblectat rea solem qui lacrimas crinem videt oscula balsam fidem.* 'Simon feeds the (divine) teacher (Christ); (however) the woman who is a sinner delights the sun; this sees tears, hair, kisses, oil of anointing, faith.' Part of a stained-glass window from Central Rhineland, second half of the twelfth century, formerly in Berlin (destroyed in 1945). Literature: Wentzel 1951, figs.16–17; Fäthke 1975, 79–90; Grodecki 1977, figs.135–7; Becksmann 1988; Schreckenberg II, 587. Illustration after Jungjohann 1935, no.1.

Si comedieuſ ſacopaigna aſpelerinſ.

◀ 8. The Emmaus disciples and Jesus (Luke 24.13–35), the former with (domed) Jewish hats, whereas Christ is distinguished from them above all by his halo. Miniature in the so-called Ingeborg Psalter, made in Paris in 1195. Chantilly, Bibliothèque du Musée Condé, Ms.9, folio verso. Literature: Schreckenberg II, 611f., 657. Illustration after Deuchler 1985 (commentary volume), no.34.

10. Circumcision of Jesus (Luke 2.21), with inscription *Circumcisio domini*. Joseph – Mary is standing behind him – is holding the child, which is showing no sign of the anxiety about the circumciser that is frequent in later depictions. His Jewish hat indicates the 'Jewish' milieu of this scene. Miniature in a composite manuscript from the monastery of Zwiefalten, c.1162. Stuttgart, LB, Cod.hist. 2°415 folio 19 verso (within a martyrology extending from 18 verso to 87 verso: 1 January, circumcision of the Lord). Literature: Schreckenberg II, 541f. Illustration after Borries-Schulten 1987, no.247.

◀ 9. Peter (with tonsure), Paul and a group of Jews. The topic of the discussion is the settling of a dispute between Jewish Christians and Gentile Christians. The Jewish hats have no negative connotation, but the two apostles are distinguished from their conversation-partners by their haloes. Miniature (pen drawing) in a Latin manuscript with legendary lives of apostles, made around 1180. Munich, SB, Clm 13074, folio 15 recto (lower half of picture). Literature: Schreckenberg II, 596f. Illustration after Boeckler 1924, no.49.

11. Flight of the holy family to Egypt. Miniature in an English psalter from the end of the twelfth century. Oxford, Bodleian Library, Ms Gough Liturg.2, folio 17. Literature: Schreckenberg II, 609, 617; Kauffmann 1975, fig.270.

12. Birth of Mary, Anna and Joachim (Apocryphal Gospel of James). Miniature in an evangeliary from the former Benedictine abbey of St Peter (in the southern Black Forest), c.1200. Karlsruhe, LB, Cod.St Peter perg.7, folio 10 verso. Literature: Blumenkranz 1965, fig.75. Illustration after Schmitt-Beer 1961, folio 10 verso.

13. Birth of Christ, in the presence of Joseph (wearing a Jewish hat) and the midwives of the post-New Testament legend. Provenance as the preceding picture, folio 1 verso. Illustration after Schmitt and Beer 1961, folio 1 verso.

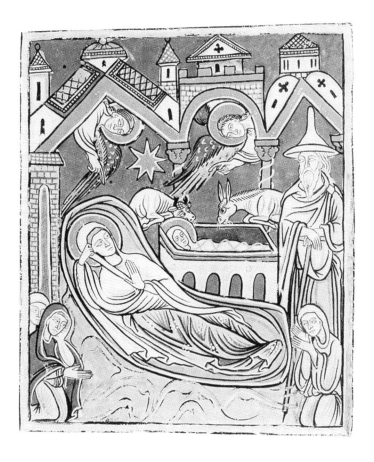

14. Adoration by the three kings. Joseph, wearing a Jewish hat, is forced right to the edge of the picture. Provenance as the preceding picture. Literature: Blumenkranz 1965, pl.84; Schreckenberg II, 615. Illustration after Schmitt and Beer 1961, folio 2 verso.

15. Resurrection of Lazarus, messianic entry of Christ into Jerusalem (John 11.1–44; 12.12–19). Miniature in an evangeliary from Speyer, c.1200. Karlsruhe, LB, Bruchs. I (evangeliary from Speyer), folio 17 recto. Literature: Schreckenberg II, 615. Illustration after Preisendanz and Homburger 1930, pl.19.

16. Jesus in the house of Simon the Pharisee (Luke 7.36–50). Stained glass in the parish church of Rone (Gotland, Sweden), middle of the thirteenth century. Illustration after Andersson 1964, pl.58.

17. Christ's entry into Jerusalem. Miniature (upper half) in a psalter from the region of Basel or Constance, second quarter of the thirteenth century. Liverpool, National Museums and Galleries on Merseyside (N 91.824), Ms 12004. Literature: Blumenkranz 1964, no.5.

18. Birth of Christ. Stained glass in the parish church of Klinte (Gotland, Sweden), c.1270–1280, now in Stockholm, State Historical Museum, Inv.no. 3086:1–2. Illustration after Anderson 1964, pl.78.

19. Christ's entry into Jerusalem (Matt.21.1–11; Luke 19.1–10 [Zacchaeus up the tree]). The 'Jewish' setting of the scene is indicated only by Zacchaeus' (funnel-shaped) Jewish hat. Miniature in a psalter made around 1220, probably in Hildesheim, from the Cistercian convent of Wölteringode near Goslar. Wolfenbüttel, HAB, Cod. Guelferbitanus 521 Helmst., folio 80 verso. Illustration after *Wolfenbütteler Cimelien* 1989, 151.

20. Christ's entry into Jerusalem. Miniature in a psalter made in Bamberg c. 1225. Bamberg, Staatliche Bibliothek, Bibl. 48, folio 61 verso. Literature: Klemm 1980, fig. p.92. Illustration after Messerer 1952, no.86.

21. Christ's entry into Jerusalem. Inscription: *Benedictus qui venit in nomine Domini* (Matt.21.9). Miniature in a Cologne evangelistary, made 1227/1235. Brussels, BR, Ms 9222, folio 19 recto. Illustration after Grimme 1989, colour plate after p.40.

22. Birth of Christ: here we have one of the (infrequent) examples of Joseph wearing a Jewish hat and at the same time having a halo. Miniature in a psalter of the Thuringian-Saxon school, c.1230–1240. Berlin, Staatliche Museen, Kupferstichkabinett, 78 A 7 (no.636). Illustration after Wescher 1931, no.15.

23. Birth of Christ. Miniature in the 'Psalter of Bonmont', made in the upper Rhineland (diocese of Basel or Constance), c.1260. Besançon, Bibliothèque municipale, Ms.54, folio 7 verso (lower half of the picture). Illustration after Leroquais 1940 (III, pl.LXXXVII).

24. Burial of Christ. Miniature in the 'Psalter of Bonmont', made in the upper Rhineland (diocese of Basel or Constance), c.1260. Besançon, Bibliothèque municipale, Ms.54, folio 17 verso. Literature: Swarzenski 1927, pl. p.93; Hauttmann 1929, fig.665; Baum 1930, pl. XX (by p.304); Dehio I, 1930, fig.343; Fischer 1942, fig.43; Baumgart 1952, fig.17; Boeckler 1952, fig. p.74; Weigert I, 1963, fig. p.161; Blumenkranz 1965, fig.97; Grodecki 1977, fig.211; de Chapeaurouge 1987, fig.30; Suarma-Jeltsch 1988, fig.16. Illustration after Leroquais 1940 (III, pl. XCII).

25. Flight to Egypt. Relief field (wood carving) of the high altar of the church in Cismar (a former Benedictine monastery), made c.1310–1320 in a workshop in Lübeck. Literature: Wentzel 1941; Goetz 1965, fig.72; Hootz 1968, fig.77; Behling 1977, fig.3. Illustration after Pinder 1956, no. 95.

26. Deposition from the cross. Small panel painting (18 x 10 cm) by a master from the circle of the Manasseh Manuscript, c.1320. Zurich, Kunsthaus. Literature: Musper 1961, pl. 41; Fritzsche 1981, fig. p.195. Illustration after Zurich 1959, no.34.

27. Entry of Christ into Jerusalem. Inscription: *Christus flevit super civitatem Jerusalem*. Miniature in the earliest manuscript of the *Speculum humanae salvationis*, dated 1324, which found its way from the former imperial abbey of the Praemonstratensians at Weissenau near Ravensburg to the Benedictine foundation of Kremsmünster (Upper Austria). Stift Kremsmünster, Codex Cremifanensis 243, folio 20 verso. Illustration after Neumüller 1972 (facsimile volume).

28. Entry of Christ into Jerusalem. Miniature in a liturgical book made around 1350 in a scriptorium in Breisgau-Alsace. Karlsruhe, Badische LB, St Peter perg.21, folio 12 (a processional and ritual, perhaps from the Dominican house of St Margaretha and St Agnes in Strasbourg). Illustration after Beer 1965, 83.

29. Birth of Christ. Erfurt, Angermuseum. Painting on the wing of the altar of the Augustinian church, c.1370 (photograph D.Urban). Literature: Brückner 1931, fig.118b; Schardt 1941, fig. p.574; Pinder II, 1956, fig.231; Musper 1961, pl.159; Schiller I, 1966, fig. 183; Stelzer 1985, fig. p.398; Bremer 1986, fig.3; Blumenkranz 1965, no.80.

30. Birth of Christ, Joseph with a Jewish hat. Font relief from the end of the twelfth century. Bochum, church of St Peter and Paul. Literature: Schreckenberg II, 656. Illustration after Ludorff 1906, pl.4, no.1.

31. Circumcision of Jesus. Miniature in a sacramentary from the Benedictine abbey of Weingarten (Baden-Württemberg), made in the second quarter of the thirteenth century. Fulda, LB, Cod.Aa 32, folio 78 verso, for the octave of Christmas (the eighth day after Christmas Day, the feast of the circumcision on 1 January). Literature: Swarzenski II, 1943, fig.116; *RDK* II, 1948, 329 fig.1; Köllner 1976, fig.202. Illustration after Blumenkranz 1964, no.2.

32. Flight of the holy family to Egypt. Miniature in a *Biblia pauperum*, made c.1320–1330 in upper Austria. Budapest, Museum of Fine Arts, folio 3 recto. Literature: Schmidt 1959, pl.10; Drescher 1989, pl.51. Illustration after Blumenkranz 1965, no.91.

33. Entry of Christ into Jerusalem. Woodcut in the *Geistliche Auslegung des Leben Jesu Christi*, printed by Günther Zainer around 1485 in Ulm. The man in the city gate of Jerusalem is strikingly wearing the late-medieval Jewish hat. Illustration after Schramm 1920, V, no.364.

34. Jesus heals a sick man. Woodcut in a *Speculum salvationis* from the workshop of the printer Lucas Brandis in Lübeck, c. 1475. Illustration after Schramm 1920, X, no.443.

35. Entry of Christ into Jerusalem (Matt.21.1–10). Before the city gate a garment is spread out (cf. 21.8) which – anachronistically – shows the Jewish ring *(rota)*. This was only introduced after 1215, and thus apparently means the acceptance of Jesus by the Jews. The ring would probably be too small for the neck of a garment, which might also be suggested. Woodcut, c. 1460–1470. Literature: Field 1987, 174, figs.150–2 (the woodcut [which has been damaged] apparently shows the Jewish ring at the same point). Illustration after Heitz 1918, no.28.

36. Circumcision of Jesus. Woodcut in a German-language *Speculum salvationis* printed by Bernhard Richel, Basel 1476. Illustration after Schramm 1920, X, no.52.

(b) Jesus as a Jew (with a Jewish hat)

1. Jesus with a Phrygian cap, on the way to Emmaus. The two Emmaus disciples look as 'Jewish' as Jesus does, one because of a form of Jewish hat which was particularly common in England (a skull-cap with a bobble or stud on top), and the other because of his Phrygian cap. In the Winchester Psalter, c.1555. London, BL, MS Cotton Nero C IV, folio 25. Literature: Schreckenberg II, 554–6. Illustration after Haney 1986, fig.24 (by permission of BL).

2. Jesus with a Phrygian cap, on the way to Emmaus (Luke 24.13–32). With his Jewish cap, akin to the conical hat, Jesus is disguised as a Jew. His cruciform halo is depicted only faintly, so as not to spoil the disguise. Part of a picture with many panels in the parish church of Rosano (near Pontassieve, Florence), around 1140. Literature: Schreckenberg II, 719. Illustration after Carli 1958, pl.6.

3. Jesus and the Emmaus disciples (Luke 24.13–32). One of the few examples of Jesus wearing the Jewish hat (as a disguise). Only his halo regularly gives him as it were an indispensable distinction; and here his hat is rather bigger than those of his companions. Miniature in a psalter of English provenance, c. 1200. Leiden, UB, Hs BPL 76 A, folio 27. Literature: Schreckenberg II, 616f. Illustration after Blumenkranz 1965, no.98.

4. Jesus teaches in the synagogues
(Matt.4.23). Water-colour by J.-J.Tissot,
1896. In an exegesis of the New Testament in
terms of the present day, Jesus is depicted as a
Jew among Jews in a nineteenth-century
synagogue. Illustration after Tissot 1896, I,
101. Similarly ibid., 'Jesus heals a possessed
man' (Mark 1.21–28); illustration after
Tissot 1896 (I, 96). Cf. *The Universal Jewish
Encyclopedia* III, New York 1941, 178.

5. The road to Emmaus. Woodcut in a
Speculum Salvationis (Basel 1476). Illustration
after Schramm 1920, xxi, no. 176.

2. The use of the special form of Jewish dress to present a critical and negative description of Jews

(a) The circumcision of Jesus (Luke 2.21)

1. The picture is not yet really polemical, but a critical assessment of the circumcision of Jesus is developing in that five Jews are surrounding the child in an almost threatening way and the child is looking somewhat anxiously at what is happening to him. Panel picture (on pine) made around 1440 (perhaps near Salzburg, possibly also in central Rhineland). Karlsruhe, Staatliche Kunsthalle, Inv.no.2197. Literature: Lauts 1957 pl.1. Illustration after *Spätgotik in Salzburg* 1972, pl.20.

Plate 7 (on IV, 1b). The passage of the
Israelites through the Sea (Ex.14).
Miniature in a manuscript of the Chronicle
of the World by Rudolf von Ems, made in
Bavaria–Austria, second half of the
fourteenth century. Augsburg, UB,
Cod.I.3.2° II, folio 39 verso. Literature:
Frankenberger and Rupp 1987, no.23.

Plate 8 (on V,1). Mary (–Ecclesia–Vita) and Eve (–death–serpent of one–Jews). Here Eve is in the iconographic place usually occupied by Synagoga and is associated with a 'Jewish'-looking group of people. Death is holding an inscription, *Mors est mal(is), vita bonis inde*, i.e., with reference to Mary distributing hosts and Eve distributing apples, 'Death gives bad things and life good things'. The picture probably belongs in the iconographic context of depictions of the soteriological contrast between old covenant and new covenant. Miniature by Berthold Furtmeyr in the third volume of the missal of the Archbishop of Salzburg, 1481. Munich, SB, Clm 15170, folio 60 verso. Literature: Jacobi 1923, fig.49; *Bayerns Kirche* 1960, fig.60; *Martin Luther* 1983, fig.468; Gercke 1987, fig.10. Illustration after *Regensburger Buchmalerei* 1987, pl.75.

Plate 9 (on VI, 1a). Entry of Christ into Jerusalem (Matt.21.1ff.) with the inscription '*benedictus qui venit in nomine Domini*' (Matt.21.9). The city gate of Jerusalem is decorated with a cross, and Christ and the apostles – Peter with a tonsure – are distinguished from the Jews, whose otherness is made clear by their (funnel-shaped) Jewish hats. The scene incorporates not only the cutting off of branches (Matt.21.8) but also Zacchaeus (Luke 19.1–10). Miniature in the Brandenburg Evangelistary made in the region of Magdeburg at the beginning of the thirteenth century. Brandenburg, cathedral archive (no classification), folio 34. Literature: Gardill and Wolfson 1992, fig.5; Schreckenberg II, 621f. Illustration after Rothe 1965, pl.36.

Plate 10 (on VII, 2b). Paul as missionary to the Jews; holding the Letter to the Hebrews in his left hand, he is teaching two 'Hebrews' from on high. These are wearing the (funnel-shaped) Jewish hats of the twelfth century, one tugging his beard in perplexity, and the other, clean-shaven, making a gesture of dispute. The special form of dress emphasizes how different they are from the apostle with his halo. Miniature in the initial *M(ultifariam)* at the beginning of the (Latin) Letter to the Hebrews, which was regarded as a text by Paul. Trier, city library, HS.2/1676 gr 2°, Vol.2, folio 286 verso. Literature: Zafran 1973, 244f.; Nolden 1988, 36.

Plate 11 (on VI, 1a). Worship by the kings. Joseph is wearing a form of the Jewish hat common in the Middle Ages. Stuttgart, LB, Kodex HB XIII 6 (life of Mary, south-east Germany, first half of the fourteenth century). Illustration after a photograph by Beuroner Kunstverlag.

Plate 12 (on VI, 2a). This depiction of the circumcision – performed with a pair of scissors – is polemical, with a clear affinity to the alleged ritual murders by Jews. Initial miniature for the feast of the Circumcision of the Lord (1 January) in the gradual by Friedrich Zollner, 1438–1442. Neustift (near Brixen), Bibliothek des Augustiner–Chorherrenstiftes. Literature: Peintner 1984, fig.51; Eckert 1991, 372.

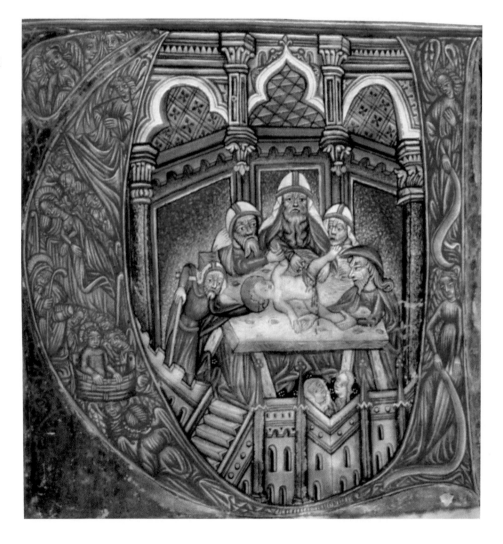

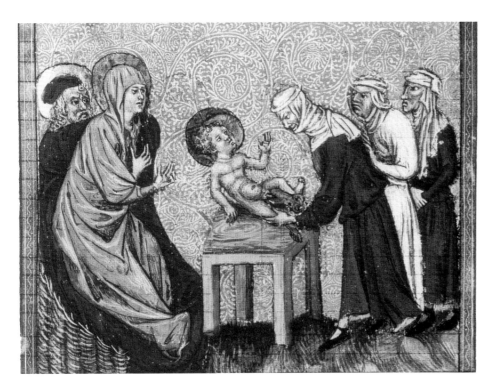

2. Joseph and Mary, anxiously stretching out her hands, watch while dark and grim older women (looking like Jewish women around 1400?) inexorably set to work. The objective account in Luke 2.21 is reinterpreted in a polemical way, and circumcision is made a cruel, repulsive ritual. Miniature in a manuscript of *The Pilgrimage of Human Life, the Pilgrimage of the Soul and the Pilgrimage of Jesus Christ* by Guillaume de Digulleville, made c. 1400 in France, perhaps the work of a German artist. Brussels, BR, MS 10176–8, folio 222. Literature: Delaisse 1959, fig.48; Blumenkranz 1964, no.1.

3. The objective report in Luke 2.21 is here made a kind of prelude to the later passion. The child is afraid of the dark and resolute circumciser (*mohel*), and the Hebrew letters on the outer garment (*tallit*) seem like a denunciation. Altar picture from the Liebfrauenkirche in Nuremberg, made c.1450 by the 'Master of the Cloth Altar'. Aachen, Suermondt-Ludwig-Museum (photograph: A.Gold). Literature: Schmitz-Cleaver, *Aachener Kunstblätter* 34, 1967, fig. p.224; Zafran 1973, II, fig .70; *Nuremberg* 1986, pl.30; Eckert 1991, 373; Suermondt-Ludwig-Museum 1982, 93.

4. The Herrenberg altar, the masterpiece of Jerg Ratgeb, made in 1519. The 'Jewish' dress of the figures (and the pseudo-Hebrew on the hem of the garment) intensifies the feeling of threat to the tiny baby. Stuttgart, Staatsgalerie, Inv.1523 c. verso. Literature: Stange 1924, fig.5; Stuttgart 1962, fig.16; Dittmar 1992, fig.8; Rohrbacher and Schmidt 1991, 279.

(b) The expulsion of the traders from the Temple (Matt.21.12–17)

1. Part of a glass window from Central Rhineland, second half of the twelfth century, formerly in Berlin (destroyed in 1945). Literature: Wenzel 1951, figs.16–17; Fäthke 1975, 79–90; Becksmann 1988; Schreckenberg II, 587. Illustration after Blumenkranz 1964, no.6.

2. Expulsion of heretics and unbelievers from the church. The moralizing exegesis of Num.12.15 (temporary exclusion of the leprous Miriam from the camp) presents the pope – with a funnel-shaped tiara, which also appears elsewhere in contemporary descriptions – driving out heretics and unbelievers from the church (a reminiscence of Matt.21.12f.: expulsion of the traders from the temple). Those who are expelled are apparently all Jews (with Jewish hats, money-bags and sacrificial animals as their attributes). Miniature in a *Bible moralisée*, c. 1240. Oxford, Bodleian Library, cod.270b folio 75 verso (last picture, bottom right). Literature: Blumenkranz 1965, fig.31; Erbstösser 1984, fig.50; Laborde 1, 1911, pl.75.

3. Expulsion of the traders from the temple (Matt.21.12–17). From as early as the time before the exile (cf. Zech.14.21) there had been a custom of having a market for the needs of pilgrims in the temple forecourt. There merchants used to sell the creatures needed for sacrifices (doves), and money-changers changed money of all kinds for shekels or didrachms, i.e. into the currency needed for paying the temple tax. Jesus was probably not attacking the tradition as such, but possible abuses arising from it. Stained glass, c.1390. Vienna, Österreichisches Museum für angewandte Kunst, Inv.no.Gl.2840/29091. Literature: Dworschak 1963, pl.53; Legner 1978, II, fig. p.434. Illustration after Frodl-Kraft 1962, colour plate after 128.

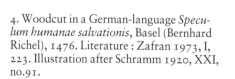

4. Woodcut in a German-language *Speculum humanae salvationis*, Basel (Bernhard Richel), 1476. Literature: Zafran 1973, I, 223. Illustration after Schramm 1920, XXI, no.91.

◄ 5. Woodcut in a *Speculum salvationis* from the workshop of the printer Lucas Brandis in Lübeck, c.1475. Illustration after Schramm 1920, X, no.369.

► 6. Woodcut in *Tresoro de la passion* by Andres De Li, which appeared in Saragossa: Pablos Hurus 1494. Here for once the change of physiognomy marking a preliminary stage to the dehumanization of the Jewish opponents of Jesus, which elsewhere tends to occur in depictions of the passion (scourging and crucifixion), appears in connection with Matt.21.12–17. Illustration after Lyell 1926, fig.26.

(c) Jesus and the woman taken in adultery (John 8.2–11)

1. Unlike Jesus, the New Testament Jews ('scribes and Pharisees') are anachronistically wearing the special form of medieval Jewish dress (rings and hats) and so are defined as enemies. Jesus is writing on the ground (John 8.6) from left to right, and therefore not in Hebrew (?). Pen drawing (with water–colour: 23 x 29.5cm), sketch for a mural in the Grand Council Chamber in Basel. Work from the school of Hans Holbein the Younger (c.1525). Basel, Öffentliche Kunstsammlung, Kupferstich-kabinett, Inv. U.II.19. Literature: Pleister-Schild 1988, no.235.

2. Miniature in a lectionary made c.1330 in Austria. Schaffhausen, Stadtbibliothek, Ms.germ.8: *RDK* IV, 1958, 796 no.4.

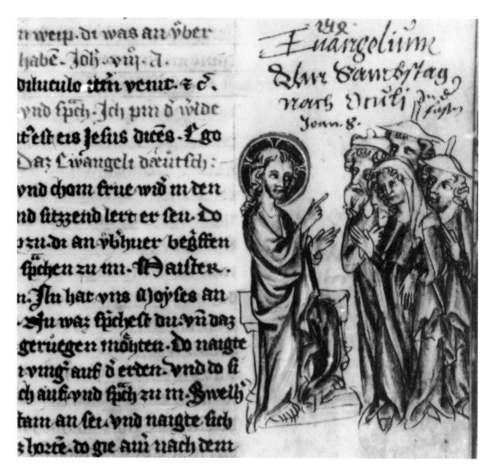

▼ 3. Woodcut in a *Speculum salvationis* from the workshop of the printer Lucas Brandis in Lübeck c.1475. Here the Jewish hat is the conical hat (with a turban-like brim). It is an earlier form of this head-dress, which was retained throughout the Middle Ages and was not completely displaced by kindred types of hat (pointed, narrow shaft with bobble). Illustration after Schramm X, 1920, no. 365.

4. Text: *dis is das frowelin das die E het gebrochen*: *Juden* ('This is the maiden who has broken the E; Jews'). Miniature in a German illustrated Bible made in the area of Strasbourg c.1430–1440. Freiburg im Breisgau, UB, MS 334 (and M.719–720 of the Pierpont Morgan Library, New York), folio 21 recto. Illustration after Beckmann and Schroth 1960 (facsimile volume), folio 21 recto.

(d) The Jews want to stone Jesus (John 8.59)

1. By their special medieval form of dress the Jews of the thirteenth century are also characterized as enemies of Christ. The (pointed) Jewish hats are white, as is usual in coloured miniatures of the twelfth and thirteenth centuries. Here, too, the Jews are depicted as a group, since there are more hats than faces. Miniature in a Cologne evangelistary, 1227–1235. Brussels, BR, MS.9222, folio 58. Literature: Grieme 1989. Illustration after Blumenkranz 1965, no.54.

2. Panel painting (extract from the panel of the life of Jesus) from Cologne, c.1410–1420. Berlin–Dahlem, art gallery. Illustration after Schawe 1988, no.4.

3. Two of the Jews, perhaps the instigators, are wearing the medieval Jewish ring (*rota*) as a distinguishing mark – a polemical anachronism. Woodcut by Urs Graf in the *Passion* of the humanist Matthias Ringmann (Strasbourg: Johann Knoblich 1503 [Latin edition] and 1506 [German edition]), a free narrative treatment of relevant New Testament texts. Illustration after Worringer 1923, no.1.

4. Text: *die juden woltent ihesum steinen* ('the Jews wanted to stone Jesus'). Miniature in a German illustrated Bible made c.1430–1440 in the area of Strasbourg. Freiburg im Breisgau, UB, MS 334 (and M.719–720 of the Pierpont Morgan Library, New York), folio 21 verso. Literature: Blumenkranz 1965, fig.53. Illustration after Beckmann and Schroth 1960 (facsimile volume), folio 21 verso.

(e) The Jewish opposition (e.g. Pharisees)

1. Peter and John before the Supreme Council (Acts 4). The representative of the Supreme Council wears the dress of Jews of the fourteenth cenutry; the apostles are distinguished from him above all by their haloes. Miniature in a manuscript of the *Historia evangelica* of Petrus Comestor (died 1178), written in 1399. Karlsruhe, LB, Codex Tenn.8, folio 110 verso. Illustration after Stamm 1981, no.87.

2. Illustrations on the New Testament. The first of the four scenes on this picture page with a caricature of the New Testament opponents of Jesus relate to Matt.22.15ff. (above left); Matt.22.23ff. (above right); Matt.23.34ff. (below left); Matt.23.1ff. (below left, hypocrisy of the scribes and Pharisees): someone sitting on the 'seat of Moses' is holding the two tables of the law before his eyes like a pair of spectacles which distort his vision (cf. II Cor.3). Two other Jews, one of them a woman, have this twofold table roughly on their foreheads, where otherwise at morning prayer they would be wearing the cube-shaped capsules containing a small parchment scroll with the Hebrew text of Ex.13.1–10, 11–16; Deut.6.4–9; 11.13–21 (i.e. the *tefillin* [or phylacteries, really amulets]); this, too, is meant as a parody, as the tables are not in the proper place on the right side, but at the level of the eyes (making them blind). In accordance with a line of exegetical tradition beginning with Jerome (the Pharisees wore thorns on their hems so that they would often get pricked and thus reminded of the law), one of the Pharisees is tugging at the hem of his garment and a second is looking at a thorn twig in his hand. Miniatures in the Holkham Bible made in England between 1325 and 1330. London, BL, Addit.MS 47682, folio 27 verso. Literature: Blumenkranz 1965, fig.46; Mellinkoff 1974, fig.20; Marrow 1979, fig.129; for 'Moses' seat' see K.G.C.Newport, *Andrews Univ.Sem.Stud.* 28.1, 1990, 53–8. Illustration (by permission of BL) after Hassall 1954 (facsimile volume), folio 27 verso.

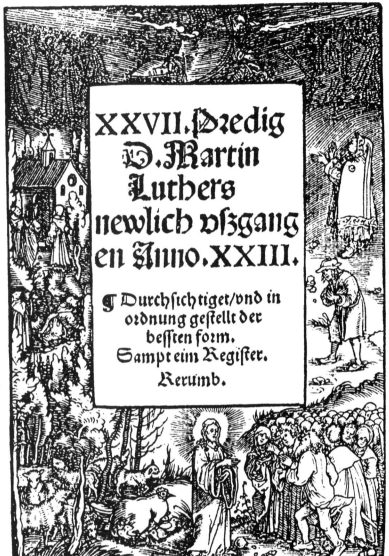

3. Title page to the edition of 27 sermons by Luther (Strasbourg: J.Schott 1523). On the upper right a pious Pharisee (with Jewish ring and pseudo-Hebrew script on his upper garment) is depicted polemically as a Jew of the sixteenth century (on Luke 18.9–14); below on Matt.11.18; left on Matt.24.23; above on II Thess. 2.8. Literature: Kristeller 1888, fig.36. Illustration after Forbes Johnson 1929, pl.41.

4. Messianic entry of Jesus into Jerusalem (Matt.21.1–10). A group of (discontented?) Jews are standing by the city gate; the one in front is anachronistically wearing the Jewish ring (*rota*) which was introduced after 1215. Here he makes the opposition to Jesus iconographically visible. Woodcut c.1460–1470. Literature: Field 1987, 172 no.150; 124, nos.150–2. Illustration after Pfister 1922, pl.26.

5. The Pharisees criticize the plucking of ears of corn on the sabbath (Matt.12.1–18). They have oriental Jewish dress, which distinguishes them from the apostles and Jesus, who have haloes. The depiction of the latter thus to some degree ignores their Jewishness, whereas the Jews appear as an alien group. Woodcuts in Ludolphus, *Life of Christ* (Antwerp: Gerard Leu 1487; Antwerp: Eckert 1503). Illustration after Friedman 1950, nos.5–6.

◄ 6. Resurrection of Lazarus (John 11.1). Haloes and Jewish hats characterize membership of the two respective groups. According to this understanding, Christ and the apostles are no longer Jews. German single-leaf woodcut, c.1460–1470. Literature: Field 1987, 169, no.146. Illustration after *Nürnberg 1892*, 16.

► 7. Jesus attacks the 'hypocrites'; Matt.6 mentions Jews and Gentiles. The dress of the two people standing in front of Jesus is oriental Jewish. Jesus stands out because of his halo, which makes him different. Carved bas-relief on the back wall of a choir-stall dated 1586. Valbert (south-east of Altena in Westphalia), village church. Illustration after Ludorff 1911, 72.

(f) The passion of Jesus, the apostles and saints

1. Eleventh to thirteenth centuries

1.The arrest of Jesus. Verona, San Zeno, door with bronze relief c.1100–1130 (in part later, c.1200). Literature: Schreckenberg II, 530–2. Illustration after Mende 1983, pl.64.

2. Death sentence of the high priests and elders on Jesus (Matt.26.3–5). Two of the group are wearing the Jewish hat (domed or bell-shaped) customary in south Germany in the eleventh century. The treatment of the picture associates the Jews of its time with those of the first century. Miniature in the Reichenau Evangelistary, c.1055. Berlin, Kupferstichkabinett, 78 A 2, folio 26 verso. Literature: Schreckenberg II, 718. Illustration after Bloch 1972.

3 The scourging of Jesus. Verona, San Zeno, door with bronze relief c.1100–1130 (in part later, c.1200). Literature: Gosebruch 1975, figs.22–23; Schreckenberg II, 530–2. Illustration after Mende 1983, pl.66.

4. The scourging of Jesus. Men wearing Jewish hats also appear in the group of those watching the scourgers. Miniature in the antiphonary of the Benedictine abbey of St Peter, Salzburg, c. 1160. Vienna, ÖN, Cod.Ser.nova 2700, p.630. Literature: Schreckenberg II, 563f. Illustration after Lind 1870, pl.XXXVI.

5. The stoning of Stephen (Acts 7.55–60). Two men wearing Jewish hats indicate the involvement of the Jews. Miniature in the antiphonary of the Benedictine abbey of St Peter, Salzburg, c.1160. Vienna, ÖN, Cod.Ser.nova 2700, p.186. Illustration after Unterkircher and Demus 1974, 186.

6. Crucifixion (nailing) of Jesus by four Jews with their typical conical hats. Font relief (twelfth century), in St Georgs-Kirche, Dortmund-Aplerbeck. Literature: Schreckenberg II, 544. Illustration after Bergner 1905, no.431 (copy). Cf. below the very similar font relief in the neighbouring city of Bochum.

7. The passion of Jesus inflicted by men wearing medieval Jewish hats. The persons carrying the spear and the sponge with vinegar (Longinus and Stephaton in post-New Testament legends) are clearly characterized as Jews, thus transferring the collective guilt foisted on the Jews of the New Testament to the Jews of the eleventh century. Miniature in a Bavarian psalter from the last quarter of the eleventh century. Karlsruhe, LB, Aug.perg.161, folio 55 verso (on Ps.52). Illustration after Beer 1965, 78.

8. Jesus is denied by Peter (Matt.26.69–75). Those wearing Jewish hats here (with the different forms that were customary: cone, pointed Phrygian cap, funnel-shaped hat) charcterize the hostile 'Jewish' background to the whole passion event. Inscription: *Abnegat ecce fidem Petrus, quod Christus eidem ante prophetavit, quod galli voce probavit.* Miniature in a Latin poem (about the significance and performance of the mass) in a manuscript perhaps made in Austria, twelfth century. Würzburg, UB, M p.th.q.50, folio 7 recto. Literature: Schreckenberg II, 655: Mälzer and Thurn 1982, 89.

9. The arrest of Jesus (inscription: *S Petrus † Iudas tradidit Christum*). Novgorod, St Sophia. Relief on a bronze door made c. 1154 in Magdeburg. Literature: Goldschmidt 1932, pl.1.22; Appuhn 1963, fig.50; Knapinski 1991; Schreckenberg II, 553f. Illustration after Mende, pl.108.

10. Conspiracy of the high priests and scribes against Jesus (Luke 22.1). Miniature in a Latin Bible from south-west Germany, third quarter of the twelfth century, Stuttgart, LB, Bibl.fol.60, folio 43 recto b. Literature: Schreckenberg II, 569. Illustration after Butz 1987, no.41.

11. Arrest of Jesus (Matt.26.47–56). The Jews are wearing the conical Jewish hats of the twelfth century. Miniature in the 'Liutold Evangeliary', which was made in the third quarter of the twelfth century in the Benedictine abbey of Mondsee. Vienna, ÖN, Cod.1244, folio 184 recto. Literature: Schreckenberg II, 568f. Illustration after Blumenkranz 1964, no.11.

▼ 12. Crucifixion, upper half of the picture. The man with the sponge of vinegar and his counterpart are wearing funnel-shaped Jewish hats. Miniature in the 'Liutold Evangeliary', which was made in the third quarter of the twelfth century in the Benedictine abbey of Mondsee. Vienna, ÖN Cod.1244, folio 188 verso. Literature: Schreckenberg II, 568f. Illustration after Hermann 1926, pl.XXVI, 1.

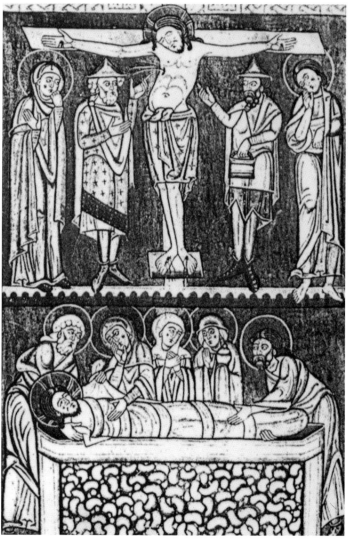

13. The scourging. The agents of the passion are wearing Jewish hats (shallow taper, a bobble on top). Relief on the narrow rear side of the reliquary shrine of the three kings made between 1181 and 1230. Cologne, cathedral treasury. Literature: Legner 1982, figs.30,39; Schreckenberg II, 627f. Illustration after *Mon.Jud.Handb.*1963, no.54.

14. Stoning of Stephen (Acts 7.55ff.), upper half of the picture. The inscription is *Quam bene Saule furis sane furor iste salutis. Amittis Christum, si non lapidaveris istum* ('How well you rage, Saul; truly this rage is for your salvation. You would not have found Christ had you not stoned this man'). Miniature (pen drawing in brown and red ink) in a breviary from the convent of Seckau (Steiermark), second half of the twelfth century. Graz, UB, Cod.832, folio 17 verso. Literature: Schreckenberg II, 724. Illustration after Unterkircher and Demus 1974, no.24.

Flagellacio

15. The scourging (Luke 22.70; 23.22). The inscription associated with Pilate reads *nullam causam mortis invenio in eo* (I find no reason for condemning this man to death); that associated with the foremost Jew, *hic dixit, filius dei sum* (He said, 'I am the son of God'). The many (funnel-shaped) Jewish hats in the background and the statement 'He said, "I am the Son of God"' both define the Jews as a hostile group whose anti-Christian activities are motivated by their rejection of the divine sonship of Jesus. Miniature in a psalter fragment from lower Saxony c.1210–1220 (in private possession). Literature: Schreckenberg II, 628. Illustration after *Zeit der Staufer* II, 1977, no.557.

16. The death sentence passed by the high priests and elders of the people on Jesus (Matt.26.1–5). Initial miniature *S(citis quia)* in a Latin Bible of the third quarter of the twelfth century from south-west Germany. Stuttgart, LB, Bibl.fol.60, folio 26 recto b. Literature: Schreckenberg II, 569. Illustration after Butz 1987, no.23.

17. Crucifixion by four Jews who are wearing the funnel-shaped hat of the twelfth century. A polemical picture with a suggestive effect, since here Christ seems to be encircled by his enemies. Font relief from the end of the twelfth century. Bochum, Catholic deanery church of St Peter and St Paul. Literature: Schreckenberg II, 607. Illustration after Ludorff 1906, pl.3.

18. Scourging by people wearing Jewish hats. The picture (a rough piece of work and badly preserved) differs from Matt.27.26 in depicting the scourgers as Jews (bearded, with tall medieval Jewish hats). Among the Romans scourging (*verberatio*) usually preceded crucifixion (i.e. the cruellest and most dishonourable death, inflicted on slaves and non-Romans in cases of murder, sedition, etc.). There was a Jewish custom of flogging (blows inflicted with a stick on an offender who was made to lie down, see Deut.25.2), for example in cases of slander (Deut.22.18). Mural in the church of Dechtice (Slovakia, around 30 miles north of Bratislava), first third of the thirteenth century. Illustration after *Pamitky na Slovensku. Súpis pamiatok zväzok švtrý, Obzor*, Bratislava 1978, 243.

19. The stoning of Stephen. Tympanum relief, west portal of the minster at Breisach, c. 1230. Literature: Zafran 1973, I, 243f. Illustration after Schmitt 1922, pl.45.

20. The arrest. Miniature in a psalter made in Bamberg c.1225. Bamberg, Staatliche Bibliothek, Bibl.48. Literature: Klemm 1980; Engelhart 1987 (II, fig.244). Illustration after *Franconia sacra* 1952, no.39.

21. The scourging. The Jewish scourgers are holding (stylized) bundles of reeds. Miniature in a Latin psalter made in Germany in the first half of the thirteenth century. Dresden, Staatsbibliothek, Ms.A 165, folio 8. Literature: Bruck 1906, fig.56. Illustration after Blumenkranz 1965, no.58.

22. The passion. His special dress clearly identifies one of the agents, with a sword in his hand, as a Jew. Miniature (folio 61 recto) in a psalter from the monastery of Marienthal near Zittau, first half of the thirteenth century. Illustration after Bruck 1906, no.64.

23. Jews mock the crucified Christ. Matthew 27.39 is interpreted pointedly: the blasphemies are not uttered by passers-by, but the Jews – and only the Jews – gather around the saviour and act with gestures and words. The (anachronistic) use of the special thirteenth-century form of dress burdens all Jews collectively with the guilt of their forefathers. Miniature in a *Bible moralisée*, c.1230. Toledo, cathedral treasury, Ms.III, folio 66. Illustration after Blumenkranz 1964, 18.

24. The betrayal by Judas (Matt.26.14–16), cf. VI, 2g below, Miniature (lower half of the picture) in a psalter from the area of Basel or Constance, second half of the thirteenth century. Liverpool, Ms.12004. Photograph by the National Museums and Galleries on Merseyside, Liverpool.

25. The arrest of Jesus (Matt.26.47–56). Miniature (lower half of the picture) in a psalter from the region of Basel or Constance, second quarter of the thirteenth century. Liverpool, Ms.12004. Literature: Blumenkranz 1964, fig.12. Photograph by the National Museums and Galleries on Merseyside, Liverpool.

26. Jesus before Pilate (Matt.27.11–26). Miniature in a psalter from the area of Basel or Constance, second half of the thirteenth century. Liverpool, Ms.12004. Photograph by the National Museums and Galleries on Merseyside, Liverpool.

27. Jesus' passion. Miniature in a psalter from the area of Basel or Constance, second half of the thirteenth century. Liverpool, Ms.12004, folio 9 verso. Literature: Swarzenski II, 1936, fig.650; Blumenkranz 1965, fig.59. Photograph by the National Museums and Galleries on Merseyside, Liverpool.

28. The arrest of Jesus. Miniature in the fragment of a psalter made around 1240 in Franconia (Würzburg?). London, BL Add. 17687. Literature: Swarzenski 1927, fig. p.83; Engelhart 1987, II, fig.91. Illustration (by permission of BL) after Boeckler 1952, 70.

29. The arrest of Jesus. The Jewish agents are characterized as evil by their physiognomy (the face as a reflection of the soul; cf. Revel-Neher, 'typical Jewish "profile"'); instead of a bobble, the Jewish cap of the man carrying a lantern has a small devil's head, a sign of affinity between the Jews and the devil. Inscription: *Mitte gladium in vaginam* (John 18.11). Miniature in the Chichester Psalter, middle of the thirteenth century. Manchester, John Rylands Library, Lat.24, folio 150 verso. Literature: Revel-Neher 1992, fig.75. Illustration after Mellinkoff 1982, fig.4.

30. Scourging by a man wearing a (white) Jewish hat. Stained-glass fragment in the chapel of La Sarraz castle (canton of Waadt). Illustration after Beer 1965, pl.202.

31. The scourging by Jews. Not only the Jewish hat but also their special physiognomy characterizes the scourgers, giving the picture the effect of a polemical denunciation (Jewish = evil). Miniature in a Latin breviary from the Cistercian monastery of Aldersbach (near Vilshofen, Lower Bavaria), thirteenth century. Literature: Zafran 1973, I, 11. Illustration after *Deutsche Buchmalerei* 1938, pl.4.

32. Arrest of Jesus. Miniature in the Neuburg Psalter, Neuburg, Danube. Literature: Horn-Meyer 1958, 291; Steingräber 1963, 23. Illustration after Engelhart 1987, II, no.246.

33. Jesus before Pilate (Matt.27.11–26). Here Pilate has the same group characteristic as the Jews (in a form of head-dress developed from the Phrygian cap; it is particularly widespread in French-speaking areas in the high Middle Ages), so that the Romans appear fully involved in guilt for the death of Jesus. Miniature in a psalter from Lüttich, thirteenth century. Paris, BN, Lat.1077, folio 163. Illustration after Blumenkranz 1965, no.57.

34. Crucifixion of St Andrew. Contrary to the account in the New Testament Apocrypha (Acts of Andrew), here Jews are acting as agents in the martyrdom (in the sense of Jewish = evil). Miniature in the psalter of a Cistercian monastery (Bonmont Psalter, named after the abbey in the canton of Waadt; made in the upper Rhineland, in the diocese of Basel or Constance, c. 1260). Besançon, Bibliothèque municipale, Ms.54, folio 22. Literature: Swarzenski II, 1936, fig.560; Eydoux 1971, fig.p.121. Illustration after Leroquais 1940, III, pl.XCIV.

35. Bearing the cross and resting before the cross. Miniature in the psalter of a Cistercian monastery (Bonmont Psalter, named after the abbey in the canton of Waadt; made in the upper Rhineland, in the diocese of Basel or Constance, c. 1260). Besançon, Bibliothèque municipale, Ms.54, folio 22. Literature: Swarzenski II, 1936, fig.568. Illustration after Blumenkranz 1965, no.60.

36. The passion inflicted by Jews. The man piercing Jesus with the lance and the man holding the sponge (in post-New Testament legends Longinus and Stephaton) are characterized as Jews by the medieval group characteristic. Mural in the village church of Gossa (in the region of Halle), fourth decade or middle of the thirteenth century. Literature: Nickel 1979, no.6. Photograph by H.L.Nickel.

37. The stoning of Stephen (Acts 7.55–60). Four bronze figures (two of which are illustrated here) served as feet for a reliquary of Stephen (which has not been preserved). By their Jewish hats, even medieval Jews are burdened with the guilt of their forefathers. The small bronze figures were made between 1210 and 1220. Halberstadt, Protestant cathedral (treasury, inv.no.36). Literature: Lenger 1982, fig.338; Schreckenberg II, 627. Illustration after *Zeit der Staufer* II, 1977, no.371.

38. The scourging of Jesus. Miniature in a psalter which was perhaps written for a nunnery, probably in the Alsatian part of the diocese of Basel, around 1260–1270. Donaueschingen, former Fürstlicher Fürstenbergischer Besitz, Cod.186, folio 13 recto. Illustration after Mittler and Werner 1988, 623.

39. Scourging of Jesus (John 19.1–3; cf. Matt.27.26–31). According to the New Testament text this was carried out by the execution squad composed of the Roman soldiers of the governor Pilate. Many Christian depictions distort the situation by making Jews (with Jewish hats) perform the scourging. Miniature in a Latin manuscript of the twelfth century. Laon, Bibliothèque municipale, Ms.550, folio 6 recto. Literature: Schreckenberg II, 546. Illustration after Green 1979, II, no.558.

2. Fourteenth to fifteenth centuries and an example from the nineteenth century

1. Nailing to the cross by persons who are wearing the Jewish head-covering particularly customary in French-speaking areas. Initial O (height 6.7 cm) of a manuscript from Lüttich, c.1300. Münster, Westfalisches Landesmuseum, inv. no. WKV Kdz 2862.

2. Crowning with thorns. Miniature in a *Biblia pauperum* made in upper Austria between 1320 and 1330. Budapest, Museum of Fine Arts, folio 11 recto. Literature: Schmidt 1959, pl.12a; Drescher 1989, fig.50. Illustration after Blumenkranz 1964, no.17.

3. The bearing of the cross. An executioner characterized by his Jewish hat is holding the hammer for nailing Christ to the cross in his left hand, and with his right hand he is impatiently grabbing Christ's robe to hurry him on. Miniature in the gradual from St.Katarinental (house of Dominican women near Diessenhofen, Switzerland), c.1312. Zurich, Landesmuseum, folio 90 recto: initial *N(os autem gloriari)*. Literature: Beer 1959, figs.66, 86; Knoepfli 1961, I, pls.116, 119; Mittler and Werner 1988, II, 343f. Illustration after Schmid and Beer 1983 (facsimile volume).

4. The arrest of Jesus. Stained glass in the parish church of Dalhem (Gotland, Sweden), second quarter of the fourteenth century. Illustration after Andersson 1964, pl.31.

◀ 5. The bearing of the cross (inscription: *Hora sexta* [i.e. at the hour of sext] *Christus crucem propriam baiulavit*). Miniature in a *Speculum salvationis* manuscript made in 1324 in the upper Rhineland/German-speaking Switzerland. Kremsmünster, Stiftsbibliothek, Cod.Crem.243, folio 50 recto. Illustration after Neumüller 1972 (facsimile volume).

▶ 6. The synagogue laughed at Christ; Saul's daughter Michal mocked her husband David (typological link between the NT and the OT). Inscriptions: *Synagoga derisit Christum regem suum et Dominum; Pater dimitte illis etc.; Consummatum est; si filius Dei es, descende nunc de cruce et credimus; confidit in Deo; liberet eum nunc, si vult; Abach, qui destruit templum. Michol subsannavit virum suum David*, etc. Miniature in a *Speculum salvationis* manuscript made in 1324 in the upper Rhineland/German-speaking Switzerland. Kremsmünster, Stiftsbibliothek, Cod.Crem.243, folio 30 verso. Illustration after Neumüller 1972 (facsimile volume).

7. The passion inflicted by Jews (inscriptions *Hora prima* [i.e. at the time of Prime] *ductus est Jesus ad Pylatum; Hora tertia* [i.e. at the hour of Terce] *fuit Christus ad statuam ligatus et flagellatus*). Miniature in a *Speculum salvationis* manuscript made in 1324 in the upper Rhineland/German-speaking Switzerland. Kremsmünster, Stiftsbibliothek, Cod.Crem.243, folio 4930 verso. Illustration after Neumüller 1972, folio 49 verso (facsimile volume).

8. The passion of Jesus (Matt.26.67) is typologically associated with the fate of Hur (husband of Miriam and son-in-law of Aaron, who was attacked by the Jews because of his opposition to the making of the Golden Calf). Inscriptions: *Christus fuit velatus, consputus et colaphizatus; atque dixerunt ei: prophetiza nobis, Christe, quis est qui te percussit – Hur vir Marie sputis Iudeorum suffocatur.* Miniature in a *Speculum salvationis* manuscript made in 1324 in the upper Rhineland/German-speaking Switzerland in 1324. Kremsmünster, Stiftsbibliothek, Cod.Crem.243, folio 30 verso. Illustration after Neumüller 1972 (facsimile volume).

9. Jesus is arrested and taken away. The perpetrators are characterized by their oriental-Jewish appearance as members of an alien group. Miniature in the Rohan Book of Hours, made between 1420 and 1427 by an anonymous artist. Paris, BN, Lat.9471, folio 61 verso. Literature: Thomas 1973; *Kunst-Brockhaus* II, 1983, 361. Illustration after Blumenkranz 1965, no.28.

10. Miniature in the Rohan Book of Hours, 1420–1427. The inscription under the picture emphasizes the involvement of the Jews (who are already indicated as such by their dress*): 'Ce sont les felons Juifs qui mettent ihesucrist en la croix'*. Paris, BN, Lat.9471, folio 165 verso. Illustration after Blumenkranz 1965, no.64.

11. Text: *man het ihesum gegeyschelt*. Miniature in a German illlustrated Bible made in the region of Strasbourg between 1430 and 1440. Freiburg im Breisgau, UB, Ms 334 (and M.719–720 of the Pierpont Morgan Library, New York), folio 34 recto. Illlustration after Beckmann and Schroth (facsimile volume) 1960, folio 34 recto.

12. The bearing of the cross. The executioners, some of whom are identified as Jews by pointed hats, do their work as wicked men. The minion at the front on the right has barely human features. Miniature in a German *Speculum salvationis* manuscript made around 1440 in Upper Rhineland or around Lake Constance. Berlin, Kupferstichkabinett, Ms.78 A.178. Illustration after Lehmann-Haupt 1929, pl.9

◀ 13. The Hebrew characters and the scorpion – in the late Middle Ages often a symbol of Judaism – on the fabric of the standard are meant to identify the passion of Jesus as a Jewish action which was a collective burden even on the Jews of the fifteenth century. Panel painting on a winged altar from central Rhineland, made after the middle of the fifteenth century by an unknown master. Speyer, Historisches Museum der Pfalz, Inv.no.HM 1979–38b. Illlustration after Speyer 1983, 85.

▶ 14. The mount of Calvary. Engraving (dated 1482) by a master known only by his monogram. 'One of the Jews is grinning as he holds the stick with the sponge of vinegar, while another holds a banner with a Jewish hat between Jewish characters... Behind them... around fourteen Jews, mostly bearded, shrieking and laughing, scribes, the people, and executioners armed with lance, club and flail. Next to the cross two standards tower above the crowd, one with a half moon and three stars' (Lehrs). The wickedness of the enemies of Jesus is evident from their faces, the physiognomy of which has some similarities to that of animals (nostrils like those of apes?), so that this picture, too, is perhaps an example of a certain tendency towards dehumanization. Illustration after Lehrs 1908 (VIII, no.557).

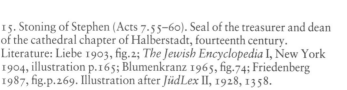

15. Stoning of Stephen (Acts 7.55–60). Seal of the treasurer and dean of the cathedral chapter of Halberstadt, fourteenth century. Literature: Liebe 1903, fig.2; *The Jewish Encyclopedia* I, New York 1904, illustration p.165; Blumenkranz 1965, fig.74; Friedenberg 1987, fig.p.269. Illustration after *JüdLex* II, 1928, 1358.

16. The mount of Calvary. Here New Testament Jews are given the medieval Jewish ring, a deliberately polemical anachronism. Woodcut, south Germany, first half of the fifteenth century. Literature: Zafran 1973, I, 15; Rohrbacher and Schmidt 1991, fig. p.236. Illustration after Hind I, 1935, fig.56.

17. The council of the Jews against Jesus: here as often elsewhere the high priest has a kind of mitre. Woodcut in a German-language *Speculum salvationis* printed by Bernhard Richel, Basel 1476. Illustration after Schramm 1920, XXI, no.93.

18. Crucifixion. This is being done under the instructions of a man with 'Jewish' dress. Woodcut by Michael Wolgemut (or the Wolgemut–Pleydenwurff workshop) in the 'treasury' of the Franciscan Stephan Fridolin (Nuremberg: A. Koberger 1491). Illustration after Kunze 1975, no.365.

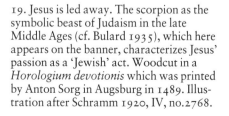

19. Jesus is led away. The scorpion as the symbolic beast of Judaism in the late Middle Ages (cf. Bulard 1935), which here appears on the banner, characterizes Jesus' passion as a 'Jewish' act. Woodcut in a *Horologium devotionis* which was printed by Anton Sorg in Augsburg in 1489. Illustration after Schramm 1920, IV, no.2768.

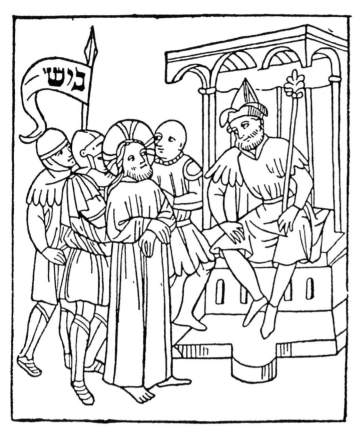

20. Jesus being interrogated. The Hebrew letters are meant to denounce Jesus' passion as a human action. German woodcut, c.1450. Literature: Zafran 1973, I, 19; Field 1987, no.267. Illustration after Heitz 1918, no.46.

21. The passion of Jesus. The late medieval 'Jewish' head-dress of the two persons involved also includes the Jews of the Middle Ages in the collective guilt. Woodcut in the 'Spiritual Exposition of the Life of Jesus Christ' printed in Ulm by Günther Zainer in 1485. Literature: Schramm 1920, V, no.381. Illustration after Muther 1884, II, pl.59.

22. The crowning with thorns. Panel painting on a winged altar from a church between Mainz and Oberwesel, c.1410. Utrecht, Rijksmuseum Het Catharijneconvent. Literature: Liebrich 1926, fig. 12: Zafran 1973, I, 11f.; *Europäische Kunst* 1962, pl.89; Getzener 1928, figs. on pp.4–5, 13–14.

23. The Jews take counsel against Jesus (Matt.26.3–5). Woodcut in *De nye Ee und dat Passional van Jhesus und Marien levende* by the printer Lukas Brandis, Lübeck 1478. Illustration after Schramm 1920, X, no.168 (cf. ibid., X, no.371).

24. Jesus before the high priest Annas: Peter's denial. The physiognomy of some of the (Jewish) agents of the passion of Jesus is abnormal, as is common at this time. Woodcut by Urs Graf in the *Passion* of the humanist Matthias Ringmann (Strasbourg: Johann Knoblich 1503 [Latin edition] and 1506 [German edition]). Illustration after Worringer 1923, no.11.

25. The nailing to the cross. To depict Jesus' passion as a 'Jewish' act it is often enough for just one of those involved or a bystander (as a guiding spirit) to have the group characteristic of medieval Jews or to look 'Jewish'. Single-leaf woodcut by an unknown artist from the time before 1500. Illustration after Field 1989, no.669–1.

26. The nailing to the cross. Watercolour by Johann Friedrich Overbeck (1789–1869), made in 1854. Overbeck was a member of the group of artists called 'Nazarenes'. In 1813 he became a Catholic, and above all the pictures painted later in his life are governed by a rigid dogmatic religious sense. In this watercolour the guilt of the Jews – represented by three bearded figures – in the passion of Jesus is strongly emphasized, contrary to the accounts in the New Testament. The artistic means are new, but the statement is the same as that in many medieval depictions of the passion. Illustration after *Duitse tekeningen* 1964, Cat.119.

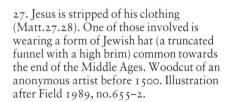

27. Jesus is stripped of his clothing (Matt.27.28). One of those involved is wearing a form of Jewish hat (a truncated funnel with a high brim) common towards the end of the Middle Ages. Woodcut of an anonymous artist before 1500. Illustration after Field 1989, no.655-2.

(g) Judas and the high priests; Judas' punishment

1. The payment of the thirty pieces of silver to Judas (Matt.26.14f.). The high priest and his companions, one of whom is almost concealed by Judas, wear the medieval Jewish hat, but the traitor does not. The payment of the money is perhaps meant to recall the business activity of Jewish money lenders of the thirteenth century. Naumburg, cathedral, sandstone relief on the west front of the choir screen, c.1245. Literature: Beenken 1989, fig.83; Feulner and Müller 1953, fig.103; Schiller II, 1968, 34; Baier 1982, fig.270; Eckert 1991, fig.374. Illustration after Jantzen 1925, no.116.

2. The betrayal by Judas. Miniature in a manuscript of the *Historia evangelica* of Petrus Comestor (died 1179), written in 1399. Karlsruhe, LB, Cod.Tenn.8, folio 75. Illustration after Stamm 1981, no.77.

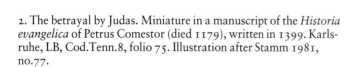

3. Judas sells Christ (inscriptions: *Judas cum argento: Judei*); the Old Testament prefiguration is the sale of Joseph by his brothers and the further sale to Potiphar (Gen.37.12–36). The Jews negotiating with Jesus are represented by a person wearing the medieval Jewish hat, so that the Jews of the fifteenth century also seem burdened with the guilt of their forefathers. Miniature in a *Biblia pauperum* from the second quarter of the fifteenth century made in North Hessen or Thuringia. Rome, BAV, Cod.Pal.lat.871, folio 10 verso. Literature: Unger 1986, 65f. Illustration after Wirth 1982, I, folio 10 verso (with II, 64).

4. The torments of Judas Iscariot. Woodcut in *Brandans Buch* (printed in 1476: Schramm 1920, IV, no.223: Judas with a black halo, similarly V, no.466) and in the *Meerfahrt des Hl. Brandan* (printed in 1491 by Michael Furter, Basel; Schramm 1920, XXII, no.518: Judas with a Jewish hat). The widespread medieval Brendan legend describes numerous fantastic adventures of the Irish saint (who lived in the fifth and sixth centuries) on his journey into the 'Promised Land of the Saints'. Brendan learns from a book of three heavens, two paradises, nine purgatories and a land under the earth in which it is day during our night. He does not believe what he reads, burns the book and therefore as a punishment has to go to sea for nine years to experience for himself what is described in the book. He voyages with twelve monks as his companions. Among other things he sees a forest growing on the back of a fish; meets souls who constantly run round a lake in great heat without getting to it; he meets the devil, hears the laments of the

souls in purgatory and finds Judas Iscariot, who is suffering fearful torments. Judas has a black (i.e. negative) halo, the opposite to the well-known aura of a saint, or a Jewish hat – which indicates a certain equivalence of the two attributes and perhaps explains

why Jewish hat and halo are only relatively rarely connected (e.g. in the case of Mary's husband Joseph); usually one excludes the other. Illustrations after Schramm 1920, IV, no.233 and XXII, no.518.

5. Judas and the high priests (Luke 22.3–6). The depiction corresponds to the widespread view that the Jews are instigated to their wicked deed by the devil or are in league with him. Miniature in a *Biblia pauperum*, c.1355–1360. Munich, SB, Cgm 20, folio 11 recto. Literature: Cornell 1925, pl.63; Wirth 1963, fig.6; Bremer 1986, fig.37. Illustration after Blumenkranz 1965, no.55.

◀ 6. Judas and his thirty pieces of silver. A miniature in a manuscript of a *Biblia pauperum* from the Benedictine abbey of Tegernsee, middle of the fourteenth century. Munich, SB, Clm 19414, folio 162 recto. Literature: Cornell 1925, pl.60; Zafran 1973, I, 223f. Illustration after Blumenkranz 1964, no.10.

▲ 7. The betrayal by Judas (Matt.26.14–16). The milieu of the scene is emphatically 'Jewish' (pseudo-Hebrew text above left, special form of late medieval dress for some high priests). Woodcut by Urs Graf in the *Passion* (a free narrative treatment of the relevant New Testament passages) by the humanist Matthias Ringmann (Strasbourg 1503 [Latin edition] and 1506 [German edition]). Literature: Bremer 1986, no.38. Illustration after Worringer 1923, no.8.

(h) Devotional pictures ('Arma Christi')

1. Fresco fragment in a former working courtyard (Erlahof) of the Benedictine abbey of Niederaltaich near Spitz (lower Austria), c.1310. Literature: Zafran 1973, I, 11; Suckale 1977, fig.4. Illustration after Lanc 1982, no.493.

▲ 2. 'The Marienstatt Foundation Document' (one of two leaves commemorating the consecration of the abbey of Marienstatt on 27 December 1324, decorated with paintings). Among the agents and instruments of the passion of Christ, as usual the bust of a Jew (with Jewish hat and beard) appears. Bonn, Rheinisches Landesmuseum, Inv.no.791. Literature: Budde 1986, fig.8. Illustration after Deckert 1928, pl.171.

▶ 3. Engraved scene on the outside of a diptych reliquary. Acording to the inscription running round the edge it was commissioned by Thile Dagister of Lorich who came from the Rhineland and was living in Elblag, Poland, as commander of the German Order; it is dated 1388. Warsaw: Museum Wojska Polskiego, Inv.no.129. Illustration after Legner II, 1978, 522.

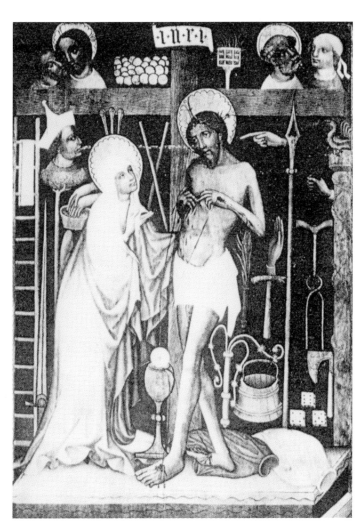

4. Votive picture: the Man of Sorrows with Mary. Panel painting from St Nicolas' church at Brieg (about 20 miles south–east of Breslau), dated 1443. Warsaw, National Museum, Inv. no.Sr.343. Literature: Behrens 1941, fig.3. Illustration after Dobrezeniecki 1977, 228.

5. Christ as the Man of Sorrows bleeding from many wounds in front of an open sarcophagus. Peter and the serving girl, Judas (with his bag of money), Caiaphas, Pilate and an executioner also appear in the picture: bottom left is King Matthias Corvinus (with the inscription *Pie Jesu miserere nostri*), above him two angels holding a crown and a sword: a bundle of reeds, a noose, a hammer, pincers, a sponge soaked in vinegar and a lance are depicted as *arma Christi*, and bottom right are Christ's cloak and dice. The high priest in 'Jewish' dress documents the responsibility of the Jews for the death of the Lord. Miniature in a missal made for the king in Vienna, dated 1469. Rome, BAV, Codex Rossianus 1164, folio 126 verso. Literature: Tietze 1911, fig.25; Farkas and Bogyai 1986, fig.18; Csapodi 1969, pl.LXXXV; *Franz von Assisi* 1982, pl.16; Plotzek and Surmann 1992 (facsimile volume), folio 126 verso. Illustration after Kühnel 1985, 383.

6. Indulgence poster c.1440. Literature: *TRE* XV, 1986, pl.2 (with p.524); Field 1991, 156; Eder 1992, 167. Illustration after Rill 1982, 395.

7. Part of a winged altar from Buxheim, c.1510. Inscription: '*Wer disen krantz wil gewinnen und den mit recht sol tragen der sol jhesum von hertzen minnen und sine sünd mit grossen rüwen and laid klagen*' (He who would win this crown and wear it rightly must love Jesus with all his heart and repent and bewaily his sin deeply). Literature: *Ulmer Museum* 1981, 195. Ulm, Museum, Inv.no.1992.5109 (photograph B.Kegler).

8. Mural under the west gallery (organ gallery) of St Stephen's Cathedral in Vienna, first half of the fourteenth century (drawing from 1888). Illustration after Tietze 1931, no.153.

9. Miniature in the vernacular prayer-book of George II of Waldburg (died 1482) (the 'Waldburg Prayerbook'), which was made in upper Swabia in 1476. Stuttgart, LB, Cod.brev.12, page 23 verso. Illustration after Heinzer and Stamm 1992, no.34.

10. The back of a triptych panel by the 'Master of Cologne', c.1350. Hamburg, Kunsthalle (photograph E.Walford). Literature: Hoffmann 1986, 43 fig.8; Marrow 1979, no.43.

VII. The Christian Message and the Jews

1. The twelve-year-old Jesus among the Jewish teachers (Luke 2.41–50): the prelude to and anticipation of the role of Jesus as teacher of Israel

1. Two of the Jewish teachers (all of whom have beards) are wearing the characteristic Jewish hat, which emphasizes the otherness of the whole group. Here the boy Jesus is not sitting on a higher level, as he usually does, but both his central position and the halo with cross emphasize him as the dominant figure. Miniature in a fragment of a psalter, to be dated between 1150 and 1170. Berlin, Kupferstich-kabinett, Cod.78 A 6, folio 9 recto. Literature: Klemm 1973, fig.17. Illustration after Kopp-Schmidt 1992, 50.

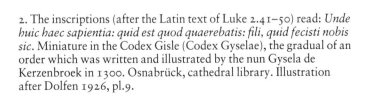

2. The inscriptions (after the Latin text of Luke 2.41–50) read: *Unde huic haec sapientia: quid est quod quaerebatis: fili, quid fecisti nobis sic*. Miniature in the Codex Gisle (Codex Gyselae), the gradual of an order which was written and illustrated by the nun Gysela de Kerzenbroek in 1300. Osnabrück, cathedral library. Illustration after Dolfen 1926, pl.9.

3. Miniature in Queen Mary's psalter, c.1310–1320. London, BL, Ms Royal 2 B VII, folio 151. Literature: Grimme 1980, 187, fig.64; Zarnecki 1986, fig.p.368: Stanton 1992. Illustration (by permission of BL) after Warner 1912, pl.188.

4. Stained glass, c.1320. Friesach (Carinthia), parish church of St Bartimea. Illustration after Frodl 1950, 86.

▲ 5. Stained–glass window in the choir of the monastery church of Hauterive (near Fribourg, Switzerland), c.1320–1330. Illustration after Beer 1965, pl.62.

6. Stained-glass window in the parish church of St Leonard (Carinthia), made around the middle of the fourteenth century. Illustration after Frodl 1950, fig.48.

7. Stained-glass window in the Frauenkirche at Esslingen (near Stuttgart), before 1350. Illustration after Wentzel 1958, no.306.

8. Inscription: *Tertia tristitia beate Marie virginis: Jesus sedet inter doctores* (i.e. the third of the 'seven sorrows' of Mary is her missing her son and having to look for him). Miniature in a *Speculum salvationis* made in 1324 in Upper Rhineland/German-speaking Switzerland. Kremsmünster (Austria), Stiftsbibliothek, Cod.Crem. 243, folio 51 verso. Literature: *Verfasserlexikon* IX.1, 1993, 52–65. Illustration after Neumüller (facsimile volume).

9. Miniature in a prayerbook made in Cologne around 1330 and presumably intended for a convent. Hanover, Kestner Museum, Inv.no. WM.Ü 22, folio 18 verso. Illustration after *Franz von Assisi* 1982, pl.17 (before p.499).

10. Woodcut in a German-language *Speculum salvationis* printed by Anton Sorg, Augsburg 1476. Illustration after Schramm, 1920, IV, no.172.

11. Stained-glass window in Strassengel (Steiermark), pilgrimage church, before 1366. Illustration after Bacher 1979, no.340.

12. Miniature in a book of hours *(Tres Belles Heures de Notre Dame du Duc de Berry)*, made by the 'Master of the Parament of Narbonne' c.1375–1380. Paris, BN, nouv.acqu. lat.3093, folio 62. Literature: Sterling I, 1987, fig.136; facsimile edition (with commentary by E.König), Lucerne 1992. Illustration after Meiss 1969, pl.11.

13. New Testament scenes including 'the twelve-year-old Jesus among the Jewish teachers', some of whom have the medieval Jewish ring (*rota*) as a group characteristic. Miniature in a manuscript of the *Breviari d'amor* of Matfre Ermengaud (died after 1322), made in the middle of the fourteenth century. Illustration after Laske-Fix 1973, 165, pls.75–80 (= Codex M, folio CLXXII).

14. Woodcut in a German-language *Speculum salvationis* printed by Bernhard Richel, Basel 1476. Illustration after Schramm 1920, XXI, no.66.

15. Panel painting, part of the wing of an altar, c.1420. Fröndeberg (near Unna, Westphalia), Stiftskirche (formerly the church of a Cistercian convent). Literature: Thümmler 1959, fig.p.137; Fritz 1970, fig. 62; *Cleveland* 1974, p.29. Illustration from a photograph by Westfälischer Amt für Denkmalspflege, Münster.

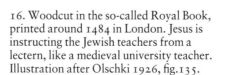

16. Woodcut in the so-called Royal Book, printed around 1484 in London. Jesus is instructing the Jewish teachers from a lectern, like a medieval university teacher. Illustration after Olschki 1926, fig.135.

17. Panel painting of the high altar of the city church of Schotten (between Fulda and Giessen), a masterpiece of Gothic in Hessen, c.1390. Illustration after Deckert 1928, pl.195: cf. Zafran I, 33.

18. Altar painting (part of a large winged altarpiece with many panels), made in lower Saxony, and placed on the high altar of the church of the Discalced Friars in Göttingen in 1424, now in Hanover, Niedersächsiches LM, Inv.no. WM XXVII, 3–8. Illustration after Schawe 1988, no.1.

19. Panel painting with scenes from the Gospels and the apocryphal Gospels: Mary's wedding, annunciation by the angel Gabriel, stay in Egypt (fall of the idols), the twelve-year-old Jesus in the temple. Soester Meister, c.1400–1420. Münster, LM, Inv.no.691.

▶ 21. Woodcut in the 'Spiritual Exposition of the Life of Jesus Christ' printed by Günther Zainer in Ulm around 1385. Literature: Schramm 1920, V, no.338. Illustration after Muther 1884, II, pl.56.

20. Panel of a winged altar by the 'Master of Schloss Lichtenstein', named after Schloss Lichtenstein south of Reutlingen in Swabia, c.1445. Vienna, Österreichische Galerie, Inv.no.4908 (photograph by Otto). Literature: Baldass 1935, fig.6; Baum 1971, no.20.

Wie maria ihesum fand im tempel

 O nun alt was wordē das kind ihesus zwelff iar fůg er uff mit vatter vnd mütter nach gewonhait der gesaçt zů dem hochzitlichen vest gen iherusalem in den tempel. Vnd wañ es sů

22. Mural in a chapel in Lanslevillard (arrondissement Saint-Jean-de-Maurienne, Savoie), fifteenth century. Illustration after Gardet II, 1965, 35.

23. Woodcut by Urs Graf (died 1527/28) in the *Cosmographey* of Sebastian Münster (1598 edition) as an illustration to a text about the Jewish school in Eger. Graf uses the topic to illustrate the popular motif of Luke 2.41–50 (Jesus and Mary have haloes). By way of a comparison there is a sixteenth-century woodcut without Christianizing elements. Both pictures show an 'ABC table' on the wall as a didactic aid to reading. E.g. Adolph Menzel (died 1905) followed Urs Graf's line of interpretation very much later with his lithograph 'The Twelve-year-old Christ in the Temple'. Literature: Mertens 1991, 169f. Illustration after Schiffler and Winkeler 1988, no.33 (Urs Graf), and *The Jewish Encyclopedia* V, New York 1903, 44. For Menzel see Dittmar 1992, 291f.

24. Engraving by Francesco Rosselli (died before 1513), c. 1470–1490. London, BM, classification: B, I,5,II. Literature: Roberts 1987, 204, fig.18. Illustration after Hind 1938, pl.176.

25. Woodcut in a German-language prayer book (composed by Ludwig Moser) and printed by Michael Furter in Basel around 1495. Jesus is on a kind of pedestal. Many Christian theologians and artistts (working on their instructions) were not content with the boy Jesus 'sitting in the midst of the (Jewish) teachers' and 'listening' to them.

Thus the depiction of Luke 2.41–50 is one of those areas in which the iconographic exegesis of the New Testament frequently deviates most from the given text (the passion scenes are perhaps an exception here). Literature: Schramm 1920, XXII, no.440; Field 1987, nos.128–9. Illustration after Heitz 1918, no.25.

26. Engraving (27.4 x 19.2 cm) by Israhel van Meckenem (died 10 November 1503). Berlin, Kupferstichkabinett L.59, B.39 (Inv.887–1: photograph J.P.Anders). Literature: *Hans Holbein* 1965, fig.207; Jászai 1993, fig. p.553: Shestak 1967, no.225.

27. The 'Jewish milieu' is depicted by the pseudo-Hebrew writing and the Jewish hat of one of the teachers. Painting (on pine, 128 x 74 cm) by the so-called Hausbuchmeister, end of the fifteenth century. Mainz, Landesmuseum, Inv.no.417, 419. Literature: *Vom Leben in späten Mittelalter* 1985, 253 pl.132g; Bookmann 1986, 289 fig.434; Hutchinson 1976, 101 fig.6; Dittmar 1992, fig.5; R.Wohlfeil (in Herzig and Schoeps) 1993, no.3.

28. Woodcut by Mair of Landshut dated 1499, 27.7 x 17.1 cm. Literature: Field 1987, 154. Illustration after Bock 1930, 167.

29. Woodcut in a *Plenarium* by the printer Thomas Anshelm (Strasbourg 1488). Illustration after Schramm 1920, XX, no.1705.

30. One of the Jewish 'teachers' is anachronistically wearing the fifteenth-century Jewish hat and Jewish ring. The boy Jesus is sitting like a university teacher in front of his students, as is customary in the depictions of Luke 2.41–50 at this time. Woodcut in a *Plenarium* (Gospels with interpretation) by the Strasbourg printer Johann Grüninger, 1498. Illustration after Schramm 1920, XX no.478.

[No illustration] 'The Finding of the Saviour in the Temple', painting by William Holman Hunt, completed c. 1865. Birmingham, City Museum and Art Gallery. Literature: Sudley 1971, pl.39; Dittmar 1987, pl.3. Illustration in *Bilder sind nicht verboten* 1982, 164.

2. The activity of Jesus and the apostles among the Jews; Jesus and the apostles as preachers of the Christian message and as 'missionaries to the Jews'

(a) Jesus

1. Jesus, John the Baptist and the Jews. The latter are wearing the conical hat which is part of medieval Jewish dress. Their special form of dress and the fact that more hats than faces can be seen emphasize the group character of the Jews. By contrast, Christ and John (the inscription has the text of Matt.3.3: *vox clamantis in deserto, parate viam Domini*) are hatless and have haloes, which stresses their otherness. Fresco in the church of Jellinge, Denmark, c.1100. Illustration after de Boor 1934, no.25.

2. Miraculous multiplication of the loaves and fishes (Matt.14.13–21). In the characterization of the group as Jewish it is often enough for one or a small number of the group to be given the medieval group characteristic (Jewish hat or Jewish ring). Woodcut in a *Speculum salvationis* from the workshop of the printer Peter Drach (Speyer 1478). Illustration after Schramm 1920, XVI no.368.

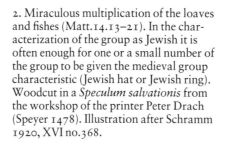

3. Jesus predicts his death to the Jews. Miniature in a prayerbook in French from the diocese of Angers, fourteenth century. Brussels, BR, Ms 5513–17, folio 305. Illustration after Gaspar and Lyna 1984, pl. LXVIII.

4. Jesus addresses the Jews from the cross. Miniature in a manuscript with readings from the Gospels in German for the forty days of Lent. Regensburg, c.1430. London BL, Ms.Egerton 1122, folio 15 verso. Illustration after *Regensburger Buchmalerei* 1987, pl.154 (by permission of BL).

5. Jesus preaches to the Jews (Luke 4.14ff.). Miniature in a German illustrated Bible made in the region of Strasbourg, c.1430–1440. Freiburg im Breisgau, UB, Ms 334 (and M.719–720 of the Pierpont Morgan Library, New York), folio 2 recto. Literature: Blumenkranz 1964, fig.3; Blumenkranz 1965, fig.53; Bremer 1986, fig.14. Illustration after Beckmann and Schroth (facsimile volume), folio 2 recto.

6. Illustration on John 8, at the beginning of this chapter, in which Jesus engages in sharp controversy with the Jews. Woodcut in a *Plenarium* (private devotional book with texts from the Gospels) printed by Günther Zainer (Augsburg 1473). Illustration after Schramm 1920, II, no.316.

7. Jesus and the Pharisees. Woodcut in a *Plenarium* printed by Günther Zainer, Augsburg 1473. Illustration after Schramm 1920, II, no.342.

8. Jesus in conversation with the Pharisees (who are in the special medieval Jewish form of dress, with Jewish hat and ring). Woodcut in a *Plenarium* printed by Günther Zainer, Augsburg 1473. Illustration after Schramm 1920, II, no.347 (cf. ibid., III, no.122).

9. Jesus converts Mary Magdalene. Jesus' Jewishness and the Jewish background have been Christianized. Buldings have crosses on like Christian churches, and Jesus is like a Christian preacher in a pulpit. Woodcut from the *Tesauro spirituale* of Petro Ferraro da Viglevano, Milan: Signerre 1499. Literature: Lipmann 1888, pl. after 144. Illustration after Lippmann 1884, 308.

▶ 10. Jesus in conversation with his Jewish opponents. Here it is again evident that towards the end of the Middle Ages the special Jewish form of dress takes on more marked oriental features. At around the same time the humanist Conrad Celtis can state polemically that the Jews are really an alien 'people from over the seas' (*gens trasmarina*), i.e. have their home on the far side of the Mediterranean (A.Werminghoff, *Conrad Celtis und sein Buch über Nürnberg*, Freiburg 1921, 198f.). Woodcut in the *Postilla Guillermi super epistolas et evangelia* (Michael Greyff, Reutlingen 1494). Illustration after Schramm 1920, IX, no.476.

11. Jesus discusses with the Jews. His opponents are wearing two forms of the medieval Jewish hat frequent in the late Middle Ages. In this way the Jews of the fifteenth century are also characterized as opponents of Christ. Woodcut in a *Plenarium* of the Strasbourg printer Heinrich Knoblochtzer (Strassbourg, nd [c.1480–82?]). Illustration after Schramm 1920, XIX, no.388 (cf. Schramm VIII, no.711; XIX, nos.705, 736).

12. Jesus in dispute with his Jewish opponents. One of the Jews is wearing –
anachronistically – the medieval Jewish
ring on his outer garment, and two others
have Hebrew characters on their hems; this
was similarly a favourite iconographical
symbol of Jewishness and the Jewish opposition to Christ at this time. To the left, in
the background, the disciples of Jesus are
standing before the withered fig tree
(Matt.24). Woodcut by Urs Graf in a *Passio
Christi* which appeared in Strasbourg in
1506 (see below on VI, 2 f 2). Literature:
Zafran 1975, fig.15. Illustration after Worringer 1923, no.7.

13. A leper asks Jesus to heal him
(Matt.8.2). Woodcut in the *Postilla Guillermi super epistolas et evangelia* printed by
Michael Greyff, Reutlingen 1494. Illustration after Schramm 1920, IX, no.455.

◀ 14. Jesus warns against false prophets. Woodcut in a *Speculum salvationis* in German, printed by Bernhard Richel, Basel 1476. Illustration after Schramm 1920, XXI, no.264.

▶ 15. Jesus heals a deaf and dumb man. Woodcut in a *Speculum salvationis* in German, printed by Bernhard Richel, Basel 1476. Illustration after Schramm 1920, XXI, no.266.

(b) John the Baptist, Stephen, the apostles

1. Peter's preaching at Pentecost (Acts 2.14–36). Peter, with a book in his hand, as is customary in depictions of disputations, is the spokesman of the twelve apostles (who are with him) to a group of people, three of whom are identified as Jews by their conical hats. Miniature in an antiphonary of the Benedictine abbey of St Peter, Salzburg, c.1160. Vienna, ÖN, Cod.Ser.nova 2700, 668. Literature: Schreckenberg II, 721. Illustration after Unterkircher and Demus 1974, 668.

2. Paul, preaching to Jews and Gentiles, is being mocked (cf. Rom.9.12f.). Here the Jews are not yet wearing the special form of medieval dress as they often do later in scenes of this kind. Miniature in a Latin manuscript of the letters of Paul, first half of the tenth century. St Gallen, Cod.64, folio 12. Literature: Schreckenberg II, 491f. Illustration after Goldschmidt I, 1928, pl.78.

3. Matthew and twelve Jews who represent a kind of disgruntled audience, while the apostle is preaching his Gospel; i.e. he is writing the Vulgate text of his Gospel beginning with Matt.1.1 (*Liber generationis Jesu Christi*). The Jews are wearing their traditional dress customary in the twelfth century; this includes the charactistic hats (in the form of truncated cones or domes). The difference between them and Matthew, with a halo, is emphasized. Miniature in a manuscript of the four Gospels, around 1125. Dresden, MS A 94, folio 1. Literature: Schreckenberg II, 719. Illustration after Bruck 1906, 35.

4. Paul as missionary to Jews and Gentiles. Two Jews are also depicted alongside the Greeks (wearing stylized Phrygian caps; is there a third Jew without a Jewish cap?). One of those in front has an inscription, *revincebat Judaeos*, whereas an inscription with *disputabat cum Graecis* is issuing from Paul's left hand. While the Gentiles are rather more passive, the two Jews are active with gestures of disputation. Enamel plate, around 1170. London, Victoria and Albert Museum, Inv. No.223–1874. Literature: *The Year 1200*, I, 1970, pl.p.162; Schreckenberg II, 577. Illustration after *Victoria and Albert Museum* 1927, no.16.

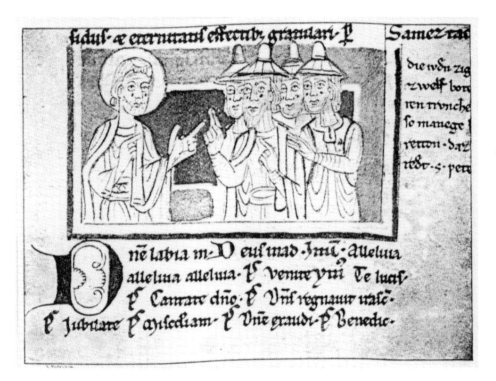

5. Mission to the Jews by an apostle. This is Peter, who in iconography is regularly recognizable by his tonsure; he is carrying on a didactic conversation with four Jews (= Acts 2.14ff.; for Acts 2.11–13 appears in the context of the miniature) who are wearing a form of the Jewish hat widespread above all in south Germany and Austria. As often, so here too the apostle is no longer a Jew among Jews. The latter are defined as a different social group by their dress. Miniature on the fragment of a leaf from a Latin parchment codex with prayers and texts of the mass, last third of the twelfth century. Nuremberg, GNM, Signature Mm 173 kl.F. Literature: Schreckenberg II, 656. Illustration after Bredt 1980, pl.1.

6. Paul preaching to the Jews (the inscription refers to Acts 9.22: *affirmans quoniam hic est Christus, dicit sanctus Paulus apostolus*). Brandenburg, Cathedral of St Peter and St Paul, painting on the predella of the former high altar, c.1380. Literature: Eichholz 1912, pl.48; Legner II, 1978, fig.p.546. Illustration after Hootz 1971, no.21.

7. Dialogue with the evangelist John, aimed at conversion: baptism of Drusiana (text above: *conversi ab idolis per predicationem sancti Johannis, Drusiana et ceteri*). The idolaters in this illustration on New Testament apocrypha are iconographically depicted as Jews. Woodcut in the 'Haarlem Apocalypse (block book)', c.1420. London, BL. Literature: Schreiber XI, 1926, fig.160; Musper 1964, fig.46. Illustration after Musper 1938, no.52.

8. The twelve apostles discuss with the Jews. Peter (with the tonsure) is the spokesman in dialogue with a group of Jews (the group characteristic is the Phrygian cap or conical hat). Miniature in a *Bible moralisée*, c.1240. Oxford, Bodleian Library, Cod.270b, folio 121 verso. Literature: Blumenkranz 1965, no.42.

9. Disputation of Stephen with the Jews (Acts 6–7). The Jews are identified as opponents of the Christian message by their special dress and corresponding iconographic symbols (Jewish hat, Jewish ring, pseudo-Hebrew writing on the hems of garments). There is an iconographic affinity to the depictions of Luke 2.41–50 (the twelve-year-old Jesus discussing with the Jewish teachers). Panel picture by Jan Polack (died 1519). Literature: Zafran 1973, I, 244. Illustration after Lutz and Wiegand 1937, no.265.

▶ 10. John the Baptist and the priests and Levites of the Jews (John 1.19). The Jews are depicted as being essentially different from John: his halo is so to speak a contrary group characteristic. Woodcut in a *Plenarium*, a devotional book with texts from the Gospels, printed by Konrad Dinckmut (Ulm 1483). Illustration after Schramm 1920, VI, no.31.

11. Jude, brother of James, warns against false teachers. The foremost listener is wearing a form of Jewish hat fairly common in the later Middle Ages (tapered in steps or terraces). Initial letter at the beginning of the New Testament letter of Jude, *I(udas ein knecht iesu)*, in a German Bible printed in Augsburg around 1475 by Günther Zainer. Literature: Strand 1966, 41. Illustration after Wendland 1967, 43 pl.13.

3. Religious disputations, dialogues aimed at conversion, sermons (compulsory), efforts at a mission to the Jews

1. Sermon by a Christian to Jews. Miniature in a *Bible moralisée*, c.1240. Paris, BN Lat.11560, folio 83 verso. Literature: Laborde 1911; Grodecki and Brisac 1985, fig.16. Illustration after Blumenkranz 1965, no.50.

2. Dispute between Christians and Jews at the feet of enthroned Ecclesia. Miniature in a *Bible moralisée*, c.1240. Paris, BN, Lat.11560, folio 87 verso. Literature: Schiller IV,1, 1976, fig.137; Hoffmann 1871, 353, fig.16. Illustration after Weber 1894, 113.

3. Disputation between a Christian and a Jew. The Christian is taller than the Jew and towers over him even when sitting down, so that the conversation has more the character of instruction. He has a tonsure and is clad in a monastic habit (the figure is the abbot Peter of Cluny), while the Jew is similarly characterized as such by his dress. He is arguing modestly and more defensively with his left hand and seems to be concealing his right hand. Miniature in the initial *V(os ego, vos inquam, ego convenio, o Judei, qui usque in hodiernum negatis filium dei)*, at the beginning of a manuscript of the *Adversus Judaeorum inveteratam duritiem* of Peter the Venerable, abbot of Cluny (died 1156), made between 1156 and 1166. Douai, Bibliothèque municipale (and Paris, Centre national de la recherche et d'histoire des textes), Ms 381, folio 131. Literature: Zafran 1973, I, 246: Schreckenberg II, 614. Illustration after Černý 1985, 53.

4. Religious disputation between the converted Jew Peter Alfonsi and his *alter ego* Moses (i.e. the Jewish name of Petrus Alfonsi before his baptism). Miniature at the beginning of a manuscript *Disputatio Petri Alfonsi contra Moysen pro defensione catholice fidei*, thirteenth century. Bruges, Major Seminary, Ms 26/91, folio 1 recto. Literature: Swarzenski I, 1936, pl.II (after p.18), no.11; Ausubel 1964, fig.130; Bloch 1965, pl.13; Jochum 1993, fig.47; Schreckenberg II, 70. Illustration after *Mon.Jud.Handb*.1963, no.58.

hoc signifi\
cauit q deus\
dat uiuo carbo\
nco uerbum et\
sapientiam ut\
possit conuer\
tere disputatio\
ne sua agmina\
contraria fidei\
xpiane.

5. Disputation of a Christian with Jews. Miniature in a *Bible moralisée*, c.1240. Paris, BN, Lat.11560, folio 121 verso. Literature: Erbstösser 1984, fig.p.37. Illustration after Blumenkranz 1965, no.39.

6. La chiesa militante e trionfante. Fresco in the Spanish chapel of the church of S.Maria Novella in Florence (section), painted in 1369 by Andrea di Bonaiuto da Firenze (died c.1377/78). On the right of the picture Thomas Aquinas is in discussion with Jews and Muslims. Below, the dogs are an allusion to the popular etymology 'Dominicani = Domini canes', i.e. 'Hounds of God'. Literature: Endres 1909, pl.XII; Kaftal I, 1952, fig.1107; Eckert 1968, 30f.; Kirschbaum II, 1970, 453; Erbstösser 1984, no.48. Illustration by Foto Fratelli Alinari, Florence.

7. Christian-Jewish disputation under the direction of a king. The picture perhaps represents the disputation moved to Paris by King Louis IX on 24 June 1240, which took place under the presidency of the Queen Mother Blanche of Castile. Miniature in a *Bible moralisée*, c.1240. Paris, BN, Lat.11560, folio 5 verso. Illustration after Blumenkranz 1965, no.40.

8. Refutation of the false arguments of the Jews by clerics. The Jews (their attributes or group characteristic are pointed Jewish hats, a sacrifical animal as a symbol of the Old Testament sacrificial cult, a circumcising or slaughtering knife). The Christians are referring in their argument to a book which is being held up (the New Testament?), while the scriptural scroll of the Jews (i.e. the Old Testament?) seems to be falling. The departure of the Jews to the left (in the heraldic sense) recalls the similar departure of Synagoga. Miniature in a *Bible moralisée*, c.1240. Oxford, Bodleian Library, Cod.270b, folio 43 verso. Literature: Blumenkranz 1965, no.43.

9. Christian-Jewish religious dialogue. The participants are each operating with their texts (book, scriptural scroll, tables of the law). No agreement between the bishop and the Jewish spokesman (with beard, locks and oriental turban) seems to be in sight. Miniature in a *Bible moralisée*, c.1410. Paris, BN, Fr.166, folio 21 verso. Literature: Weber 1894, 114; Meiss 1974, II, fig.320; Hoffmann 1981,351,fig.14. Illustration after Blumenkranz 1965, no.27.

10. The preaching of Berthold of Regensburg (died 1272). Because of the great throng of hearers, the Franciscan popular itinerant preacher used to preach from a portable pulpit in the open air in front of churches, with the support of the Holy Spirit (a dove is flying down towards him from heaven). His audience occasionally also included Jews; here at any rate a woman listener, below left, is wearing a pointed hat of the kind known as the head-dress of Jewish women in the late Middle Ages. Miniature in a manuscript containing sermons of Berthold in German from 1444. Vienna, ÖN, Cod.2829, folio 1 recto (coloured pen drawing). Literature: Kirchbaum V, 1973, fig.p.396; Rosenfeld 1978, fig.161; Mazal 1980, fig.23; Unger 1982, fig.14; *Franz von Assisi* 1982, fig.p.174; Glöger and Zöllner 1985, fig.21; Mazal 1987, 62, fig.9. Illustration after Mazal 1975, no.56.

11. Fictitious religious dialogue aimed at conversion, between a rabbi becoming a Christian and his colleague who remains true to Judaism. Miniature in a German edition of the *Epistola ad R.Isaac de adventu Messiae quem Judaei temere expectant* (Letter of Rabbi Samuel to Rabbi Isaac on the Advent of the Messiah whom the Jews Vainly Await). This is a letter to a colleague allegedly composed around 1072 by a rabbi: in fact it is a work wholly composed by Alfonsus Bonihominis in 1339. Copenhagen, Kongelige Bibliotek, Ms.Thott 942°, folio 21 recto. Literature: Ben-Sasson II, 1979, fig.36 (after p.390): cf. Zafran 1973, I, 254–6. Illustration after *Mon.Jud.Kat.*1963, no.B 270.

12. *Ars moriendi* illustration (temptation in faith). A dying man is pressed by four devils to deviate from the right Christian faith. Those around the deathbed include three non-Christians (probably a Muslim, a Jew [recognizable by his hat] and a pagan, engaged in a religious disputation). The inscriptions are: *Fac sicut pagani* (act like the pagans), *Infernus fractus est* (hell is no more), *Interficias te ipsum* (kill yourself). Woodcut in a block book made c.1460–1470 in the Netherlands or West Germany. Berlin, Staatliche Museen Preussischer Kulturbesitz, Kupferstichkabinett. Literature: *LGB* I, 1988, fig.p.145. Illustration after Meister E.S.1986, fig.36.

13. Sermon by the Franciscan John of Capestrano (died 1456) at the market place of Bamberg, in 1452. Above left in the background of the picture a Jew is being forced by two Christians to come and hear the sermon. Oil painting (on wood), painted around 1480. Bamberg, Neue Residenz (loaned by the Historisches Museum, Bamberg, Inv. no.62). Literature: *Franz von Assisi* 1982, pl.3; Deneke 1988, fig.p.172; A. Herzig, in Herzig and Schoeps 1993, fig. alongside p.18; *Reformation in Nürnberg* 1979, 58 no. 63; G.Jaritz, in *Anzeiger des Germanischen Nationalismus* 1993, 209.

14. Disputation between the poet Hans Folz (died 1513) and a Jew. Frontispiece (woodcut) at the beginning of Folz's poem *Christ und Jude* (Nuremberg 1429), in rhyming couplets. Literature: Fischer 1961, pl.2; Zafran 1973, I, 251f. Illustration after Schramm 1920, XVIII, no.360.

15. Frontispiece, woodcut, by Hans Burgkmair for the *Dialogue de diversarum gen-
cium sectis et mundi religionibus* by Johannes Stammler (Augsburg: Erhard Oeglin
and Jörg Nadler 1508). *Sancta Mater Ecclesia* here – in a triumphalistic view – is the
mistress of the world; the emperor is receiving the sword from her and the pope the
keys. Further down are seated the allegorical personifications of the subjected
powers: *Sinagoga, Saracena, Gentilitas*
(with turban and crown), *Tartarica*; Saracena is holding the banner which belongs to
Synagoga (with a Jewish hat), while
Machometus is inscribed on Synagoga's
banner (a mistake, or the symbol of the
anti-Christian conspiracy). Below, there is
a learned religious disputation led by
Doctor Oliveri, and also Samuel Iudeus
(with a Jewish ring [*rota*]). Literature:
Weber 1894, 142; Garber 1915, fig.p.XLV;
Geisberg 1930, II, fig. 737; Seiferth 1964,
fig.60; Zafran 1973, I, 256; Jochum 1993,
fig.29. Illustration after Butsch 1881, pl.19.

16. Disputation between a Christian and a
Jewish scholar. Woodcut in *Der Seelen
Wurzgarten* (Ulm 1483). The depiction is
matter-of-fact and unpolemical. The
subjects of such discussions included the
justification for christological biblical
exegesis, the proofs of the Trinity, the Incarnation of Christ, etc. Illustration after
Schramm 1920, VI, no.93.

NE IVDICATE, VT NE IVDICEMINI. QVOMODO DICES FRATRI TVO, SINE EIICIAM FESTVCAM EX O-CVLO TVO, ET ECCE TRABES IN OCVLO TVO: HYPOCRITA, EIICE PRIMVM TRABEM ILLAM EX OCVLO TVO, ET TVM DISPICIES VT EIICIAS FESTVCAM EX *etc.* SI CAECVS CAECO PRAEIERIT AMBO IN FOVEAM CADENT.

17. Dialogue between a Capucin and a rabbi aimed at the latter's conversion. Engraving (end of the fifteenth century) by the Flemish painter Karel van Mander (died 1606), who spent the last decades before his death in Harlem. An ironically topical exegesis (in rhyming couplets) of Luke 6.39ff. ('blind leaders of the blind' and 'beam in your brother's eye'). This is one of the rare testimonies to criticism of the mission to the Jews within Christianity, which was more possible in the liberal Christian Netherlands shaped by the Reformation than elsewhere in Europe. In his *Disputation*, Heinrich Heine ironically remarks that 'the knights in this battle are Capucins and rabbis'. Illustration after *JüdLex* IV, 1930, 1344–5. Plate CXLIII (Art Collection of the Berlin Jewish Community; for Karel van Mander see *Lexikon der Kunst*, 1989, 6).

18. Frontispiece to *Liber Nizachon Rabbi Lipmani. Conscriptus anno a Christo nato MDCCCXCIX, etc. Editus typis academicis curante Th.Hackspan,* Nuremberg 1644 (first printing of the Hebrew text; for the Christian scholar Hackspan see Friedrich 1988, 67f.). Jomtob ben Salomo Lipmann from Mühlhausen lived mainly in Prague in the fifteenth/sixteenth century, and wrote his *Sefer ha–Nizzachon* (Disputation Book or Book of Victory) as a compendium of Jewish theology and for apologetic use in disputations with non-Jews. It continued to make an impression and after being translated into Latin provoked various Christian responses. Below left, the frontispiece shows a Jew with a Jewish ring. Illustration after Stock 1939, 191.

19. Initial miniature (as an illustration of a legend about the conversion of a Jewish family by St Basil [fourth century]) for a Life of Basil in the *Magnum legendarium Austriacum,* a thirteenth-century manuscript. The picture demonstrates vividly an object of the Christian mission to the Jews in the special form of dress typical of the thirteenth century. Zwettl (Austria), Stiftsbibliothek, Cod.Zwettl 13, folio 4. Literature: Kühnel 1985, fig.305. Illustration after Lohrmann 1982, 304, no.52.

20. *Pugio fidei.* Frontispiece engraving by I.A.Baener in *Raimundi Martin Pugio fidei adversus Mauros et Judaeos*, Leipzig, Friedrich Lanck, 1687. The engraving relates to remarks by the Dominican Raimundus in the preface of his work (completed in 1287): he wants to compose a work 'which can be a dagger at the disposal of preachers of the Christian faith and its servants, to cut the word of God when they speak to them, but another time to cut off the head of their godlessness and their perverse faith and abolish their pride and shameless folly directed against Christ'. The hand with the *pugio fidei* coming from the clouds of heaven thus threatens the Jew sitting at a table (with prayer shawl and *tallit*) and the Muslim lying on the floor in an attitude of prayer, very much in the spirit of the often aggressive mission to Jews and Moors (i.e. Muslims). Illustration after the Leipzig edition of 1687.

21. Roman Jews at compulsory preaching in a church. Lithograph (38.7 x 32.4 cm) by Friedrich August Fricke (died Leipzig 1858), c.1850. Fricke gives a distorting, condescending picture of the Jews, who look almost like 'a horde of beasts' (Dittmar). The artist has probably also chosen his theme to promote anti-Jewish feelings: the Jews are beings who seem to lack any organ for receiving the Christian message, and their spiritual degeneration is visible in a corresponding physiognomy; they make grimaces, indeed they have grotesquely distorted faces which are quite different from normal Christians, like the monk in the pulpit. Literature: Dittmar 1988, fig.11. Illustration after *JüdLex* IV, 1930, 1474.

22. Disputation between monks and Jewish scholars. Woodcut by
Friedrich Wilhelm Bader (born 1828 in Heilbronn and active in
Vienna from 1851) for an edition of Heine published by Sigmund
Bensiger. This information and the illustration come from *The
Universal Jewish Encyclopedia* III, New York 1941, 570 (not listed
in Horst Banke, *Illustrationen zu Heinrich Heine*, Leipzig 1972; the
woodcut seems to refer to Heine's poem 'Disputation').

23. Frontispiece woodcut by Robert Engels (died 1926), in Liebe
1903. This historicizing and psychologizing modern depiction of a
medieval disputation between Christian and Jewish scholars shows –
like Liebe, who commissioned it – a sympathetic understanding of
the situation of the Jews as a persecuted minority. The Jews (with the
usual group characteristics of Jewish hat, ring on the upper garment
and beard) are in the minority and seem to be being put on the
defensive by the Christians, some of whom appear arrogant. We may
infer that the argument was concerned with the traditional themes of
such dialogues: the exegesis of the Bible – both sides are holding
texts in their hands – and above all its christological exegesis; Trinity
and Incarnation and Mary's virginity; and above all the question
whether the Messiah has or has not already come (in the figure of
Jesus Christ). Illustration after Liebe 1903, frontispiece; cf. Eigen-
stein 1969, frontispiece.

24. Compulsory preaching for the Jews in a church in Rome, water colour by Hieronymus Hess, 1823. The Jews of Rome had regularly to listen to compulsory sermons aimed at converting them (here apparently in S.Angelo). Hess depicts this from a liberal, emancipated standpoint. Literature: *EJ* 1971, III, 201f.; Ben Sasson III, 1980, fig.17 (before p.197); Dittmar 1988. Illlustration after *JüdLex* V, 1930, 1647f.

25. Disputation between Christian and Jewish scholars. Woodcut by Johann von Armssheim in *Der Seelen Wurzgarten*, a German collection of examples orientated on salvation history, which was made in 1466/67 in the monastic foundation of Komburg (near Schwäbisch Hall), printed by Konrad Dinckmut, Ulm 1483. The subject of the portrayal is perhaps a disputation held in Regensburg by Petrus Nigri, which took place (or was intended) at this time. Literature: Schramm 1920, VI, fig.95; Weil 1929, 57–62 (with illustrations); *EJ* 1971, VI, 86; Zafran 1973, I, 254; Lazar 1991, fig.5; *Verfasserlexikon* VIII, 1992, 1027–9. Illustration after Liebe 1903, no.42.

26. The Dominican Petrus Nigri (died c.1483), in dialogue with the Jews of Regensburg. The latter are distinguished from the group of Christians not only by the prescribed special form of medieval dress but also by their physiognomy (which is repulsively ugly, and makes clear the inner wickedness which is imputed to them). Woodcut in the work *Der Stern Meschiach* by Petrus Nigri (Peter Schwarz), printed in the workshop of Konrad Fyner, Esslingen 1477. Literature: Olschki 1926, fig.88; Schreiber 1929, fig. p.22; Friedman 1950, fig. before p.433; Zafran 1973, I, 248–51; Kunze 1979, II, no.214; Mälzer 1986, fig. p.293. Illustration after Schramm 1920, IX, no.2.

27. Mocking medallion for the baptism of a Jew (minted by Christian Wermuth, died 1739 in Gotha), end of the seventeenth cenutry. On the obverse is a priest with a prayer book, baptizing a Jew kneeling on the edge of water. A millstone is hanging round his neck. A minion is ready to push him into the water after his baptism. Inscription: *So bleibt er am beständigsten* (i.e., if he is immediately executed, he cannot lapse into his own faith). Inscription on the reverse: 'Rarely does a Jew become a Christian unless he has done something; he usually does it for money, in order not to hang. For if he steals from anyone else he is punished too sharply.' There is also an inscription round the outside edge of the coin: 'If the cat does not eat the mouse, a Jew will become a true Christian.' This is a sarcastic comment on the optimism over conversion widespread for a time in Christian circles. Literature: Deneke 1988, 294f.; Eckert 1991, 383. Illustration after Kirschner 1968, 27.

4. The 'citadel of faith', overrun by Jews and heretics, pagans and demons

1. Woodcut at the beginning of the first edition of the *Fortalicium fidei* (citadel of faith) by Alfonsus de Spina, which appeared in Strasbourg (from Johannes Mentelin, 1470). In a way the picture sums up the content of the work: the square tower of faith, guarded by two Christians, is attacked by Jews (with the Jewish hat and with blindfolds, because they are blind to the Christian truth), pagans (or Muslims, below left) and demons. Literature: *Philo-Lexikon* 1936, fig. col.723. Illustration after Schramm 1920, XXI, no.553.

2. Illustration in a French translation of the *Fortalicium fidei*, second half of the fifteen century. Jews are also among those attacking the 'citadel of faith' protected by the Christians (some of them blind and in chains, i.e. without a chance). Brussels, BR, Ms.1714, folio 122. Literature: Eckert 1991, 384: Blumenkranz 1965, no.49.

3. Illustration (by an unknown artist) for the *Spiegel der Bruderschaft vom Rosenkranz* by Marcus of Waida, Leipzig 1514. The assailant below right seems to be wearing the Jewish ring – which usually characterizes Jews as such. Illustration after Muther 1894 (II, pl.203).

Der zweiflenden zanck von der waren kirchen Gottes.

4. Opponents of the Catholic faith, including Jews, Turks and pagans. Flysheet (with a woodcut) from the end of the sixteenth century with 232 rhymed verses. Below left, *jud türk und haid*, among whom the Jew has his typical dress (with Jewish ring). In this pictorial depiction in one of the rare Catholic pamphlets of the sixteenth century the church of the old faith is built on the rock of Christ and Holy Scripture. 'The insignia of the papacy are inscribed in the rocks. The typological association of *tau* and cross, Noah's ark and the ship of the church, the brazen serpent and the crucifix, demonstrate the correlation between the Old and New Testaments in the Catholic Church. The group of Protestants is depicted as divided; they are fighting over the legacy of Luther, who sits in the middle (with a small black devil on his head), and is having his arms pulled by his followers' (Harms 1983). In the middle of the picture is the sea of the world, in which apostates are swimming. Munich, SB, Einbl. III, 52. Illustration after Harms 1983, 73.

5. Illustration in a French manuscript of the *Fortalicium fidei*, second half of the fifteenth century. 'The "fortress church", defended by the pope, emperor, members of orders and clerics, supported by the hands of others and attacked by blind heretics and harlots and ne'er do wells' (Seibt, 340). The assailants also include Jews (who can be recognized by the Jewish ring, below left). Literature: Zafran 1973, I, 257–8; Erbstösser 1984, pl.86; Seibt 1987, fig. p.340. Illustration after a photograph of the Archiv für Kunst und Geschichte, Berlin.

5. Harmonizing statements

1. A Jew (with Jewish hat) prays to the crucified Christ (in a cycle of illustrations of the Antichrist legend). Stained glass in the choir window of the church of St Mary of Frankfurt an der Oder, c.1370. Illustration after Seeger 1977, no.17.

2. Joint Christian-Jewish prayer to God. Woodcut in *Der Seelen Wurzgarten*, a collection of examples orientated on salvation history, printed by Konrad Dinckmut (Ulm 1483). Illlustration after Schramm 1920, VI, no.98.

6. A comparison: preaching of the Christian faith among Muslims

1. Raymond Lull, the missionary to Islam and the Jews, in prison in the place of his missionary activity, in Bugia (Bougie, Algeria). Although a prisoner, he is still disputing with a Muslim. Woodcut, Valencia 1560. Illustration after *Europa und der Orient* 1989, no.176.

◀ 2. Repudiation of the Qur'an by a learned monk. Here, too, a book is needed for apologetic argumentation. The Muslims do not remain passive but maintain their standpoint – backing it up by argumentative gestures. Frontispiece woodcut of the work *Improbatio al–corani* by Ricoldus (Seville: Stanislao Polono 1500). Illustration after Lyell 1926, fig.51.

3. According to tradition Raymond Lull, active among other things in the mission to Islam and the Jews, was killed by stoning in the harbour of Bugia (Algeria) in 1316. Woodcut in a printing of his *Ars inventiva veritatis* (Valencia: Diego de Gumiel 1515, folio 100). Illustration after Lyell 1926, fig.17.

Dis ist der vinster berg do die roten Juden hinder ligent vnd ist
in yndia do Sant Thomas der Apostel lit.

Plate 13 (on VIII,1). The Jews in hell. Whereas the pains of hell are chosen for most offenders on the principle of 'an eye for an eye' (e.g. the punishment for the deadly sin of gluttony is that the offenders have to eat toads), the Jews are punished *qua* Jews (i.e. because of their stubborn unbelief), and here too the 'characterization of the damned, which deviates completely from the gospel, must contribute to the defamation of minorities' (H.Vorgrimler, *Geschichte der Hölle*, Munich 1993, 359). Miniature in the *Hortus deliciarum* of Herrad of Landsberg, c.1185 (Paris, BN), folio 255 recto. Literature: Schreckenberg II, 601–4. Illustration after Green II, 1979, 439. pl.146.

◀ Plate 14 (on IX, 8). Between the thirteenth and the sixteenth century, a legend developed about the whereabouts of the ten tribes of Israel who had disappeared after the fall of the northern Kingdom (in 722 BCE). These sinful tribes, who had sacrificed golden rams, had been imprisoned by Alexander the Great in the Caspian mountains, from which they would emerge with the Messiah (there is a mixture with the tradition of Gog and Magog here), liberate Jerusalem from the Muslims, take the Christian yoke from the Jews of Europe, and so on. Such speculations were sparked off by the Mongol advance into Europe in the thirteenth century, with which the ten tribes were connected. This led to a strengthening of messianic hopes among the European Jews or to support from the Muslims from the Jews. How the term 'red Jew' (for the ten tribes) arose in this web of legend is unclear. Perhaps one contributory factor was that according to a variant of the legend these apostate and renegade Jews lived far to the East 'beyond the Red Sea'. Miniature in a medieval German book of weapons (Strasbourg, c.1400–1410), *Uffenbachsches Wappenbuch*, which included fabulous biblical and geographical weapons (i.e. imaginary weapons of biblical figures and oriental rulers). The heading reads: *Dis ist der finsterberg do die roten Juden hinder ligent unde ist in Yndia do Sankt Thomas der Apostle lit* ('This is the Finsterberg under which the red Jews lie; it is in India, where St Thomas the Apostle is buried[1]). Hamburg, UB, Cod. in scrin.90b. folio 51 recto (photograph E.Horváth). Literature: Geiger 1888, 364f.; Aronius 1902, 227–30; Brandis 1972, pl.4; Stamm 1981, fig. 132; Birkhan 1992, 149f.; Gow 1993; cf. Zafran 1973, I, 25f.

▲ Plate 15 (on XI,2). Messianic procession. Engraving in *Detectum Velum Mosaicum Judaeorum nostri temporis*, with the explanatory title 'The Jewish cloak of the Mosaic Law, under which the Jews of the present time practise all kinds of knavery, vice, harm and financial dealings, discovered by Dietrich Schwab, a Jew who became a Christian in Paderborn', [nd] 1666 (first published in Paderborn in 1615). The author tells us that he saw the motif in Friedberg (north of Frankfurt am Main) on the Mainzer Tor, and that there was a similar picture on the Brückenturm in Frankfurt. The ugly anti-Jewish tendency which can often be noted in the works of baptized Jews can be seen not least in the explanatory title; for nothing is further from the text of Paul in II Cor.3 than to make the 'veil' of Ex.34.35 the cloak for alleged Jewish misdeeds. Frankfurt am Main, Historisches Museum, Inv no.C 10154 (photograph Zeitz–Gray). Literature: Shachar 1974, fig.53.

Plate 16 (on XII,2). Illustration in the City Book of Landshut (Lower Bavaria), 1361. It has a (mocking) annotation by the scribe and artist: 'Feifelein der Judenchunch'. In his right hand Feifelein has a Torah scroll, which had to be held when making an oath. The writer polemically notes important areas where the Jewish oath is applied. The term 'king of the Jews' which appears in the text probably refers to the head of the Jewish community. Landshut, Stadtarchiv, Vol.11/1361, folio 57 (photograph: H.Zdera). Literature: *EJ* 1971, X, 1412; Gidal 1988, 48; Deneke 1988,176.

VIII. Jews and the Devil, Jews and Hell, Jews and Witches; the Jews at the Last Judgment; the Jews and the Antichrist

1. The Middle Ages

1. Christ treading the grapes: Elijah and Enoch are preaching to humankind, including the Jews, to arm them against the final coming of Antichrist. Christian exegesis referred Isa.63.6 (*torcular calcavi solus*, I alone trod the wine–press) to Christ. Revelation 19.13–15 (Christ with 'garment soaked in blood', 'the one who treads the wine', cf. e.g. also the traditional interpretation of the grapes in Num.13.23 in terms of Christ) was also thought of in this context. A comprehensive view of salvation history is connected with the typological interpetation of Isa.63.3: the grapes are brought by the two groups of the people of God (pope, bishops, monks, hermits, nuns, king, laity); below Christ, Paul, Peter and Stephen are emptying their baskets into the winepress. The text of the *Hortus deliciarum* declares that this is the church 'in which the fruits of righteousness and holiness are gathered... the winepress is also the holy cross; he alone trod for all, that all might be saved'. Below left Christ is leading 'the healed lepers', i.e. the heretics and penitent sinners, back into the vineyard; below right is a group (including two Jews) to whom Elijah and Enoch are speaking in order to arm them against the eschatological attack of the Antichrist. Miniature in the *Hortus deliciarum* of Herrad of Landsberg, c. 1185. Literature: Schreckenberg II, 601–4. Illustration after Gillen 1979, no.77, p.119 (folio 241 recto).

2. The descent of the Jews to hell (detail below right). The foremost in the line of Jews who are going to the gates of hell – flames are issuing from them – is holding the inscription *Sinagoga* (which defines the whole group). The inscription round the outside edge explains what is happening: *Que reprobat Christum Sinagoga meretur abissum* (the synagogue which rejects Christ merits hell).

Engraved drawing round the edge of the underside of a paten (the centre depicts a crucifix with Mary and John) from the monastery of Wilten (Tirol), c.1160–1170. Vienna, Kunsthistorisches Museum (KK 8924). Literature: Schreckenberg II, 571–3; Blumenkranz 1965, no.69.

3. Crucifix with Christians and Jews. On Christ's right are believing Christians; on his left the Jews – without heeding Moses, who is pointing faithfully to Christ – are turning from the crucifix towards hell; they are disappearing into its open jaws, forced there by a devil. They are recognizable from their group charcteristic (conical or funnel hats). Moralizing miniature in the poetical *Bestiaire divin* by Guillaume le Clerc, made between 1210 and 1217 (see Kindler III, 1971, 1470f.). Paris, BN, Ms.fr. 14969, folio 9. Literature: Weber 1894, 106; Wehrhahn-Stauch 1967, 119, fig.17 (a similar miniature of the same provenance: a devil is forcing Jews with funnel hats leftwards into hell); Lewis 1986, 561 figs.23 and 14. Illustration after *Revue de l'art chrétien* 5, 1861, 33 fig.5 (copy).

4. The Antichrist raises the dead. Among the amazed audience is a Jew in his typical dress. Window of St Mary's Church in Frankfurt an der Oder, c. 1370. Illustration after Wentzel 1951, no.151.

▼ 5. The descent of hardened Jews to hell. The text (not illustrated here) explains the picture: 'It means the unbelievers who are damned and are led by devils to hell' (*significat infideles, qui dampnati sunt, quos diaboli deferunt in infernum*). It looks as though the descent into hell was preceded by a vain attempt at conversion by monks (with tonsures). These are holding books (as proof-texts for the argumentation), while the Jews can be seen to have a scroll. Miniature in a *Bible moralisée*, c.1240. Oxford, Bodleian Library, Ms 270b, folio 16 recto. Literature: Blumenkranz 1965, no.33.

► 6. Descent of the Jews into hell. A variant of the earlier iconographic type of Ecclesia and Synagoga. The moralizing Latin text on this says that just as the dying Samson killed the Philistines, so the crucifixion of Christ means the downfall of his enemies (*inimici*), the 'Jews and unbelievers' (*Judei et infideles*). However, the jaws of hell, which are wide open below left (heraldically, in the sense of the left-right symbolism of Matt.25.33,41) are swallowing only Jews, the last of whom is looking back defiantly, as Synagoga often does elsewhere. They are wearing conical, funnel-shaped hats or skull-caps, while the 'good' alongside Ecclesia are depicted as tonsured monks. Miniature in a *Bible moralisée*, c.1240. Oxford, Bodleian Library, Ms 270b, folio 119 verso. Literature: Blumenkranz 1965, no.35.

◀ 7. The descent of the Jews into hell. The two pictures on folio 34 of the manuscript relate to the theme of Gen.18.14; 19.1, 29, 31; 50.11–12, i.e. the evening of Jacob's life and his death in Egypt. The second picture from the top in the series of pictures on the right illustrates how after their death Jacob and the other Israelites in the biblical period had to go to hell, from which they were freed only by Christ on his descent into hell (cf. Matt.12.10) – an aspect which is left out of account here. Rather, the use of the special medieval form of dress shows that the Jews are as it were compelled to go to hell. Miniature in a *Bible moralisée*, c.1240. Oxford, Bodleian Library, Ms 270b, folio 34 recto. Literature: Blumenkranz 1964, fig.34; cf. Ehrenstein 1923, 300, fig.19; Laborde I, 1911, pl.34.

8. The archangel Michael drives the wicked to hell (with a Jew right at the front), assisted by a devil. Miniature in a psalter made in Augsburg after 1235. New York, Pierpont Morgan Library, M.280, folio 53. Literature: Harrsen 1958, pl. 11; Zafran 1973, I, 27f.; Blumenkranz 1965, no.37.

9. The devil blindfolds a Jew. Because of the bad state of preservation it is also conjectured that here the devil is seizing the Jew to drag him off to hell (see the similar depiction of a relief on the tympanon of the cathedral of Autun, twelfth century, illustration in H.Weigert, *Geschichte der Europäischen Kunst*, I, Stuttgart 1951, 162), but this is improbable. Bamberg, cathedral, Prince's Portal (immediately below the statue of Synagoga), 1230–1240. Literature: Bremer 1986, fig.16; Suckale 1987, fig.36. Illustration after Viollet–le–Duc V, 1875, 157 (copy) and Jantzen 1925, no.76.

10. The Antichrist and the Jews. The Antichrist, who appears before the end of the world, does miracles (a withered tree blossoms, fire rains down from heaven, the sea is churned up by storms), and thus leads the astonished people astray, is also followed by the Jews (*Judei*). The opponents of the Antichrist are punished (they have their eyes put out, are stoned, a dragon swallows them or they die from snake-bites). Finally – not pictured here – the followers of the Antichrist, including the Jews, are converted and have themselves baptized. This legendary material, widespread in the Middle Ages, is based on II Thess.2.3–9 (or related passages like John 17.12 and Deut.11.36). Miniature in the *Hortus deliciarum* of Herrad of Landsberg, c.1185. Literature: Schreckenberg II, 603f. Illustration after Gillen 1979, 147 no.89 (folio 241 verso and 242 top).

▶ 11. Oath by a Jew on the inverted cross which is being held out to him by the Antichrist (a T on his head defines him as the devil). The Jew is wearing the special form of dress usual in the fourteenth century. Stained-glass window in the choir of St Mary's Church, Frankfurt an der Oder, c.1370. Illustration after Seeger 1977, no.11.

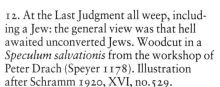

12. At the Last Judgment all weep, including a Jew: the general view was that hell awaited unconverted Jews. Woodcut in a *Speculum salvationis* from the workshop of Peter Drach (Speyer 1178). Illustration after Schramm 1920, XVI, no.529.

13. The devil with a 'Jewish nose' and pig's ears. He is vainly approaching the deathbed of St Martin, whose soul, rather, is destined for the security of Abraham's bosom. The 'Jewish' physiognomy of the devil shows that an affinity between Jews and the devil is assumed. Similarly, the devil is sometimes given the Jewish ring (*rota*) as a group characteristic (see the section on the Frankfurt 'Judensau'). Oil painting on wood (86 x 90cm) by Derrick Baegert, c. 1518. Münster, Westfälisches Landesmuseum, Inv.no.383, WKV (photograph WLMKuK, no.6163). Literature: Jászai 1977, 24f. (who argues, against the previous interpretation as the death of St Nicholas, that this portrays the death of St Martin).

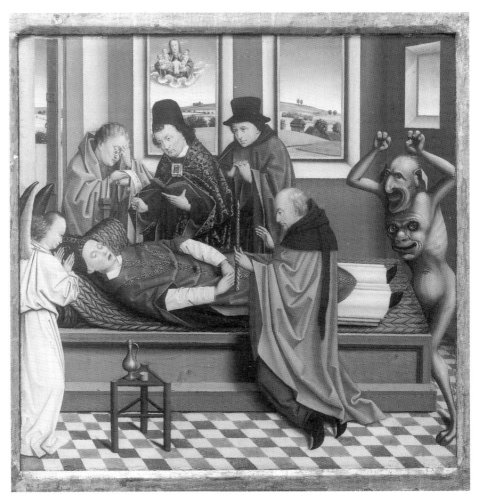

◀ 14. The Antichrist takes the Jews over the water. Stained-glass window in the choir of St Mary's Church, Frankfurt an der Oder, c.1370. Illustration after Seeger 1977, no.12.

15. The Last Judgment. Punishment awaits not only the foolish virgins (cf. Matt.25.1–13) and other groups but also (unconverted) Jews and pagans (*Judei et Pagani*). After the judgment they have to begin their journey to hell; their tearful pleas are to no avail. Miniature in the *Hortus deliciarum* of Herrad of Landsberg (Paris, BN). Literature: Schreckenberg II, 604. Illustration after Green 1979, 434 no.336 (folio 253 verso), pl.145.

16. The blinding of the Jews to the christological statements of their own prophets. An illustrated compilation of Old Testament prophecies in Latin, Provençal and (in three manuscripts) also in Hebrew. Each of the three versions of the saying has a small miniature. On the right, alongside each of the Hebrew quotations – because the Hebrew is read from right to left – stands a Jew (with a polemical use of the special Jewish form of dress [*rota*]), whose eyes the devil is closing in various ways. Miniatures in manuscripts of the *Breviari d'amore* of Matfre Ermengau (died after 1322), fourteenth century (a selection of 7 miniatures, made from a far larger number by Laske-Fix, 158); these miniatures are placed in the part of the text of the *Breviari* (from v.11765) which is about the Jews' lack of faith in Mary and Christ (the models for the surviving miniatures were already in the original, which was made around 1292). Literature: Blumenkranz 1965, fig.45; Zafran 1973, I,24; Lazar 1991, fig.8; Blumenkranz 1977, fig. 352. Illustration after Laske-Fix 1973, 158 no.49.

17. The Jews weep at the Last Judgment. Woodcut in a German-language *Speculum salvationis* printed by Bernhard Richel, Basel 1476. Illustration after Schramm 1920, XXI, no.245.

2. Modern times

1. Fairings for the Jews, or the Jewish Yellow Ring, an illustrated seventeenth-century flysheet (in rhyming couplets with etchings). A subsidiary theme is the well-deserved punishment of the Jews, their fall into hell. They are denigrated, in that spurious reasons are given for the introduction of the yellow ring which identifies the Jews as Jews. Another edition of the same pamphlet contains two additional strophes. 'The fox wants to kill the hen, but must himself be killed. That will happen (if God wills), and all unbelieving Jews will perish. The Jews slander us Christians with their mockery, and even think to exterminate us; we shall be patient, though you mock us.' Literature: Liebe 1903, fig.19; Fuchs 1921, fig.21; Schnur 1939, 8; Stock 1939, 168 pl.24; Flemming 1960, fig. p.51; *Mon.Jud.Kat.*1963, B 361; Paas II, 1986, fig. p.171; Zimmermann 1986, fig.p.367. Illustration after *Flügblätter* 1983, 207. Cf. *Anzeiger Germanischer Nationalismus* 1992, 177: someone wearing a Jewish ring before hell.

2. Witches' Sabbath (Witches' Kitchen) by Hans Baldung Grien, made 1510 in Strasbourg. The polemical assumption of an essential affinity between witches and Jews (and the devil) which was widespread at this time is expressed in the pseudo-Hebrew script decorating the pot in which a magic potion is being brewed. Literature: Strauss 1973, fig.32; Baldung 1981, fig.p.116; Glöger and Zöllner 1985, fig. 51; *Renaissance* 1986, fig.p.380; von Dülmen 1987, fig.p.180; *LGB* II, 10, 1988, fig.p.134. Illustration in Winckler 1936, pl. alongside p.156. This is one of the old engravings by Diederichs I, 1908, no. 387 (which is suitable for reproduction).

Wir Mauschel müssen jetzt in Chalers Loche sitzen;
Au weymer! noch darzu auff Schweinen Leder schwitzen
Warum! wir haben einst zu vielen Schmuh gemacht,
Und ließ an Galgen hin der Gojim Gott veracht.

3. The Jewish hell. German eighteenth-century engraving. On earth the misdeeds of the Jews are punished by hanging (upside-down with a dog); in hell, which is depicted as a mine (see the picture in *Lexikon des Buchwesens* III, Stuttgart 1955, 40), they have to endure a similar humiliating punishment: they have to ride on the pig, which they abhor (according to Lev.11.7f.; Deut.14.8f. it is unclean) but may still read while doing so. This is presumably directed satirically against the study of the Talmud as a chief passion of the Jews, which does not prevent them from going to hell. Riding on a beast totally unsuitable for the purpose – absurd behaviour – is meant to illustrate the perverse thought of the crazy Jews. The contempt of the God of the Goyim (i.e. non-Jews, pagans, Christians) is directed against the traditional objections of the Jews to central doctrines of Christian faith (Trinity, Incarnation of God, virginity of Mary and the like). The Jews are also mocked for their jargon, Yiddish: *au wey mer* = 'woe is me'; *Mauschel* for Moses; *schmuh* = (dishonest) profit. Literature: Fuchs 1921, fig.60; Schnur 1939, fig.41; Shachar 1974, pl.55a. Illustration after Liebe 1903, no.63.

IX. The Jews in Christian Legend

1. The discovery of the cross (the legend of Helena)

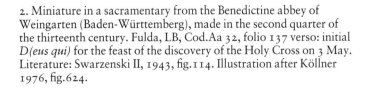

1. Miniature in a Low German manuscript from the first quarter of the fourteenth century. Berlin, SB, Ms.germ.fol.129, folio 46 recto. Illustration after Wegener 1928, no.105.

2. Miniature in a sacramentary from the Benedictine abbey of Weingarten (Baden-Württemberg), made in the second quarter of the thirteenth century. Fulda, LB, Cod.Aa 32, folio 137 verso: initial *D(eus qui)* for the feast of the discovery of the Holy Cross on 3 May. Literature: Swarzenski II, 1943, fig.114. Illustration after Köllner 1976, fig.624.

3. The special form of dress for Jews in the Middle Ages is emphasized in pictures of this kind because they are valuable testimonies to the truth of Christianity from the enemy camp. Sunk enamel panel from the triptych of the Benedictine abbey of Stavelot (Province of Lüttich). New York, Pierpont Morgan Library. Literature: Schreckenberg II, 561f.; *The Stavelot Triptych* 1980, pl.3.

2. The Theophilus legend

1. Under the influence of a Jew, the Christian Theophilus makes a pact with the devil. Miniature in the so-called Scheyer Matutinale, made in the Benedictine monastery of Scheyer (Upper Bavaria), 1225–1226. Munich, SB, Clm. 17401, folio 18 verso. Literature; Zafran 1973, I, 23–24; Hauke and Kroos 1980; Diemer 1992, 33 fig.20. Illustration after Wittelsbach I, 2, 1980, cat. no.157.

2. The Christian Theophilus sells himself to the devil. A Jew is the intermediary here; he is not depicted, but his decisive influence on the event is perhaps indicated by the 'Jewish' head-dress of Theophilus, a form of Phrygian cap, customary above all among Jews in France. Miniature in the so-called Ingeborg Psalter, made c.1195 in Paris. Chantilly, Bibliothèque de Musée Condé, Ms.9 folio 35 verso. Literature: Schreckenberg II, 611f. Illustration after Deuchler 1985 (commentary volume), nos.39–40.

3. Jewish fathers kill their Christianizing sons

1. The basis of this is legendary material from late Christian antiquity (which can be detected e.g. in Gregory of Tours [died 594], PL 71, 714–15): the son of a Jewish glass-blower receives the sacrament of the altar along with his Christian playmates; furious at this, his father throws him into the burning oven of his workshop, but under the protection of the Mother of God he remains unharmed. Miniature in a French collection of legends from the thirteenth century. Brussels, BR, Ms 9229–30, Vol.II, folio 12 verso. Literature: Blumenkranz 1965, no.9.

2. Legend of the Christianizing Jewish boy whom his angry father wants to burn in the oven. However, he is saved by a miracle. The boy's communion (together with his Christian friends and with the benevolent presence of Mary) is depicted in the left half of the picture. Miniature in an English prayerbook ('Book of Hours'), end of the fourteenth century. Copenhagen, Kongelige Bibliotek, Ms.Thott 574, folio 44 verso. Illustration after Blumenkranz 1965, no.10.

3. Flysheet with a picture by Michael Störitz, 1694. Legends like this about Simon (Schimon, Schmiele) Abeles (1682–1694) contributed to the anti-Jewish mood among the Christian population of Prague. Literature: Schnur 1939, fig. p.51; *EJ*, 1971, 700, fig.33; Rybar 1991, fig. p.48; Berger 1992, fig.22; illustration after Liebe 1903, no.68.

4. Miniature in a French collection of legends about Mary. The Jew is wearing the round skull-cap has locks). Paris, BN, Nouv.acqu.fr. 24541, folio 35. Illustration after Blumenkranz 1965, no.8.

4. Profanation of images (pictorial representations of Christ, Mary and the saints)

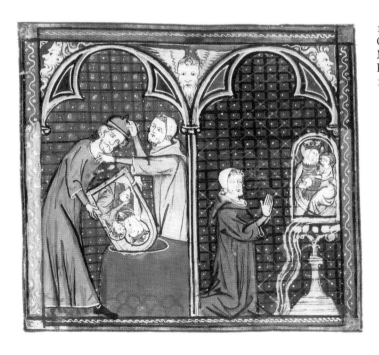

1. Jewish profanation of a picture of Mary and the boy Jesus. A Christian chastizes the Jew and then prays in front of the image. Miniature in a French manuscript of the fourteenth century. Brussels, BR, Ms 9229–30, folio 30 verso. Literature: Zafran 1973, I, 205.

2. A Jew strikes the statue of St Nicholas. Stained glass in Tours Cathedral, third quarter of the thirteenth century. Illustration after Grodecki 1981, fig. 109.

3. Maltreatment of an image of St Nicholas by a Jew. Ceiling painting in the church of St Maria Lyskirchen in Cologne, c.1250–1260. Literature: Geiger 1931, 147f.; Goldkuhl 1954, fig. 57; Deuchler 1975, fig.169; Meisen 1981, fig.142; Zarnecki 1986, fig.365. Illustration after Clemen 1930, p.5 fig.4 (cf pl.1).

4. Profanation by Jews of an image of the crucified Christ. Boeckler 1923, 52, comments: 'Jews find an image of Christ and crucify it, as their fathers crucified Christ. A crucifix, the *imago Christi*, has been suspended in the upper part of the S. A Jew is putting a sponge to the lips of the crucified Christ, and another is stabbing him with a lance. Finally, a third is catching the blood from the wound in his side in a bowl and using it to heal a paralytic, who is depicted lying in bed in the lower curve of the S. Blood is flowing from the wounds in the feet of the crucified Christ on to the eyes of a blind man, whose sight is thus restored.' But the almost devotional expression on the face of a Jew at the foot of the cross and his attitude of prayer, along with the hope of salvation associated with the blood of Christ, are perhaps also an anticipation of the conversion of the Jews after the miracle of the blood. Miniature in a Passionale (i.e. book with legends of the martyrs), made in the Benedictine abbey of Zwiefalten, between 1160 and 1165. Stuttgart, LB, Bibl.fol.56, folio 131b. Initial S at the beginning of an *Omelia facta a beato Athanasio archiepiscopo de miraculis, quae fecit imago dei nostri Jesu Christi*. Literature: Aronius 1902, 146f.; Kretzenbacher 1977; Thornton 1986; Bunte 1989, 366–82; Schreckenberg I, 283, 343, 376, 543; II, 570f. Illustration after Boeckler 1923, no.109.

5. Chastizing of an image of Nicholas by a Jew. An image of St Nicholas has been put on an iron-bound money chest to guard the money which a Jew has entrusted to the saint before setting out on a journey. However, while the Jew (recognizable from his group characteristics, a white hat, beard and long garment) is away, a thief steals the money and carries it off in the kind of money-belt that merchants wore round their bodies. On his return home the Jew, furious at what has happened, strikes the image of the saint as a punishment. Stained glass on the south side of the cathedral of Freiburg im Breisgau, first half of the fourteenth century. Literature: Geiger 1931, fig.370; Krummer-Schroth 1967, pl. XIII. Illustration after Meisen 1931, no.177.

6. Profanation of a crucifix by Jews and the baptism of Jews who are converted as a result of a miracle (blood from the image of Christ). Legendary material of this kind is known from Christian antiquity (e.g. in Gregory of Tours [died 594], PL 71, 724: *De Judaeo qui iconicam Christi furavit et transfordit)*; cf. also the *Historia imaginis Berytensis* (Ps.Athanasius, in Schreckenberg I, 218). Miniature in a thirteenth-century French collection of legends. Brussels, BR, Ms 9229–30, folio 89 recto. Literature: Blumenkranz 1965, no.65.

7. A Jew stabs a crucifix. Blood flows from it, and the perpetrator is stoned. Woodcut from the workshop of Michael Wohlgemut and Hans Pleydenwurff in the World Chronicle of Hartmann Schedel, Nuremberg 1493. Illustration after Schedel, folio 149 verso (relating to the period around 600 CE).

Das sechst alter

Diser zeit hat ein iud das bild eins crucifix gestochē dz dz plūt mitli gelich herauß floße vn de iude besprenget also dz man des iude füßstapffen plütig spūret. die cristen die das sahen volgten dem gespor der plütigen fußtritt nach bis sie zu dem plütflüßigen pild komen. als sie das funden do verstaynten sie den iuden.

IN dem sechsten iar des kaisers mauricy was ein sölche wasser güß das man maynet dz die syntfluß noe vernewet wer. dann dise synt fluß was in der venediger. foriaul oder andern gegente welsch lāds also das sich die weg vnd straßen verluren. acker. wysen. dörffer vnnd ander menschliche wonung zu seegrüben warden vnd vil menschē vn vih verdürben vnd ertranken. Der fluß der etsch lieff dessinals also außdas in sant zenonis des martrers kirchen außerhalb der mawin d statt Bern oder Verona gelegen das wasser bis zu den öbern fenstern raichet. vnd solche wasserguß beschahe am. xvij. tag des monats octobris. Aber es warn solch hagel. thonr vnnd plyze die kawm zu sumer zeit geschehen mugen. So was auch die Tyber zu rom also groß das das wasser dauon vber die mawin hynein floße vnd vil örtter dariñ beschwemmet. do schwimme auch ein wundergroßer drack mit vil schlangen in dem rechten wasser gang vnnd fürt des fluß der Tyber

▶ 8 a–l. Profanation of an image at Cambron (in 1322), directed against an image of Mary in the church of the Cistercian monastery in Cambron, Belgium. Twelve woodcuts in Thomas Murner's *Entehrung Mariä*, an anti-Jewish poem, printed in Strasbourg in 1515 by the printer Hüpfuff (Hupfuff, for whom see *LGB* III, Stuttgart 1991, 546). The model for these woodcuts was provided by a cycle of pictures commissioned in 1477 by the later Emperor Maximilian I in the Franciscan church in Colmar (destroyed in 1792). Literature: List 1987; Zafran 1973, I, 213f.; Güde 1981, frontispiece; Po-Chia Hsia 1988, fig.p.25; Bunte 1989, 51–61; Treue 1992, 113f.; cf. Simonsohn 1988, 357f. Illustration after Klasser 1905, 98–109.

Wie die falschen iuden die bildung
Marie verspottet vnd verspuwet haben.

Wie die falschen juden das bild
Marie durch stachen vnd blüt vsher ran.

Wie der schmidt und brüder die
Badten von den juden eynem apt klagten.

Wie ein engel dem schmydt beualhe
die Baden gegen dem Juden zü rechen.

Wie der pfarer dem schmydt mitz
riedt die sachen zů klagen/ die er jm für geleyt hatt.

Wie Marie dem schmydt des nach,
tes erschein vnnd ym sein fürnemmen sterkte.

Wie der schmydt dem Grauen die
vbeldadten klagte von den falschen juden.

Wie der Graue den schmydt vnd
brüder Lehörer vnd erdiget sy vor dem apt.

Wie der Graue den iuden wyter
peinlich ließ frage · vñ der iud sich eins kampffs erbodt.

Wie der schmydt den erbottenen
kampff gegen dem Juden an nam vnd jn ob lag.

Wie der Graue den iuden ließ
schentlichen vß schleyffen zů dem galgen.

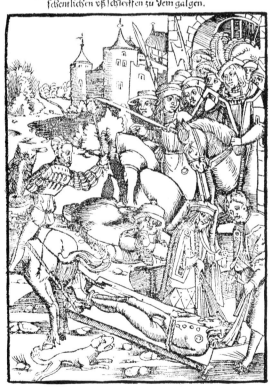

Wie der Graue den iuden ließ er-
hencké mit zwey ruden · vnd verbrient vñ dem galgé.

5. Profanation of the host

1. Profanation of the host in Lauda, twenty miles south-west of Würzburg, end of the thirteenth century. The story 'documented' in this picture probably rests on a legendary local tradition, the history of which can apparently no longer be clarified: at all events, *Germ.Jud.* (I,153f.; II, 1, 470f. [a legend of desecrating the host is mentioned only in 1638]; III, 1, 720f.) offers little on the subject, and Simonsohn (1988ff.) knows no relevant bull for the period in question. Illustration after Hahn 1988, 350.

▶2. Profanation of the host in Passau, 1477. In pictures of this kind the medieval form of Jewish dress, especially the ring (*rota*), has the polemical function of denunciation. The illustrated narrative of such legends often reports how a bad Christian sells the Jews a host which they then torture, allegedly to establish whether the Christian faith is true, but without performing any miracles. In the supposition of 'torturing' the host a role is also played by the Christian assumption that in this way the Jews are repeating the passion of Christ inflicted by the Jews of the New Testament. The doctrine of transubstantiation promulgated by the Fourth Lateran Council (1215) and the introduction of the feast of Corpus Christi (1264) were probably essential presuppositions for the rise of such legends. Broadsheet by Caspar Hochfeder, Nuremberg, c.1495. Literature: Liliencron II, 1866, 142–66 (cf. *Verfasserlexikon* II, 1980, 721f.); Heitz 1919, fig.49; Schramm 1920, XVIII, fig.713; Bauerreiss 1931, 38f., 99; *Mon.Jud.Kat.* 1963, B 293–6; Kunzle 1973, fig.p.26; Mayer 1955; Boockmann 1986, fig.429; Deneke 1988, 188–90; Po-Chia Hsia 1988, 50–6; Schuder and Hirsch 1990, fig. p.295; Eckert 1991, fig. p.389; Rohbacher and Schmidt 1991, fig. pp.296f.; Eder 1992, 104, 261–75. Illustration after Liebe 1903, pl.2; cf. *Germ.Jud.* III, 2, 1089.

Ein grawsamlich geschicht Geschehen zu passaw Von den Juden als hernach volgt

Hye stylt Cristoff acht partickel des sacramēt auß der kirchē. legt das in sein talchē. hat dy darinnē drei tag behaltē

Hye schuet er die sacrament den juden auff den tisch die vnucrmaßigt gewesen sein. darumb sy im ein guldē gaben

Hye tragen die judē vn schulklopffer. die sacrament yn ir synagog. vnd vber antwurtden dye den Juden.

Hye sticht pfeyl Jud das sacrament auff irem altar. ist plut daraus gangen das er vn ander juden gesehen haben.

Hye teyltē sy auß dye sacramēt schicken zwen partickel gen Prag. Bwē gen saltzpurg. zwen yn die Mewenstat

Hye verprenten sy die sacramēt versuchen ob vnser glaub gerecht wer floge auß dem offen zwen engel. vñ .ij. taubē

Hye vecht man all Juden zu Passaw die dy sacramēt gekaufft verschickt gestolen vnd verpzant haben.

Hye furt mā sy fur gericht. verurtaylt die vier getaufft. fackel mand. kolman vnd walich. sein gekopft worden.

Hye zereyst man den pfeyl vnd vettel die das sacramēt behyltē. dz darnach gestochen vnd verpzant haben.

Hye verpzent man sy mit sampt dē juden. die yn yrem glauben blyben. vnd vmb das sacramēt gewyst haben.

Hye wirt der Cristoff des sacramentz verkauffer. auff einem wagē zeryssen mit gluenden zangen.

Hye hebt man an zw pawen. vnserm herren zu lob eyn gotzhaus. Auß der juden synagog ꝛc.

Nach christi gepurt. M.CCCC.LXX

Nvij. iar Regirende zu den zeytē der hochwirdig furst vñ herr Her Ulrich zu passaw geborn vonn Außdorff. Es hat sych begeben das ein leychsfertiger vñ verzagter mensch weylandt genant Cristoff eysengreißhamer / vergessende seiner sel selygkayt / nach Judas syten auß begyer zeytlichs guts Mit den juden dye zeyt wonede hye zu passaw / bey der Jlcz alda hinder sant Jorgen perg. seynd vnd lesterer des gecreutzigten waren lebentigen gots vñ Marie seiner gepereryn yn ein vozrd vertrag gemacht hat. Nach dem als sy yn etwo offt in yren potschaffte genutzt vñ gebraucht nahendt vnnd verr geschickt hetten. ob er yn precht das hochwirdig sacrament. den leychnam vnsers herren Jhesu christi ob sy den icht kauffen wolten. darzu sy ym als die begyrgen hunot. auß grossem neyd so sy zu dem herren Jesu vnserm heyland haben. antwort gaben. Er solt in leychsfertig darum wolten sy ym ein benugen thun. nach solchem geding der verkauffer vnnd verstockt sunder yn seiner poßhayt nach dem hoch wirdigen sacrament stellet. des bemelten sybenundsybenzigsten iars. Am freytag vor sant Micha els tag die kirchen vnser lieben frawen yn der freyung der abtey. das stock geheuß auff gebrochen. dar yn. viij. partickel des hochwirdygen sacramēts gestollen. das mit seinen sunoigen henden an gegryffen. vñ yn eyn tuchlein gewickelt von dem freytag byß an den suntag Jorgen bey ym getragē dar nach den Juden falschafftig vberantwurdt. vmb eyn reynischen guldē verkaufft. eyn partyckel gepurt vmb dreyssig pfennig. zu schmach der heyligen christenlich kyrchen. dye Juden vnd lesterer gots wolltē zu zweyfel yn ir synagog pracht den leychnam christi mit iren sundigē benden. gryffen

mit grymmiger gier zu creutzigē. christē glaubē zu werē. Ein jud ein scharpfes messer genumē den leychnā xpi auff irem altar in der synagog gestochē daraus plut geflossen. Eins kindes angesicht erschynē. Die judē sere erschracken. wurdē zu rabt. vñ schicktē .ij. partickel gen Prag. ij. in die Mewestat. ñ gen Saltzpurg. ij. partickel worffen sy yn einē gluende packoffen. haben sy gesehen. ij. engel. ij. tauben aus dem ofen flygē. nachmals ist der vbeltreter vor der fasten im sybenundsybentzigstē iare. bey einē kyrchstock zu Germal perg begryffen. vñ den gefangē gefurt auff das oberhaus bey passaw. Da selbst er vngezwungē solch groß vbel gesagt vñ mer auff die Judischayt. dar auff der obgenant hochwirdig yn got vater. vñ herr Ulrich byschoff zu pas saw. Als ein christēlicher furst dem solch vbel pillich zu hertzen ist gangen. vñ rechtlich zu straffen erkant hat. schuff durch denckeln vñ gestrenge Ritter herr Sebastian võ der alben. die zeit seiner genadē marschalck. die selbē Juden hye zu passaw all zu fahen vnd vmb die warhayt zu fragē. die doch also gemeynicklich einhellig vñ bekantlich wurde. vñ zaygtē das messer. dē stein. die stat vñ den ofen da sy solch handlūg mit dem hoch wirdigen sacrament volbracht vñ begangē habē. Also bekertē sych yr vier zu dem Christē lichen glaubē. vñ wurde am Erichtag nach Judica yn der fasten des syben vndsybentzigstē iars fur recht gestelt. Die newē christē mit dem schwert ge richt. die Judē yn dem fewer. auch ir zwen mit zangē gerissen. Nach dē alle vber etlich wochē wardt der verkauffer auch nach ordnūg des rechtē mit gluendē zange gericht. das er als mit grosser gedult rew vñ andacht erlydē hat. wie das durch yn gehandelt ist. offenlich vor menigklich bekannt. got wol sych vber sein vñ alle glaubig sel erbarmen. Amen.

Wo de Jode dat hillige Sacramente stelt

Wo de Jode dorch gotlike Schickinge vnd gewalt nicht vorgbaen kondt

Wo de Jode dat hillige Sacrament vnder de galgen begroff 8

Wo de Jode wanckerbh myt blodigen henden nach Brssnalck

3a–e. Profanation of the host in 1285 at the tomb of a saint near Techow (Prignitz district, Brandenburg). Five coloured panel paintings (tempera painting on wood) in the porch of the monastic church of Heiligengrabe, made some years after the Reformation (seven of the original fifteen have been preserved). This legend about the profanation of the host – like others – only came into being some time after the date of the alleged event. It was disseminated in the first quarter of the sixteenth century, first in Latin in 1516 and then in 1521 in a Low German version by Ludwig Dietz in Rostock. The content of the legend is that a Jew from Freiberg (in the Meissen region of Saxony) lived in Techow and on 16 May 1285, the Friday after Ascension Day, stole from the church of Techow a monstrance with a consecrated host which he wanted to take the Jews of Pritzwalk. However, it bled, and in a miraculous way became increasingly heavy on the journey. So he was unable to carry it further, and had to rest under an oak – which still existed in the sixteenth century. Finally he continued to a gallows outside Techow (the place of execution for the town), where he buried the host – having previously broken it into pieces. The peasants of Techow noticed the burglary of the church, heard of a Jew who had arrived at Pritzwalk with bloody hands, and by a trick got out of him where he had buried the sacrament. The Jew indicated the place to them with the words 'here lies your God'. He was condemned by the judge to the punishment of the wheel (i.e. to be bound to the spokes of a wheel, after which his limbs were crushed and shattered and the wheel was put on a post). Various miracles took place at the spot where the sacrament had been buried, so a chapel or a monastery was built there. This monastic church had a so-called holy sepulchre (i.e. a copy of the legendary tomb of Jesus in Jerusalem – a widespread form of piety at that time, focussed on the passion and on grief). Thus the whole story of the miracle of the host is probably an aetiological legend, since the miraculous bleeding host is said to have lain in this holy sepulchre. Literature: Bauereiss 1931, 56; Zafran 1973, I, 184f.; Kötzsche 1987. Illustration after Schuder and Hirsch 1990, 1234–7. For blood-red colonies of bacteria (*serratia marcescens*) growing on old bread see *Lexikon der Biologie* VII, Freiburg 1986, 411.

4. Woodcut in *La rappresentazione d'uno miracolo del corpo di Christo* (miracle play) printed in Florence around 1500. The illustration shows two stages of the action simultaneously: a woman (Kristeller: a monk) has pledged a garment with a Jew and is redeeming it (with a host which she has brought). On the right Jews – here the Jewish ring functions as polemical denunciation – are torturing the host, which is moving in order to avoid the pain, in a way customary in such pictures. Literature: Zafran 1973, I, 141–3. Illustration after Kristeller 1968, no.48.

Das heilige Sacrament wird von
einer Christin nach der h. Communion offtermahlen in ein
Schnupftuch gethan, glaubens ver-
gessnerweiß umb ein Versetztes
Kleid welches sie zu lösen nit ver-
mögend denen Juden vertauscht

Die heilige Hostien werden von
denen Gottlosen Juden mit einer
spitzigen Schuchahl, so heut noch
gegenwärtig, bis zu vergiessung
des Allerheiligsten Bluts gestochen

Die heilige Hostien werden von
den verschalckten Juden biß auf
das heilige Blut mit Dörnern
gefrätzt, und es erscheint unter
solcher Marter ein kleines Kindlein, ein dergleichen Dorn ist
noch zu sehen

Das heilige Sacrament wird in einen geheitzten Bach-Offen geschos-
sen, bleibt doch mehrmall die gestalt eines Kindlein vorbildend un-
verletzt, der Stein von dem Mund
loch dieses Bach Offens wird
noch heut gewißen.

5. Profanation of the host in Deggendorf
(1337). 12 engravings in the work *Das
obsiegende Glaubens-Wunder des ganz
christlichen Chur-Landes Bayern*, edited
and published by the Deggendorf citizen and
bookbinder Johann Georg Siegmund Drien-
dorfner in 1776. These pictures (which
make no claims to being art) report a
fictitious story. Jews had probably lived in
Deggendorf since the beginning of the
fourteenth century. There is historical evidence only of the sudden murder (without any
previous trial) of the Jews of Deggendorf at
the end of September or the beginning of
October 1338 (probably for economic
reasons: failure of the harvest and subse-
quent debts). Quite unconnected with this
event, in the second half of the fourteenth
century a church was built in Deggendorf
dedicated to Peter and Paul and the Body of
Christ: this 'Holy Sepulchre Church', as it
was also called, apparently contained an
imitation of the sepulchre of Christ in
Jerusalem (as was customary at that time).
In the framework of this contemporary piety
centred on the passion, the local legend of
profanation of the host arose after 1370 (!);
it soon developed a life of its own and was
fancifully elaborated. Miraculous hosts
which were said to bleed became the object
and centre of eucharistic pilgrimages, pro-
cessions, indulgences, songs, poems,
dramas, paintings and devotional images of
various kinds. The whole development was
started off by the arbitrary association of the
historical murder of the Jews with the contemporary cult of the Man of Sorrows (or
the cult of the sepulchre). The requisites for
authentication (miraculous hosts, instruments of martyrdom) were added only later:
presumably the hosts had to be changed
frequently in the course of the centuries. The
motive for the genesis of this legend was the
quest for scapegoats in times of distress and
crisis (e.g. famine, pestilence). As uninteg-
rated aliens and a marginal group, the Jews
were candidates for this role. Since in any
case the Jews were regarded as wicked
enemies of Christ and the Christians, the
reddening of hosts (through bacterial infec-
tion) was interpreted as the result of their
misdeeds and a repetition of the passion of
Christ by the descendants of the New Testament Jews. Thus a later legend justified the
murder of the Jews in 1338 and sparked off a
lucrative pilgrimage tourism which produced many hundreds of thousands of
visitors down to the twentieth century.
Literature: Graetz 1853ff., VII, 326-8;
Krotzer 1964; *Germ.Jud.* II.1, 1968, 157;
Geissler 1976, 223-5; *Verfasserlexikon* IV,
1983, 893-6; Lotter 1988, 568ff.; Frey
1991, 41f.; *Tribüne* 129, 30-4. Illustration
after Eder 1992, 567-70.

Die unmenschliche Judenhänd er-
greiffen die Hämer schlagen die
heiligen Hostien doch mehrmall
unverletz auf einem Schmid ampoß
dessen Stock biß dato zu sehen ist.

Umb ihren Muthwillen ein End zu
machen und ihre unmenschliche Ubel
thaten sambt dem heil. Sacrament zu
vertuschen wollen solches die Iuden in ihre verfluchte Rachen ver-
schlucken aber ein widerum erschei-
nendes kleines Kind widersetzet sich
mit Händ und Füßlein dan dieses
Brod gehört nit vor die Hund.

Die heilige Hostien werden in
einen Brunnen geworffen daß
Wasser vergifft das daran viele
Christen gestorben.

Die heilige Hostien werden von
einem Neu geweichten Priester so
von Niederaltach gebürtig bey ange-
stellter Procession (weilen sie sich
frey eigens Gewalt von dem Wasser in die Luft erschwungen und
in den Kelch nidergelassen) in das
Gotteshause getragen.

Die Nachtwächter und folgend
andere nehmen bey der Nacht
umb die gegend des Brunen
einen unvergleichlich schönen
glantz gewahr, und hören ein
Lamentirliche Stime.

Die Bürger schweren Zusam-
men einen theuren Eyd sich an
denen Iuden zu rächnen.

Die Juden werden von denen Chri
ften, aus rechtmäßigen Gott ge
fälligen Eifer ermordet und aus
gereutet. Gott gebe das von die
sem Höllen geschmaiß unser Vater
land jederzeit befreyet bleibe.

Wie viel und große Ablaß, dem
allhiesigen Orte sind ertheilet wor
den ist in der von Jahr 1749. Neu
auffgelegten Relation viel meh
rers zu ersehen.

▶ 7. The Pressburg (Bratislava) case of 1591. A roughly contemporaneous flysheet with a woodcut describes the event in several scenes depicted synchronously: 'The church on the left and the synagogue on the right represent the two opposing religious forces with the castle on the hill in the centre as the secular authority. Divine punishment is meted out by a fire from heaven which burns the synagogue, and earthly punishment by the quartering and impalement of Jews' (*EJ* 1971, VIII, 688). Berlin, Kupferstichkabinett (Inv.no. D–139–8: photograph J.P.Anders). Literature: *The Jewish Encyclopedia* X, New York 1905, 188; *JüdLex.* IV, 1930, 1099f.; Schnur 1939, 17; Strauss 1975, II, 703; Liebe 1903, no.17.

6. The trial for profanation of a host in Berlin, 1510. Woodcut: Burning of the Jews. Literature: Geiger 1888, 312–14; *EJ* 1971, IV, 642, fig.1; Zafran 1973, I, 185–7; Bürger 1987, fig.p.150; Schuder and Hirsch 1990, 427–35; Nachama 1992, fig.p.145. Illustration after *EJ* 1929, IV, 218; cf. *Germ. Jud.* III, 1, 146.

Ein erschröckliche Newe Zeitung/so sich im 1591. Jar zu Preß-

burgk in Vngern zu getragen/wie daselbst etliche Juden zwey Consecrierte Ostien vberkommen/damit einen
schendlichen mißbrauch vnd Gottslesterung geübt aber hefftig von Gott gestrafft worden/allen fromen Christen zu einer warnung.

ES hat sich im lauffenden 91. Jar zu Wormbs am Reinstrom zugetra-
gen das ein Jude mit namen Leo/ein erfahrner in allerley Sprachen/
sonderlich aber in Hebreischer / Griechischer vnnd Lateinischer/zum
Christlichen glauben ist bekert worden/ sich tauffen lassen/den warhafftigen
Messiam bekent/das er der gecreutzigte Christus/der Juden König/vnd aller Menschen Erlöser vnd Seligmacher sey. Diser/ nach dem er die tauff em-
pfangen/begibt sich daselbst zu Wormbs ins Frawekloster zu eim Münch/
deß Name Petrus Rodamus war/dazu bestelt/das er die Krancken besucht/
jhnen das Hochwirdige Sacrament Jesu Christi reicht vnnd gibe. Wie nun
obgedachter getauffter Jud eine zeytlang im selben Kloster verharret bey diesem Münch sich auffenthalten/zu wol in acht genomen/wo die Consecrierten
Ostien behalten vnd verwaret worden. Nimbt er auff ein zeit mit list vnd be-
hendigkeit der selben drey/wickelt sie in ein brieff/hebt sie fleissig auff/vnd sich
macht damit daruon/vn kompt endlich biß gen Preßburgt in Vngern/da er
sich zu ein Juden zur Herbrig eingelegt/vnd bey im etlich tag verharret/vn
da sie derhalben eins in disputation gerathen/von der Menschwerdung/vn
dem H. Sacrament des leibs vnd bluts Jesu Christi vnderredung gehalten/
fraget in der Jud/weil er getaufft wer/vnd Christum bekent/ob er auch das
H. Nachtmal empfangen habe. Darauff hat der getauffte Jud geantwort/
Er hette es empfangen. Nach mehrer vnterredung/ sind sie auch endlich so
weit komen/dz der getauffte Jud die 3. Consecrierte Ostien/so er zu Wormbs
im Kloster gestolen/eussert vnd herfür thut/vnnd sagt/ er hab die von einem
Christen gekaufft/Als die der Jud gesehen/hat er derselbigen zwo von jhm be-
kommen/auffgehaben vnd verwaret. Wie nun gedachter getauffter Jud
der Leo widerumb von Preßburge weggereiset/vn sich nach Nickelsburg be-
geben/fordert dieser Jud etliche andere Juden zu sich/zeiget jnen die Ostien/
vnd saget/es were ein getaufter Jud bey im gewesen/der het dieselbigen bey
sich gehabt/vnd sie von einem Christen gekaufft/von dem er sie empfangen.

Wie nun diese Juden also bey einander/beschliessen sie/sie wolten andere
Juden mehr zu sich nemen/wie auch geschehen/vn probieren/ob auch betrug
vnter der Christen Sacrament were oder nit. Nemen der wegen die Consecrierten zwey Ostien/ legen sie auff den Tisch/vnnd ein messer darneben / mit
welchem alß bald einer vnter jnen die Ostien/so auff dem Tisch gelegen/durch
stochen/vnd gesagt/bistu der Christen Gott/ so beweise es. Als bald ist Blut

auß den Ostien gesprungen/vnd auff den Tisch geflossen/darüber sie alle nicht
wenig erschrocken. Vber diser grewlichen vnd erschröcklichen that/ hat Gott
sein zorn/aber die Jude sehen lassen/mit doner vnd plitz in das Hauß geschla-
gen/ vnd ist dasselbige in grosser eyl vom Fewer verzehret worden/ der Jud/
sein Weib/zwey Kinder/auch andere Juden mehr: mit verbrandt/vnd sind
nur drey dem Fewer entrunnen/Der Tisch aber/ darauff die blutend Ostien
gelegen/ ist vnuersehret stehen blieben. Als nun der Statthalter/der ausserhalb der Statt auff eim Schloß wohnet/solch grewlich Fewer gesehen/hat er
als bald seine diener in die Statt geschickt/ der meinung/das sie das Fewer
solten helffen leschen/denen als bald in der Statt bericht worden/ wie das in
dem brennenden Hauß etliche Juden bey einander gewesen/was sie aber da-
rin gehandelt könte man nit wissen/deren etliche weren verbrandt drey aber
daruon kommen. Wie nun die diener jhrem Herrn dem Statthalter solches
berichtet/hat er nach diesen 3. Juden forschen lassen/dieselben auch endlich
bekomen/vn für sich gefordert/sie gefraget/Was sie im selben Hauß gemacht
oder gethan hetten. Vnd wiewol sie sich lang geweret/vnd nichts sagen wöl-
len/hat doch einer endlich vnder jhnen angefangen/vn vor dem Statthalter
den gantzen handel/wie sie mit den Consecrierten Ostien vmbgangen weren
bekent vn erzelet/darüber der Statthalter seher schrocken/ vnd als bald die
drey Juden gefenglich lassen einziehen/ sich hin vnnd wider bedacht/was er
jhnen für solche schröckliche that/ für Marter wolt anlegen/bey sich aber be-
schlossen/vnd sie auff folgende weise tödten vnd vmbringen lassen.

Erstlich hat er sie halb lassen schinden/vnd also eine Nacht ligen lassen/
des ander tages hat er jhnen die Füß lassen in Pech sieden/vnnd endlich des
dritten tags lassen spiessen vnd an die Landstrassen setzen.

Gott der Allmechtige gebe/dz wir solche vnd dergleichen Exempel betrachten vnd vns zu gemüt führen/nicht so leichlich in Wind schlagen/ verachten
vnd gedencken/Es sey wol ehr so vil geschehen/es sey nichts newes/Aber ein
jeder sey gewarnet/vnnd enthalte sich des leichtfertigen schwerens/mißbrauch
Göttliches Namens/ vn der heyligen hochwirdigen Sacrament/ mit welch-
en man eben so wol Christi Wunden verneweret vnd eröffnet/das sie täglich
bluten/welches ein jeder zu seiner zeit befinden wirdt. Gott verleihe vns sempt-
lichen ein bußfertiges leben/t das wir endlich selig werden/AMEN.

Gedruckt zu Nürnberg/bey Lucas Mayer/Formschneider.

Sterneberch.

8a -d. Sternberg (Mecklenburg), 1492. The priest Peter Dähne has pledged an iron pot to the Jew Eleazar (also called Elihard or Eligard): he gives two consecrated hosts to redeem it. As the hosts are tortured by the Jews with knives, they begin to bleed. In terror the Jews return the hosts, but the news has got around, and after a short trial, on 27 October 1192 the Jews – twenty-seven in number – are burned on the

Sternberg. Around six months later (on 13 March 1493), Dähne is burned in Rostock. Literature: Geiger 1888, 309–12; Liebe 1903, fig. 27; Fuchs 1921, fig.10; Bauer-reiss 1931, 62; Baron IX, 1965, 370; Peuckert 1966, I, 132f.; Zafran 1973, I, 177–81; Schuder and Hirsch 1990, 129–44; Rohrbacher and Schmidt 1991, 299f.; *Verfasserlexikon* IX, 1, 1993, 306–8. Illustration after various contem-

porary publications: Schmidt 1981 (facsimile volume), folio 167 verso (in two parts: below the profanation of the hosts and above the burning of the Jews); Schramm 1920, VIII, no.748 (text: 'All Christian people', etc.): XII, no.668 (text: 'Sternberg. The wicked Jews...'); XII, no.668 (text: 'This is what happens to the Jews on the Sternberg near Mecklenburg'); *Germ.Jud.* III, 2, 1413.

Die geschicht der Jüden zum Stern
berg im landt zu Mecklenburg.

9. A Christian woman gives a Jewish pawn-broker a consecrated host to redeem a garment (this relates to a profanation of the host in Paris in 1290). The Jew is wearing the prescribed sign *(rota)* on his right shoulder, but in the form customary in Italy; he is also dressed in an Italian style.

Miniature in the Florentine Chronicle of Giovanni Villani, fourteenth century. Rome, BAV, Ms.LVIII 296, folio 149 verso. Literature: Browe 1926, 180f.; Simonsohn I, 1988, 283; Eder 1992, 160–4. Illustration after Blumenkranz 1965, no.14.

6. Charges relating to blood: the accusation of ritual murder

1. Ritual murder in Bern (1294). The Jews murder the Christian boy Ruef. The body of the martyr is buried in the Holy Cross altar. The picture anachronistically depicts the crime in front of the typical late medieval façades with their balconies, as though it had taken place in public. The perpetrators are wearing late-medieval Jewish hats; the Jew on the left (with a cauldron of blood?) has a full Jewish beard (and a hooked nose?). Outside, on the right, are Christian citizens of Bern. Miniature in the Bern Chronicle of Diebold Schilling, written 1474–1483. Literature: Blumenkranz 1965, fig.13; *Germ.Jud.* II, 1, 1968, 75; Zafran 1973, I, 52, 90f.; Zafran 1979, pl.9c; cf. *Verfasserlexikon* VIII, 1992, 67–5. Illustration after Schilling I, 1943, 44.

2. William of Norwich, allegedly crucified by the Jews of Norwich on Good Friday 1144 – his body was found in a wood near the city – is regarded as the first known victim of a Jewish ritual murder. It is said that the Jews had bought the boy before Easter and had made him suffer the same passion as Jesus, crucifying him out of hatred. From a present-day perspective the Norwich case looks like the very numerous similar events in the criminal history of unsolved murders. Flavius Josephus already reports the original form of this anti-Jewish legend in the first century CE (*Contra Apionem* 2, 89–102: the Jews kill a Greek in the temple of Jerusalem every year). As a legend, the accusation blossomed on the fertile soil of prejudces against the Jews as a group. Woodcut (imaginary picture, more than three centuries after the event) by Michael Wolgemut (or the Wolgemut and Pleydenwurff workshop in Nuremberg) in the Chronicle of the World by Hartmann Schedel (Nuremberg: Anton Koberger 1493), folio CCI verso. The Jewish rings, introduced only after 1215, are anachronistic here. Literature: Schedel 1493 (facsimile edition); *EJ* 1971, IV, 1121; XII, 1226f.; Zafran 1973, I, 36–9, 80f.; Lazar 1991, fig.22; cf. Schreckenberg II, 154f.: F.Lotter in Erb 1993, 25–72. Illustration after Robert 1891, pl.V; cf. *Zion* 59, 1994, 343–50; *Aschkenas* 4, 1994, 405–17.

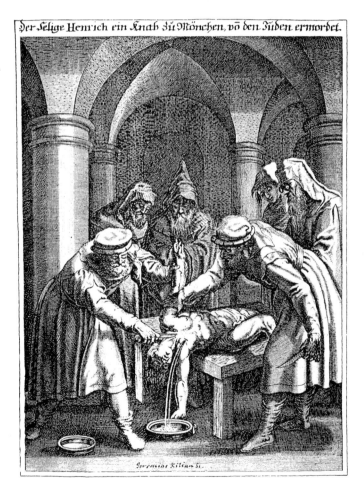

Der Selige Henrich ein Knab zu Mönchen, võ den Juden ermordet.

Der Juden Haß kont abermahl!
Sie bringen umb mit höchster qual,
Henrich den Jungen Raben.

Stirb hin, mein Kind, vor Gottes Sohn,
Von dem wirst du so grossen Lohn,
Alß ein Eißgrauer haben!

Der seelige Henricus / ein Knab/ von den Juden zu München ermordet.

Naum seynd sechtzig Jahr nach dem gleich jetzt erzehlten grausamen Mord vorüber geflossen / da hat widerum das unglückseelige Juden-Geschmäiß ein gleiche Unthat zu begehen kein Abscheuen getragen.   Es müssen die verruchte Leuth in so kurtzer Zeit gantz vergessen haben die damahls an ihnen verübte Rach/ deß ergrimmten Volcks; und also wohl verdienet haben/ daß sie auß gantz Bäyern verjagt worden.   Sie seynd auch mit disem Henrico also unbarmhertzig verfahren/ daß sie ihme alles Blut auß allen Aederlein gleichsam herauß gezäpfft/ selbigen mit 60. Wunden/ villeicht zu einem Angedencken der sechtzig / nach erstem Mord verflosnen Jahren/ zersetzt/ und auf einen Acker ausser der Stadt hingeworffen: allwo er gefunden/ Ehrentbietig aufgehebt und in Ehren/ ja Verehrung gehalten worden.   Ein Mehrers ist von disem unschuldigen Blut-Zeugen nit bekant: bey deme wir es dan auch bewenden lassen müssen.

3. Murder of a Christian boy in Munich, 1346. Engraving by Jeremias Kilian (died 1730), who produced pictures in the style of Raphael Sadeler for Rassler's German edition (Augsburg 1714) of Matthäus Rader's *Bavaria Sancta*, Munich 1615–1627: 1704). Rassler took over Rader's account of the murder, which is in turn based on the legendary account of the Bavarian historian Aventinus (died 1534). Literature: Rassler 1714, 326; *Germ.Jud.* II, 2, 1968, 557; Zafran 1973, I, 103f. Illustration and facsimile after Stock 1939, 112f.

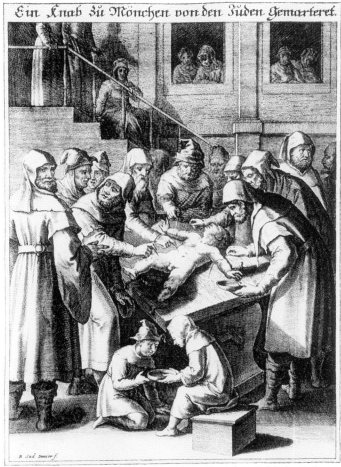

Ein Knab zu Mönchen von den Juden gemartert.

Was wütet ihr wider die Chriſtliche Kinder /
Beſchnittene Böſſwicht! kein winkel der welt
Vor euch iſt mehr ſicher: Ihr blinde Leutſchinder /
Ihr werdet bald ſürmen das ſternen Gezelt.

Was thut euch ein Kind ſo ihr alſo hinrichtet
Euch röhret der Männer mit beſſerem fug:
Was von den Megæren die Alte gedichtet /
Wahr mache an Chriſten die Neidige Handt.

Ein Knäblein von den Juden ermordet / zu München in Bayern.

ES haben die Chriſten-Blut begürige Juden in angedeutem Jahr zu München / vermittels einer alten Chriſtlichen / aber dißfalls Unchriſtlichen Rungunckel / ſich eines kleinen Chriſten-Knäbleins habhafft gemacht. Alsbald ſie ſolches umb einen ſchlechten Werth erhandlet / ſeynd ſie auß ihrem alten unerſättlichen Haß alſo grauſam und unmenſchlich mit dem unſchuldigen Kind verfahren / daß was ſie in der That verübet / die Feder zu entwerffen Abſcheuen tragt. Sie haben das ſchier noch unmündige ihrer Blut-Begürigkeit Opffer / ſeiner Kleidlein beraubt / mit allerhand ſpitzigem Werckzeug alſo am gantzen Leiblein durchſtochen / daß nit ein Tröpfflein Blut in ihme übergeblieben / und auf ſolche Weis nit ſo vaſt verwundet / als eine eintzige Wunden zuſeyn ſcheinte. Darauf haben ſie es / waiß nit wohin verſcharret. Durch diſe Mörderiſche That iſt ihr Blut-Durſt mehr angezündet / als außgelöſchet worden: derowegen ſie auf alle Weis getrachtet / wo ſie wider ein ſolch unſchuldiges Lämmlein erhaſchen / ihren Muth und Wuth daran kühlen / und das herauß gepreßte Blut / zu ihrem verdammten Gefallen mißbrauchen könten. Gehen derohalben mehrmahlen zu jener Gott und Ehrvergeſſenen alten Kinder-Krämerin / verſprechen ihr wiederum umb ſolche Schand-That / einen wenigen Lohn. Diſe ſo Geld-begürige / als Blut-begürig die Juden waren / läßt ſich mehrmahl zu einem Kauff bereden / ab deme alle menſchliche Natur ein Grauſen und Abſcheuen tragen ſolte. Siehet umb / wo ſie ein mit Chriſtlichen Tauff

gereinigtes Lämmlein finden / und auf die mehr dan Teufliſche Schlacht-Banck / umb ihre wenige Kreutzer lifferen könte. Hat auch nit über lang eins dergleichen erſehen / und die Gelegenheit in Obacht genommen / in dero ſie ihr vermaledeytes Vorhaben in das Werck richtete. Hat ſich aber übel betrogen befunden; dan als ſie vermeinte unwiſſend aller / das Kind hinweck zu ſtehlen / iſt ſie an der That von dem Vatter deß Kinds ertappet / und ſogleich der Obrigkeit überlifferet worden. Als ſie von diſer mit ſcharffer Betrohung befragt worden / zu was End ſie ein ſolchen Kinder-Raub vollbringen wollen / hat ſie nit allein den jetzt-vorgehabten / ſonder auch vorigen Raub beſtanden / auch zugleich angezeigt / wo die Mörderiſche Juden das erſte Knäblein hin verſcharret haben. Sie empfangt darauf ihren verdienten Lohn. Das ſo grauſam ermordete Knäblein wird außgegraben / oder hervor gezogen. Als nun das Volck zu München / eines ſo erbärmlichen Weis zugerichteten Leibleins anſichtig worden / iſt gleich ein dermaſſen unaußlöſchliches Rach-Feur in ihnen entbrunnen / daß ſolch unmenſchliche an einem aller Schuld unfähigen Kind verübte Mord-That ſie angetriben / die Thätter bey dem Kopff zu nemmen / ja wie diſe ſo zartem Alter nit zu ſchonen gewußt / alſo auch ohne alle Barmhertzigkeit auf das grauſamſt wider ſie zu verfahren. Derowegen ohne weiteres Rathſchlagen / halb wüthig laufften ſie herumb / was ſie immer von Juden / Schuldigen oder Unſchuldigen (wan anderſt einige unſchuldig zu nennen / in dem keinem an dem Willen / ſonder nur an der Gelegenheit mangelt / ſolche Unthaten zu verüben) antreffen / ſchlagen ſie zu Boden / ſtechen / hauen darein wie ſie nur können zukommen. Alles Abmahnen der Obrigkeit ware umbſonſt / und ware kein Mittel / ſolches Wüthen in etwas innzuhalten. Auf Rath der Aeltern auß den Juden / oder auch der Obrigkeit / laufft alles was Jüdiſch war / zuſamen in ihr mehr Mörder-Grub als Synagog. Aber diſe gleichſam Veſtung / ware zu ſchwach / die Anſtürmende außzuhalten: weilen ſie nit gleich Werckzeug genug an der Hand hatten / einzubrechen / und all diſes verruchte Geſündlein außzureiben / tragen ſie zuſamen Hartz und Pech / Kohlen / dürres Geſträus / mit einem Wort / alles was tauglich war eine Brunſt zuerwecken / zünden ſelbiges an / und verbrennen alſo lebendig die 180. bey ihnen verfluchte Juden. Freylich iſt ſo erſchreckliche Rach nit Lobſam: allein wer will einem ergrimmten Volck Maaß und Weis fürſchreiben / wie es die Rach verüben ſoll? Es ſcheinte halt unerträglich / ſolch Mörderiſches Geſündlein länger unter der Chriſtlichen Gemeind zu gedulden / und ihre Kinder alſo erbärmlich mißhandlet anzuſehen. Aber da hätte alle Rach der Obrigkeit ſollen überlaſſen werden; welche ſchon gewußt hätte / welche Straff ſothaner Schuld gemeſſen wäre. Wie dan zu andern Zeiten und Orthen / dergleichen Begünnen / durch Obrigkeitlichen Gewalt genugſam begegnet worden: wie erſcheint auß ſo vilen Städt und Länderen / auß welchen diſes Chriſten-häſſige Geſchmäiß außgeſchafft und vertriben worden: weilen es auch anderſtwo an derglei-
gleichen Unmenſchen nicht ge-
manglet.

4. Murder of a Christian boy in Munich, 1285. The Jews had a Christian boy lured away by an old woman and then killed him by repeatedly lancing his veins. When this became known, the Christians invaded the Jewish quarter and burned the Jews, 180 in number, who had fled to the synagogue. The picture shows affinities to late medieval depictions of the circumcision of Jesus (Luke 2.21), which polemically sought to see this act as a kind of prelude to his later passion. Engraving by Raphael Sadeler (died 1632), in a *History of the Saints* by the Jesuit Matthäus Rader, *Bavaria Sancta*, Munich 1624 (reprinted in Rassler 1714, on p.322; Stock 1939, 111 pl.10). Facsimile from Rassler 1714, 322, 325 (in Rassler [or Rader] this is taken over from the Bavarian historian Aventinus [died 1534]), who used Salzburg annals. Literature: Rassler 1714, 322–5; Geiger 1888, 320; Bauerreiss 1931, 32f.; Zafran 1973, I, 103f.; *Germ.Jud.* II.2, 1968, 556; Deneke 1988, fig.p.184. Illustration and facsimile after Stock 1939, 109–11.

5. Werner of Oberwesel (Werner of Bacharach). In April 1287 the boy Werner (born in 1273 around Womrath, Simmern district) was found murdered in a field near Bacharach. According to the legend he was being employed by a Jew in Oberwesel, and having received communion on Maundy Thursday was seized by the Jews who wanted to get hold of the host, hung up by the feet, tortured, and finally murdered. According to another version of the legends the Jews wanted to drain off the boy's blood. The murder was blamed on the Jews of Oberwesel and this provoked persecutions amounting to pogroms in the Rhineland. Werner was venerated in the diocese of Trier as a martyr from 1761 (on 19 April; his festival was abolished in 1963). Werner's body was buried in the chapel of St Cunibert in Bacharach; the Gothic Wernerkirche was built on the spot and became the goal of great pilgrimages. This picture also shows the customary display of the venerated dead person in the inner wall of the church. In 1621 Werner's relics were carried off by Spanish troops. Heinrich Heine treats a similar theme in his narrative 'The Rabbi of Bacherach', which remained a fragment. Literature: *Acta sanctorum*, April, Antwerp 1675, 697–710; Bauerreiss 1931, 66f.; *Mon.Jud.Kat.* 1963, B 298–30 (with fig.21); *LThK* XI, 1965, 1055f.; *Germ.Jud.* II, 2, 1968, 618; Zafran 1973, I, 109ff.; Bunte 1989, 390–6; Schuder and Hirsch 1990, 145f.; Eckert 1991, 378; Rohrbacher and Schmidt 1991, 12–14, 287–8, 307–13. Illustration 1 (engraving with two scenes one above the other: pilgrimage to Werner's tomb), after *Acta sanctorum*, p.737, fig.2 (relief in the Spitalkirche of Oberwesel [1968]) after Rohrbacher and Schmidt 1991, 309.

6. The two-year-old Christian boy Simon (for a long time venerated as a holy Christian martyr on 24 March), son of a tanner in Trent, disappeared on 23 March (Maundy Thursday) 1475. His mutilated body was discovered by the Jews in the night between Easter Day and Easter Monday in a ditch running past a Jewish house. Although they immediately reported this to the local bishop, they were suspected of having killed the boy. The Jews Samuel, Angelus, Tobias (a doctor), Israel and Bonaventura, who allegedly took part in the murder, were immediately arrested, along with the Jew Joaff (Joff). When asked about the Jewish Passover rites, a baptized Jew, Johann von Feltre, in prison for theft at this time, indicated that in preparing the unleavened bread and mixing the Passover wine the Jews used the blood of a Christian boy and while doing so cursed Christ and Christianity. Ten further Jews were arrested (Israel, son of Samuel; Moses the elder; Mohar his son; Solomon son of Mendelin de Ysprecho; Lazarus de Seravallo; Moses son of Solomon of Hospoch; Isaac son of Jacob de Vedera; Brunetta, Samuel's wife; Vitalis; and Israel son of Mohar of Brandenburg). Fourteen Jews in all were executed after making confessions in the interrogations, which were accompanied by torture. Through the new medium of printing (including the possibility of xylographic pictures) the case was given publicity far beyond the region. The most publicity came from texts by Johannes Matthias Tiberinus (personal physician to the local bishop, Hinderbach; he noted the medical evidence after the discovery of the body): 1. provisional report by letter (on 1 April 1475), of which some impressions soon appeared under different titles (e.g. *Passio Beati Simonis pueri Tridentini*); two German translations appeared independently of each other as early as 1475–6: *Die Geschichte und Legend von den seyligen kind und marterer genant Symon* ('The story and legend of the blessed child and martyr called Symon', Augsburg, Günther Zainer); *Johannes Mathias Tuberinus der freyen kunst und Ertzney doctor*, etc. (Nuremberg: Friedrich Creussner); Middle Low German versions of it also appeared. 2. *Historia completa de passione et obitu pueri Simonis* (one edition of this appeared in Trent in the workshop of Albert Kunne, dated 9 February 1476). The tendency of Tiberinus' reports is to see Simon as a martyr in the footsteps of the passion of Christ, which in any case was regarded as an act of the Jews. There is more on contemporary journalistic and literary agitation in *Verfasserlexikon* VII, 1992, 1262–74. Literature: Schedel 1493, fig.

folio CCLIII verso (woodcut by Michael Wolgemut); Graetz 1853, VII, 258ff.; Liliencron II, 1866, 13–21; Scherer 1901, 596–615, 643–67; Liebe 1903, figs. 12, 13, 15, 21,22; Hind 1838, II, pl.74; IV, pl.133; Friedman 1950, figs.439–41 and alongside 444; *Mon.Jud.Kat* 1953, B 137–6, 302–3; *LThK* IX, 1964, 772; Eckert 1964 (with illustrations): Baron XI, 1967, 148f., 359f.; Eckert 1968, 269f.; *EJ* 1971, II, 97f.; VII, 167; XV, 1122, 1374f.; Kunzle 1973, figs.1–19; Zafran 1973 (passim); Shachar 1974, pl.33; Rosenfeld 1978, fig.p.85; *Reformation in Nürnberg* 1979, fig. p.50; Schubert 1979, fig. 28; Zafran 1979, pl.9; Lohrmann 1982, 77;

Stemberger 1983, fig. p.366; Timmermann 1986, 361–3, 368f.; *Germ.Jud.*III, 1, 1987, 358: Seibt 1987, fig. p.304; Po-Chia Hsia 1988, 43–50 (and fig.8); Dundes 1989; Battenberg I, 1990, 160f.; Esposito and Quaglioni 1990; Hernad 1990, fig. p.214; Schuder and Hirsch 1990, 149–53; Simonsohn III, 1990, 1226–34, 1246f., 1276–8; Eckert 1991, 90f., 379f.; Puppi 1991, pl.71; Rohrbacher and Schmidt 1991, 283–7; Po-Chia Hsia 1992, figs. pp. 128, 134; *Verfasserlexikon* VIII, 1992, 1260–75; Wenzel 1992, fig. p.308; W.P.Eckert, in *Die Macht der Bilder* (exhibition catalogue), Vienna 1995, 86–101.

6a. Assembly of the Jews of Trent in their synagogue. Woodcut in a printing of the 'Complete Story of the Passion and Death of the Boy Simon' by Johannes Matthias Tiberinus, Trent (printer Albert Kunne), 1475–76. Illustration after Liebe 1903, no.21.

6b. The Jews at a meal. Woodcut in a printing of the 'Passion Story' by Tiberinus, Trent (Albert Kunne), 1475–76. Illustration after Liebe 1903, no.22.

6c. Simon of Trent. Woodcut by Michael Wohlgemut in the Chronicle of the World by Hartmann Schedel, Nuremberg (Koberger) 1493, folio CCLIIII verso. Illustration after Liebe 1903, no.115: facsimile after Schedel.

6d. Woodcut in the Trent printing of the passion story of Simon by Albert Kunne. Illustration after Lohrmann 1982, no.53.

Symon das sellig kindlein zu Trient ist am. xxi. tag des Mertzen nach der gepurt Cristi. M.cccc.lxxv. iar. in 8 heiligen marterwochen in der statt Trient von den iuden getödt vnd ein martter Cristi worden. dann als die iuden in derselben statt wonende ir ostern nach irem sytten begeen wolten vnd doch kein cristenlichs plůt zu gepiauch irs vngestwiten piots hetten do biachten sie dijs kindlein verstolens in Samuelis eins iuden haws. in solcher gestalt. an dem dritte tag voi ostern vmb versperzeit saße dijs kindlein voi seins vaters thür in abwe= sen seiner eltern do nehnet sich Thobias ein iüdischer verreter zu disem kindlein das noch nit dieymal zehen mo= nat alt was. dem redet er mit schmaychlenden worte zu vnd trüg es pald in das haws Samuelis. Als nw die nacht herfiele do frewten sich Samuel Thobias Vitalis Moyses Jsrahel vnd Mayer voi der synagog vber vergiessung cristenlichs plůts. Nw entplößeten sie das kindlein vnd legten ime ein faciletlein vmb sein helßlein das man es nit schieyen höien möcht vnd spanneten ime sein ernlein auß. schnytten ime eistlich sein mälich glid lein ab vnd auß seinem rechten wenglein ein stücklein vnd stachen es allenthalben mit scharpffen spitzigen sta= cheln hefflein oder nadeln. einer die hend der ander die füßlein haltende. vnd als sie nw das plůt grawsamlich gesamelt hetten do hůben sie an lobsang zesingen vnd zu dem kindlein mit hönischen bedroeworten zesprechen Nym hin du gehangner Jhesu also haben dir ettwen vnßer eltern gethan. also sollen alle cristen in hymel. auff eiden vnd meer geschend werden. dieweil verschied das vnschuldig mertterlein. die iuden eyleteं zum nachtmal vnd assen von dem plůt das vngesewerte zu schmahe Cristo vnßerm hayland vnd wurffen den tote leichnā in ein fließends wasser nahent bey irem haws vnnd hielten ir ostern mit frewden. Die bekümerten eltern suchten ir verloins kindlein. das funden sie vber diey tag in dem fluß. Als solchs an Johannßen von Salis den edeln burger von Bixien kaiserlicher rechten doctoi vnd deßmals obersten pfleger gelanget do hieß er nach den iude= greiffen vnd sie mit marter anziehen. also das sie nach ordnung ansagten wie sie dise mißtat beganngen hett en. vnd darauff waiden sie mit gepürlicher straff außgetilgt. Als der leichnam auff befelhe Johaßen hinderbachs bischoffs daselbst bestattet waidt do fieng er alßpald an in wunderzaichen zescheinen vnd auß allen cristenlich en gegenten zu dises heilliges kindes grab ein zulawffzewerden. davon dañ dise statt nicht kleine auffung vnnd zunemung empfunden hat. vnd die burger daselbst haben disem leichnam ein schöne kirchen auffgerichtet.

6e. Woodcut in the passion story of J.M.Tiberinus on Simon of Trent (cf. *Verfasserlexikon* VIII, 1992, 1263f.). Illustration after Stemberger 1983, 366 (photograph from Munich, SB).

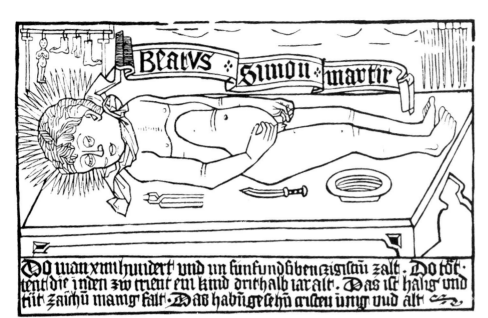

6f. German wood-block print c.1475–1480 (Schreiber 1926, no.1968). Illlustration after Diederichs I, 1908, no.107.

6g. Woodcut in the Trent printing of the passion story of Simon by Albert Kunne (1475–76). Illustration after Diederichs I, 1908, no.133.

6h. Woodcut in an edition in German of the Latin account of the events in Trent by J.M.Tiberinus, the most influential source, Nuremberg [nd], by Friedrich Creussner (active as printer in Nuremberg 1470–1500). Illustration after Schramm 1920, XVIII, no.343.

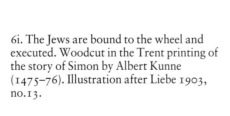

6i. The Jews are bound to the wheel and executed. Woodcut in the Trent printing of the story of Simon by Albert Kunne (1475–76). Illustration after Liebe 1903, no.13.

6j. The Jewish ring (*rota*), which was part of the special form of Jewish dress in the Middle Ages, here has a picture of a pig inside it: this makes a bridge to the sphere of the Christian iconographic polemic which is defined by the 'Judensau' pictures. Engraving made in 1475–1485, probably in Florence. Illustration after Hind 1938, II, pl.74.

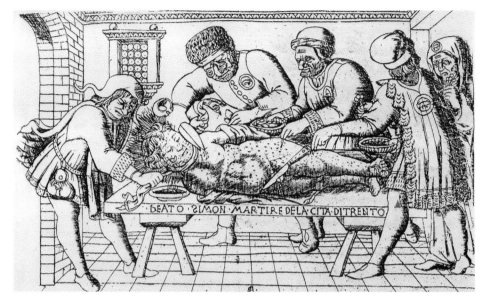

6k. Woodcut in the Nuremberg edition of the passion story in Friedrich Creussner [nd]. Illustration after Schramm 1920, XVIII, no.344.

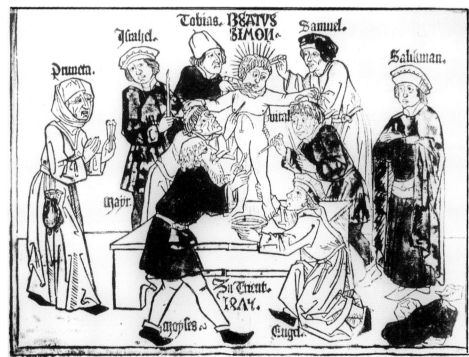

6l. The Jews are taken to the place of execution and tortured with glowing tongs on the way. Woodcut in the Trent printing of the passion story of Simon by Albert Kunne (1475–76). Illustration after Liebe 1903, no.12.

▶ 6m. Beginning and end of the German edition of 'The Story and Legend of the Blessed Child and Martyr Named Simon' (translated from Tiberinus' Latin version), Augsburg (printer: Günther Zainer), c.1476. Illustration after Schramm 1920, II, pl.68, nos. 529–30.

¶ Die geschicht vnd legend von dem sepligen kind vnd matterer genant Symon von den Juden zu Triente gemarterer vnd getödtet võ worē zewor volget hie nach mit figuren vnd brewtnuß diser geschicht

Ohannes Mathias Tiberinus der frepen kunst vnd ertznep ein todtor den Großmechtigen regierrn vnd weplen des volcks tzü Briten Epn groß geschicht deßgleychen von dem leptrn hr vnsers hrn ihesu xp̄i vntz auf die zept hat nge kain alter erhört Schrepb ich euch zu Ir großmechtigen regierer vnd furnäm burger die in nägst vergangen tagen vnser herr ihus xp̄us dem menschlichē geschlecht senftmü tigklichen sich uber dz erbarmet in vil vnd groß grausam misse tat So haben die iuden wider die cristenmenschen krapbsamlichen wider sp zurtr end gethan vnd vol bracht offengewatr das dardurch der criste gelaub ob er ia etwas in einē tail in dem menschn schwach ist werde als ein starcker turen vnd der alt grimmig zorn der iuden auß dem gantzen krapb der cristenmen schen abgetilgt werde vnd von der erden der lebendē ir gedächtnuß gantz vergange Hörend die ir regierend das volck ein vngehörtt ubel vnd wachend in massen als die güten hürten flepßlich über das Es sullen erfaren alle die die wonend auf erdn vnd sch awen wellicherlap vipernatur sp in ier argen schoß ernerend ¶ Die grausamen vnd hörtn iuden nit al lain der cristenmenschē gütter mit wüttende hunger des wüchers verzerend Sunder auch in vnsere herw ter vñ tödtliche schaden haben sp zusamen geschwor dz sp wöllen erneret werdn von dem lebentigen blüt vnser Kinder die sye in iren iudenschülen mit grau samer matter pepnigend vnd gleich in massen des

schwerts lassen richten als ir dan hie inn diser figur wol sehend Damit hatt die legend diß vnschuldige matterers xp̄i Symõs ein ende mit dem Christus der herr allen vnsern kummer hie ab vns wende vñ gebe vns mit disen Säligen matterer dz ewig iebē durch sein bitter mart vñ sterben fur vns alle amen ¶ Geben zü Trient ij nõns april am vierden tag in dem apeill von xp̄i vnsers obengemelte herrn geburte Tausent vierhundert vnd darnach in dem fünffund sibentzigisten Iare.

¶ Gedruckt durch Gintherum Zainer Burger tzü Augspurg ersten außgang diser Translation tzü teutsch.

Warhafftiger bericht von zweyen Juden die zwey Weiber bestelt haben das sie inen ein Christen Kind solten bringen vnd wie die sach offenbar ist worden vnd die Weiber sampt den Juden sind gericht worden in der Stat Litomischel In der Kron Behem gelegen den dreytzehenden Januarij 1574.

7. The case in Leitomischl (Bohemia), January 1574. Single leaf with woodcut. Illustration after Strauss 1975, II, 831.

Sechs Knaben zu Regenspurg von den Juden ermordet.

Waß für ein wüt zu Christen Blut
Köndt euer Herd antreiben,
daß ihr mehr-mal mit höchster quäl
sechs Knaben dürft aufreiben.

Ihr Cainß, und Herodiß Hünd
Gebt ursach ab den Kleinen,
Durch euren haß ohn underlaß,
Der Rachel gnüg zu weinen!

Sechs seelige Knäblein / welche die Juden zu Regenspurg hingerichtet.

EIne Löbliche damahlen noch Christ-Catholische Obrigkeit zu Regenspurg / hat in angezognem Jahr (Joan. Eckius setzet 10. Jahr weniger) 17. Juden / deren damahls in selbiger Stadt ein zimliche Anzahl ware / in Verhafft nemmen lassen / welche auf der Reck-Banck gestanden / daß sie 6. Knäblein von Christlichen Eltern gebohren / und durch das heilige Tauff-Wasser abgewaschen / auß angebohrnen Haß / und auf gewöhnliche grausame Weis umb ihr unschuldiges junges Leben gebracht. Solchen Kinder-Mord / und dessen abscheuliche Unmenschlichkeit haben wir bey dem ersten Knaben gleich oben zu Gnügen beschrieben / wan anderst einige Feder zu Gnügen herfür streichen kan / ab deme auch die wildiste Thier einen Grausen haben wurden. Vor disesmahl hat die besagte Obrigkeit einige abgeschickt / jenes Orth in Augenschein zu nemmen / wo solche Metzgerey so viler unschuldigen Lämmlein / verübet worden. Sie haben dan in dem Hauß eines gewisen Jossel / eine Höhle unter der Erden gefunden und alldorten noch einige Uberbleibsel von sechs (Eckius zehlet acht) erwürgten Knäblein / welche sie samentlich auf das Rath-Hauß gebracht haben. In der Crufft ware ein blatter / runder Stein / auf einen gleicher Materi Fuß gesteiffet / anderthalb Elen brait / auf welchen sie dise unschuldige Opfer zu schlachten pflegten. Diser Stein ware damahls mit allerhand Unrath beschmitzt: als man ihn aber in etwas gesäuberet / hat sich gleich das Blut darauf zu Zeugnus der da verübten Mord-Thatten sehen lassen.

Wan jemand etwan zweiflen solte / und zu wissen begehren / was doch dises verstockte Gesindlein zu solcher Grausamkeit wider so unschuldige Kinderlein / denen die ärgste Feind / ja die wilde Thier oft zu verschonen pflegen / anraitze. Gibt Joan. Eckius an oben angeregter Stell die Antwort / es geschehe darumen / weilen der Juden Weiber / ohne Christen Blut nit gebähren können. Also solches sein frisch in Menge zu haben / stehlen sie entweder selber junge Christen-Knaben / oder bestellen alte Vetteln / oder andere Unmenschen / denen umb ein kleines Geldlein zu erhaschen / kein Unthat zu groß und abscheulich ist / welche ihnen dergleichen Kinder zubringen / denen sie hernach die Adern öffnen / mit Zangen zerreissen / an ein Creutz naglen / oder unter eine Preß legen / selbigen alles Blut auß den Adern herauß trucken / ja alle Grausambkeit an ihnen verüben. Auf die Frag / wie dan die Juden-Weiber unter Heyden/ Türcken/ Abgötter in allerley End der Welt gebähren / gibt bemelter Author die Antwort / andere unter den Christen wohnende Juden / lassen das Blut der Christen / so sie zu Handen gebracht / dörren / in kleines Pulver verreiben / und also schicken sie es denen / welche sonst unter ihnen dergleichen Blut nit haben können. Wir lassen dise Meinung in jenem Werth / den sie ohne uns hat.

Sonsten ist auch in besagter Juden-Crufft eine Müntz-Werckstatt gefunden worden / in welcher sie nit gelaugnet falsche Müntz geschlagen zu haben. Sie haben auch an der Folter bekant / daß sie Lauff-und Schöpff-Brunen vergifftet / daß widerum wohl nit zu bewundern / daß sie an so vilen Orthen der Christenheit nit mehr geduldet werden: mehr aber zu bewundern / daß sie noch an einigen sicher und unverhindert zu bleiben haben: welches Zweifels ohne der Göttlichen Vorsichtigkeit zuzuschreiben / welche dises in die gantze Welt verstreute Völcklein Zeugnus geben laßt / deß von ihren Vor-Eltern verübten GOttes-Mord / welchen sie lang büssen / bis zu End der Welt aber nicht abbüssen werden.

8. Trial for ritual murder in Regensburg (1476–1480), following the charge of ritual murder in Trent (1475). Attributions of blame in Trent and the finding of six children's corpses in Regensburg led to proceedings against the Jewish community there. After a trial lasting several years the emperor Frederick III was finally able to persuade the city of Regensburg to drop the unfounded charge and to release the imprisoned Jews. Literature: Zafran 1973, I, 103f.; Deneke 1988, 185; Po-Chia Hsia 1988, 66–85; Schuder and Hirsch 1990, 232–50; Eder 1992, 104–6. Illustration after Stock 1939, 115 pl.12 (taken over with the facsimile from Rassler 1714, 327–30); cf. *Germ.Jud.* III, 2, 1200).

9. The case in Benzhausen/Waldkirch (north-west or north-east of Freiburg im Breisgau), 1604. On Good Friday the body of a boy, Matthew Bader, was found in a field near Benzhausen by the young shepherd Andreas, a friend of the dead boy. Andreas raised the alarm in the village (see the first picture). In the course of the investigation by the village judge Philipp Bader, the father of the dead boy, came under suspicion and finally confessed. Jews from Waldkirch had offered him money for a Christian boy to draw blood from him – evidently without the intention of killing him. The village judge first involved in the matter and the Freiburg magistrate passed the case over to the judge within whose competence it fell (Konrad Stützel, who lived in Buchheim; cf. the second picture: he is a worldly man, endowed with the symbols of his power; in the background of the picture the Jews are polemically depicted as devil-worshippers). On 30 May 1504 Bader was executed as the guilty person, although he had made contradictory statements. The Jews of Waldkirch, who had been accused and meanwhile arrested, constantly asserted their innocence and were finally freed at the end of October 1505 – above all because the emperor Maximilian I interceded for them. The illustrations appeared in the contemporary poem *Ein seltzam kouffmanschatz wie ein man sein leiplich kind nüwlich den Juden verkaufft hatt und das kind zu tod gemartet worden ist* ('A strange story of how a man recently sold his own child to the Jews and the child was tortured to death', anonymous, no place and date; perhaps written by the Franciscan Thomas Murner). Literature: Po-Chia Hsia 1988, 86–110; W.Treue, *Aschkenas* 2, 1992, 96, 105f. Illustration after photographs in the city archive of Freiburg; cf. *Germ.Jud*.III, 1, 397.

Am tag der himelfart Christi im thausent funffhundert vñ neune
undzwenßigsten jar/ist zu Pösing/ein Marckt in Hungarn/so
den wolgebornen Herrn/herrn Franßen vnd.Wolffgang gebrüe-
dern/Graffen zu S.Jörgen vnd Pösing zc. zugehörig/ein kneb-
lein mit namen Hänßel / im neunden jar seines alders / verloren
worden/welches Gregor Meylingers/eines mitwoners doselbst/
kind gewesen.Vnd so aber durch vleissig suchen der Burger vñ
einwoner doselbst/das knäblein vnter den Jüden / so da wonhafft gewesen/gesucht/auch sunst an vil andern orrten vnd enden
nachgefragt/auff ettliche tage verloren bliben.Welches knäblein
widerumb am mitwoch nach der himelfart Christi zwischen sie-
ben vnd acht vren/vor mittag/außerhalb bestimpts Marckts/in
einer dicken dornhecken/mit gebunden hendlein/in einem hembd-
lein/auff sein angesicht ligend/durch Göttlich schickung/ein ald
weib on gefar gefunden.Welchs sie dem Gericht vñ Marckteme-
nig doselbst fürgebracht/vnd angezeigt.Dorauff solch kind/gen
Pösing inn Marckt/in seines Vattern haws/tode / mit vil wun-
den/stichen vnd schlegen/getragen worden.Darein die geschwor-
nen Burger vñ Gemaind doselbst ernstlich gesehen/dorauff weiß-
lich gehandelt/vnd von stund die ganß jüdischeit/jung vnd alt/
so darzumal doselbst wonhafft gewesen/berzüchtigt/vnd gefenck-
lich (von wegen des kinds) angenomen / Behalten vnd Bewart.
Dornach am Donstag/den achten tag vorschinen/wie solchs Be-
schehen/die obgemelten wolgebornen Herrn/herrn Franßen vñ
Wolffgangen gebrüeder/Grauen zc. Die zwo Freystet in Hun-
garn/ nemlich Bießburg vnd Tierna / Auch daneben die zween
Marckt Worldperg vnd Moder/ersucht/begert / vnd erfordert/
als das begangen vbel vnd mord/so an dem knäblen beschehen/
Besichtigen vnd schawen/vnd wo das von nöten sein würd/dar-
umb zeugnus zugeben.Hierüber aus bemelten zweyen Freysteten
aus yeder Stadt sonderlich zween Radtsgeschworne / Nemlich
von Preßburg Merten Semler / vnd Sigmund Goldner . Von
Tierna Endres Höffelmair/vnd Hans Koschub.Dergleichen vö
den vorgedachten Marckten/nemlich von Worldperg zween ge-
schworne

Left panel (facsimile pamphlet)

Ein erschrockenlich geschicht vnd Mordt / so von den Juden zu
pösing (ein Marckt in Hungarn gelegen) an einem
Neunjärigen Knäblein begangen/ wie sie das iämer-
lich gemartert/geschlagen / gestochen / geschnitten vnd
ermordt haben. Darumb dann biß in die dreissigk Jü-
den/Mann vnd Weibs personen / vmb yhr mißhand-
lung / auff Freitag nach Pfingsten / den.xxi.tag May /
des.M.D.vnd.xxix.jars/verprennt worden seind.

Form vnd gestalt eines Messers
damit sie das Kind gemartert haben.

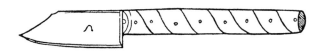

Captions

10. The case in Pöwing (Hungary) in 1529. The most important
contemporary testimony is a pamphlet reproduced here as a reduced
facsimile (with a frontispiece woodcut: a knife of the type used in the
crime), consisting of four folios (now in Munich, B, Sammelband Jus
4937, classification: a⁴). It reports *cum ira et studio*, but nevertheless
is of high documentary value as a typical example of a ritual murder
trial because it was composed on the basis of the court records and
involuntarily shows the vicious circle in the proceedings.

On Ascension Day a nine-year-old boy (Hänsel, son of Gregory
Meylinger) went missing. After some days his mutilated body was
found in a state which seemed to show the signs of the kind of Jewish
ritual murder often attributed to the Jews (four stab wounds, the
veins partly opened, the penis cut off). Thereupon the Counts of St
George and Pösing (the brothers Franz and Wolfgang), one of whom
was in debt to the Jew Esslein Ausch from Pösing and to Jews from
Marchegg (in Lower Austria), had all the Jews in Pösing and around

schwozne als Mertein Behem/vnd Nicolasch schusser.Vnd von Moder/Wolffgang schneider/Ambzosius Mayr/vnd Wolffgang hautzinger/auff ersuchen merbemelter zweyer Herren vnd Grauen ꝛc.zu Pösing erschinen seind/doselbst yhnen das knäblein fürgetragen wozden ist/welchs sie nottürfftiglich besichtiget vnd beschawet/an allem seinem leib vil stich/wunden vñ schlege befunden vnd gesehen/als auff seinen hendlein alle seine äderlein abgestochen/deßgleichen auff seinen füeßlein vnd gantzem leib/die adern zerschnitten vnd zerstochen/vnd sein mennlich glydlein abgeschnitten/dergleichen seine hödlein heraus geschnitten/sein halß vnd gnick zerstochen/sein hewpt gar zerschlagen/das alles am höchsten zuerbarmen gewesen. Nach solcher beschaw des kindes/Sie/die vozgemelten Steth e vnd Merckte/nicht anders vozmercken noch erkennen haben mögen/dañ für jüdische arbeit vnd von den jüden beschehen vnd verbzacht sein.Vber solches/die verdachten/Betzichten/vnd gefangen jüden/von stund an wie sichs gepürt/notürffciglich/mit strenger frag/samptlich angetzogen wozden seind/Sie/die jüden selbenmals/an strenger frag/all in sonders durchaus/der missethat vnd mozds/noch anderer sachen/nichts Bekent haben.Alßdann vber solches die zwo Stett vnd zween Merckt widerumb/zum andern mal/auff Begeer vnd erfozdern egemelter Herrn vnd Grauen von S.Józgen vnd pösing etc.erschinen/da denn abermals die gantz Betzicht jüdischeit mit ernstlicher vnd strenger frag fürgewendt/vñ gefragt wozden. Haben sie all einhellig Bekent vnd veriehen/in massen vñ gestalt wie hernach folgt/vnd Begriffen ist.

Item nach hierabuermerckten vnd vornomen vigichten Bemelter jüden/sein sie am freitag nach pfingsten/Anno vt supza/zu Pösing für recht gefurt vnd gestellt wozden/ßo dann offige dachter zweyer Herrn vñ Grauen etc.yhrer genaden zweyer Merckt/von S. Józgen vnd Pösing/die geschwoznen Richter vnd Burger zu Recht gesessen/an offnen platz/da auch neben zugesessen/obbemelt zwo Freystet/vnd der zweyer Märckt verozdent

a ij   geschwoz

geschwozne leuthe/als das zu einem getzeugnus/vnd sunst auch vil ander Erbar leuthe/ßo vmbstendig/als von der Neissa/Ölmitz/Wienn/vnd aus andern Stetten/Merckten/Dözffern/Biß in die ettlich thausent menschen/vnd hierüber in offem Rechten ir vigicht vozlesen wozden ist.Vnd nach vozleßner vigicht/durch den Richter die jüdischeit gefragt wozden ist/Ob dem also sey/wie sie Bekennt/vnd die vigicht außweist/Des die jüdischeit also mit einhelliger stimme/voz dem Rechten/vñ voz aller meniglichen vmbstender geschzey/vnd gesagt/Dem sey also/wie dann die veriehung innhelt.Darauff recht vnd vzteil gefellt/gangen vnd gesprochen/Mit dem fewer die gantz jüdischeit/ßo daselbst/jung vnd alt/zuuertilgen etc.Doch nach ergangem vzteil/haben die vil gedachten Wolgeboznen Herrn vnd Grauen von Sanct Józgen vnd Pösing etc.die jungen jüdischen kinder/ßo vnter acht vnd zehen jarn alt/Begnadt.Welche kinder/die Christen zu sich genommen/außgeteilt/vnd getaufft.Aber die alten jüden/Mann/weib knaben/medelein/Biß in die dreissig/hinaus für den Marckht zu Pösing/auff einen weytten platz gefurt wozden/auff ein fewer gesetzt/vnd zu puluer verpzennt.

Der Juden bekentnus.

Im Thausentfunffhundert vñ neunvndzwentzigistem jar am Dinstagabent/inn Pfingstfeyertagen/hat Duid/ein Jüd/Graff Wolffgangen zu Pösing/an strenger frag Bekant/wie er am freytag nach der Himelfart Christi/in die Synagog der Jüden/daselbst zu Pösing/komen/sey da auff dem tisch in der Sinagog/geschziben gestanden/Es hab ein man ein kind/wo er es mit yhn wöll halten/soll er es zuuersteen geben. Mit dergleichen wozten seind sie an yhn komen.Hat er geantwort/Ich bin nicht daheym gewesen/vnd will mit dißen sachen nichts zuschaffen haben.Aber ich hab wol vozstanden das sie solchs gethan haben.Item im gefengknüs/auch außerhalb ee sie gefangen wozden/sein an yhn kõmen die jüden Samuel vñ Dauid saiffenmacher/auch der Michel jüd/haben an yhn Begert vñ gesagt/Lieber Dauid du hözest das

geschzey

---

arrested and tortured until they made the desired confessions, and then had around thirty men and women executed. The Count of Pösing pardoned the children 'below eight and ten years' and distributed them among Christian families where they were baptized. The adult Jews were 'put on a fire and burned to powder' on the Friday after Pentecost, 21 May 1529. A charge against the Jews of Marchegg who were similarly accused in this connection came to nothing because the Jews of Vienna successfully made representations to King Ferdinand of Hungary and Bohemia, Archduke of

Austria (by pointing out the great debt owed by Count Wolfgang and the fact that Esslein Ausch's statements had been extracted by torture).

The principal defendants in the Posen show trial, which drew 'several thousand people', were the Jews Samuel, David Saiffenmacher and Michel, in whose house the group murder of the child was alleged to have taken place. The torture led to contradictory statements. Thus Jacob Schwertfeger named only his three fellow-Jews as perpetrators, whereas these also incriminated all the other

geschrey/so vnter den Christen ist/des kinds halbe/man lest vns aus der verdacht nicht/Wir bitten dich/dieweil du so ein gnedigen herrn an Graff Wolffen hast/handel doch mit sein gnaden/das man das alt weib/die das kind gefunden hat/auch des Wagners knecht/des solch kind seines meisters gewest ist/annehme/vñ mit yhn so streng handel/ob sie sich durch die martter zu solcher that bekenten/so würden wir erledigt. Vnd soltestu gleich seinen gnaden dreissigk/vierzigk/adder hundert gülden zugeben zusagen. Sölchs hat obbemelter Dauid den gedachten jüden vnter yhre augen gesagt/auch auff sein letze hinfart genomen vnd dorauff gestorben als ein fromer jüd/das sie solchs (wie hieroben vornohmen) gethan haben.

Item an dem abent/hat bekent Jacob Schwerdtfeger/jüd/an strenger frag/wie er dieselbig zeit/do das kind verloren ist worden/nicht anhaim gewest/des er sich an die Jüden vñ Christen laß. Aber am Freitag nach der Himelfart Christi/haben sich die Jüden all vorsamelt in die Sinagog/yhn vnd Jacob jüden/des Kolmans bruder/aus der Synagog/zu zweyen malen getrieben/also sey er wider an sein arbeit gegangen. Vnd so er doheim in des Dauid Jüden hauß gearbeit hat/ist zu yhm gemelter Jacob komen/vnd sich hintter die thür auff ein tägken gelegt/sprechende/Lieber gesell/schaw was haben die Jüden angefangen/Do hat er yhn wider gefragt/Lieber was ist geschehen. Antwort yhm obgedachter Jacob/sprechend/Des Kolmans bruder/Samuel/vñ Dauid saiffenmacher/habe das kind getödt in des Michel jüden hauß/im keller. Aber am selben freitag hat man das verloren kind gesucht/do sein yetzgemelt zween jüden bey einander gelegen/hat Jacob des Colmans bruder/an den Schwerdtfeger jüden begert/Lieber gesell/die sach sicht mich nicht wol an/wir wöllen vns daruon machen. Hat yhm Schwerdtfeger jüd geantwort. Ich bin der sach vnschuldig/ich hab ein gnedigen herrn/ich ways niergent hin zufliehen. Weytter hat er auch bekent/der selbig Schwerdtfeger jüd/dieweil alle Jüden in dem gefengknus

a iij   Bey

Bey dem Michel Schneider/yhrem jüdenrichter gelegen seind/das sich jetzbemelter Samuel/Dauid saiffenmacher/vñ Michel Jüd/vor allen andern jüden haben lassen hören/Lieben Brüder/wir wissen/das wir die ersten drey müssen sein/an die martter/wir wöllen vns lassen reissen vnd reckhen/vnd nichts bekennen/damit werdt yhr all ledig. Dorauff haben sie sich all zusamen verpunden/vnd geschworn/das keiner auff den andern nichts sagen vnd bekennen soll. Alle hierüber bekentnús/des Jacob schwerdtfegers jüden/hat er auff sein letze hinfart genomen.

Item Mitwochen nach Pfingsten/hat zu Sanct Jörgen jm Schloß/der Jacob/des Colmans bruder/an seiner strengen frag nichts wöllen bekennen/allein das er gesagt hat/er sey kein jüd von Pösing/er were des willens gewesen heimzuziehen zu seinem weib vnd kindern.

Item Dauid Saiffenmacher/Jüd/hat erstlich bekannt/an strenger frag/wie der Michel jüd/das kind in sein haws gepracht hab/das er yhn/vnd den Samuel/auch all ander Jüden darzu erfordert/vnd das kind haben sie all in des Michel jüden keller gemartert/das blut von dem kind also bey dem Michel jüden gelassen. Weytter hat bemelter Saiffenmacher bekannt/wie den nehsten Grünen donrstag vier jar vergangen/weyl er noch zu Tierna wonhafft gewesen/yhm/bey nechtlicher weyl/ein todter gemarterter Christ/auff seinn wagen/on willen vñ wissen gelegt/vnd mit mist verdeckt gewesen. Zu morgens haben yhm die jüden/Schlammen vñ Colman beuolhen/er soll den mist auß füeren/das hab er gethan/aber yhm sey vnwissend gewesen das der todt Cörper ader leichnam darinn gelegen sey. Vñ so er aber den Cörper im abladen des mists gefunden/ist er erschrocken/vñ alßbald er in die Stat ist komen/hat der klein Veitl jüd võ Tierna gesagt/wie denselben tag/der Isaac jüd/Sogedi genant/zu zweyen tischen jüden in seinem hauß zu gast gehabt/mit geschrey Daselbst im keller seines hauß/der Christ gemartert worden ist.

Item

Jews and said that part of the blood which had been drawn off had remained in Pösing, and part had been sent elsewhere, There was agreement only over the hiding-place of the body, a thorn hedge, evidently because this place was known *a priori*.

The recto of the first page (a picture of the implement used and a brief headline-type report in telegraphic style) indicates that this was a 'mass media' pamphlet intended to have a wide circulation. Its author was presumably convinced of the truth of his account, according to which the Jews are people who 'martyr' Christian children, as a means of symbolically mocking and paining Christ – from the twelfth century on a commonplace in legends of ritual murder.

The pamphlet is full of detail; thus among other things it reports correct legal procedures and the immediate call for sworn councillors mentioned by name (two each from Pressburg, Tyrnau, Wordperg and Moder), who were to act as assessors or witnesses. But it is silent, for example, about the large debt owed by Count Wolfgang – known from another source – who thus had a motive for doing away

Item am Donrstag dornach/hat auch bemelter Dauidj jüd/ an der gestrengen frag bekant/vnd gesagt/Wenn sie das kind gestochen/haben sie solchs blut mit federkülen vnd rhor aus dem kinde gesogen.

Item am Mitwochen hat weytter bekant an strenger frag/ der Michel Jüd/wie er am tag der himelfart Christi/das kind in sein hawß gelockt hab/alßdenn solch kind verhalten/dem Samuel/vnd Dauid Saiffenmacher/auch allen andern Jüden zu kundt gethan/haben sie dasselbig kind all miteinander gemartert vnd hab yhm Michel jüd den ersten schlag mit einer hacken an das haupt gegeben.Vnd alßdann hat yeder jüd das kind ein weil gestochen/vnd ein weil gehalten.Das blut hat Michel jüd behalten.Nachmals hab er das todt kind in einem Stall verhalten vñ mit rhor bedeckt.Vnd am dinstag zu nacht/mit gebunden hendlein/hinaus/hinder der Haffner gassen/in ein dornhecken/dobey ettlich Nußboum stehen/tragen/vnd gelegt/ da zum teyl ettlich jüden auff der schgart gestanden seind/ vnd das blut dornach in die Synagog getragen/darab sie ein groß frolocken gehabt. Auch hat er bekent/wie Jacob/des Tschecho jüden Sohn/aus beuelh aller jüden/das blut gen Marcheckh gefüert/dem schilhenden Löbla vnd Nästl zuuberantworten.

Item Jacob/des Tschecho jüden Sohn/hat bekent/er hab aus befelh aller Jüden/das blut dem schilhenden Löbla Jüden/ vberantwurtet.hab yhm Löbla jüd/ein gülden zuuertrincken geben. Er bekent auch/das er bey der martter des kinds gewesen/vnd das kind hinaus in dornstauden helffen thun. Auch gesagt/das ettlich jüden auff der schgardt gestanden sein.

Item am Mitwochen hat der jüden Meßner/Ysaac genant bekent/das er dapey gewesen/vnd das kind helffen marttern.Vñ yhm sey auch wissend/das dem Jacob jüden/des Tschecho son/ aus beuelh der jüden/des kinds blut/beuolhen sey worden/gen March

Marcheckh zufüren.Vñ zeigt an/das die Jüden der Christen blut müessen haben/denn damit bestreichen die Tempelherren yhre finger/zu yhren hochzeitlichen tagen.

Item am Mitwoch mehr hat Samuel jüd/den man sunst Schmölderl heyst/an der strengen frag bekant/er hab auch das kind helffen marttern/sampt andern jüden.Zeigt an/das die Jüden müessen Christenblut haben/damit bestreichen die fürnembsten Jüden/in Ebreisch Colman/die da segen sprechen/Auch Peischa genant.

Item Wölfl Jüd/Pfora genant/bekent/wie yhm die Jüden den mord vnd todt des kindes angezeigt haben/des hab er sich hoch beschwärt vñ bekömert/sprechende/Yr habt nicht wol gehandelt.Dorauff yhm die Jüden geantwort/Es sey geschehen dürff sich nicht bekömern.Ober solchs ist er heym gangen/zum Tisch nidergesessen/den ganzen tag gewaint.

Item Wölfl jüd/der Trostler orden/bekennt an strenger frag/das er dem kind einn stich in das genick hab gegeben. Vnd sagt auch/wie die Jüden sampthlich desselbigen kinds blut/einem Jüden/mit namen Ysaac/von der Freystat (bey Tierna ligend) mitgeteilt haben/do er am zug heraus aus Merhern gewest/das er solchs blut mit yhm gen Tierna füeren wöll.

Item Leiphart jüd/hat bekant an strenger frag/das er bey des kinds tod vnd martter nicht gewest ist/aber yhm sey gut wissend/das die Jüden solchs gethan haben.

Item Tschech Jacob/jüd/hat bekent vñ gesagt an strenger frag/das er bey des kinds tod nicht gewesen ist. Aber trag des gutt wissen/das solchs von den Jüden geschehen sey.

¶ Lob vnd Ehre sey Gott in der höhe.

with his Jewish creditors. On the other hand it reports as true a fantasy statement made under torture, that the Jews had sucked the blood from the Christian boy whom they had tortured with 'quills and reeds' – a legendary element which the Jewish artist Lilien treats ironically at the beginning of the twentieth century (see below).

Around 1529/1530 the well known Nuremberg reformer Andreas Osiander, beginning from the Pösing case, composed a fundamental refutation of the anti–Jewish assertions of ritual murder. This work (in the form of a legal opinion), which appeared in print in 1540, provoked a very polemical response from the well-known Catholic theologian Johannes Eck (died 1543), who extensively supports, develops and promotes the charge of blood-guilt. Literature: Zafran 1973, I, 97f.; Andreas Osiander der Ältere, *Gesamtausgabe*, Vol.7, ed. G.Müller and G.Seebass, Gütersloh 1988 (216–48: opinion on the accusation of blood guilt, ed. K.Keyser); Hägler 1992, 9–23; J.F.Battenberg in Erb 1993, 95–100. Illustration and facsimile after Stock 1939, 125–32.

11. Murder of a Christian boy in Diessenhofen (near Schaffhausen, Switzerland) in 1401. The picture shows, synoptically, below right, the servant (Zan or Zon) of the mayor of Diessenhofen, who is being given three florins by the Jew Michel for procuring a Christian boy; below centre is the murder (some of the perpetrators have Jewish rings on their hats). Above are examples of the punishment: the wheel for Zan and the burning of the Jews. 'Thirty Jews, man, woman and child' were burned in Swabia, and 231 in Winterthur. Miniature in the Lucerne Chronicle of Diebold Schilling who, with the painter Hans von Arx, also painted the miniatures, in 1513. Lucerne, Zentralbibliothek, Cod.S.23 fol., folio 22 recto. Literature: Zafran 1973, I, 91f.; W.Treue, *Aschkenas* 2, 1992, 98f. Illustration after Schmid 1981 (facsimile edition), folio 22 recto; cf. *Germ.Jud.* III, 1, 230.

12. In 1429 in Ravensburg (not 1422 in Augsburg, as Schilling reports), the Jews murdered a boy, Ludwig Etterli (from Brugg in the Aargau). They hanged him on a tree, making it look as if he had committed suicide. Miracles happened in conjunction with this. The Jewish perpetrators were burned, and other Jews in the region were also called to account (a general or collective arrest of Jews as a group). The synoptic depiction shows: above right the dead Christian boy; in front of him and below him three Jews (in Jewish dress with Jewish rings and pseudo-Hebrew letters on the hems of their garments); in the foreground, left, the burning of the miscreants, fettered (three chained together at the neck and the waist) and immediately recognizable as Jews by their special garb (hat and ring). An executioner is stoking the fire and a minion with a sword is standing in a group of onlookers (official persons?), two of whom are holding their foreheads in dismay (?). Miniature in the Lucerne Chronicle of Diebold Schilling, 1513. Lucerne, Zentralbibliothek, Cod.S.23 fol., folio 36 recto. Literature: Fehr 1923, fig.110; Zafran 1973, I, 52f.,91f.. Illustration after Schmid 1981 (facsimile edition), folio 36 recto; cf. *Germ.Jud.*III, 2, 1174.

13. Murder of Andreas (Anderl) Oxner of Rinn (died 12 July 1462). See *Freiburger Rundbrief*, XII Folge, 1959–60, 66: 'in the foreground right, immediately beside the steps up to the pulpit, is a giant stone block surrounded by a screen. On this, some colourfully painted figures, almost life-size, depict quite realistically the slaughter of little Andreas. One Jew has raised a knife and another is grinningly preparing a noose. With greedy eyes a third is falling on the innocent little boy with a slaughtering knife, while the fourth Jew is holding a vessel to receive the blood in a container. (As we know, the rumour was spread among the people that the Jews needed the blood of Christian children for ritual purposes; they were accused of "ritual murder".) Further light on the macabre proceedings is shed by a large picture on the left wall of the nave. A series of thirty pictures with accompanying text tells of "St Anderl", as he was known throughout the Tyrol. The Jews spy out Andreas. They get the guardian of the child on their side. The widow (his mother) goes to cut corn and entrusts the child to his guardian. The guardian is given a hat full of money by the Jews. The guardian hands over the innocent little boy to the Jews. They entice him into a wood. They stretch him out and put him on a large stone. They lance his veins and catch the blood. They cut his throat and take all

the blood from him. They hang the dead child on a birch tree. They flee, taking the blood with them. The following pictures depict the mother's search for her child, the discovery, the solemn burial, and some miracles. The twenty-fifth picture shows the guardian lying in chains. He has gone mad.' Literature: *Ars Sanctorum*, July III, 1728, 462–70; Scherer 1901, 592–6; *LThK* I, 1957, 519; *Freiburger Rundbrief*, XII.

Folge, 1959–60, 66; XXXVII–XXXVIII. Folge, 1985–6, 87–9; Kirschbaum V, 1973, 158; Zafran 1973, I, 104–9; Andies 1988, fig. p.181; Erb-Lichtblau 1989–90; Schuder and Hirsch 1990, 154–9; Eckert 1991, 380f.; Ginzel 1991, 18; Rohrbacher and Schmidt 1991, 286f. Illustration after Körber and Pugel 1935, 83.

14. Ironic replica by the Jewish engraver Ephraim Moses Lilien (pseudonym: his name was Lipaciewiez) on the alleged ritual murder in Kichinev (north-west of Odessa) in 1903: Jews are sucking the blood from a Christian child. Literature: *EJ* 1971, X, 1064f.; Heyd 1980, 65, fig.14; for Lilien cf. Deneke 1988, 408; Künzl 1988; Gelber and Finkelstein 1990. Illustration after Fuchs 1921, no.226.

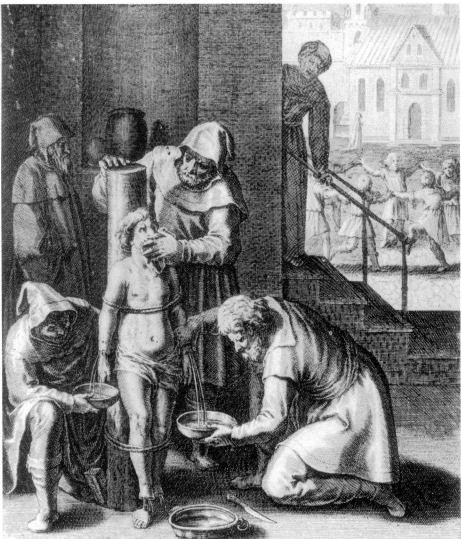

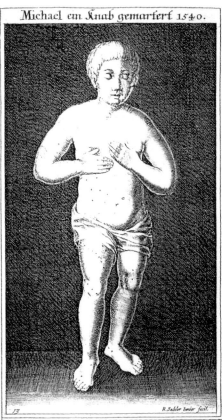

Michael ein Knab gemartert 1540.

15. The Sappenfeld case, 1540. On Passion Sunday, two weeks before Easter 1540, a four-and-a-half-year-old boy, Michael, son of Georg Pisenharter (Bisenharter), got lost in Sappenfeld (near Eichstätt in Bavaria). By chance he was found dead by a shepherd on the Friday after Easter: there were wounds all over his body and his foreskin had been cut off. Suspicion for the act fell on the Jews, and an investigation was held; however, this showed that the Jews had been wrongly accused. Two works were written in connection with the Sappenfeld case, a pro-Jewish treatment by the Nuremberg Reformer Andreas Osiander (probably already composed in 1529/30 in connection with a ritual murder alleged to have taken place in Pösing, Hungary in 1529: this work was used in their own defence by the Jews under suspicion in Sappenfeld) and a response by the Catholic theologian Johannes Eck (*Ains Judenbüechlins verlegung* [it appeared around 1540 with no indication of place or date]). Here are three illustrations. The first is after Stock 1939, p.121, pl.13 (the boy, standing, is having blood drawn off him into dishes by three Jews: in Stock taken from Rasseler 1714 [= German translation of Rader 1615ff.]). The second is after Po-Chia Hsia 1988, p.60 fig.7 (a single Jew with a knife is drawing blood from the boy [= frontispiece woodcut from the anonymous anti–Jewish poem 'Ein hübsch new lied....', Ingolstadt: Alexander Weissenhorn, 1521, which was composed shortly after the events in Sappenfeld, photograph by permission of BL]). The third is after Stock 1939, 122 pl.14 (from Rassler, engraving by R.Sadeler, 'Shape and size of the body, etc.'). Literature: Stock 1939, 51–107 (esp. 71f.); Zafran 1973, I, 98f.: Po-Chia Hsia 1988, 125–31; Andreas Osiander der Ältere, *Gesamtaufgabe*, Vol.7, ed. C.Müller and C.Seebass, Gütersloh 1988 (216–48: opinion on charges relating to blood, ed. K.Keyser); Raddatz 1991, 177; Rohrbacher and Schmidt 1991, 302.

16. The case in Mies (Stříbro, west of Plsen, in Bohemia), 1675. Contemporary engraving with nine scenes. Above centre: the Jews attempt to abduct a Christian child in the absence of his mother, but are prevented by a woman passer-by. Above left: the Jews bribe a woman to bring them another child. Above right: the child is killed by having his throat cut. Centre left: the body is thrown in a river. Centre: the abduction of the child becomes known. Centre right: the Jews want to exonerate themselves by pointing to another child. Below left: the decapitated head of the first child is discovered. Below centre: an eye-witness appears and confirms the crime of the Jews. Below right: the Jews are arrested. Literature: Kunzle 1973, 181, nos.6–32. Illustration after Diedrichs 1908, II, no.1220.

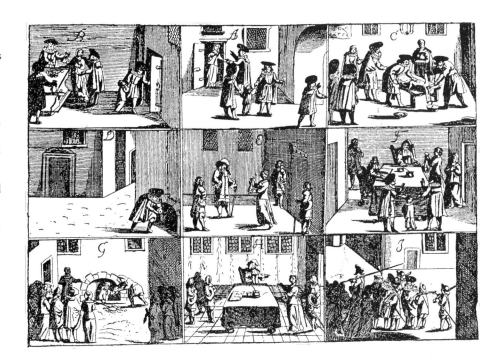

7. The Eternal Jew (Ahasuerus, The Wandering Jew)

1. Christ and Cartaphilus. According to the legend, when Jesus was being dragged to the cross by the Jews, Cartaphilus passed by him, hit him and told him to go more quickly. Thereupon Jesus said to him, 'I am going, and you shall wait until I return'. Cartaphilus became a Christian, was baptized in the name of Jesus, and by returning to his then age of thirty every hundred years kept living as a pious witness to the passion of Christ, hoping for his redemption at the end of the world. In this early stage of the legend Cartaphilus is not yet described as a Jew, but this is doubtless the nucleus of the legend of the Eternal Jew (Ahasuerus). Miniature in the *Chronica maior* of the English Benedictine Matthew Paris (died c.1259) from the hand of the author. Cambridge, Corpus Christi College, Ms.16, folio 70 verso. Literature: Lewis 1986, fig.1; van Run 1987, fig.6. Illustration after Lewis 1987, 301 fig. 188; M.Körte, *Jahrbuch für Antisemitismus Forschung* 4, 1995, 39–62; M.Tilly, *Zeitschrift für Religions- und Geistesgeschichte* 47, 1995, 289–303.

2. Woodcut, Paris 1616. The Eternal Jew is wearing the Jewish ring on his cloak as a sign of his Jewishness. Illustration after Adhémar 1968, pl.2.

Comme le Iuif errant rencontra deux Gentilhommes françois ces iours paffez au pres Chaalons.

Comme vn Iuiftenant fon fils repouffa Iefus-Chrift, qui fe vouloit repofer deuant fa porte & fut faict errant.

3. This French woodcut (c.1770–1800) shows, above left, the workshop of the Eternal Jew – one version of the legend makes him a cobbler who did not let Jesus, laden with the cross, rest at his house as he passed by – and below it Jesus on the way to the mount of Calvary. At the bottom of the picture is the eternally wandering Ahasuerus. Literature: Adhémar 1968, fig. p.12 and pl.3; Hasan-Rokem 1985, fig. p.71. Illustration after Champfleury 1869, frontispiece.

4. Flemish picture (before 1865). Illustration after Champfleury 1869, 62.

5. The Eternal Jew with a Jewish ring. German picture, 1602. Illustration after Champfleury 1869, 49.

6. Picture from Jonköping, Sweden, 1833/1857. Literature: Hasan-Rokem and A.Dundes 1986, 168. Illustration after Champfleury 1869, 60.

7. Picture by Desfeuilles, Nancy (before 1869). Illustration after Champfleury 1869, 97.

8. French engraving from Metz (c.1830?). Illustration after Champfleury 1869, 37.

9. French picture from Épinal (before 1869). Illustration after Champfleury 1869, 169.

10 .Title picture of a *Légende du Juif-Errant*, southern France [nd (before 1869)]. Illustration after Champfleury 1869, 7.

11. a–d *La Légende du Juif errant.* 12 compositions by Gustave Doré (illustrations for the poem by Pierre Dupont), Paris: Michel Lévy 1856. This cycle by the French illustrator and painter Gustave Doré made a deep impression in its time as a significant depiction of the beloved legendary material. Literature: Fuchs 1921, plates after pp.144,152; Becker 1964, pl.9; *EJ* 1971, V, 173, fig.1; Mellinkoff 1981, pls.5–6; Cooper 1986, fig. p.208; van Run 1987. The four illustrations chosen here are after Forberg 1975, 118–61. 1. Poster announcing the appearance of the book (the Eternal Jew is going through a dark forest, as though hunted by terrifying manifestations

of the Christian faith); 2. = no.1 of the cycle = Forberg, 150 (the Eternal Jew, a cobbler in Jerusalem, shows no compassion for Jesus); 3. = no.11 of the cycle = Forberg, 151 (the eternal Jew, a bearded old man, holding a money-bag as an attribute of his Jewishness, is

going bowed but unswervingly past a crucifixion on his route); 4 = no. XII of the cycle = Forberg, 161 (the redemption of the Eternal Jew at the end of days).

12. Seventeenth-century French picture (Musée de Caen): the Eternal Jew (with a Jewish ring) survives even the greatest danger to his life, because he has to continue wandering until the Last Day. Illustration after Champfleury 1869, 67.

13. Woodcut (after 1870, from an earlier print [Epinal: Pellerin, c.1830]). The Eternal Jew is forced to wander without looking at the landscape, his gaze directed as it were to a distant goal. The name Ahasuerus is derived from the name of the Persian king in the biblical book of Esther; in Belgium and France he is usually called Isaac Laquedem. That someone lives until the Last Day is a notion which perhaps goes back to points of contact in the New Testament (John 21.22f.: 'If I will that he remains until I come, what is that to you?'; Matt.16.18: 'There are those standing here who shall not taste of death until they see the Son of Man coming with his kingdom'); the influence of Gen.4.14 is also possible (Cain: 'I shall be a fugitive and a wanderer on earth'). At all events, the Eternal Jew is not caricatured here, but is seen more as a tragic figure of the Christian salvation history, who has to wait for redemption – according to legend – until the end of days. In this view Ahasuerus is a Christian allegorical personification of the Jewish people, with the same status as Synagoga in the Middle Ages. Literature: Champfleury 1869, fig. p.25 (cf. some further pictures of Ahasuerus in Champfleury 1869, and Hasan-Rokem 1986, 167–8; see also Schuder and Hirsch 1990, fig. p.697); *EJ* I, 1928, fig. col.1150; *Bilderbogen* 1972, p.73 no.56. Illustration after Champfleury 1869, 25.

IVD *AHASVERVS*

14. A German engraving from 1618. Illustration after Champfleury 1869, 51.

8. The ten lost tribes of Israel; the Queen of the Amazons and the Jews

1. God imprisons the Jews in the Caspian mountains, and only the Queen of the Amazons can get to them. A legend connected with the stories widespread in the Middle Ages about the hiding place of the ten tribes of Israel, lost since the Babylonian captivity (sixth century BCE). This narrative material belongs in the context of the messianic expectations of the Jews. Woodcut in the travel journal of John of Montevilla, who among other things reported fabulous beings and botanical peculiarities in distant lands (animals growing on trees, creatures which were half bird and half lion, apples as big as horses' heads, and so on). Picture in the Basel printing by Bernard Richel, c.1481. Literature: Zafran 1973, I, 25–6. Illustration after Schramm 1920, XXI, no.519 (cf. XX, no.1153).

9. 'Miraculous delivery by a pregnant Jewish woman'

Ain Gewisse Wunderzeitung von ainer Schwange-
ren Judin zu Binzwangen/vir meil von Augspurg/welche kurzlich den 12. Septem-
bris/des nächstverschinenen 74. Jars/an statt zwaier Kinder zwai leibhafte Schweinlin
oder Fürtlin gepracht hat.

SO wunderlich laut die geschicht
Das wa ichs nicht wer wolbericht
Würd ich mich scheuen die zu schreiben/
Dan man möcht denken/das wirs treiben
Vileicht den Juden nur zu spott:
Aber es hat der ware Got
For augen es so klar gestelt
Das daraus greif die ganze Welt
Wie Christus der Messias recht/
Das verplent Judisch Talmutgschlecht
For seiner andern zukunft nun
Zur lez will zu spott pringen thun:
In for der ganzen Welt nun weisen
Das da sie seine Ehr nicht preisen
Was sie sind für Messias werd/
Nainlich der Säu/der wüsten herd/
Weil sie ain Irdisch Reich doch warten
Da sie inn wollust nur erzarten:
Weil sie den Höchstgsalbten entehren/
Mögen mit Sauschmär sie sich schmeren:
Dan die sind nicht werd Christi Gaist
So sinnen flaischlichait vnd flaisch.
Derwegen wißt/Sich hat begeben
Den nächstverschinen Christmont eben
Vir meil von Augspurg zu Binzwangen
Aim Dorf/welches thut angelangen
Dem Hauptmä Ludwig Schärtlin aige/
Da that ain Jüdin sich erzaigen
Sehr schwäres leibs/vnd ging damit
Nach schwanger Weiber Monatsitt/
Als nun die zeit verloffen war/
Da kam sie nider vnd gebar.
Was aber? Da hört libe Leut
Was Juden Kinder deiten heut:
Zwai Säulin namlich sie gebar
Für ir zwai Sönlin/das ist war:
Ja zwai Natürlich Färklin recht
Daran kain Menschlich glid war schlecht/
Gar glatt von haut/vnd gar nichts harig/
Wie solchs ward vllen offenbarig.
Das erst ist von stundan gestorben/
So bald es das Licht hat erworben/
Das ander hat gelebt ain stund/
Darnach zum Sduhauf es verschwund:
Darauf hat man dis Judenplütlin
Die Judenfärlin vnd Säusüdlin
Inn ainen garten bald vergraben/
Da sie dan fre rhu noch haben:
Auch zihen täglich Leut dahin
Zu schen die Säubetterin/
Vnd all vmständ recht zuerfaren/
Bei allen die dabei auch waren.

Vnd gwiß es ist ain wundergschicht
Wan man es inn dem grund besicht.
Dan wer erschrocken schon das Weib
So wer kain Sau doch der ganz leib,
Vileicht so wer ain glid daran
Welchs Menschenart möcht zaigen an:
Zu dem so wer es nicht ain par/
Auch mißgeboren mit gesar:
Aber da sicht man nichts dergleichen
Damit es sich lis was verstreichen:
Drum ists zuhalten für ain wunder
Welchs vns zur warnung gschicht besunder:
Was nun daßelbige bedeit:
Hab ich for etwas angedeit:
Doch ists am besten Got bekant
Der nie vmsonst kain wunder sant/
Der auch durch vnglaubige ermanet
Das man auf Gläubiger stras recht bauet:
Dan vns der Juden stockverplenden
Soll zu dem waren Licht mee wenden/
Vnd denken/was dort Paulus spücht/
Das so Got hat geschonet nicht
Sein Volk/den Natürlichen Zweigen/
Was er den Einimpfling werd zaigen/
Vns die wir an ir stat sind komen
Vnd nicht thun was wir han vernomen.
Derhalben sollen dise zaichen
Christen vnd Juden zur warnung raichen/
Vom Säuischen leben zulasen
Vnd nach nüchterem vns zumasen/
Das wir wacker mit Nüchterkait
Erwarten Gots zukunft berait.

Zu Strasburg

1. Illustrated flysheet with a poem by the German satirist Johann Fischart (died c.1590) and a woodcut (by Tobias Stimmer?), printed in Strasbourg: Bernhard Jobin 1574. This malicious anti-Jewish legend – akin to the 'Judensau' theme – is presented as contemporary reporting, since the giving of a date (12 September 1574) and place gives the impression of historicity. The rhyming verse (four-stress, rhymed in couplets) describes the three scenes presented in the picture: the birth, the inspection (by a man with a Jewish ring), the burial in the garden. This kind of denigration was thought to be particularly effective because the pig – in the Middle Ages a symbol of impurity and sin – was regarded by the Jews as unclean (according to Lev.11.7; Deut.14.8). Literature: Hauffen II, 1922, 6f.; Stock 1939, 48f.; Trachtenberg 1961, fig. p.53; de Boor-Newald V, 1967, 106–18; Shachar 1974, pl.48; Strauss 1975, I, 462; Kosch V, 1978, 47–64. Illustration after Liebe 1903, no.46; cf. I. Ewinkel, *De monstris*, Tübingen 1995.

X. Jewish Professions: Merchants, Businessmen, Pawnbrokers, Physicians

1. Jewish slave traders. Bishop Adalbert of Prague (died 997) treats with Count Boleslav of Bohemia for the release of Jews in slavery to Christians. Christians and Jews were involved in the slave trade – which was quite common. The slaves here are wearing the conical Jewish hat of the twelfth century. Relief on a bronze door of the cathedral at Gniezno, c.1170. Literature: Grimme 1985, fig.29; Zarnecki 1986, fig. 151; *DMA* XI, 1988, fig. p.337; Schreckenberg II, 574f. Illustration after Goldschmidt 1932, pl.86.

2. A man sells or pawns his outer garment to a Jew in Jerusalem. Sketch from life in the *Peregrinationes in Terram Sanctam* (Mainz 1486, folio 76 verso) by Bernhard von Breydenbach, Dean of Mainz; Erhard Reuwich made the woodcuts for this work, basing them on sketches and drawings which he had made as Breydenbach's travelling companion (1483–4). Of the Jews in Jerusalem Breydenbach writes, among other things: 'At this time four hundred Jews were dwelling in Jerusalem who lived in their unbelief and persisted in a great error, as they first believe that God is corporeal and deny the Trinity of persons in the Godhead. They believe that Christ or the Messiah has not come. They do believe that Christ was born of the Virgin Mary, but from the seed of Joseph. They also deny purgatory and original sin. So they believe that their Messiah will restore the promised land to them. They understand their law only in accordance with the letter, which kills, and not the spirit, which brings life. So they are entangled in many other errors, which anyone can note who reads their Talmud, which contains many foolish fables, all of which they firmly believe' (Geck 1961, 26). Literature: Muther 1884, II, pl.149; Davies 1911, pl.34; Olschki 1926, fig.44; Solms-Laubach 1935, fig.113; Fischer 1951, fig.140; Geck 1961, fig. p.26; *EJ* 1971, VIII, 674, fig.25; Zafran 1973, I, 228–30; *Verfasserlexikon* I, 1978, 752–4; Borst 1979, fig.69; Lülfing and Tietge 1981, fig. p.221; *Vom Leben im Spätmittelalter* 1985, 286, no.142; Schramm 1920, XV, no.11 (cf. IV, no.2404). Illustration after Muther 1894, II, pl.149.

Von den juden berten auch eyn gůt teyl zů difer zytt zů Jerufalem wonen·

3. A cleric engaged in speculative business with a Jew (handing over money, presumably in order to earn interest on it). Such business was forbidden by canon law. In the Middle Ages and in early modernity the European Jews found it difficult, if not impossible, to acquire land or engage in crafts (organized into guilds); therefore many of them shifted from this to trade and lending money against interest. For a long time canon law did not allow Christians to engage in the latter – at least in principle – so that there was a window of economic opportunity here. Miniature in a manuscript of the *Decretum Gratiani* from the Benedictine monastery of Schäftlarn (south of Munich), c.1165–70. Munich, SB, Clm 17161, folio 91 recto. Illustration after Klemm II, 1988, no.297.

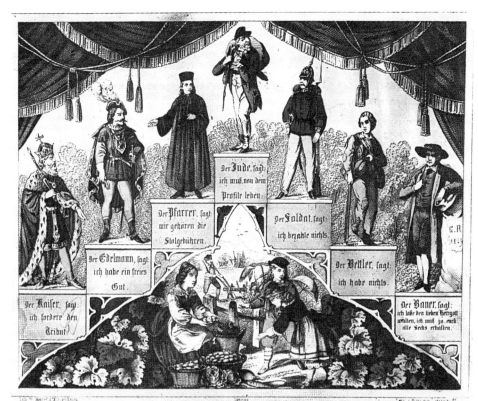

Die verschiedenen Stände im menschlichen Leben.

4. Hierarchy of estates, with a Jewish peddler (with satchel and walking stick) at the top. Jews active in this profession were a familiar sight in the nineteenth century, so that itinerant trade can be regarded here as a prototype of Jewish existence. The depiction has no striking antisemitic tendency. The Jewish trader is so to speak one member belonging to society as a whole. Coloured lithograph from the publishing house of F.Wentzel, Wissembourg, Alsace, 1868. Bad Windsheim, Museum im Ochsenhof. Illustration after Deneke 1988, 204.

5. The sick Basil, archbishop of Caesarea in Cappadocia (330–379), is treated by a Jewish physician. For a long time canon law forbade Christians to consult with Jewish doctors. But little notice was taken of such regulations in cases of emergency, and even some popes had Jewish personal physicians. Woodcut in an early printing of the *Legenda sanctorum* (Golden Legend) of Jacobus de Voragine (thirteenth century) in the workshop of Konrad Fyner (Urach 1481; repeated in the *Plenarium* of Hans Schobser, Augsburg 1487). Literature: *EJ* 1971, XI, 1182, fig.1; Weidinger 1986, 98f.; Schoeps 1992, 332. Illustration after Schramm 1920, IX, no.234.

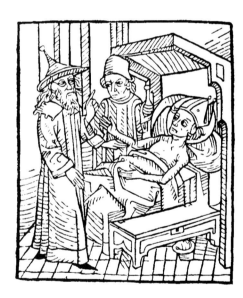

6. A Christian asks a Jewish money-lender for credit. Woodcut in *Der Teutsch Cicero* by Johann von Schwarzenberg, Augsburg: Steiner 2535, folio 122 verso (the same woodcut apparently appeared earlier in an edition of Cicero's *De officiis* from the same publishing house in 1531). The picture is completely objective. It has a caption: 'I beg you, Jew, lend me money against a guarantee or a pledge. Let me know what your terms of credit are.' The Christian, dressed simply but neatly, perhaps a farmer, enters as it were the office of a Jewish 'banker' who is wearing the Jewish dress customary in his time. The pseudo-Hebrew characters on the hem of his garment were really unnecessary to define him as a Jew. On the table, with an abacus, money is ready to be paid out. Although the woodcut has no polemical intent, it could be understood as anti-Jewish, especially by those who used such pictures to confirm prejudices against the Jews (a people who enriched themselves at the expense of Christians). However, the lending of money was a financial necessity, and the Jews engaged in this activity, which was open to them, mostly with the approval of the secular authorities, who regarded them as substantial taxpayers. The social need for banks already led Christians to found the so-called *montes pietatis* in late medieval Italy (with prescribed and moderate rates of interest). Literature: *Mon.Jud.Kat.* 1963, B 208; *EJ* 1971, IV, 171, fig.4; Zafran 1973, I, 230; Schubert 1979, fig.328; Bienert 1982, fig.20; Deneke 1988, 179. Illustration after Liebe 1903, no.8.

Ich bitt euch Jud leicht mir zů hand/   Was euch gebürt gebt mir verstand/
Bar gelt auff bürgen oder pfand/

XI. Social and Religious Denigration, Caricatures

1. Medieval caricatures of Jews (some not polemical)

1. Miniature in a manuscript of the Psalm Commentary by Peter Lombard (died 1160: made in south-west Germany in the third quarter of the twelfth century). 1. Seven prophets' heads in the initial *C(um omnes prophetas)* at the beginning of the commentary; 2. Heads of Jews and Gentiles in the initial *Q(uare fremuerunt gentes et populi meditati sunt inania)*. Such pictures, usually painted from life, can provide information about what European Jews actually looked like in the Middle Ages. Here, too, the miniaturists usually depicted figures from the Old and New Testaments in terms of appearances in their own day. The heads of the prophets are not yet polemical caricatures in the narrower sense, but the 'Jewish' appearance in the miniature on Ps.2.1 perhaps already has negative connotations, since the psalm text speaks of 'plotting' against the 'Lord's anointed', i.e. against Christ, of whom Christian theologians found mention in Ps.2.7, and whose main opponents were always identified as the Jews. Stuttgart, Württembergische LB, Cod.theol. et phil. fol.341, folio 2 verso and folio 5 recto. Illustration after Butz 1987, nos.247 and 252.

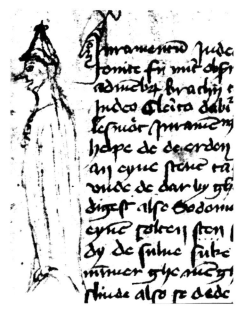

2. Spontaneous sketch of a scribe from a section of text which prescribes keeping sealing wax for Jewish documents in a particular container (inscription: *provisio*). London, Public Record Office, The King's Remembrancer Memoranda Roll (for the 56th year of the reign of King Henry III [i.e. 1271/72], relating to the 24th year of his reign [i.e. 1240]), E 159/47 Mem.4 dorse. Literature: Roth 1962, fig.8; Rokeah 1972, fig. p.61; Revel-Neher 1992, fig.70. Illustration after Blumenkranz 1965, no.19.

3. Cartoon in the margin of a thirteenth-century Latin Bible which was perhaps written in Paris. Prague, National Museum, MS XII A 10, folio 179 verso. Illustration after Bohatec 1970, fig.107.

4. Caricature of a Jew connected with the text of a Jewish oath (*Juramentum Judeorum*), in the initial *J(uramentum)* there is just a head with the pointed Jewish hat, then on the left the whole figure, also with Jewish hat (and with Jewish ring?). Latin and Low German text in a composite manuscript of the second half of the fifteenth century. Wolfenbüttel, HAB, Cod.Guelf. 381 Helmst. Literature: Boockmann 1987, fig. p.244. Illustration after Meckseper 1985, II, 504.

5. Demons and the devil drag Jews of Norwich to hell. Caricature in a Roll of the Issues of the Exchequer (Exchequer of Re- ceipt, Jew's Roll, no.87), London, Public Record Office, 1233. Literature: Trach- tenberg 1961, fig. p.53; Roth 1962, 83 fig.5; Mellinkoff 1970, fig.12; Zafran 1973, I, 221f.; Rubens 1981, fig.126. Illustration after Friedman 1950, 434.

7. An English Jew. The drawing is in the margin of a manuscript which contains a list of sums of money (owed to Jews by various people) claimed by the royal treasury. The caricature is on the same level as the sub-heading *De Judaismo*. A note calls the Jew 'Hake' (i. e.Yitzhak or Isaak), but he is not mentioned again within the text, so his identity is unclear. He displays three group characteristics: the beard, only indicated with strokes; the typical hat customary in the region, the peak of which points sharply upwards (cf. similar forms of Jewish hats in Hassall 1954); and the hooked nose. His apparently dark evil-looking eye and a kind of forelock are also striking. English document from 1289 (private possession of C.Roth, Oxford). Literature: Roth 1962, fig. 6 (after p.82). Illustration after Blumenkranz 1965, no.20. Mention should be made here in passing of the unfriendly caricature of a New Testament Jew in an English liturgical manuscript of the late thirteenth century (Cambridge, St John's College, MS 262, folio 50 verso [illustration in Alexander 1992, fig.90]).

6. An English Jew with the two tables of the law (prescribed special dress). The tables are enlarged in caricature. The context (*interdicta est iudeis licentia usurandi*, Jews are forbidden to levy interest) indicates that a typical money-lender is being depicted. The white two-fold tables – ultimately going back to Ex.31.18 – were the usual equivalent in England for the Jewish ring (*rota*) customary on the Continent. Miniature (perhaps a spontaneous caricature from life) in a chronicle from the reign of the English King Edward I (1272–1307), relating to the ban issued in 1275 against the levying of interest by English Jews. London, BL, Ms. Cotton Nero D.2 folio 180. Literature: Roth 1962, fig.3; Rubens 1981, fig.111; *DMA* III, 1983, fig. p.621; Lazar 1991, fig. 4. Illustration (by permission of BL) after Mellinkoff 1974, fig.19.

8. Caricature of Aaron, son of Leo. This Aaron was present as a surety at court proceedings, and the court clerk evidently found time to caricature him from life as *Aaron fil Diaboli Colecester*, i.e. as a 'devil's son'. He, too, is wearing the sign prescribed for Jews in England, in the form of two-fold tablets of the law in white. Drawing in the Essex Forest Roll of 1277 (Colchester is part of the county of Essex). London, Public Record Office. Literature: Friedman 1950–51, fig. by p.436; Roth 1962, fig.7; Mellinkoff 1970, fig.125; *EJ* 1971, III, 93–4, fig.2; IV, 63 fig.2. Illustration after *EJ* IX, 1932, 964.

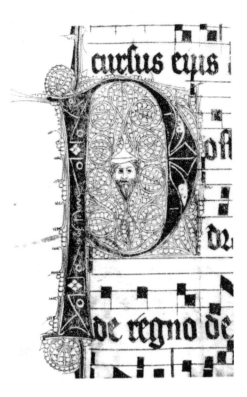

9. Initial miniature *P(ost)* in an antiphonary made in central Rhineland around 1323. Koblenz, Bibliothek des Staatlichen Görres-Gymnasiums, Vol.II, folio 48 recto. Illustration after Kessel 1992, no.15.

11. Figurative jug (*aquamanile*, used above all for washing the priest's hands before mass; neck of a clay flask [17.5 cm.], fifteenth century). Krems (Lower Austria), Städtisches Museum. Illustration after Dworschak 1963, pl.216.

10. Denigration of the Passover ritual. In the initial *P(ascha)* there is a caricature (with an affinity to the 'Judensau' theme) which contrasts the bloodless, spiritual Christian sacrifice of the mass polemically with the 'fleshly' Jewish Passover ritual. Six Jews are greedily surrounding a lamb which has been hung up – though it looks more like a calf. The Jew to the left on the outside is wearing a valuable fur on his cloak, like Süsskind of Trimberg in a well-known miniature of the Manasseh Song Manuscript (c.1310–1340). Miniature in the Codex Gisle (*Codex Gyselae*), the gradual of an order written by the nun Gysela de Kerzenbroek in 1300 and illustrated. Osnabrück, Cathedral Library. Illustration after Dolfen 1926, pl.18.

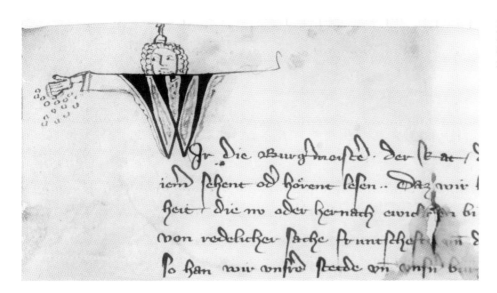

12. Jew scattering money (with Jewish hat). Initial miniature in a document from Speyer, 1532. Literature: Debus 1981, no.16.

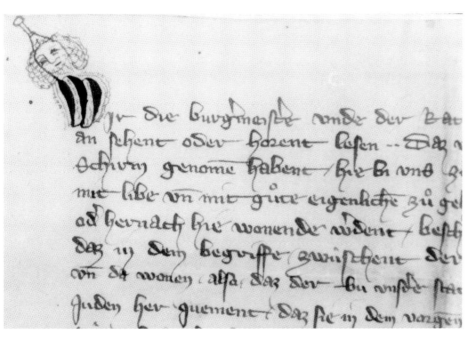

13. Heads with Jewish hats as initial decoration (initial M; Speyer city archive 1 U 280, dated 18 August 1354) or alongside a civic entry (Speyer city archive 1 A 694, folio 22, fifteenth century). Literature: Debus 1981 nos.29 and 30.

2. The Jews as usurers, cheats, enemies of the Christians, accomplices of the devil, advocates of deviant religious notions, etc.

1. Warning against Jewish usurers. On the bottom left a Jewish woman is sitting, wearing the hat typical of Jewesses and witches in the late Middle Ages (pointed hat made of straw?) It is drawn down over her eyes, a symbol of blindness (to the truth of Christian belief or to Christ). The pseudo-Hebrew on the open book and the Jewish hat and Jewish ring are also intended to mock Jews. Woodcut from Moravia, c.1475. Literature: Zafran 1973, I, 225f.; Zafran 1979, pls.6f.; Braudel 1986, fig. p.621; Wenzel 1992, fig.10. Illustration after Liebe 1903, no.5.

2. Single-leaf woodcut by Hans Wandereisen (with rhymes by Hans Sachs?), Nuremberg 1520. The Jewish businessman – the *gsuch* is the demand for interest on credit given – is characterized by the ring (*rota*) and the pseudo-Hebrew scripture on the hem of his garment; his attribute is the money-bag. Literature: Fuchs 1921, pl.23; Zafran 1973, I, 230. Illustration after Liebe 1903, no.23.

Der Jüd.

Bin nicht vmb sonst ein Jüd genannt/
Ich leih nur halb Gelt an ein Pfandt/
Löst mans nit zu gesetztem Ziel/
So gilt es mir dennoch so viel/
Darmit verderb ich den loßn hauffn/
Der nur wil Feyern/ Fressn vnd Sauffn/
Doch nimpt mein Handel gar nit ab/
Weil ich meins gleich viel Brüder hab.

Der Geltnarr.

Ein Geltnarr so werd ich genannt/
On ruh ist mein hertz/mund vnd hand/
Wie ich nur groß Gelt vnd Reichthumb
Vnverschempt listig vberkumb/
Mit dem Jüdenspieß thu ich lauffn/
Mit Wucher/ aufsätzn vnd verkauffn/
Bin doch darbey sehr genauw vnd karck/
Ich spar das gut vnd friß das arg.

3. Woodcut by Jost Amman in *Eygentliche Beschreibung aller Stände auff Erden* by Hans Sachs (Frankfurt 1568): *Der Jüd; Der Geltnarr*. The second of the two pictures depicting a Jew and a swindler does not actually portray a Jew, but is on the Jewish theme in so far as there is a metaphorical reference to Jews (levying excessive interest and cheating) in the poem below. This metaphor already presupposes a widespread unfriendly picture of the Jews. Literature: Sachs 1568 (reprint); Liebe 1903, figs.19–20; Fuchs 1921, figs.19, 22 (with p.132); Azfran 1973, I, 235; Bein 1980, I, 158; II, 86f.; Petzoldt 1985, 52. Illustration after Stock 1939, 39f., nos.5–6.

4. Fettered Innocentia oppressed by allegorical personifications (Envy, Persecution, Greed), while Justitia and a judge sit passively by. Greed (Avaritia) is denounced as a typically Jewish trait by a ring on the right upper arm. Possibly the artist was also thinking of Christian depictions of alleged Jewish ritual murder. Emblem of Christoph Murer, end of the sixteenth century (for Murer [died 1614] see Thieme and Becker XXV, 1931, 238). Illustration after Vignau-Wilberg 1982, no.116 (cf. ibid., nos.117, 119).

Die rechnūg Ruprecht Kolpergers vō dē gesuch der iuden auf 30 dn̄

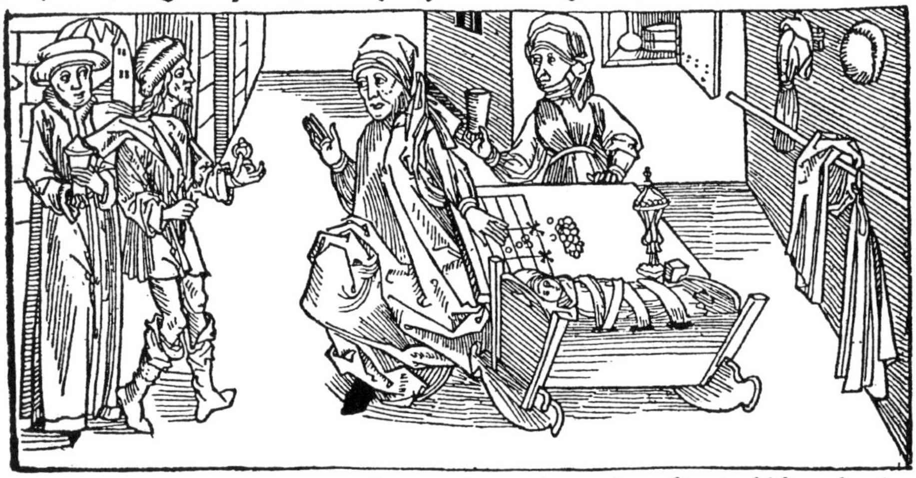

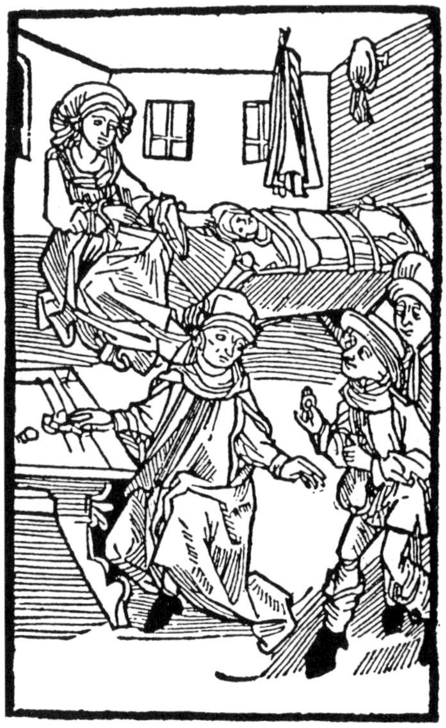

1 Jar	61	dn̄
2 Jar	124	dn̄
3 Jar	244	dn̄
4 Jar	423	dn̄
5 Jar	1082	dn̄
6 Jar	2241	dn̄
7 Jar	4645	dn̄
8 Jar	9630	dn̄
9 Jar	19908	dn̄
10 Jar	41403	dn̄
11 Jar	85840	dn̄
12 Jar	178017	dn̄
13 Jar	369134	dn̄
14 Jar	765434	dn̄
15 Jar	1587201	dn̄
16 Jar	3291218	dn̄
17 Jar	6824667	dn̄
18 Jar	14151628	dn̄
19 Jar	29344813	dn̄
20 Jar	60849403	dn̄
Suma	2433597 fl 5 lb 3	dn̄

Etwas zu sagē von den iüdē
vñ den vflūchtē teüfels rüden
so merckt wie trot ir eim ei kit
gepoin wirt ist er trauf besint
das er im xxx pfenig lehen dut
doch anders nit dan in dem mut
vnd eigentlich der meinung nach
das es aln cristen sei ein schmach
dar vm das vnser schöpfer zart
vm xxx pfening verkauffet wart
des halb er mer noch minder nimpt
dar auff vns dan hin wider zimpt
zu sagen das xxx iüden plint
vm einen pfenig verkauffet sint
des halb ich plint sie nēnen mag
wan sie nie hant erkant den tag
dar in sie got do selbst der straffen
vnd hant die hirten pfeiff vschlaffē
irs messias halben die narn
dar auff sie ye seit lauttn vnd harn
Nun das be stee nach seiner war
die xxx pfening leicht er ym dur
all virteil iars vm sechs gesuch
vnd im zu eim ewigen fluch
wan yn das zehend pot dut lern
du solt nit fremdes guts begern
Nun slecht er vier mol vm ym iar
als sie über al thū für war
vnd ist geflissen tag vnd nacht
gar zu verderben cristlich macht
praucht doch dar pei des fortels sich
er sagt dem cristē wie freüntlich
ym in der rechnung sol gescheen
er well ym gar vil übersehen
lest im gleich wol nit wenig nach
das man destminnd merck sein rach
war aber es die xx iar raichet
stet in den ziffern klar verzaichet
vnd nimāt glaupt d sum auff erdē
des halb es offenbar muß werden
So aber nū nit ider man
sich noch den ziffern richtten kan
hab ich das auch von iar zu iar
zu reym gesatzt gantz offenbar
Das erst iar ein vñ sechtzg .dn̄.macht
das and hundert xxiiii sacht
das drit ccl vnd fir
fünfthundert xxiii mir
das fird nach worer rechnūg stipt
dē funfften .m. zwei vñachtzig zipt
so macht das .vi. nach rechtē schik
zwei .m. zwei c ein vnd firzick
Fier .m. vnd vi hundert wist
vñ funf vnd xxx pringend ist
das sibēd iar Das acht merck fleisig
neün .m. sechs .c. vnd treissig
das neünd neünzehen tausent hot
neün .c. acht vnd sechtzg von not
Daß .x. ein vnd virtzig tausent
do fier hundert vnd treü pei hausent
Fünf vñ achtzig tausent acht hūdt
vñ .l. das eylft iar macht wil wüdt
hūdt tausent das .xii. iar mist
mit acht vñ sibentzg tausentē wist
vnd sibenzehen auch dar pei
Merckt was das .xiii. iar aus schrei
wol trei mol hūdt tausent ich
mit neün vñ sechtzg tausentē sprich
dar pei hūdert vñ fier vnd treissig
sint auch dar zu bestimet fleisig
Das fierzhent iar zu siben moln
hundert tausent pfenig dut holn
mit fünf vnd sechzig tausent der
fierhundert fier vnd treisg sint mer
Das fünfzend iar ist dar bestimpt
dein zu tausent moln tausent zimpt
vnd fünf mol hūdttausent me

Nach dem vñ iüdisch listikeyt
yr fursetzt gar on all arbeyt
mit gātzer faulkeit sich zu nern
wellē ploß vō dē rochrauß zern
die zehen pot mit wiln verachten
so sie den frefel nit petrachten
welchs pot mā vō den zehē swecht
synt auch die neün dar mit gesmecht
welt pey einr gleichnus das verstan
wer vnert einen orden man
der smecht dar mit ei gantz convent
so dan das letzer pot bekent
nicht fremder güter zu begern
ich sweig mit wucher sich zu nern

5. A town-dweller and a farmer deposit pledges with a Jewish pawnbroker. Woodcut at the beginning of the poem *Jüdischer Wucher*, in rhyming couplets, published by Hans Folz in Nuremberg in 1491. The caption of the picture, 'The Calculation by Ruprecht Kolpergers of the Interest earned by the Jews on 30 Denarii', refers to the calculation of interest under the picture by the Nuremberg actuary Kolperger, who helped with the calculations in the rhyming couplets. But the picture has its setting in the very anti-Jewish text by Hans Folz and the apparently exact calculation of interest – though in reality it is quite remote from reality (about a debt of 30 pfennings which in twenty years grows like a snowball into an avalanche). Literature: Liebe 1903, figs. 7, 32; Fuchs 1921, fig. p.8; Schramm 1920, XVIII, figs.374, 392; Gümbel 1926; Stock 1939, 177–81; Fischer 1961 (310–18: 'Jüdischer Wucher', with pl.5 and p.XXIX); *Mon.Jud.Kat* 1963, B 207; *EJ* 1971, III, 139f.; VIII, 462; Zafran 1973, I, 228; Rosenfeld 1978, fig.54; Zafran 1979, pl.6 c; *Verfasserlexikon* II, 1980, 787; Debus 1981, fig.52; Wenzel 1982, 9f.; Seibt 1987, fig.p.306; Deneke 1988, fig. p.180; Wenzel 1992, fig.11. Illustration after Stock 1939, 178 (narrow picture at the beginning of the rhyming couplets) and 177 (wide picture with the table of interest below it = single-leaf, Nuremberg: Hans Mair, c. 1493).

dar mit der nid sich schuldig gipt
das er got nit ob alm ding libt
so er mit willen sweiß vnd plut
leib leben sel eer vnd das gut
gern als mit wucher zu ym precht
dar mit er auch das drit pot smecht
wan fur vnd fur sein wucher get
kein sabat er den feyern let
dan das sie kein hant würkung thun
do sint sie sunst faul kotzen sun
des feyerns mag der teufel lachen
suln aber sie ein gantz nacht wachen
zu lestern alle kristenheit
do sint sie eilends zu bereit
weiter zu sage von den iüde
vñ den vsluchtë teüfels rüden
so merkt wie trot ir eimei kynt
gepom wirt ist er trauf besint
das er im xx pfenig leihë dut
doch anders nit dan in dem mutt
vnd eigentlich der meinung nach
das es aln cristen sei ein schmach
dar vm das vnser schöpfer zart
vm xxx pfening verkauffet wart
des halb er mer noch minder nimpt
dar auff vns dan hin wider zimpt
zu sagen das xxx iüden plint
vm ein pfenig verkauffet sint
des halb ich plint sie nenen mag
wan sie nie hant erkant den tag
dar in sie got do selbst det straffen
vnd hant die hirten pfeiff vschlaffë
irs messias halben die narn
dar anff sie ye seit laurn vnd harn
Nun das bestee nach seiner war
die xxx pfening leicht er ym dar
all virteil iars vm sechs gesuch
vnd im zu ein ewigen fluch
wan yn das zehend pot dut lern
du solt nit fremdes guts begern
Nun slecht er viet mol vm ym iar
vñ machts allweg zu haupt gut gar
vnd ist geflissen tag vnd nacht
gar zu verderben cristlich macht

6. Epitaph of Good Money. Denigration of the Jews – two are wearing the ring on their upper arms – as forgers. Engraving from 1618, printed by Martin Wörle in Augsburg. Augsburg, Staats- und Stadtbibliothek, classification: 2° Lw Einblattdrucke nach 1500, no.120. Literature: Alexander-Strauss II, 1979, 693.

Der Jud stellt sein sinne natyt vnd mey Wie er den cristen verderben may

Der Korn vnd Wein Jud

Das ist: Nachdenckliche figur vnd Bildnus, der Korn, Wein, vnd Geldwucherer, Leudtschinder vnd Leuttfresser, mit ihren Manniren vnd
Panniren. Aus dem buchlein Tobi: Syrach, propheten Michea, Ezechiele, vnd andern biblischen hypotiposib9:
Warnungs halben vor Augen gestellet.

7. German single–leaf against Jewish merchants (section, with the inscription 'The Jew calculates night and day how to cheat the Christians'), which expresses a sweeping prejudice against the Jews as a group. The extensive calculation of interest added to the picture is meant to show that the credit given by Jewish pawnbrokers carries excessive interest. On the right is an abacus, in the centre the acceptance of the pledge, and on the left perhaps a Christian scholar who is inviting an official (with a servant) to come in. Literature: Zafran 1973, I, 227; Boockmann 1986, fig.428; Seibt 1987,179. Illustration after Fuchs 1921,16.

8. 'The Corn and Wine Jew'. Illustrated flysheet from 1629. Literature: Liebe 1903, fig.51; Schnur 1939, fig.34; Coupe II, 1967, pl.64. Illustration after Fuchs 1921, pl. after p.32.

9. The Jewish 'cheaters' and 'changers'. The 'changer' made a profit from money-changing or from advantages in the rate of exchange, when for example a larger number of new coins of the same denomination were minted from old and better coins, i.e. there was a debasement of the currency. Illustrated pamphlet (with 76 lines in rhyming couplets and an engraving/etching), 1622. Wolfenbüttel, HAB (classification: I E 194). Literature: Liebe 1903, fig.54; Stock 1939, 103 pl.8; *Mon.Jud.Kat.* 1963, B 206; Coupe II, 1966, fig.107; Harms I, 1985, fig. p.343; Fuchs 1921, no.46.

10. The Jewish Bathhouse. Philipp von Allendorff's *Der Juden Badstub*, which appeared in 1535 bearing no indication of place (with a frontispiece, the first of our illustrations), provided the material for a flysheet of the same title with eighteen engravings in all (= the second and third of the illustrations above), which were disseminated in different versions – the earliest appeared in Frankfurt in 1611/1614. The 'bathhouse', in which bleeding was practised as a medical therapy, is a kind of parable of the Jewish usurer, who draws the blood out of Christians, and thus an allegory of the activity of the Jews which

was harmful to Christians. The Jews appear as accomplices of the devil and all have the Jewish ring as a symbol denouncing them. Literature: Geiger 1881, 333–5; Fuchs 1921, figs.24–41; Stock 1989, pl.35; Trachtenberg 1961, 28f.; Kunzle 1973, figs.6–31; Shachar 1974, pls. 50–51; Oberman 1981 (in *Flugschriften*), 289; Oberman 1981 (*Wurzeln*), 121f.; Harms I, 1985, fig. pl.349; Paas 1985, II, fig. p.173; Frey 1989, 268, 270–6; Frey 1991, 46f.; Rohrbacher and Schmidt 1991, figs. 158f.; cf. Coupe 1966, II, pl.79, and Harms 1983, fig.131. Illustration after Liebe 1903, nos.25–26, 33.

Der Juden badstub.

Ein anzeygung irer manigfeltigen

schedlichen hendel/zů warnung allen Christen/
iten trieglichen listigkeyten zů entweychen
vnd zůuermeyden.

Wer wissen wil was schand vnd schad
Entspringet auß dem Juden bad/
Der selb durchleß mich biß zum ende
Von jn wir sehend sind verblendt.

1 5 3 5.

Der Juden Er=
barkeit.

ALhie siehstu der Juden Tantz/
Jr Gottes Lesterung vnd Finantz/
Wie sie den Son Gotts verspeyen/
All Christen vermaledeyen.
Darzu all Christlich Oberkeit/
Weils nicht gerhet so ists jn leid.
Auch jr grewliche Wucherey/
Noch sind sie bey alln Herren frey.
Betracht doch solchs du fromer Christ/
Du seyst gleich hoch / odr wer du bist.
Las dir dis Buch zu hertzen gan/
Gott wird eim jeden gebn sein lohn.

ANNO. M. D. LXXI.

11. Frontispiece woodcut of a poem against the Jewish usurer (printing of 1571). The Jews here are no longer accomplices and minions of the devils but have themselves become devilish mixed beings who do absurd things. Literature: Geiger 1888, 335f.; Trachtenberg 1961, 30; Mellinkoff 1970, fig.127; Shachar 1974, pl.47a; Zafran 1979, pl.8d; Rohrbacher and Schmidt 1991, fig. p.160; Wenzel 1992, fig.13. Illustration after Fuchs 1921, no.20 (with 176–8).

Der Juden zukünfftiger Messias groß/
Sein Hoffgesind vnd Schelmen genoß/
Welche vnsern Herrn Christum verspeyen/
All Christen vnd Oberkeyt vermaledeyen/

Die kommen auff irem Talmuth reyten/
Jucken in wol auff allen seyten/
Sie folgen irem Engel der sie fürt/
Wie jetzt hernach gelesen würt.

Teuffel. 1.

Hernach/hernach/ir lieben Gesellen/
All mit einander in die Hellen/
Da will ich euch gut kurtzweil machen/
Das ewer keiner nit soll lachen.
Ich hab so lang darnach gerungen/
Biß das es mir einmal ist gelungen/
Ewer Messias soll der erste sein/
Die Badstub will ich euch wermen ein.

Schalckreyper. 2.

Thu gemach/thu gemach/mein lieber gesell/
Wir seind nu weit mehr von der Hell/
Thu vns so geschwind vbereylen nit/
Auff das wir bringen den anhang mit.
Das Thier/so vnser Messias reyt/
Das kan geschritten nit so weit/
Es hat anhangen ein wüste rott/
Daran es gnug zuziehen hat.

Krautrihrer. 3.

Ich pfeyff vnserm Messias disen Tantz/
Wiewol der Rey ist noch nit gantz/
Wir wöllen allgemach hiemit fort trollen/
Bruder Rausch wirt die andern auch holn/
Die vnserm Messias nach sollen kummen/
Auff das erfüllet werd die summen/
Es besteht im Talmuth buch gar fein/
Wie vil der Schelmen noch dahinden sein.

Herodes. 4.

Wir werden sehet willkom vnserm Gott/
Der vnser so lang begeret hat/
Sich erfrewen vnsers Messias doch/
Weil er mit bringt solch ehrlich geloch/
Denn sie seind alle von edler art/
Mit jm genommen auff dise fart/
Bey jm zuhaben solch Ritterschafft/
Den gybt der Talmuth grosse krafft.

Messias. 5.

Ich reyt daher/doch nit allein/
Vnd bring mit mir ein arg gemein/
Die ich mein Vorfar dem Lucifer/
Ins Reich der Hell zustellen beger.
Am berg Horeb haben wir so lang gebrochen/
Biß das wir seind herdurch gekrochen/
Mit trucknem fuß durchs Rote meer/
Bring ich das heylig Volck hieher.

Rabi Jekoff. 6.

Ich reyt auff vnserm Talmuth auch/
Vnd befund/das er will werden schwach/
Darumb kompt der jr Raben all/
Versucht wie euch der Talmuch gefall/
Ich thu auch den fürbang die auff decken/
Rabi Süßkind soll jn zum ersten schmecken/
Damit er könn anzeigen frey/
Wie doch dem Talmuth geschehen sey.

Rabi Dofurt. 7.

Dich dunckt bey Adonay auch wol/
Das der Talmuth schwach sein soll/
Darumb Süßkind will ich dir zeigen/
Wo du jm die schell solt feigen/
Halt eylends den groß Waffel dar/
Damit nichts auff der erden far/
Er gehbet in solchen heyligen Mann/
Der die schrifft so wol gemeystern kan.

Rabi Süßkind. 8.

Amen der Talmuth ist sehr kranck/
Sein othem hat ein bösen gestanck/
Ich glaub es mache das warm gewitter/
Dieweyl er schmeckt so härb vnd bitter/
Oder ist mit Schelmen so hart beschwert/
Darvon sich also sein kranckheit mehrt/
Er solt sonst schmecken wie süsse milch/
Sonderlich dunckts dich nit auch billich.

Rabi Senderlein. 9.

Ich will jn melcken in disen Krug/
Mein findling saugt jm auch genug/
Ob er ein krafft davon mög bekummen/
Christen zuuerfluchen mit grossen summen/
Er will bey vns so gar nit wircken/
Je mehr wir fluchen/thun sie sich stercken/
Joseph Artzt soll jn besehen wol/
Wie man dem Talmuth helffen soll.

Joseph Artzt. 10.

Ich besehe wol das er krafftloß ist/
Im gebrechen noch mehr Fluch vnd list/
Es erscheinet mir hie der Engel im glaß/
Der vns eingibt zuuerfluchen baß/
All Goyim/mit jrem gedenckten Gott/
Mit dem wir treiben vnsern spott/
Rabi Seydel in vnser Cantzley soll bleiben/
Den Talmuth noch vil stercker beschreiben.

Rabi Seydel. 11.

Was ich jnnen darinn hab vergessen/
Soll jetzundt doppel werden gemessen/
Mit fluchen/lestern/vermaledeyen/
An sie mit vns all Teuffel speyen/
Ist dann der fluch nit krefftig gnug/
So finden wir ein andern fug/
Mit falschen brieffen vnd siegeln fein/
Juncker Siegeldieb kan die meister sein.

Juncker Siegeldieb. 12.

Die Siegel wie ich sie schneiden thu/
Bring ich euch gar viel Ducaten zu/
Ich beschess damit groß Fürsten vnd Herren/
Kan sie gar fein vnd meisterlich narren/
Das sie nit anderst können dencken/
Ich brauch mit jnen kein falsche rencken/
Mannus der fromme nachbaur mein/
In vnser gesellschafft auch soll sein.

Mannus Jud. 13.

Juncker Siegeldieb lieber nachbaur mein/
Wir wöllen nun mehr gut gesellen sein/
Wir haben einander offt selbs belogen/
Felschlich verhalten/vn dieblich betrogen/
Biß wir das handtwerck recht gelebt/
Dz wir für meisterlich Dieb seind gewebt/
Ich zünd dir/daß das Siegel wol gerath/
Zu wem wir kommen frü vnd spath.

Rabi Lefer. 14.

Wir müssen eins beym andern treiben/
Auff das keyn Gou bey vns thu bleiben/
Des Talmuthe hab ich gesoffen so viel/
Darumb verfluch ich sie ohn maß vnd ziel/
Darzu die höchste Oberkeyt/
Hat es kein krafft so ist mirs leidt/
Auch Keyser/König/Fürsten vnd Herren/
Thut vns der heylig Talmuth lernen.

Die arme Saw. 15.

Ach wehe/ach wehe/mir armes Thier/
Das dich die hellisch gesellschafft für/
Zum Lucifer gar in die Hellen/
Ein banckett mit jm sie halten wöllen/
Sein will ist jm gantz wol gebraten/
Ich muß jn geben ein guten Braten/
Das sie von mir haben zu essen/
Bruder Rausch wirt je auch nit vergessen.

Bruder Rausch. 16.

Ich will euch dem Braten recht zurichten/
Das ewer keiner soll erschrecken/
Will auch in solchem geloch mit sein/
Das hellisch fewr nich schüren ein/
Daran solt jr kein mangel haben/
Fort fort/vnd laßt vns eylends traben/
Dann ich der Gesellen mehr muß bringen/
Ehe vns den Brägel ich heissen singen/
So wöllen wir tantzen vnd Jubilieren/
Ob wir jm klappern/das ist holtselig/
Das wäre dann fein in rechter Ley/
Den sie so lang verdienet han/
Ho da/soll ich des spiels nit lachen/
Ich könte doch besser mit gemachen/
Dann wen allbie zusamen/ab bracht/
Jch mit mein feinn gute nacht.

1563

◀ 12. The 'Future Messiah of the Jews'. A mockery of the Jewish messianic expectation. The absurd behaviour of the group – joining in a procession with devils and pigs – is meant to illustrate what from a Christian perspective was the deviant faith of the Jews. The regular appearance of the Jewish ring (*rota*) in pictures of this kind confirms that its function is mainly that of polemical denunciation. Woodcut (flysheet), 52.5 x 41 cm, dated 1563 (Halle an der Saale, Staatliche Galerie Moritzburg). Literature: *Mon.Jud.Kat.* 1963, B 311; Lazar 1991, fig.27. Illustration after Shachar 1974, pl.46.

14. Caricature against the cheats and swindlers. Good money is collected and reminted as bad money (on the right above, new coins are being minted with a press). Some of those involved are prominently wearing the Jewish ring or even appear in the form of devils (with birds' feet), so that here too the assumption of an essential affinity between Jews and the devil becomes clear. Engraving of 1623. Literature; Schnur 1939, fig.37; Trachtenberg 1961, fig p.185; Hoofacker 1988, fig.11. Illustration after Liebe 1903, no.55.

13. Frontispiece woodcut by Lucas Cranach. The strange head-dress of this representative of the lying Jews suggests devil's horns, and he is fingering the abacus, the instrument that he needs for his business. This woodcut probably played its part in shaping the contemporary portrayal of the Jew. Literature: Fuchs 1921, fig.17; Körber and Pugel 1935, fig. p.213; Stock 1939, 32 no.4; Mellinkoff 1970, fig.126; *EJ* 1971, III, 105, fig.5; *Luther* 1973, pl.39; Zafran 1973, I, 266f.; Mellinkoff 1984, fig. 12. Illustration after Liebe 1903, no.31.

Exsultat Juvenis; sed serto Virgo triumphat: *Judaeus fraudat; ludere Miles ovat.*

Der Jüngling dantzt und springt daher
Jhrs krantzes frewt sich die Jungfraw sehr.

Der Jüd thut nichts als betrügen wil:
Der Kriegsman abr frewt sich zum spiel.

15. Engraving in D.Meisner, *Politisches Schatzkästlein*, Frankfurt: E.Kiesner 1624. Absurd behaviour (riding the wrong way round on a mount unsuitable for riding [the he-goat is also an animal associated with the devil]) and deception are defined as essential features of the Jews. Their special dress (with Jewish ring) also reinforces the impression that the Jew is a strange outsider in Christian society. Literature: Trachtenberg 1961, fig. p.45. Illustration after Liebe 103, no.74.

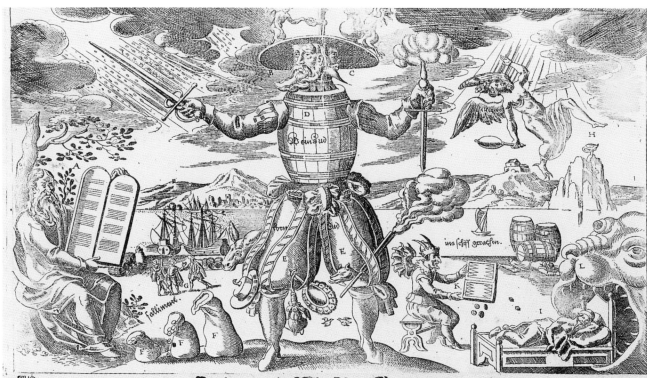

Geitz- vnd Wucher Spiegel.

In welchem sich die jenigen wol zubeschawen haben/ so mit dem abschäwlichen Laster deß vnersättlichen
Geitzes vnd Wuchers behafftet/zur trewhertzigen Warnung für Augen gestellet.

Wie können jetz zu dieser Zeit/
Mehr fortkommen die gmeinen Leuth?
Dieweil es gibt der Wucherer viel/
Die als auffkauffen in der Eil/
Korn vnd Wein mit grossen Summen/
Das man schier nichts kan bekommen.
Es sey dann vmb vierfaches Gelt/
Drauff ist deß Wuchrers Sinn gestelt.
Wann aber kombt der liebe Gott/
Vnd den Armen errett auß Noht/
Den Reichen fordert bey seim Gwissn/
Ob er auch hab an jhn bewissn/
Das gut Werck der Barmhertzigkeit/
So wirdt kommen ein andrer Bscheide/
Anders als hie auff dieser Welt/
Dieweil es jedem so gefelt/
Zu wucheren mit Korn vnd Wein/
Dann es vilen so geht hein:
Denen soll man aber zur Hauben
Greiffen/ vnd die Zecken wol klauben/
Vnd rupffen die Flugfedern auß:
Wer hinder sich kaufft in sein Hauß/
All Wein vnd Korn im gantzen Land/
Vnd förchtet weder Sünd noch Schand/
Damit ein armer Mann nichts findt/
Bald Hungers stirbt mit Weib vnd Kindt:
In dem er jhm als ein Böswicht/
Sein Leibs Narung vnd Krafft entzeucht/
Welchs jhn auffhalt in seinem Lebn/
A. Da Moses jhm doch die Lehr gebn/
Daß er seins Nechsten Ehr vnd Gut.
Soll lieben als sein eigen Blut.
Er aber acht keins Armen Noht/
B. Vnd streit muthwillig wider Gott.
Ist also sein gantzes Gedicht/
Nuhr auff den Mammon abgericht.
Demselben dient er Tag vnd Nacht/
Vnd seines Schöpffers wenig acht.
Dieweil er nuhr nach seinem Willn/
Alhie mag Kasten vnd Keller füllen.
C. Darumb sicht er ins Gbürg hincin/
Ob auch die Rebn tragen viel Wein/
Vnd gibt dem Rebman gern Gelt drauff/

Verläst sich/ obs schon nicht geht ab/
Daß er doch guten Eßig hab:
D. Der wirdt jhm gnommen auß dem Paß/
Wa er nicht vom Wucher ablast.
Sondern verhart im bösen Wesn/
Da jhm doch Moses das Gsetz glesn/
Vermeint er hab gleich gnug daran/
Die Seel mag fahren wa Sie kan.
Derhalben braucht er ohn Verdrieß/
Sein wolgebutzten Judenspieß/
Sticht mit demselben vmb sich her/
Vnd wirdt jhm gantz kein Reich zu schwer.
Ja/sein mit Wucher gwonnen Guth/
Jhm selbst den grösten Schaden thut:
Macht jhn zu einem Sünden Knecht/
E. Daß er von Lastern börsten möcht.
Er ist ein solcher träger Gsell/
Zu gutem faul/ wie ein Esel.
Gut Speiß macht jhn so schleckerhafft/
Zu Marckt er alles zu sich rafft.
Empfindt gar nichts in seim Gewissn/
Meint/ er müß alles zu sich reissn.
Das macht sein Neid/sein Geitz vnd Zorn/
Daß er nicht denckt heut oder morgn/
Werd sein Seel von jhm genommen/
Wa wirdt hernach Sie hinkommen?
Die gute Koß macht jhn so geil/
Daß er versuchet all sein Heyl.
Mit Gelt vnd Gaben auch verführt/
Wa er die gringste Armuht spürt.
F. Der Hochmuht treibt jhn auch dahin/
Daß er jhm nimbt in seinen Sinn/
Zu thun alles was jhn nuhr glust/
Dann der Wucher wärmbt jhm sein Brust.
Vnd weil sein Sinn in Lüfften schwebt/
Er gar ohn ein Gewissen lebt/
In Geitz/ Finantz darzu Hochmuht/
Aber es selten lang gut thut.
Dann Gott von Himmel stürtzen thut/
Der Engel hoch- vnd stoltzen Muht.
Also auch solcher Leuthe Pracht/
Gott der HErr bald zu schanden macht.
Da jhn Gotts Straff solt schrecken ab/

Vnd sticht mit dem Schindmesser sein/
An alle Ort vnd End hinein/
Ob er schon manchen Fählstich thut/
Dann Gott offt rächt des Armen Blut:
Vnd kombt der Fluch mit grossem Spott/
Daß er muß spilen Banckeroht.
In das Schiff sitzen vnd falliren/
G. Sich plötzen lassen vnd Thurniren.
Da ist dann gfallen sein Reichthumb/
Vnd groß Credit ist kommen vmb.
H. Gleich wie der Habich alls außspeit/
Was er sein Lebtag hat gebeut.
I. Endlichen er dann auch wird kranck/
Vnd fährt stracks in der Höllen gstanck.
Damit der Teuffl das Spiel gewonnen
K. Im Brett/weist jms/weil er vnbsonnen/
Sein zeitlich Heyl nicht wol betracht/
Vnd sich vmbs ewig auch gebracht.
L. Da sperr die Höll den Rachen auff/
Vnd kommen jhm all Sünd zu hauff/
Daß er mit Leib vnd Seel zugleich/
Dem Teuffel dient in seinem Reich.

Warnung.

Die lieben Alten vor viel Jahren/
So nicht viel Ränck haben erfahren/
Von Wucher/ Geitz vnd auch Finantz/
Die haben solchen Gsellen gantz/
Die Sacramenta nicht spendirt/
So ein solch gottloß Leben gführt/
Jetz gehn Sie all zum Tisch deß Herrn/
Ja truz/ der jhn solches solt wehrn.
Aber das gschicht zu jhrem Gricht/
Weil kein Besserung drauff geschicht.
Darumb du Christ zu jeder Zeit/
Den Geitz vnd losen Wucher meidt/
Der in der Schrifft/ wie jeder list/
Bey Seelen straff verbotten ist.
Auff daß dir das nicht widerfahr/
Davon ich jetz gantz offenbahr/
Nach meinm Verstandt/ gar vnverzagt/
Auß Gottes Wort hab geweissagt.

E N D E.

◄ 16. The Corn and Wine Jew. Illustrated flysheet (128 rhymed verses with an etching), c.1620. Warned in vain by Moses, who is holding out the tables of the law in an attempt to deter the cheat, and unimpressed by the fall of the angel (a punishment for arrogance), the Janus-headed usurer continues in his actions until, fatally ill, he falls into the jaws of hell. Wolfenbüttel, HAB, classification: I E 193. Literature: Liebe 1903, fig.30; Fuchs 1921, fig.44; Schur 1939, fig.24; Harms I, 1985, 341.

17. The 'fortune berries' (which were alleged to put the Jews in a position to predict the advent of the Messiah). They are the title and subject of a very polemical poem in rhyming couplets by the Nuremberg poet Hans Folz (died 1513), published in 1485 (a first, less polemical, version had already appeared in 1479). A Christian charlatan sells the stupid Jews dried lumps of dung as miraculous berries. Narratives and caricatures of this kind fooled or tricked Jews – to the delight of Christians. Woodcut for the print of Folz's poem. Literature: Zafran 1973, I, 252–4; Zafran 1979, pl.8 e; Bunte 1989, fig. p.459. Illustration after Schramm 1920, XVIII, no.397.

18. 'The New Swarm of Enthusiasts'. An illustrated flysheet which appeared soon after 1651(etching and engraved text). It is directed against the efforts at tolerance in England and mocks four representatives of religious minorities, including a Quaker (lying in ecstasy) at the front of the picture, and a Jew in the background. The Jew is pointing to a church which he wants to buy with money, some of which he is holding in his hand and some of which is lying at his feet. In a stereotypical way the Quaker is defined by his ecstatic raptures and the Jew by his money (as an instrument of power), which he is also prepared to use against Chrisitianity. Illustration after Harms II, 1980, 609.

Geystliche Gleyssnerey.

Ach wie hat sich mein glück verkert
Mich hat verwundet vnd versert
Das wort Gottes das scharpffe schwert
Ich lig gantz trostlos auff der ert
Dem esel bin ich gantz vnrein
Der vor mein stym gar geren hert
Vnd alles thet was ich jn lert
Der mich sanfft drug vnd lieblich nert
Vnd mir mein schen gantz reychlich mert
Das ich mein zeyt in rü verzert
Jetzund der esel mich auffkert
Vnd sein futter vor mir züspert ꝛc.

Menschliche vernunft.

Esel schau vmb es leyt im schranck
Gleyssnerey die dir thet gros dranck
Noch leydest du gar bitter zwanck
Von gwalt vnd wucher anne wanck
Die haben dich an jren stranck
Vnd reytten dich machtlos vnd kranck

Vnd verdienst doch vmb sie kein danck
Was hilfft des wort Gottes gesanck
Du bleybst beschwert wie im anfanck
Darumb schlag auff mackes nit lanck
Ob du sie sturmst mit eim ranck
Dann wir gering dein schwerer ganck ꝛc.

Tyrannisch gewalt.

Esel du bist darzü geboren
Das du solt barren weytz vnd korn
Vnd du doch essen distel dorn
Darumb geh hin an alles zorn
Wilt nicht mit lieb so müst mit zorn
Wann ich sü gwaltig auff dir born
Vnd schlag dich dapffer vmb die oren
Snipff dich darzü mit scharpffen sporn
Du bist mein engen vnd geschworen
Du müst tantzen nach meinen horen
Der vernunfft ratt ist gar verloren ꝛc.

Finantzscher wucher.

O esel schon selb deiner beyt

Das dich in das fleisch nit schneyt
Ich schinde vnd schab zü beyden seyt
Titus Liuius j.) Darumb rufft ich von Rom verleyt
Jetz hastu mich dragen lang zeyt
Gedulglich an widerstreyt
Sag was dein gumpen noch bedeyt
Du wirst dardurch gar nit gefreyt
Wie starck dir die vernunfft eyn schreyt
Gewalt mich vber rucken dreyt
Vnd nimbt mit mir gleyche beyt
Des halb ich sicher auff dir reyt ꝛc.

Der arm gemein Esel.

Kein emer thee auff ert man vint
Ich mus arweytten regen wint
Vnd grawen was all welt verschlint
Des haberstro man mir kaum gynt
Es sten auff mir zwey bösse kint
Das foder schlecht mich vmb den grint
Sein scharpffen spren ich mercktint
Der hinder mich lebendig schint
Das bluet täglichen von mir rint

Ach grechtigkeyt hilff mir geschwint
Es ich in dem iamer erplint
Schlag vmb mich vnd werd vnbesint

Natürliche gerechtigkeyt.

Ach esel ich erbarm mich dein
Ich merck dein not die ist nit klein
Ich thet dir meiner hülffe schein
So schreyt nymer das schwerte mein
Damit ich Tarquinum bracht peyn
Jetz muß ich selb gefangen sein
Von wucher tyraney vntrein
Valerius Ir hertz ist verhert wie ein stein
Maximus In darff gar nymant reden eyn
am.6. Dein vnd mein ellent ich bewein
Darumb so klag es Got allein
Der kan auß noch dir helffen sein ꝛc.

Das wort Gottes.

Rom.13. Esel dich hat vernunfft verplent
Bar... 3.2. Das du dem gwalt wilt widerstent
Esaie.3. Den Got zü straff deiner sünd hat gsent

Matth.5. Darumb so sey nit wider spent
Luce.9. Drag dein selb kreuz in dem ellent
Mat.24. Vnd bleyb gedultig biß ins end
Apoca.2. Wer vberwint der wirt gekrent
Psal.37. Halt du Got still biß er dir wend
Wucher tyrannisch regiment
Rom.12. Laß im die rach in seiner hend
Deut.32. Die rach ist sein die schrifft bekent
Sap.6. Die grwelig er mit krafft zürrent
Exodi.14. Pharo stürst er in meeres grunt
Judicü.3. König Eglon wurt dödlichen wundt
3.Reg.22. König Achas bluet leckten die hunt
Da Israhel in yeder schunt
Also noch heüt zü disser stunt
Erret Got sein volck auß dem schlunt
Psal.37. Der tyrannen wie grausams thunt
Job.24. Auch von des wuchers schwinden sint
Macht Got sein armes volck gesundt
Esaie.40. Balt sie Got rüret durch sein munt
Deutro.7. Got helt getrewlich seinen bunt ꝛc.

Hans Guldenmund. 1525.

19. 'Who has heard your great lament?' The 'poor common ass' is being mocked by 'Spiritual Hypocrisy', 'Tyrannical Power' and 'Financial Usury', the latter personified ironically as a Jew with a Jewish ring (and dragon's wings, which the devil is often given elsewhere). The 'word of God' can only console to the degree that it points to God's omnipotence and vengeance. Single-leaf woodcut of 1525 (picture by Peter Flötner, text by Hans Sachs). Literature: Zafran 1973, I, 231f.; R.Wohlfeil, in Herzig and Schoeps 1993, 30. Illustration after Geisberg and Strauss III, 1974, 775, G.813.

20. Warning to the usurers. Illustrated flysheet (54 lines in rhyming couplets with woodcut), printed in 1622. Perhaps the sequence of scenes is meant to depict the career of a money-changer whose end the devil awaits. At any rate, on the right a Jewish money-changer or money-lender is recognizable by his clothing and beard; he is engaged in writing up his books. The devil (with a pig's face) seems to be surveying the whole scene with pleasure. Ulm, Stadtbibliothek (Einblattdruck 327). Literature: Harms 1983, 103. Illustration after Diedrichs I, 1908, no.913.

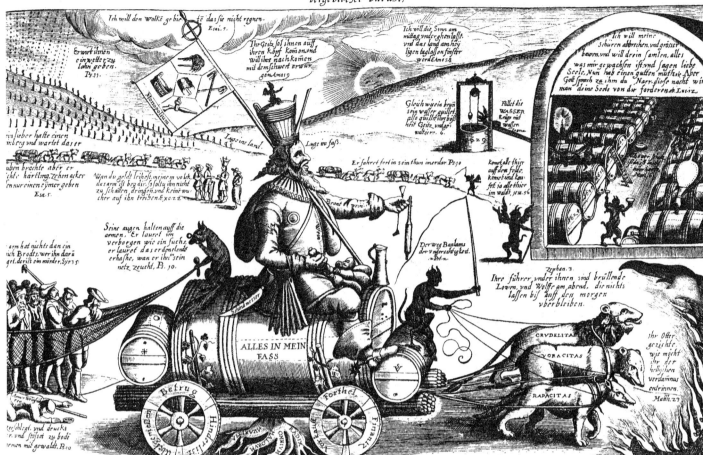

21. 'The Wine Jew'. Illustrated flysheet (with an etching and numerous engraved inscriptions in German and Latin, including some from the Old and New Testaments), 1629. The Janus-headed 'Wine Jew' (i.e. wine merchant) with the Jewish ring, who exploits the vintners by his monopolistic domination of the market, is acting in community with devils, who are controlling him and almost driving him into hell. This flysheet was probably made in the terrible years of the Thirty Years' War in a region of vineyards (Rhine and Moselle, Trier?). As a result of the increase in intermediaries who were free from the influence of the guilds, Jewish as well as Christian businessmen could engage in the trade. In the emergency after 1618, impoverished vintners were often compelled for example to sell their harvest in advance – at prices dictated by intermediaries – and take credit, which made them dependent and perhaps led to ill-feeling. Wolfenbüttel, HAB (classification: 38.2 Aug.2°). Literature: Stock 1989, 167 pl.20; Bosbach 1992, fig.3; Harms I, 1985, 347.

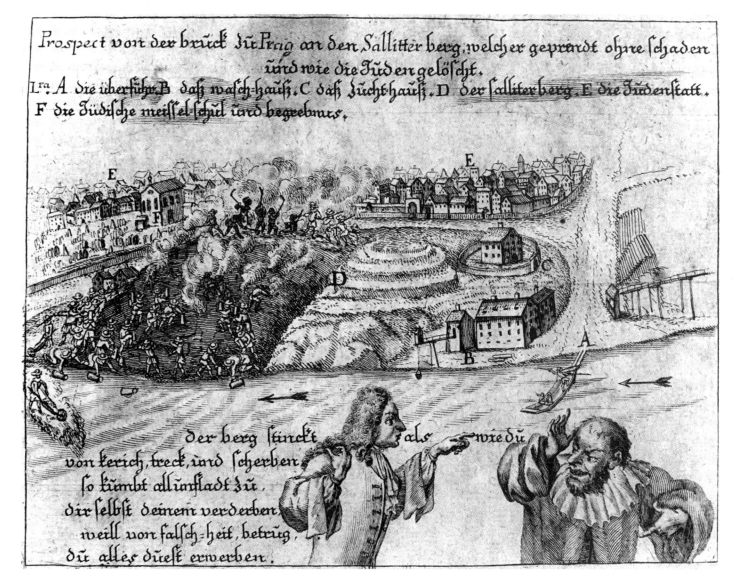

22. The Salliterberg on the edge of the Prague ghetto in flames. This event, an accident which could take place anywhere and at any time, aroused latent anti-Jewish prejudices: 'The hill stinks, like you, of rubbish, filth and old pots. Such an end awaits all filth, and you in your perdition, since you will reap the rewards of falsehood and deceit.' Engraving from Prague, 1750. Tel Aviv, Beth Hatefutsoth. Literature: Rybar 1991, fig. p.56; Berger 1992, 38 no.23.

23. Frontispiece of an anti-Jewish work by Wilhelm Marr (died 1904). Its theme is the infiltration and take-over of Germany by 'alien' Jews and the anxiety which that foments. There is harsh polemic behind the apparently witty picture: the Arminius of the Hermann Monument (dedicated at Detmold in the Teutoburg Forest in 1875, i.e. four years before Marr's work) has been cast down and replaced by a Jewish businessman: the *vae victis* (woe to the conquered) is parodied in Yiddish as *waih victis*.

Lied vom Levi

mit 51 Originalzeichnungen von Siegfried Horn
und
einem Geleitwort von Dr. Hermann Bartmann

24. Frontispiece of a book by Eduard Schwechten, *Das Lied vom Levi* (Düsseldorf: J.Knippenberg 1988 [first edition 1895]). The young Levi, son of a Jewish family, is going out into the world – with useful advice – to make his fortune as a businessman. The frontispiece of this antisemitic poem has been influenced by a similar scene in Sessa's satirical farce, *Unser Verkehr* (first performance in Breslau in 1813), which had an enormous influence.

25. The activity of swindlers. Jews (recognizable by the symbol of the ring on their outer garments) and Christians are engaged in exchanging better coins for worse. Engraving c.1680. Illustration after Diederichs 1908, II, no.915.

Der Judenſpieß bin ich
genant/
Ich far daher durch alle Lande/
Von groſſen Juden ich ſagen wil
Die ſchad dem Land thün in der ſtill.
Der Geiſtlich feſlt vnd würt zü nicht
Der weltlich mechtig hoch auff bricht/
Vnd w aindern vmbher in dem Land
Vnſer wahr iſt laſter/ſünd vnd ſchand.

26. Woodcut frontispiece of a poem printed in Strasbourg in 1541. A Jewish businessman is sitting behind his 'bank', on which coins are heaped high. There is perhaps more money in the sacks at the back of the room. Two borrowers are entering the room, where the Jew continues to sit waiting. Both the picture and the text are anti-Jewish polemic, because they strongly exaggerate the Jewish involvement in money matters and narrow the picture of the Jew to this. Literature: Geiger 1888, 335; Fuchs 1921, fig.13; Zafran 1973, I, 233; for the term 'Judenspiess' see Wander II, 1870, 1041; Grimm IV.2, 1877, 2357. Illustration after Liebe 1903, no.34.

Wie der Deutsche sieben Mal arbeitet und der Jude neun Mal dabei verdient.

1. Der Jude bringt die Einstell-Kuh: —
   Das Kalb, Hans Jörg, erziehest Du;
   Erwuchs zum Jungvieh dann das Kalb
   So theilen wir auf halb und halb.

2. Hans Jörg erzieht das Kalb mit Müh,
   Schmuhl kommt dann, eines Morgens Früh,
   Taxirt das Rind. Hans Jörg nun zahl' er
   Die Hälfte mir; macht 20 Thaler.

3. Der Nachbar Michel braucht 'ne Kuh,
   Schmuhl schmust das Rind vom Jörg ihm zu,
   Und Jörg und Michel drücken Beide
   Dem Schmuhl die Hand. Gott! was 'ne Fraide.

4. Der Michel schaffet spät und früh,
   Macht dick und fett das liebe Vieh.
   Schmuhl bringt zur Zeit den Schlächter an,
   Macht sein Geschäft als Mittelsmann.

5. Des Schlächters Arbeit ist vollbracht,
   Schmuhl hat die Haut sich ausgemacht
   Und hat dem Gerber sie verhandelt,
   Der sie in Leder drauf verwandelt.

6. Das Leder kauft vom Gerbermeister
   Nun unser Schmuhl; zur Messe reist er.
   In Leipzig kauft's der Schuster Witt,
   Schmuhl macht dabei 'nen tücht'gen Schnitt.

7. Der Schuster macht für Hungerlohn
   Nun Schuh und Stiefel für Herrn Cohn...
   Dort prangen sie dann Paar an Paar
   Im Schleuder-Ausverkauf-Bazar.

8. Hans Jörg kauft seine Stiefeln dort,
   Und sind sie schlecht, wirft er sie fort.
   Schmuhl schleicht vorbei und nimmt sie mit,

9. Er macht auch dabei noch Profit.

Und die Moral merkt jedes Kind: Der Deutsche schafft — der Jud' gewinnt!

(left margin) Wählt Paul Förster an Friedenau bei Berlin!

(right margin) Alle Mann zur Wahl! Keiner darf am Wahltag fehlen!

Gegen jüdschen Wucher und Ausbeutung trkt ein die

Deutsch-soziale Antisemiten-Partei.

Unser Candidat für den Wahlkreis Cassel-Melsungen ist

Oberlehrer Paul Förster in Friedenau.

Wer den Bauer und Handwerker schützen, und den Kaufmann vor unehrlicher Concurrenz bewahren will, wer dem ehrlichen Arbeiter seinen verdienten Lohn gönnt, der

 **wählt Förster!**

27. Election pamphlet for the German Social Antisemitic Party, one of the party groups with an antisemitic platform – it included the Antisemitic Popular Party, the German Reform Party and the German Social Reform Party, which wanted to abolish the emancipation of the Jews or limit their civic equality and prevent their immigration. This pamphlet, intended for the electorate of Kassel-Melsungen (1893),

contrasts the alien 'Jewish' nature with the 'German' nature and attempts to create hostility to Jewish merchants among the poor country population of Hessen. The social discontent is focussed on an apparently obvious target by a great simplification and distortion of the social situation (in the period of crisis after the period of rapid industrial expansion). Kassel, Gesamt-Hochschul-Bibliothek, 2° Ms.Hass. 763. Literature: *Juden in Kassel* 1986, 182.

¨BILDERBOGEN· des Kikeriki!

Mieses Geschäft.

Hier steht der Salo Zwiebelduft.
Der voll Sehnsucht „Handeln!" ruft.

Kühn auch lauert dort am Eck,
Handeln ist sein Lebenszweck.

Es winkt vom Fenster die Frau Bolte
Weil sie etwas verkaufen wollte.

Eine Hose ist 's nur, leider,
Und sie spornt die Kauflust beider

Ein Wunderlicher Streitt/
zwischen einem Kipperer vnnd Juden/
Wellicher der beste sein wirdt/ Werdet jhr inn
disem Gesang v. ruemmen.

Im Thon: Venus du vnd dein Kind/ıc

Jud.   **Chrift.**

Getruckt zu Kempten/ im Jahr 1622.

Sie feilschen hin und zerren her —
Ach, die Hose ist nicht mehr!

Und die Moral von der Geschicht'
Rauft nie um eine Hose nicht! —
Denn es stört wie überall.

Zum Schluss mengt sich die Wache ein
Und jeder zahlt ein — Hosenbein! —

Die Konkurrenz auch diesen Fall!
Würden einzeln beide wandeln,
Könnten sie erfolgreich „Handeln!"

28. Frontispiece woodcut of 1622 which refers to the cheats and swindlers. It employs terms used in the seventeenth century for money-changers who melted down good money (silver) and substituted bad money (e.g. copper) for it, at the same manipulating the coins when weighing them or trimming them at the edge; cf. Fuchs 1921, pl.200. Illustration after Hoofacker 1988, no.5.

29. Antisemitic cartoon strip in the journal *Kikeriki*, Vienna (c.1900?), here with the regular theme of the Jew who is tricked despite his acute business sense, one which delighted those hostile to the Jews. As is customary in the antisemitic journal, he is depicted as being physiognomically repulsive. Illustration after Fuchs 1921, no.209.

30. Frontispiece woodcut for Luther's work *A Sermon on Usury* (Wittenberg: Grunenberg 1520). Luther's work is not about the Jews at all; rather, he is attacking the sale of goods at exorbitant prices and the excessive use of capital – here governed by the traditional church prohibition against leying interest. The publisher gave the work this bold title page without Luther's knowledge, evidently to achieve better sales. It in fact depicts a Jew, as is shown by the pseudo-Hebrew on his upper arm and his oriental appearance; the sentence 'Pay or give interest, since I desire profit' is meant to suggest the behaviour of a Jewish creditor to a Christian debtor. Literature: Zafran 1973, I, 232; Bienert 1982, fig.11; Börnert 1983, figs.26–27; Rohbacher and Schmidt 1991, fig. p.83; Wenzel 1992, fig.12. Illustration after Bunte 1989, 448.

Fünftes Capitel.

Kurz die Hose, lang der Rock,
Krumm die Nase und der Stock,
Augen schwarz und Seele grau,
Hut nach hinten, Miene schlau —

So ist Schmulchen Schievelbeiner.
(Schöner ist doch unsereiner!)

Er ist grad vor Fittigs Thür;
Kauwauwau! erschallt es hier. —
Kaum verhallt der rauhe Ton,

So erfolgt das Weitre schon.

Und, wie schnell er sich auch dreht,
Ach, er fühlt, es ist zu spät;

Unterhalb des Rockelores
Geht sein ganze Sach kapores.

31. Caricature of a Jew by Wilhelm Busch (1832–1908) in *Plisch und Plum*. There is some dispute as to whether Busch is expressing his own prejudices against the Jews as a group or just circulating or ironically quoting the mockery of the Jews widespread in the cultured circles of his time even outside antisemitic groups. Literature: Kosch II, 1969, 406–12; Stoffers 1939, 768f.; Bein 1980, II, 192f.; Pleticha 1985,98f., 110f.; Dittmar 1987; Gidal 1988, 236; Dittmar 1992, figs.238–9. Illustration after Fuchs 1921, no.181.

Nathan Kohn, der Wundersohn.

Hier stell' ich vor den Nathan Kohn,
Den genaien Wundersohn,
Von dem die Judenstadt erzählt,
Er werd' emol das Licht der Welt,
Wan is der Nathan Kohn — wie haißt?
Hait' is er schon e Ries' im Gaist!

Der Nathan war erst alt e Johr
As er e Stolz der Mamme war
Der Cateleben, de Mischpoch'.

Es weren alle stolzer noch,
Dos Jüngel mit an' Johr — af Ehr'! —
Platischgelt wie e alter Herr!

Wie's geht so in der Zeiten Lauf,
Der Nathan wachst schön langsam auf,
Er hat jetzt schon e sainen Witz

Und werst herum mit Geistesblitz',
De Christenmadeln foppt er gern,
Weil die sich können doch nix wehr'n.

Bald sucht er sich im Nachbarhaus
Die holde Zukunfts-Kalle aus
Es is Rebetta Veilchenfeld,

Die kriegt emol e bißl Geld,
Er schwört ihr d' Lieb' se is vergnügt,
Daß se den g'scheiden Nathan kriegt.

Der klane Nathan wachst heran,
Da fängt er denn ze handeln an.
Wie er sich räuspert wie er spuckt.

Vom Tate hat er's abgeguckt.
Son Rebbach hat er längst den Sin,
Drum bringt der Mazzes ihm Gewinn.

Und bald entsteht e groiß' Geschäft,
Wo mer de schönsten Sachen trefft.
O Wunder — Chef und Persoual

Vertrogen sich in jedem Fall:
Denn beide stellt der Nathan vor —
Der haut die Goim über's Ohr.

32. 'Nathan Kohn, the Wonder Son',
Vienna 1910 (from the antisemitic journal
Kikeriki). Illustration after Fuchs 1921, pl.
after p.200.

Auch in der Schul' geht Nathan gern
Do glänzt sei' Weisheit wie e Stern
Do zeigt dos gold'ne Wunderkind,
Wie hell sei' Gaist is und gsünd.
Ja, in der ganzen Judeng'schicht',
Do is er trefflich unterricht't.

Die Lehren, wos der Talmud pre
hat tief und ganz erfaßt sei' Go
Und Alles lauscht, wenn er geräh
Den „Schulchan Aruch" memorirt,
Wenn er mit Pathos spricht esoi
Vom dummen, vogelfreien Goi!

Auf diesem Bild zeigt, wie Ihr seht,
Der Nathan Genialität.
Das Opfer seiner Klugheit ist

E Ganserl, dos er gern genießt.
Doch diesesmal ward es arg — de Schand'! —
Des Nathan's Genius verkannt.

Die Polizei — vor der ihm graust —
Packt Nathan Kohn mit roher Faust.
Reactionäres Instinkt.

Das einsperrt, wenn man mausen thut!
Vom Nathan glaube ich jedoch,
Der Fall passirt ihm öfter noch!

3. Association with Saturn, the god of disaster

1. The Jew as one of the 'children of Saturn'. Woodcut by Sebald Beham (or Georg Pencz, the attribution is disputed) in *Die Kinder des Planeten Saturn*, a series of seven woodcuts made around 1531. One picture in this series shows farmers working in the fields and slaughtering pigs, along with cripples, beggars and people receiving alms (distribution of soup by a monk); above right there is a place of execution, and centre left a well (?); behind it are fishermen with rods by a stream. A Jew is talking to the offender in the stocks; the Jew is identified by the Jewish ring (it is yellow in one coloured print which has survived), his beard and the cowl (very often worn by Jews); presumably this is a conversation between debtor and creditor – the prison in the background (cf. the old term 'debtor's tower') fits this. Above, out of the illustration, is the planetary god Saturn swallowing his children, with the poem, 'Saturn old, cold and impure, my children are wicked; I can encompass the twelve signs in thirty years'. This recalls the orbit of Saturn round the sun, which lasts for thirty years, and the twelve signs of the Zodiac. The picture sets the Jews in the harsh world of life and work in early modern times, not without some understanding of their social role as pawnbrokers and givers of credit, but also contributes to reducing the public picture of the Jew to a kind of 'Shylock' type. The popular literature of the Middle Ages generally held that 'the planet which controls the fate of the Jews is the most malign – Saturn' (Zafran 1979, 18). In a way this led to an 'inter-relationship and even identification between Saturn and the Jews' (Zafran 16). Literature; Zafran 1970, pl.5a; Myter 1983, fig. p.101; Müller 1984, fig.19; R.Wohlfahrt in Herzig and Schoeps 1993, fig.8; cf. Tinkle 1987. Illustration after Diderichs 1908, I, no.178.

2. Saturn (i.e. Kronos, in Greek mythology the father of Zeus; he swallowed his own children in order to maintain rule over the gods; in the late Middle Ages and early modern times he was often regarded as a hostile star and the god of disaster, or as the deity above all asociated with meanness, the harsh life of business, and toil in earning one's living) pictured as a Jew (with Jewish hat and Jewish ring). The basis of the picture is probably the assumption of an affinity between Jewishness and disaster or evil. Woodcut in the Almanach of the Nuremberg printer Peter Wagner, from 1492. Literature: Zafran 1979, pl.8b. Illustration after Schramm 1920, XVIII, no.409 (section).

4. The 'Judensau'

(a) Depictions connected with Christian churches

1. Badly weathered sandstone relief outside the choir of the city church in Wittenberg, c.1305. The inscriptions Rabini, Schem-Hamphoras, i.e. 'of the rabbi, an expounded (or true, authentic) name (of God)', were chiselled in only after Luther's death. They refer to Luther's work under this title and his comments on this relief in it (Weimarer Ausgabe, Vol.53, Weimar 1920, 87f.) or to kabbalistic statements about God (see Junghans 1979, fig.10.) This picture is a copy: some details are inaccurate (thus the hats were funnel-shaped, as can still be seen from good modern photographs), but it is largely exact, even to the Jewish rings. Literature: Fuchs 1921, fig.16; Holdschmidt 1935, frontispiece; Güde 1973,1; Shachar 1974, pls. 26–27, 39; Strauss 1975, II, fig. p.167; Bott 1983, fig. 278; Schouwink 1985, 87f.; Schuder and Hirsch 1990, fig. p.408; Wenzel 1992, fig p.299. Illustration after Wolfius 1600 (II, 1031).

RABINI, SCHEMHAMPHORAS,

2. Magdeburg, cathedral. Capital frieze on the interior on the south wall of the Ernestine chapel, c.1270. Literature: Bergner 1905, fig.483; Fuchs 1921, fig.1; Shachar 1974, pls.13a–15a; Schuder and Hirsch 1990, fig. p.168. Ilustration after Otte I, 1883, fig.257 (copy).

4. A Jew (Jewish boy?) recognizable by his Jewish hat, typical of the time, is holding a young pig in a friendly, even loving, way. This picture imputes to the Jews almost a certain affinity to pigs. At any rate the viewer is meant to think that Jews are quite a different kind of people from normal Christians. Badly weathered relief in the Lutheran collegiate and parish church of St.Mary in Lemgo (Lippe), made around 1310. Literature: Thümmler 1970, fig. 198; Gaul and Korn 1983, pls.243–8; Schouwinck 1985, 76. Illustration after Shachar, pl.7.

5. Judensau (with allusion to a ritual murder). Choirstall relief, Cologne, cathedral, c.1222. Literature: *EJ* 1971, III, 117; Shachar 1974, pl.16b; Ben–Sasson II, 1979, fig.26; *Juden in Köln* 1984, fig.83; Wenninger 1984, fig. p.83; Wenninger 1984, fig. p.26; Eckert 1991, 381f.; Rohrbacher and Schmidt 1991, 312. Photograph: Rheinisches Bildarchiv, Cologne.

3. Capital relief in the choir of Uppsala cathedral, middle of the fourteenth century. Literature: Blumenkranz 1965, fig.48; Wenzel 1992, fig. p.298. Illustration after Shachar 1974, pl.20.

6. Regensburg, cathedral, relief on a southern buttress (at a height of around seven metres). The badly weathered picture seems to be an allegory of gluttony (*gula*) in the framework of a series of depictions of vices and virtues. An older bearded Jew is holding by the ear a large sow to which two young Jews are lovingly attached (almost like her piglets), sucking or wanting to suck on her dugs. This almost familiar juxtaposition and combination of pig and Jews suggests to the viewer that there is a natural affinity between the Jew and the pig. Literature: Mader 1933, I, fig.21; Shachar 1974, pl.18b; Eder 1992, 113. Illustration after Schuegraf 1848 (copy of its condition around 1848).

(b) Other

1. Anonymous woodcut from south Germany c.1470, only preserved in some uncoloured copies of a later date (reprinted from the original stock). One example is in Nuremberg, Germanisches Nationalmuseum, Inv.no. HB 24631/1269. The inscriptions read: 'We Jews should all note well how it stands between us and the pig. We should never forget that we should not eat swine's flesh. Now see, dear people, how I make use of our mother. Suck hard, dear brothers, and I will blow in her arse. We don't eat roast pork, and that is why we are yellow and our breath stinks.' The special Jewish form of dress, the mock-Hebrew on the hems and the absurd action of the Jews, who are gathering like a family around their 'mother', make the statement of the picture very polemical: the pig is an allegory of the Jewish religion, whose adherents lack the reason (*ratio*) of a thinking Christian because they are unwilling to see the truth of the Christian faith, and are closer to beasts without reason than to human beings. In addition to the combination 'pig-unclean-sinful-Jew' known since the time of the church fathers, there is also the absurdity of the Jewish religion (the pig has the udders of a sow and the tusks of a boar), which can also be seen from the way in which the medieval Christian theologians often speak of the *stultitas* and *perversitas* of the Jews. The Jewish rider is

also sitting wrong way round on the backside of the pig. Literature: Major 1908, pl.18; Hollstein 1954, IV, fig. p.149; *Mon.Jud.Kat.* 1963, B 306; Shachar 1974, pl.30; Schubert 1979, fig.26; Sievers 1981, fig. pp.78f.; Schouwinck 1985, fig. 13; Paas 1985–86, fig. p.324; Deneke 1988, 174. Illustration after Liebe 1903, no.11.

2. Single-leaf print, Frankfurt 1618. The general denigration of the Jews is here combined with the 'Judensau' motif. Literature: Stock 1939, 81, pl.6; *Mon.Jud.Kat.* 1963, B 309; Shachar 1974, pl.49; Paas II 1986, fig. p.178;. Illustration after Fuchs 1921, no.42.

Der Juden Synagog,

Vff Teutsch Kirch oder Schul genandt,
Damit es werd im Reich bekandt,
Zu gefallen also das erdicht,
Der Leser wolts verachten nicht

A   Arawenos der gelehrte Narr
    Zeigt an den Seckel vnd Brieffe fern,
    Die Spitzköpff zu vnterweisen,
    Wie sie die Christen sollen bescheissen.

B   Butzmann der galgendieb,
    Stöst den Heber in Arß fein tieff.

C   Cuntzmann schlecktauß, wart mit fleiß,
    Biß die Sauw jhm ins Maul scheiß,

D   Doctor Hünereyer kam auch herbey,
    Damit der Rath fein gantz sey.

E   Ertzmann spitzbub in der Karten,
    Thut des fressens vñ schlemmens auch warte.

F   Fortz fresser fang auff, friß geschwindt,
    Es ist gut für vnser Gesindt.

G   Gumbel zum Sewtrog macht sich leicht,
    Freylich ein Sauw die ander reucht.

H   Hermann Stutz ist mein Namen,
    So kompt die Gesellschafft zusammen.

I   Judas verrieth Christum behendt,
    Auch das Kindlein zu Trynt.

K   Krotzebeisser steht mit weil,
    Sicht an das Kalb an der Seul.

L   Lortzartz Rotzaff heiß ich,
    Die Sauw mit dem Strick führ ich.

M   Mutzkopff bey der Stiegen,
    Hat ein Buch, kan frey drauß liegen,
    Letzlich vnser Freyheit nichts benommen,
    Weil die Gesellschafft ist beynander kömen.
    Also bleibt wer ihr seyd,
    Daß euch der Teuffel reit.

Ein Ehrliebenden Christ die Noth zwingt,
Der Judt singt,
Vnd der Teuffel springt,
Letzlich das Fewr brint.

(c) The 'Frankfurt Judensau'

On the old Brückenturm in Frankfurt am Main there was a fresco (made between 1475 and 1507 and destroyed in 1801) which was evidently a kind of tourist attraction; at any rate it was publicized in a great variety of different ways in flysheets and other publications between the seventeenth and the nineteenth centuries: the earliest known (or extant) version dates from 1618. The copies which have been preserved – and which are a good substitute for the lost original, like extant manuscripts of a lost archetype – have in common a connection between the Judensau motif and the motif of ritual murder (Simon of Trent), and it is this combination in particular which seems to have made this picture so extraordinarily effective. In these depictions the Jews are evil beings who do quite incomprehensible things and are closer to beasts and the devil than to Christians. Indeed their obscene nature (including coprophagy and scatology) can raise doubts as to whether they are still people at all. Not only does the devil have a Jewish physiognomy in some pictures, but his Jewish ring identifies him as a Jew; in keeping with this, the Jewess who usually forms part of the group rides on a he-goat (a symbol of the devil). Goethe also mentions the picture in the Brückentum once (*Dichtung und Wahrheit*, Book 4), which confirms how well known this fresco was. Literature: Liebe 1903, fig.28; Diedrichs II, 1980, fig.1183; Fuchs 1921, fig.50; Körber and Pugel 1935, fig. p.212; Stock 1939, fig. pp.86, 209; Trachtenberg 1961 (frontispiece); *Mon.Jud.Kat.* 1963, B 305; *EJ* 1971, 119–20, fig. 7c.; Zafran 1973, I, 112; Shachar 1974, pls.42–45, 61a; Lohrmann 1982, fig.83; Harms I, 1985, fig. p.351; Schouwinck 1985, fig,18; Paas II, 1986, figs. pp.175–6; Po-Chia Hsia 1988, figs. pp.175–6; Schuder and Hirsch 1990, fig. p.215 and colour plate p.632; Rohrbacher and Schmidt 1991, fig. p.17. The illustrations here, a selection in chronological order, follow Paas II, 177 (= first picture, dated 1618); Wolfenbüttel, HAB, 38.25 Aug. 2° fol.229 (= second picture, first half of the seventeeth century); Liebe 1903, no.28 (= third picture, seventeenth century); Schouwinck 1985, fig. 18 (= fourth picture, dated 1678); Fuchs 1921, no.50 (= fifth picture, beginning of the eighteenth century).

5. Caricatures relating to equal civic rights and the emancipation of the Jews

2. Confession. Lithograph c.1848 (26.5 x 20.8 cm). Bamberg, Staatsbibliothek (classification: M.v.O.C. I.88). Literature: Dittmar 1992, 192.

1. English caricature against the Naturalization Bill of 1753. The draft of this law presented to Parliament ('The Jew Bill' [according to which even Jews not born in England were to have the right to own land]) had to be withdrawn by the government because of the hostility to the Jews. Illustration after *EJ* IX, 1932, 967–8.

Reich u. glücklich soll ein jeder, Jude, auf der Erde seijn._
'Oder 'gilt nicht, _noch: 'Entweder'," Sondern, Gojem gib dich drein.
Gegen Christen Wucher treiben, ist erlaubt u. kein Betrug.
Er soll bei der Arbeit bleiben, für uns ackern hinterm Pflug.
Alle Tage, jeden Morgen, Geh der Christ zur Arbeit seijn.
Wenn wir ihm aus Gnade borgen, lass für hohen Zins nur seijn.
Das heiß ich Emanzipiren, nehmen kühn mit Fug u. Recht.
Was zu unserm Glück kann führen, u. der Christ sei unser Knecht.
Gojem kamen wie die Hunde, schändeten des Tempels Ruhm.
Ewig blutet diese Wunde: Plünderer, unsres Eigenthums,
Alle Schätze dieser Erde, sagt uns Moses heilig Wort,
Sind für uns: Jehovas Heerde! _ Er ist unserm Volk ein Hort.
Uns, aus Arons Stamm geboren, Uns gehört die ganze Welt,
Wir allein sind auserkoren, die des Himmels Licht erhellt,
Uns ward Chnaan entrißen, Tempel, Eigenthum zerstört.
Jeder Gojem hat zu büßen, Nichts ist das ihm angehört.
Heilig nur ist unser Glaub, Gott geweiht ist unser Stamm,
Selbst der Oelzweig einer Traube, deutete es wunderbar.
Der Jehova ganz zu dienen, leben unverwischt wir treu,
Und wir sehn mit stolzen Mienen, auf der Gojem Dudeldei.

3. Cartoon from Vienna (by Loeschenkohl) of the unsoldierly Jewish recruits, c.1780. This aimed to show that the Jews were cowardly and whining, and unsuitable as soldiers (and at the same time as full citizens) by virtue of their 'Jewish' nature. J.H.Loeschenkohl (from Regensburg, and active in Vienna from 1779; for him see Thieme and Becker XXIII, 1929, 323) made many woodcuts and engravings which provide information about the history and culture of his time. Many of his works were forerunners of the later illustrated journals and appeared in substantial editions. Literature: Liebe 1903, fig.98; Stock 1939, pl.45. Illustration after Fuchs 1921, no.59.

Die sich bey Erlernung des Exercitiums beklagenden jüdischen Rekruten.

Mauschel.

Verzweifelndes Geschick! au wei! wir sind verloren.
Allein zum Unglück sind wir auf die Welt gebohren.
Schau her, o deutsche Welt! schau mit Verwundrung an.
Wir ziehen in das Feld. Ach! schickt sich dieses dann?
Ein Mauschel und Soldat zugleich wir müssen werden.
Wir schwören bey dem Bart, bey Himmel und bey Erden,
Die Sache geht nicht an, weils an Kurage fehlt.
Und dennoch werden wir dem Krieger zugesellt.
Uns dieses gar nicht schmeckt, wir haben keine Freude,
Wir fühlen stete Quaal, und lauter Herzenleide.
Kurage bey uns fehlt, man lacht uns aus und ein.
Es kann ein junge Katz bey uns ein Dracke seyn.

Korporal.

Gut Herz, mein Sohn! im Feld wird sich der Muth schon mehren.
Es kann der Haßelstock euch auch Kurage lehren.

Mauschel.

Au wei, Herr Korporal! ums Himmels Wunder doch,
Was biethet ihr uns an? Ev was erzählt ihr noch?
Wie wird das Goienvolk nicht in die Hände klatschen,
Wenn uns der Haßelstock soll auf dem Buckel batschen!
Wär wider das Gesetz; wir sind es nicht gewohnt.
Ach laß von diesem doch uns Jüden seyn verschont.

Korporal.

Macht nicht viel Plauderey, schickt euch zum Exerciren;
Sonst will den Buckel euch recht tapfer runter schmieren.

Mauschel.

Hört zu, Herr Korporal! wir sind dazu entschlossen;
Ach seyd doch über uns nicht zornig und verdrossen.
Wir greifen willig an; doch sagen wir dabey,
Wie daß von unserm Fleiß nicht viel zu hoffen sey.
Wir fürchten Pulverrauch, und auch der Kugel pfeifen;
Wir fürchten uns sehr stark wenn die Kanonen streifen.
Betrachten Sie, wie tief uns dieß zu Herzen geht,
Wenn uns der tolle Feind einmal entgegen steht.
Wie leichtlich könnten wir noch über all Beschwerden
In solcher Lebensgefahr wohl gar erschossen werden.

Korporal.

Durch eine Kugel stirbt ein braver Feldsoldat.
Wenns euch nicht besser geht, ist wenig für euch Schad.

Mauschel.

Gott walt, Herr Korporal! das kann doch nicht bestehen;
Es würd in dem Gesetz ein großer Bruch geschehen.
Einmal für allemal, es kann gewiß nicht seyn,
Ihr wisset ohne das, wir essen nichts von Schwein.
Wenn wir bey Goien seyn, und mit den Türken fechten,
Wer wird uns mittlerweil zur Speis die Ochsen schlechten?
Wer giebt uns andres mehr? wer giebt uns Koscherwein?
Ich sag es ehrlich, Herr! es kann gewiß nicht seyn.

Korporal.

Im Feld ist alles frey, wo das Gesetz gehoben;
Drum macht mir kein Geschrey mit euren schlechten Proben.
Was der Soldat genießt, ihm allezeit wohl schmeckt,
Ansonst der Haßelstock euch Appetit erweckt.

Mauschel.

Mord tausend Mages wei! itzt hats den Teufel g'sehen,
Itzt heißts, den Buckel her! es hilft kein Bitt noch Flehen.
Au wei! der Teufel hat das Schlagen aufgebracht;
Au wei, Herr Korporal! hört wie die Rippen kracht.
Au wei! Meßias komm; ach laß dein Horn doch blasen,
Wie Donner vom Mittag mit Stürmen und mit Rasen.
Au wei! ach komm zu Hülf der armen Judenschaar,
Au wei! ach rette uns vor Streich und Lebensgefahr.
Au wei! Herr Korporal! ach schont mich unterdessen,
Wir wollen koscher Fleisch, Sauerkraut und Knödel fressen.
Es ist uns alles gut, es ist uns alles recht,
Ach hört doch einmal auf mit diesem Stockgefecht.
Wir fressen dünne Würst, wir fressen Speck und Plunzen;
Au wei, Herr Korporal! ich muß in d'Hosen brunzen.
Au wei, Herr Korporal! erhöret mein Geschrey.
Vor Schmerzen bekre ich, au wei! au wei! au wei!

Habts Acht ! Nehmt's euch zusam Hascheln ! mer kümen zu gehen vor unsern
Kümandanten sein Haus! Regimentstremler ! schlog ein ! trum! bum! trum!

4. Viennese caricature of the emancipation
of the Jews, 1848. Literature: Dittmar
1992, fig.68. Illustration after Fuchs 1921,
plate after p.128.

XII. The History of the Jews in Christian Europe: The Christian View

1. Law and social history

(a) The Jews under the protection of emperor and pope

1. The German emperor and the Jews. On his way back from his coronation in the Lateran to S.Sabina in 1312, i.e during his procession through the city of Rome, Henry II receives the ritual of greeting and submission from representatives of the Jewish community of Rome which these customarily performed to popes and emperors on the latters' accession – at the same time asking for the continuation of the traditional protection of Jews. Text: *Imperator redit dans Judeis legem Moysi in rotulo*, i.e. on his return (to S.Sabina) the emperor restores to the Jews their Torah scroll (which previously they had ritually offered to him), thus confirming their right to practise their religion freely. The strange appearance of the group of Jews in their special dress so impressed the miniaturist, who presumably like his bishop was a witness to this encounter, that he added this scene to the codex in Trier in 1335. Miniature in Codex Trevirensis (i.e. a collection of documents of Balduin, died 1354, Archbishop of Trier and Count of Luxembourg, into which is bound a cycle of wash pen drawings on parchment in which the journey of Balduin's brother, the emperor Henry VII, to Italy is depicted). Koblenz, Landeshauptarchiv, Balduineum I, Best. 1 C, no.1, folio 24 recto. Literature: Irmer 1881, pl.24; Eichler 1935, pl. on p.105; *Mon. Jud.Kat.*1963, B 39; Blumenkranz 1965, fig.16; Heyen 1965; *Germ.Jud.*II 1, 1968, fig. after p.XXIV; *EJ* 1971, VII, 465, fig.4;

Jmparor redit dans Judeis legē movsi ī rotulo.

Rosenfeld 1978, fig.53; *Schatzkunst Trier* 1984, 144f.; RDK VIII, 1987, 1417, fig.1a; Nolden 1988, 41; cf. Benoschofsky 1989,

11 (the same ritual for the Hungarian king Matthias Corvinus, 1476). Illustration after *Synagoga 1960*, D 120.

2. The Jews ask Pope Martin (11 November 1417 – 20 February 1431) on 21 November 1417 in Constance for the traditional confirmation of their freedom to observe the law. As a rule, at the beginning of the period of office of a new pope there was a meeting with a delegation of Jews who welcomed the new pope and sought to gain his protection. In this connection, many popes issued a *Sicut Judaeis* bull of protection at the beginning of their time in office. Miniature (coloured pen drawing) in the Chronicle of the Council of Constance by Ulrich Richental (died 1437), in one of the copies which have been preserved (the original has been lost). Constance, Rosgarten Museum, c.1456, folio 105 verso and 106 recto. The text which interests us here runs: 'Then the Jews went to meet him bringing many large lighted candles and in the dress in which they had been standing all day, bearing their ten commandments on a pole under a golden canopy with four staves, on a cushion which was of red satin and had four tassels and a bell on each tassel. And when they moved the staves, the bells sounded and almost seemed to be singing Hebrew. And when they came to the pope, they knelt before him, offered him the ten commandments and asked him to confirm their freedom, the freedoms which they had had previously. The pope did not want their commandments, but our lord the king received them and said, "Moses' commandments are good and right, but you are not willing to observe them, nor do you understand them

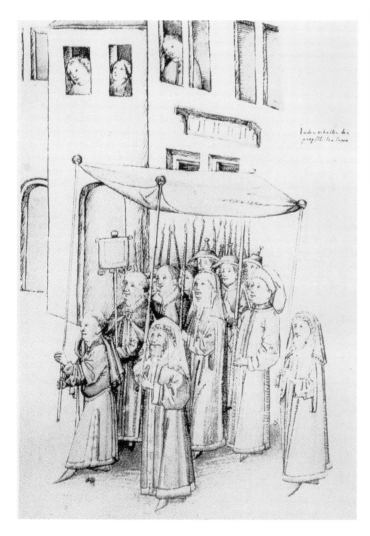

rightly." Then the pope said something secretly which I could not understand and turned to the Jews and spoke loudly, so that the crowd could hear: "*Omnipotens deus avertat velamen ab oculis vestris, ut possitis videre lumen eterne vite!* [May the Lord God remove the veil from your eyes that you may see the light of eternal life]." And then he gave them the blessing with his right hand, "*In nomine patris et filii et spiritus sancti.*" Then he went back through the streets to the upper market, from the market back to St Stephen's, and from St Stephen's to the upper court, where he gave the people his blessing and went back into the palace. Then everyone returned to their homes, and the pope sent the horse on which he had ridden to Heinrich of Ulm, who was the burgomaster. And all this took place up to the eleventh hour' (Buck 1882, 129f.). Literature: Buck 182; Feger 1964; *EJ* V, 1971, 913–14, fig.2; Bialostocki 1972, fig.87; Stemberger 1983, fig. p.502; Matthiesen 1985; Unger 1986, 142–4; *Germ.Jud.* III 1, 1987, 667; Stemberger 1990, 181–4 (F.Gregorovius); *Verfasserlexikon* VIII, 1992, 55–60. Illustration after *Mon.Jud.Kat.* 1963, B 278.

(b) The Sachsenspiegel miniatures

1. A prominent secular cleric and a Jew bearing weapons. On journeys, clerics and Jew are already protected against violence by their specific special form of dress (tonsure, Jewish hat); they may also carry weapons, but if they come to harm they lose their special rights and are treated like laity (on Landrecht III, 2). Miniature in a Sachsenspiegel manuscript (the author of the Sachsenspiegel is Eike von Repgow [died after 1233]), c.1320–1330. It attests that the gradual loss of the Jewish right to bear weapons is a development of the high Middle Ages. Heidelberg, UB, Cod.Pal.-germ.164, folio 12. Literature: Koschorreck 1977, fig 31; Kisch I, 1978, 28; Lohrmann 1982, fig.83; Schmidt-Wiegand 1986. Illustration after *Mon.Jud.Fazit* 1963, no.15.

2. Secular clerics, religious, girls, women and Jews are under the protection of the law of peace appointed by the king (on Landrecht II, 66, 1). Miniature in a Sachsenspiegel manuscript, c 1320–1330. Heidelberg, UB, Cod. Palat. germ. 164, folio 11. Literature: Schild 1980, fig.12; cf. Drescher 1989, fig.18. Illustration after *Mon.Jud.Fazit* 1963, no.16.

3. The creditor (of a defaulting debtor) transfers the pledge to a Jew: the latter pays the creditor the sum of the debt and takes the horse away (on Landrecht I, 70, 2). Miniature in a Sachenspiegel manuscript, around the middle of the fourteenth century. Dresden, LB, Sachsenspiegel, folio 21. Literature: Amira I, 1902, pl.41. Illustration after *EJ* V, 1930, 983–4.

4. A Jew, a Frank and a Saxon, as legally recognized by the law and regular assessors, stand before the judge, who is seated; as a pagan, a Wend (standing apart) cannot plead at law. Miniature in a Sachenspiegel manuscript, around the middle of the fourteenth century. Dresden, LB, Sachsenspiegel, folio 21 (on Landrecht III, 760,1). Literature: Kisch 1949, fig. p.51. Illustration after Amira I, 1902, pl.99.

5. The Christian who is killing a Jew is beheaded by the executioner on the orders of the count (on Landrecht III, 7, 2–3). A Jew upon whom church vessels are found (bought or taken as a pledge) is accused before the count and then hanged (on Landrecht III, 7,4). Miniature in a Sachenspiegel manuscript, around the middle of the fourteenth century. Dresden, LB, Sachsenspiegel, folio 37. Literature: Amira I, 1902, pl.74. Illustration after *EJ* V, 1930, 985–6.

6. Jews bearing weapons (with the Jewish hat as a group characteristic) in an armed levy before a fortress; only secular clerics, women, sextons and shepherds are exempt from conscription to a levy (on Landrecht II, 71,3). Miniature in a Sachenspiegel manuscript from the fourteenth century. Wolfenbüttel, HAB, illustrated manuscript of the Sachsenspiegel, folio 41 verso. Illustration after Scheele 1991, volume of plates, no.47.

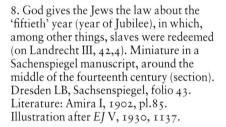

8. God gives the Jews the law about the 'fiftieth' year (year of Jubilee), in which, among other things, slaves were redeemed (on Landrecht III, 42,4). Miniature in a Sachenspiegel manuscript, around the middle of the fourteenth century (section). Dresden LB, Sachsenspiegel, folio 43. Literature: Amira I, 1902, pl.85. Illustration after *EJ* V, 1930, 1137.

7. Excommunication of the emperor. The pope may excommunicate the emperor for only three reasons: doubting the true faith (here illustrated by the emperor [the central of the five figures] discussing with a Jew); abandoning or casting off his wife; and destroying a house of God (on Landrecht III, 57,1). Miniature in a Sachenspiegel manuscript, around the middle of the fourteenth century. Dresden LB, Sachsenspiegel, folio 46. Literature: Amira I, 1902, pl.92. Illustration after *Mon.Jud.Fazit* 1963, no.14.

(c) The Jewish oath (more iudaico)

1. A Jew giving the oath in a Christian court. Here he is standing on a pig's skin, a form of this procedure customary in some places. Prague, City Archive, sixteenth century. Literature: Berger 1992, fig.12. Illustration after Rybár 1991, 42.

2. *Fide sed vide.* Seventeenth-century engraving with an allegorical depiction of the Jewish oath. The Jew is prominently wearing the Jewish ring, which here also here has the function of denouncing him. Cf. Wander 1867, II, 1037, 1038. In the twentieth century Elvira Baur, *Trau keinem Fuchs auf grüner Eid und keinem Jud bei seinem Eid. Ein Bilderbuch für Gross und Klein* ('Trust no fox in the open country and no Jew in his oath. A picture book for grown-ups and children'), Nuremberg: Stürmer Verlag [7] 1936, bases herself on the 'Jewish oath' theme. This work has been available for a decade in *Mit Hängemaul und Nasenzinken... Erziehung zur Unmenschlichkeit. Medienpaket für Gruppenleiter und Lehre. Texte*, dkv–Reihe, der kleine verlag düsseldorf 1984, ed. G.B.Ginzel et al. Illustration after Stock 1939, 215.

Fide sed Vide

Prædator, lupus et Iudæus apella, sequitur
Militiæ Libycæ conspurcant ructibus Orbem

Wer einem Wolff trawt auff der heyd.
einem Iuden auff seinem eyd,
Vnd einem Kriegsman bey seim gwißen
der wirdt von allen dreyen bschißen.

3. Woodcut (by Hans Frutenbach) in the *Laienspiegel* by Ulrich Tenngler (Augsburg: Hans Othmar 1508, folio MVI). Jews had the right to give the oath 'according to Jewish custom' (*more Iudaico*) in legal proceedings between Jews and Christians, because for religious reasons they were not allowed to repeat Christian formulae for oaths. The Jewish oath was given in the synagogue or – as here – in a Christian court. While pronouncing the text of the oath the person swearing it had to have a copy of the Torah in his hand; perhaps the relevant passage here was Ex.20.7 (the commandment against perjury). The Jew swearing has two helpers, who like him are wearing the usual Jewish dress (with the Jewish ring, *rota*); this is a book, not a Torah scroll of the kind used in the synagogue; the composition of the picture probably explains why the man is putting his left rather than his right hand (as was customary) on the text to swear the oath: the right hand would not have been so visible from the perspective chosen. Literature: Liebe 1903, fig.9; Rupprich 1970, 371; *EJ* 1971, XII, 1302 fig.1; Zimmermann 1973, 196–9; Kisch I, 1978, 140,157 (with 169f.); Deneke 1988, fig. p.175; Battenberg 1990, I, 177, fig.8. Illustration after *Mon. Jud.Kat.*1963, B.260 no.15 (Nuremberg, GNM, Inv. no.II, 4656).

Traw / Schaw Wem.

Wer einem Wolff trawt auff der Heyd/
Einem Juden bey seinem Eyd/
Einem Krämer bey seim Gewissn.
Der wirdt von allen dreyen gebissn.

Tauben bey Raben/
Meidlein bey Knaben/
Soldaten auff der Awen/
Pfaffen bey den Frawen/
Sol niemandt vertrawen.

Ach Gott wie gern ich wissen wolt/
Wem ich auff Erden trawen solt/
Judas Kuß ist jetzt worde new/
Nur gute Wort vnnd falsche Trew
Lache mich an vnd gib mich hin/
Das ist jetzunder der Welt Sinn.
Wann der Mundt spricht: Gott grüsse dich/
So dencket das Hertz/ hüte dich;
Ich sih mich vmb zu aller frist/
Kan doch nicht sehn wer mein Freundt ist.
Mich fragt offt mancher wie's mir geht/
Gieng es mir wol/ es jhn weh thet/
Mit solchen Trewen wie ers meint/
Wil ich auch lachen wann er weint.
Es heist jetzundt dein Freundt zu Hauß/
Jedoch fünff Stück nimm ich mir auß/

   traw dir
   glaub dir
Ich borg dir   nicht.
   leyhe dir
   Verbürg mich dir

Ausser diesem zu aller zeit/
Bin ich zu dienen dir bereit.
Das sind die Freund da in der Noht/
Zwey vnd dreissig gehn auff ein Loth/
Sols aber ein harter Standt seyn/
Gehn funfftzig auff ein Quintelein.
Heut so sind wir gute Geselln/
Baldt thun wir vns zu andern stelln.

Dann Trew ist vber Meer gezogen/
Die Warheit gen Himmel geflogen/
Die Frombkeit ist hinweg getriebn/
Vntrew ist vns zur letzt hie bliebn.
Wer nur den Fuchs wol streichen kan/
Hat Gnad vnd Gunst bey jedermann/
Ist auch allzeit der best am brätt/
Muß vornen seyn vnd hinden stätt.
Ob er gleich aller Schalckheit voll/
Schadt nicht/er bleibt bey Ehren wol/
Wer aber bey der Warheit hält/
Bekompt vngunst in dieser Welt/
Darzu verhaßt / muß leyden Noht/
Man gönnt jhm nicht das liebe Brot.
Dann die Welt gantz vntrew ist wordn/
Vnd jetzt getretten in den Ordn/
Da alle Gutthat baldt vergessen/
Vnd guts mit Vntrew wirdt gemessen/
Kein wunder wehrs man ließ anstahn/
Vnd würde niemand guts gethan.
So nun einer dir dancket nit /
Gedenck es ist der Menschen Sitt.
Laß drumb nicht guts zu thun von alln/
Vnd deinen Nechsten seyn zu gfalln.
Doch magstu sehen wer er sey/
Vndanckbarkeit wohnt vielen bey.
Mancher dient einm bey Tag vnd Nacht/
Der jhm darmit nur Feindschafft macht.
Auch soltu einm nicht dienen heut /
Vnd Morgen vorwerffen zum Leidt.

Volg dieser Lehr / Laß alles liegen/
Ein jeden ehr/ Was da nicht dein/
Red was ist wahr / So wirstu fein/
Was kaufft zahl bar. Können passieren/
Sey still/verschwiege/ Vnd deutlich spüren/
   Daß ein getrewe Handt/
   Gehet durch alle Landt.

Verachte nicht mich / noch die meinen/
Beschaw zuvor dich vnd die deinen.
Sih vor auff dich/ darnach auff mich/
Thu ich vnrecht/ so hüte dich.
Vrtheil auch nicht wie mich thust sehen/
Wer weiß wie fromb du thust bestehen.
Verschmäh den nicht der vngstalt ist/
Ob du am Leib gerader bist.
Laß dein Zung auch dich nicht betriegn/
Dein Nächsten fälschlich zu beliegn.

Ich wolt daß mir ein Meister klug/
Geb einen Schildt gegen Betrug /
Vnd einen Helm gegn Haß vnd Neidt/
Den brauch ich wol zu dieser Zeit.
Auch für Vntrew ein gute Salbn/
Die wolt ich streichen allenthalbn.
Vnd ein bewehrts Kraut für den Todt/
So wehr Ich sicher in der Noht.

J. V. H.   M. DC. XXXIII.

4. 'Whom do you trust?' Illustrated flysheet (engraving with eighty rhyming verses), Strasbourg 1633. The verses (with four stresses and rhymed in couplets) interpret and moralize the picture. This depicts: on the left, a wolf; below centre, a man negotiating with a Jew (group characteristics: ring on the coat, beard, beret); below right, a fashionably dressed young man who is displaying wares from a tray; above left on the veranda, a woman talking with a cleric; above centre, a girl chatting to a young man; above left, a kind of guard (soldier) with a halberd going towards the hedge which a man (a thief) is just climbing over. The verses – containing a variety of traditional proverbs – bewail the faithlessness and perversity of the world, but also warn the reader to avoid misrepresentation and flattery and not to judge others over-hastily. So current bad behaviour is described and warned against, and the reader is admonished to loyalty and honesty and a self-critical attitude. Despite this moralistic attitude the flysheet perpetuates contemporary group prejudices, the knowledge of which it can presuppose in its readers; it tends rather to reinforce these prejudices by its suggestive combination of text and picture: Wolfenbüttel, HAB, classification: IE 53. Literature: Harms I, 1985, 101.

Vorstellung/
Wie ein Jud vor Christlicher Obrigkeit in Breßlau den Eyd zu schweren hat.

Erstlich wird der Jude võ den Gerichten nothdürfftig erinnert/ dafern er einen falschē Eyd thun werde/ daß nicht allein des Allmächtigen Gottes/ sondern auch der weltlichen Gerichte Strafe zum wenigsten die Abschlagung der Faust/ damit er geschworen/ folgen würde.

Hernachmals wird ihm die Weise / so in Vollziehung des Eydes gehalten wird / angezeiget/ als nemlich/ daß er seinē rechten Arm bis an die Brust entblössen/ und dieselbige Hand auf die Hebräischen Zehen Gebot legen / auch auf

einer Säu-Haut stehend schweren soll.

Auf dieses wird ihm die Form des Eydes fürgelesen / nachmals auch beschrieben zugestellt / sich über Quer-Nacht/ oder auch nach der Gerichte Erkänntniß länger darüber zu bedencken. Und wann er sich alsdenn zum Eyde geschickt gemachet hat/ so muß er zuvor das andere Gebot in den Zehen Geboten in Hebräischer Sprache lesen / darnach muß er auf die Schweim-Haut mit blossen Füssen tretten/ und mit entblöstem rechten Arm/dieselbige Hand auf die Zehen Gebot legen/ und nachfolgender gestalt schweren.

Der Juden-Eyd.

Ich N.N. Jude/ schwere bey dem Allmächtigen GOTT Adonai, der Himmel und Erden/ auch alles/ so darinnen ist/ erschaffen hat/ der HErr ist über alle Malachim, der seinem auserwehlten Volck die heilige Torah gegeben hat/ die auch in diesem Buch/ darinnen ich meine rechte Hand liegen habe/ recht und warhafftig beschrieben sind/ daß rc. (hier wird die Sache ausgesprochen/ worüber geschworen wird.) und daß in der Warheit also/ und nicht anders sey/ denn wie ich jetzo ausgesagt habe / das bezeuge ich mit dem Allmächtigen GOTT/ Abraham/ Isaac und Jacob/ der sein auserwehltes Volck aus Eegypten/ durchs rothe Meer/ in das Gelobte Land geführet hat/ auch dem Mose im Pusch erschienen ist. Da ich aber die rechte lautere Warheit/ wie mir dieselbige aus eigener Wissenschafft bewust ist/ nicht ausgesaget habe/ so sey ich Heram und verflucht ewiglich. Es soll mich auch von Stund an anfallen der Auffatz/ mit dem Naëman der Syrer ist geschlagen gewesen/ und soll mich verzehren das Feuer/ das Sodoma und Gomorra verzehret hat/ oder mich soll das Erdreich/ wie Dathan und Abiram/ in meiner Feinde Lande verschlingen/ und sollen mich von Stund an überfallen alle Flüche/ die an der Torah geschrieben stehen/ dawider ich nicht begehren/ bitten noch aufnehmen will einige Erklärung/ Auslegung/ Abnehmung oder Vergebung von keinem Juden noch andern Menschen/ als mir der GOtt Adonai helffe/ der Himmel und Erden/ auch alles/ was darinnen ist/ erschaffen hat/ Amen !

Gedruckt zu Breßlau.

5. Breslau Jewish oath (seventeenth century). The Jew had to stand with bared chest and bare feet on a sow's hide; the right hand had to be on the open Torah, he is holding his Jewish hat in the left. Literature: *JüdLex* I, 1927, 1159; *EJ* IX, 1932, 535; Kisch I, 1978, 140. Illustration after Shachar 1974, pl.4.

2. Individual historical personalities and Jews known by name: Susskind of Trimberg, Josel of Rosheim, Sabbatai Zvi and others

1. The king or prince of the Jews *redivivus*. An illustrated flysheet (summer 1666) for the information of German-speaking Jewish comunities, with a report of the fate of the Jewish messianic pretender Sabbatai Zvi. Wolfenbüttel, HAB, classification: IE 200. Literature: Kunzle 1973, 185, figs. 6–37; Harms III, 1989, 291; Ben-Sasson 1992, 858–64.

2. Süsskind the Jew of Trimberg (thus the superscription in the Manesseh Song Manuscript, named after the Zurich patrician family whose songbooks were the model for the collection, known as the 'Manasseh' Manuscript). The interpretation of the picture is still uncertain (a dispute between a bishop and a Jew). Süsskind is wearing a yellow or gold pointed hat (*pileus cornutus*) and a blue coat with fur trimmings and also the usual Jewish beard. Miniature in a manuscript made between 1310 and 1340: Heidelberg, UB, Cod.Pal.germ. 848d folio 355 a, no.c. Literature: Liebe 1903, pl. by p.8; Fehr 1923, fig. 182; *EJ* 1971, XV, 484; Rosenfeld 1974, fig.3; Kisch II, 1979, 121; Rubens 1981, fig. 123; Metzger 1983, 150; Unger 1986, 110–12; Mittler and Werner 1988, pl.117. Illustration after Stemberger 1983, 365.

3. The prophet Nathan of Gaza anoints Sabbatai Zwi Messiah (by pouring oil on him).Illustrated flysheet in German with a picture (etching and engraving) and text; composed at the end of 1665 or the beginning of 1666, the text is probably based on a letter from Nathan in Jerusalem to European Jewish communities. We note this flysheet providing communication within Jewry here above all because it gives two significant figures of Jewish history with the Christian sign of Judaism, which was forced on the Jews. Was this symbol – known only too well to European Jews – meant to make the Jewish identity of both figures clear beyond any doubt? For Sabbatai Zvi see Scholem 1992. Wolfenbüttel, HAB, classification: IE 197. Literature: Harms III, 1989, 287.

4. Flysheet from the first half of the sixteenth century, with woodcut: Josel of Rosheim (c.1478 to March 1554), a kind of president and spokesman for the Jews in the German Empire, who interceded for Jewish interests and protested against anti-Jewish intolerance, for example by referring to the image of God in Jews as human beings like everyone else. Josel (from Rosheim in Alsace), also called Gössel and Gossel in the flysheet, is wearing the hat customary for Jews in his time and has the Jewish ring on his left shoulder; he is holding a money bag in his left hand and in his right a book (defined in the left column of the text as the Talmud) with mock-Hebrew characters. These attributes are meant to be polemical denunciation, as also is his gaze upwards (in worship?) to the Golden Calf (Ex.32). From the time of the church fathers this regularly appears in catalogues of the misdeeds of the Jews, for which they were thought to have been rejected. One indication of this was seen to be the shattering of the tables of the law (Ex.32.19); on the whole no notice was taken of the two new tables (Ex.34.1–5). Above all during the modern period, the anti–Jewish charge of greed was derived from the worship of the Golden Calf. The title and introduction to the flysheet refers to Josel's role as the advocate of the German Jews of his time (ruler of all Jewry): 'Hearken, all men, poor, rich, great and small, you won't be bored, for you shall be told wonders. I am a Jew, I don't deny it, a wicked man by nature, and I'm called Jozel, a herald of all Jewishness.' In fact on different occasions Josel energetically represented the interests of fellow Jews who were in danger and often persecuted before the emperor (Charles V) and the great lords of his time. When the Elector Johann Friedrich the Generous of Saxony banished the Jews from his land in 1536 for alleged crimes, Josel – with a letter of commendation from the Strasbourg Protestant theologian Wofgang Capito – went to Luther to ask him to intercede with the court, but in vain. The text of the flysheet is a good example of the customary vivid polemic of the time, in so far as it mentions the 'shitting' of Jews on Christians. Literature: Graetz 1853, IX, 45ff.; Geiger 1888, 339–41; Scherer 1901,

433–6; Fuchs 1921, fig.11 (with 135f.); Stern 1959; Ben Sasson 1971, 286–93; EJ 1971, III, 139–40 (cf. X, 227–9); Zafran 1973, I, 226; Bienert 1982, fig. 29; Ehrlich 1983, 138f.; Friedman 1983, 35–9; Schreiner 1983, 153f., 157, 159f.; Oberman 1985, 157 (cf. ibid., 161f., 362, 367); Battenberg 1990, I, 184ff.; Schuder and Hirsch 1990, fig p.391 (with pp.353–423); Siegele-Wenschekewitz 1991. Illustration after Liebe 1903, no.29.

5. The Jewish banker Daniel Norsa and his family, humbled at the feet of the Madonna (section). With the permission of the bishop, Daniel had taken a picture of the Madonna down from the façade of a house which he had bought in Mantua. The great indignation over this among the population led to the Jews being punished. The painting from the school of Mantegna (end of the fifteenth century) refers to this event. It shows the male Jews with the thin white ring then customary in Italy, which clearly serves to defame them. Literature: Zafran 1973, I, 215f.; Rubens 1981, fig.110; Friedenberg 1987, 346–51 (the complete picture is on p.346 with the Madonna enthroned and the Jews at her feet); W.P.Eckert in Ginzel 1991, 385. Illustration after Blumenkranz 1965, no.26.

6. The Viennese Jewish Master Lesier of Perchtoldsdorf. The axe is a sign of his office (as judge?). He was president of the Jews of Vienna and as such also mediator between the local ruler and the Jewish community. Drawing at the beginning of the *Judenbuch der Scheffstrasse*, i.e. a register of the land on Scheffstrasse (in front of the Stubentor in Vienna), or more precisely a special part of this book (drawings about Jewish believers), the *Judenbuch* of 1389. Vienna, Hofkammerarchiv. Literature: Ausubel 1964, fig. p.119; Friedenberg 1987, fig. p.296; Schubert II, 1979, fig 10. Illustration after Lohrmann 1982, 71.

7. Jobst Mellern of Prague, the 'yellow dandy'. In this woodcut the Jew portrayed is wearing the prescribed (yellow) ring (*rota*) on the typical long garment as a sign of his Jewishness; in his left hand he is holding a money bag, the usual attribute. Here the fur cap replaces the Jewish hat. His appearance recalls some modern depictions of the wandering 'Eternal Jew'. Literature: Rubens 1981, fig. 117. Illustration after *Philo-Lexikon* 1936, 384.

Der Große betrieger und Falsche MESSIAS
SABATAI-SEVI,
König der Jüden
Anno 1666.

Die Großen Ertz Betrieger.

Der Falsche Messias
JACOB NAYLOR
König der Quacker
Im 1657 Jahr.

Der Falsche Messias
SABATAI-SEVI
König der Jüden.
Im 1666 Jahr.

So siehet NAYLOR aus in seiner rechten Tracht,
Die ihn in Occident zum Quacker König macht,
Und dis ist SABATAI den in den Orient
Die gantze Jüdenschafft MESSIAS hat genennt.

9. Engraving around 1666/7. The Quaker James Naylor entered
Bristol in 1654 as 'king of Israel' to cries of Hosanna from his
followers. However, he was regarded as an outsider even by his
fellow believers. Literature: Liebe 1903, fig.60. Illustration after
Stock 1939, 225.

Deß Jüngsthin Abgestandenen überall wolbekandten ErtzDiebischen

Juden Amschel zum Schuck und seines verdambten

Jünglings Wölffgern traurige Grabschrifft; Welche zu Ehren dem noch Lebend-herum Schwebend-hin und wieder
Lands-Verwiesenen ErtzBetrieger Löwgen/ als hinderlassenen/betrübten/jedoch
vermaledeyten redlichen Erben/auffgesetzt
An die
Jüdische Anverwandten/ vornemlich an den Reiffer talma toucsem dem Rabbi Abraham zum Trachen gehorsamlich
geschrieben/ darbey gebotten worden solches in den Grabstein mit schönen Buchstaben den Vorübergehenden zur Nachricht
auffs fleissigste außhauen zu lassen.

10. Flysheet against the thieving Jew Amschel (1671). The picture is influenced by the Frankfurt 'Judensau' motif (the sow and he-goat as mounts) and contains a mocking 'epitaph'. Literature: Fuchs 1921, fig.49; Schnur 1939, 61; Stock 1939, pl.9; Shachar 1974, pl.54; Strauss II, 1975, 786. Illustration after Liebe 1903, no.85.

1.

Steh still und lese doch/was hie geschrieben steht/
Wer dieses nur anschaut/ nicht leicht vorüber geht/
Hier unter diesem Stein/liegt was verschart begraben/
Ein Amschel-Teuffels Kind/viel schwärtzer als die Raben/
Sang als sie lebte noch/ein solchen bösen Gsang/
Der durch der Christen Schweiß/ und Blut mit Wunden trang/
Sie legte wie ein Hun/viel heß und klare Eyer/
Die machten manchen Menschen/so naschhafft und so geher/
Daß zwey und dreyssig Mann/die schwere rothe Ruhr/
Daran gefressen sam/ daß noch an dero Thur/
Die Kinder liegen kranck/sind schwerlich zu Curiren/
Der Diebisch Vogel wust/die Welt so zuverführen.

2.

Das Hindle lieget auch/in diesem Teuffels Nest/
Trug selbst die Eyer auff/den armen Christen Gest/
Sie sahen auß wie Gold/und war doch Bley darinnen/
Offt solt es Silber seyn/so war es doch nur Zinnen/
Sie ist der Uebertrag/ob sie nun schon entstehlet/
Hat ihrer dannoch nicht/der Teuffel gar gefehlet/
Das Hindle schüttet auß/zu unterschiedlich mahlen
Ein Wölffgen/Löwgen/gar/die wie die Amschel stahlen/
Das Wölffgen leider auch/in dieser Diebes Rauth/
Verschart/vermodert ligt/mit der verfluchten Haut/
Die Seelen alle drey/seynd Judisch wol verwahret/
Der Teuffel selbsten sich mit ihnen schon geparet.

3.

Du Wey der Vogel wird getrupft/das Hindle auch
Geschunten in der Höll/dem Wölffgen wie Gebrauch
Der Bels wird abgezirrt/das Losament zu ziehen
Ist das nicht immer schad/die Bälg so zu verstehen/
Das Hindle Handschuch giebt/ihr jedes Hexen Fell
Den Teuffels Klauen wird anstehen in der Hell.

4.

Das Löwgen aber ach/daß wandert noch auff Erden/
Darff wie ich sorge recht/gar nicht verscharret werden/
Deß Gersono seine Straß/hat es sehr wol verdient/
Der Hencker wird ihm zwagen/sein Schelmen Diebes Grind.

Es treibt von Tag zu Tag/dergleichen Diebes Stück/
Betrieget Jung und Alt/führt sie am Diebes Strick/
Zu Hanau fing es an/er war schon an dem Tanz
Das Meister Hemerle/ den Rück wolt segen gantz.

5.

Ist das nicht Wunderwerck/ein Amschel hat bestiegen
Ein Teuffels Händelein/das kam ins Bett zu liegen/
Mit einem Wölffgen bald/darbey es noch nicht blieben
Sie warff ein Löwgen auch/das lauter Boßheit trieben/
Auch Zauten hatten sie/das Hexen Diebs Gesind/
Daß nunmehr wird zu streut/wie Spreu vom starcken Wind,
Drumb ist es wunderlich/ein Amschel Hund/ und Zaur.
O Schachele Mochepum Durch deß Wölffgens Haus
Seynd Dieb wie man weiß/ von böser Art und Sitten/
Die/welche die Natur mit Diebes Griff beschritten/
Gehören all hieher/ grad unter diesen Stein/
Der schwartze Teuffel wil/ihr rechter Hüter seyn.

6.

Beth lieber Leser beth/daß doch der Diebes Samen
Gerotter werde auß/und dieses Amschels Namen
Mit Löwgen seinem Sohn/mög kommen auff den Brand/
Daß dieses Diebs Geschlecht/nicht werde mehr genandt/
Die Juden selbsten auch/seynd froh daß er verrecket/
Er machte Christ und Juden/daß sie sich verstecket/
Der Armen Christen Schweiß/saugt er in seinen Schlund/
Nun frist deß Teuffels Aaß/der Juden Metzger Hund/
Am andern Zweiffel nicht/ sie werden ewig schwitzen/
Und vor der Welt Betrug/im hellen Ofen glitzen/
Diß war der Oberst Schaum/gar wider die Vernunfft
Ein Schelm und essig Dieb auß aller Teuffels Zunfft/
Denck lieber Leser doch/was dieser Jud geschlichtet/
Er hat deß Henckers Ampt/an Juden auch verrichtet/
Dieselb gepeinigt gar/hüt dich vor solchem Dieb/
Der diese Laster all biß an sein Ende trieb.

Off der Juden Schabes den 14. Jan.1671.
In die Judische Synagogen überschicket / dar-
bey gebeten solches dem R. Prophen Schilo
Sabathoy auffs ehst zu communiciren.

Da ich im garten wolt | begunten nach die Dorn
ver liebte Rosen brechen, | der hertzens angst bijstechen

Da ich vorn Asperg soll mit | Jo langt vieleicht mein Glück
mehr nach Stutgardt suchen | dort wieder anbli bluhen

Die jchöner Ehren Staat! | der Schinder soll mich gar
bey meinen letzten jeiten, | zum Richt Blatz hin geleitet

Das Logis jmagt mir nicht, | nie solche jchwehre band
ich hab bey meinen Tagen | und Silber- Gejchmeid getragen

Das Urtheil ist verfaßt; | und ich darf doch kein Wort
ich jeh den Stab zerbrechen; | zu meinem Vortheil jprechen

Nun jiehet man mich zum Tod; | und hang ich eine Stund
nun geht es an den Kragen, | jo kan ichs jchon vertragen

Eigentliche Abbildung des
IOSEPH SÜS OPPENHEIMERS.

Ehemahligem Hoch- | Fürstl. Württembergi-
Jten Gehaimten Rath, | Cabinets Minister und
Finantien Directorie- | In jeinem Glück
Standt. | A° 1736.

Ich war ein reicher Herr, der jelber durffte Müntzen
Und Taujchte auf der Welt nicht wohl mit einem Printzen
Laquayen, Kutjchen, Pferd meublirte Zimer gnug
hab ich mir angejchafft, wie ich begierde Trug.
Ich brauchte die Gewalt durch Land-Comijsionen
Wer einen dienst gewollt, der mußte mir vor lohnen
Man hieß mich Excellentz, uhrwar auch in der That
Von einem Großen Herrn, Fiscal, Geheimder Rath.

Eigentliche Abbildung des
IOSEPH SÜS OPPENHEIMERS.

in jeinem unGlücks | Standt, wie jolcher nach
Uatheil und Recht von | einer Hoch-fürstlich
Württembergijchen Com- | mijsion, zum Strang
Verurtheilt und dem | Schaffrichter übergeben
worden | A° 1738.

Jetzt jieht es anders aus, man hat mir abgenommen
zu was ich auf der Welt vorhero bin gekommen
Ich bin ein armer Jud, vom Würtemberger Land
Nun mehr Vermaledeyht, und in des henckers hand
Man wird aus Stuttgard mich mit Schinder Karren führen
Am Galgen muß ich hier mein Leben heut verliehren
Ich werde noch darzu ins Käfig eingethan
Daß ich im rothen Kleid fein langer langer Karr.

Ihr Juden die Ihr Euch müßt meinetwegen jchämen, Ihr Könet jetzt an mir ein gut Exempel nehmen.
Betriegt ihr Land und leut, und mijcht euch in den Staat, So wider fähret euch auch eine jolche That.

11. Joseph Süss Oppenheimer, called Jew Süss (born in Heidelberg on 12 February 1698 – died in Stuttgart on 4 February 1738). As a 'court Jew', adviser and representative of Duke Karl Alexander of Württemberg, in whose business, financial and tax interests he acted with wide-ranging powers. Because of his organization of financial and business administration on mercantile principles he incurred such hostility from the nobility that the duke, on whose instructions and wishes he was acting, finally dropped him and sacrificed him to the wrath of his subjects as a kind of scapegoat. Literature: Liebe 1903, figs.69–71; Fuchs 1921, figs.51–53; Schnur 1939, fig.5; Schnee V, 1965, 182–204; Kunzle 1973, fig. p.184; Sievers 1981, fig. p.121; Baumgart 1988; Deneke 1988, fig. p.287; Gidal 1988, fig p.109; Gerber 1990; Schuder and Hirsch 1990, 678–93; Ginzel 1991,128 (and ibid, 327–36, 383); Rohrbacher and Schmidt 1991, 132–6; Jung 1992, 27, 174–83, 209–13. Illustrations after Diederichs 1908 (II, no 1208: six individual scenes, each with a poetic legend); Stock 1939 (pl.30; Oppenheimer first as a prominent and powerful lord, then fettered and condemned to be hung); Diedrichs, ibid. (no.1207: five individual pictures: in the middle the equipment with a cage for offenders, and various texts).

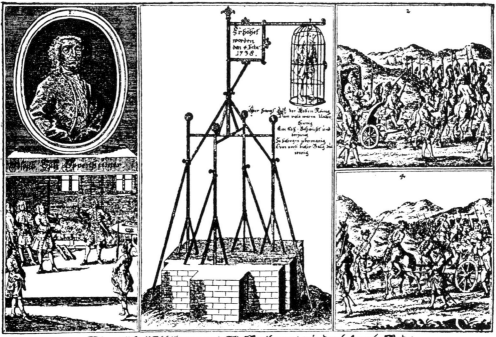

Eigentliche Abbildung und Beschreibung/ wie der bekannte Jud/

Joseph Süß Oppenheimer,

Den 30. Januarii 1738. von Asperg unter starcker Wache nach Stuttgard in das sogenannte Herrschafft-Hauß gebracht/ deß folgenden Tages darauf gleich das Leben abgekündet worden/ worüber er sich als ein rasender Mensch aufgeführet/ und viele böse Worte von sich fliessen lassen; und ob zwar zwen Herren Geistliche A.C. grosse Mühe anwendeten, seine Seele zu gewinnen, verharrete er doch, als ein verstockter Jud, in seinem Irrthum. Den 4. Februarii Morgens zwischen 8. und 9. Uhr wurde ihm das Todes-Urtheil dahin angekündet, daß er mit dem Strang vom Leben zum Tod solle hingerichtet werden: Wurde also zwischen 10. und 11. Uhr aus obgedachtem Herrschaffts-Hauß auf neun Schnorer-Karren arsenirt/ zu dem Gerichts-Platz ausserhalb der Stadt gebracht/ und an dem eisern Galgen aufgehencket/ der Leib aber in ein 6. Schuh hohes und roth-angestrichenes eisern Köficht eingeschlossen.

Süß! dein Nam ist gut, dein Tod ist aber bitter,
Du zohest selbst auf dich diß schwehre Ungewitter,
Drum klag allein dich an, nimm mit der Straff vorlieb,
Du hast noch nicht verdienet, verwegner Galgen-Dieb.

Weil nun die Juden sich auf ihre Grab-Stein schreiben,
So soll nach deinem Tod dir diese Grab-Schrifft bleiben,
Damit ein jeder mög dieselbe schauen an,
Und dein sehr böses Thun in Kürtze lesen kan.

EPITHAPHIUM.

Stehet still/
Ihr
die ihr vorüber gehet/
und betrachtet dises eiserne Gerüst/
dann
Ihr könnt hier etwas sehen/
So bey Menschen-Gedencken nicht geschen worden/
nemlich
einen abscheulichen Vogel/
welchen die Gerechtigkeit in disem Köficht eingeschlossen;
Er will zwar nicht mehr singen/
dann er hat sich ausgesungen/
und
ist jetzund in der Mauß.
Er war ein rechter Raben-Vogel/
welcher andere zu zerreissen gesucht/
darum ist er auch hieher in die freye Lufft gehängt worden/
damit er Raben genug köpffen möge/
weil es ihme dermalen daran mangelt/

dann
der Meister hat ihme das Hals-Band gar zu enge gemacht/
Es ist ein Hebräischer Vogel/
welcher auf Teutsch gar abscheulich gesungen;
Er hat dem gantzen Juden-Volck einen Schandfleck angebracht/
Er ward von ihnen sehr hoch angesehen/
Aber
als seine unglückliche Erhöhung erfolgte/
liessen ihn alle allein die Ehre.
Er pranget an einem Gericht/
welches ihn doppelt erhöhet hat/
So recht von Holtz/
sondern schon An. 1597. von starcken Eisen aufgebaut ist
Und zwar
vor einen Ertz-Betrüger/
welcher aus Kupffer Gold zu machen versprach/
und sein schändlich erfunden/
Sein Name war
Georg Honauer;

dessen Nachfolger auf diesem hohen und festen Ort ist/
Joseph Süß Oppenheimer,
ein böser Jud/
Disem ist an diesem hohen Gerüst ein eigen Zimmer eingeräumt
wohl vergittert/
Sechs Schuh hoch/ und schön roth angestrichen/
dann es mußte drei ihm im Leben alles propre dabei geben/
dahero hat er auch im Tod solche Ehre genossen/
Er war 40. Jahr alt/
Hat aber dieses Zimmer auf nicht als 40. Jahr in Bestand genommen/
Es lasse sich ja kein Jud gelüsten/
wo er anderst klug ist/
Ihn daraus zu vertreiben/
dann
es ist ihme allein zum starswehrenden Besitz eingeräumt worden/
darum
wer hier vorbey gehet/
spreye aus/
Und lasse disem Ertz-Bößwicht die Raben die Augen aushacken/
Und dessen Mist in deren Gruben tragen.

Cartouche Geistes Ansage an Jud Süssens seinen Geist.

Cartouche Geist erwacht aus seinem Staub und Erden/
Er siehet gantz verwirrt in seinem Angesicht,
Er weiß nicht, warum doch an ihn gedacht soll werden/
Weil er durch Rad und Strang schon lange hingericht,
Er sahe einen Geist mit Feur bestammten Ketten/
Es fragt sein guter Geist denselben, wer er sey?
Ob man nicht von der Qual ihn könnte noch erretten/
Und durch gesuchte Hülf ihn möchte machen frey?
Ob er dann mehr Betrug, als er selbst, hätt begangen/
Ob er aus Ehr-Geitz ihm den Ruhm wollt spannen ab?
Er fragt ihn, warum doch sein Leib sey aufgehangen?
Und daß der Galgen ihm sey worden zu dem Grab?
Warum in solchem Pracht in Köficht eingeschlossen/
Ob er dann besser wär als andre Galgen-Strick?
Warum sein Galgen sey aus Eisen ausgeflossen/
Und daß zu oberst er zu hangen hätt das Glück?
Es fielen diese Wort vom Geist auf sein Befragen:
Was fragst du Schatten mich/ was gehet es dich an;
Doch will ich diese Wort auf deine Frag dir sagen:
Ich habe als ein Jud mehr Böß als du gethan.
Ich daß zwar nicht gemordt; doch mehr dann du gestohlen/
Ich war so klug als du, verteuffelt war mein Sinn:

Ich sag dir rund und frey, aufrichtig, unverhohlen,
Daß ich ein größrer Dieb, als du, gewesen bin.
Ich hab das gantze Land durch falsche List betrogen,
Ich hatt was mehr's im Sum, doch gieng es mir nicht an,
Ich habe vieles Gut durch List an mich gezogen/
Die Bosheit, so ich übt, man kaum begreiffen kan.
Maitressen hielt ich mir, mein Juden-Fleisch zu laden/
Ich war ein geiler Bock, biß hohe Ehr an mich/
Drum muß ich auch die Ehr am eisern Galgen haben/
Weil das verhaßte Glück mich biß zuletzt am Stich.
Ich hielte Wagen, Pferd, ich wollte keinem weichen/
Mein Hochmuth war so groß, als wär ich Herr allein/
Und war doch nur ein Jud, und keinem nicht zu gleichen/
Ich müntzte vieles Geld, steckt aber vieles ein.
Ich starb als ein Jud, und wollt zur Höllen geben/
Damit das Bosheits-Maaß ich völlig füllte an.
Man wird wohl meines gleich auf Erden nicht viel sehen/
Der so viel Schelmen-Stück, wie ich gäubt, gethan.
Drum laß erblaßter Geist, Cartouche, ab mit fragen/
Du starbest in der Buß, ich fuhr verzweiflet hin/
Ist aber nöthig nicht, daß ich dir soll sagen/
Wo ich mit meinem Geist anjetzt logiret bin.

Als nun Cartouche Geist von diesem Geist vernommen,
Was auf den Erden Rund sein Thun gewesen sey,
Ist er von selbigem, gleich wie ein Blitz entkommen,
Und ware höchst-vergnügt, daß er von diesem frey.
So prange dann du Dieb auf deiner Galgen-Porten/
Lad alle Raben ein zu einem grossen Schmauß,
Sie seynd dein Hof-Gesind bey dir im Tode worden/
Hab acht, daß sie dir nicht die Augen hacken aus.
Du schöner Hamans-Sohn, wie herrlich kanst du prangen,
Es ist jetzt Mondes-Zeit, daß Purim zu begehn/
Laß deine Glaubens-Freund mit dir viel Freud erlangen,
Dann dieses Fest befiehlt in lauter Freud zu stehn.
Du kanst du in dem Tod noch grosse Ehre machen,
Ein König, Bajazeth, lag auch in solchem Hauß/
Nicht aber als ein Dieb, nicht um so böse Sachen/
Ihm blieb das Lebens-Licht, euch nicht der Hencker aus.
Du bist vor diesemal recht trefflich hoch gestiegen,
Drum trachte ferner nicht, wie du gethan, nach Ehr,
Laß dich mit dieser Gnad, so lang du hangst, begnügen,
Du hast genug jetzund, begehre ja nichts mehr.

Anmerckungen der in dem Kupffer sich befindlichen Ziffern.

No. 1. Das Portrait deß Juden in dem Herrlichem Stand.
2. Dessen Einbringung nach Stuttgard von der Festung Haben-Asperg.
3. Das Zimmer/ wie ihme angekündet wurde/ daß er sich zum Sterben bereit machen solle.
4. Seine Hinausführung auf dem Schnorer-Karren zu dem Gerichts-Platz.
5. Der eiserne Galgen/ an welchen er gehenckt/ und in den Köficht eingeschlossen worden. Dieser Galgen wurde An. 1597. für einen sich ausgegebenen Goldmacher und Ertz-Betrüger erbauet/ weswegen auch den 12. April besagten Jahrs redersich daran gehenckt worden: Das Eisen an diesem Galgen hatte ein Gewicht 41. Centner/ und kostete 3000. Oberländische Gulden.

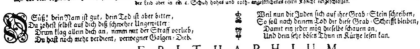

Der in seinen Leben, Betrügereyen, und verdamten Hochmuth
den Jud Süß-gleichende Jud

Isaac Nathan Ischerlen,

von Weissenbern in Francken gebürtig.

Welcher wegen seiner begangenen Missethaten und Ertzbetrügereyen 1740. zu Anspach arretiret,
an Hand und Füssen geschlossen und in Kürtze seine wohlverdiente Todes-Straffe furchtsam erwartet.

Dessen curieuser Traum und ihm erschienenes Nacht-Gespenst.

12. Dream vision of Isaac Nathan Icherlen at Ansbach. The devil in the form of a pig terrifies the offender, who is awaiting his execution. The cage is meant to recall the iron cage used for Joseph Süss Oppenheimer. Here the reader is meant to gloat over the anxiety of the Jew and be strengthened in his prejudice that Jews are more wicked than Christians. Flysheet with engraving, 1740. Literature: Stock 1939, fig. p.481. Illustration after Liebe 1903, no.72.

Nu wey was vor ein Traum
Will meine Ruhe stören,
Die Glieder sind erstart,
Es schauret mir die Haut:
Und da ich jetzt schon wach
Will doch die Furcht sich mehren,
Wann ich denck an den Geist
Den ich in Schlaff geschaut.
Er that halb einen Schwein,
Halb einen Menschen gleichen,
Sein Athem war wie Feur
So aus den Abgrund fällt.
Ich wolt und kont doch nicht
Ihm aus den Wege weichen,
Weil Ketten, Schloß und Band
Mich angefesselt hält.
Er stund im vollen Feuer,
Bespannt mit Blitz und Strahlen,
Es gienge Rauch und Dampff,
Von diesen Ungeheuer:
Mir war ob müste ich,
Mit ihm zur Höllen fallen,
Und kosten einen Tranck
Von Schwefel, Pech und Feuer.
Ich krüm und wehrte mich
Ich that um Hülffe schreyen,
Ich meint das Ungeheuer
Das werd mich packen an,
Doch hörte niemand mich
Niemand wolt mich befreyen,
Und niemand kam zu Hülff
Mir armen Juden-Mann.
In seiner Hand da trug
Der Geist ein starcke Stangen,
Wo in der andern er,

Mein Diebstahl mir gezeigt.
Und an der Stangen that
Jud Süß in Kefig hangen,
Den ich in Lebens-Zeit.
War sonderlich geneigt,
Es wird der Teufel ja
An mir nicht Schelmisch handlen;
Dem ich durch List und Trug
So treue Dienst gethan.
Vor dem mein Hochmuths-Geist
Pflegt prächtig herzuwandlen;
Ich war ein solcher Jud,
Und gleichte den Haman,
Wann ich nur nicht mit ihm
Muß auf die Laiter steigen,
Und zwischen Erd und Lufft,
Verzehren meine Zeit.
Es wird ja mir der Traum
Den Weg dorthin nicht zeigen,
Die Reputation
Gieng mit mir viel zu weit,
Wann ich gleich soll wie Süß
In Vogel-Hauß verderben,
Und auf den Galgen-Platz
Die Laiter steigen auf.
Ich wurd hierdurch gewiß
Mir wenig Ruhm erwerben,
Und in Verachtung stehn
Bey den beschnittnen Hauff.
Was hilfft mich nun das Geld
So ich zusamm gestohlen,
Ich war ein armer Mann
Eh ich nach Hoffe kahm,
Dort war ich gantz behend
Den Reichtum einzuholen,

Auf ungekehrter Banck
Ich alles zu mir nahm.
Ich armer Bettel-Hund
Ließ mich den Hochmuth blenden,
Und wolte allerdings
Befehle theilen aus.
Ich Narr wer bin ich nun,
Die Ketten mich jetzt binden,
Das Unglück lachet mein
In diesen Kercker-Hauß.
Die ich verachtet hab,
Getroget und belogen,
Die lachen jetzund mein
Und machen sich ein Freud.
Der Hochmuths-Teuffel hat
Mich armen Jud betrogen,
Strick, Galgen, Henckers-Hand,
Führt mit aus dieser Zeit.
Was wird doch der Jud Süß,
Bey meiner Ankunfft sagen,
Wann in der Todten-Reich
Er mich erblicken wird:
Was Antwort gib ich ihm,
Wann er mich so wird fragen?
Wie hat der Hencker dich
Zu mir anher geführt.
Die Antwort wird wohl seyn,
Ein Dieb, sucht seines gleichen,
Wie du warst war ich auch,
Ein Schandfleck aller Welt:
Ich thäte gleich wie du
Die höchste Spitz erreichen,
Wo Ketten und der Strick
Uns an den Galgen hält.

Sabathai Sevi ein falscher Messias. Jacobus Melstinius ein falscher Messias.

Zwey ertz-Betrüger sieht man hier beysammenstehen,
Die blinde Juden-Schaar die hat sie angesehen,
Vor dem der wahrer Gott, und aller Heyland ist,
Mein Christ! bejammre doch des Teuffels Trug und List,
Der wahre Messias der soll bey sie noch kommen
So sehr hat Aberwitz die Juden eingenommen

13. Illustrated eighteenth-century flysheet against false messianic figures, against the Jew Sabbatai Zvi and against Jacob Melstinius (apparently a distorted version of the depiction of Sabbatai Zvi and Jacob Naylor [see above]). Illustration after Shachar 1974, pl.40.

3. Acts of violence

against Jews: plunderings, expulsions, pogroms, executions of whole
groups of Jews without cause, special forms of execution for Jews

1. Burning of Jews at the time of the plague epidemic (1349). The Jews were accused of having poisoned the wells and springs everywhere to kill the Christians. The burning (i.e. a form of execution customary for heretics and Jews) takes place in a cave filled with burning wood. It was probably also regarded as an introduction to the punishment of hell awaiting these groups. Miniature in a manuscript of the *Annals of Gilles li Muisit*, Tournai, c.1353. Brussels, BR, MS 130076/7, folio 12 verso. Literature: Blumenkranz 1965, fig.23; Legner 1978, III, fig. p.74; Ben-Sasson II, 1979, fig. 265 (before p.263); Aschoff 1989, 21–2; *Germ.Jud.*II, 1,1968, p.XXXIX; Ben-Sasson 1992, 546; K. Bergdolt, *Der Schwarze Tod*, Munich 1994, 119–45.

2. Burning of Jews. A woodcut (from the workshop of Michael Wolgemut and Wilhelm Pleydenwurff) which appears three times in the Chronicle of the World by Hartmann Schedel (Nuremberg: Anton Koberger 1493), as folio CCXX versio, CCLVII verso and CCCXX verso. In the context the execution in a fiery pit – this was customary for Jews, just as the stake was for heretics, perhaps as a prelude to the fiery torments of hell – is not connected with any particular misdeeds of the Jews, but indicates that they are suffering such a punishment generally 'for their evil actions' (folio CCXX verso) or, in connection with (alleged) profanations of hosts, as 'blasphemers of the divine majesty of Christ and our faith' (folio CCLVII verso). On folio CCCXX verso the picture of the burning is connected with the profanation of the host at Deggendorf in 1337 and the great pogrom prompted by the plague epidemic of 1348: on the latter it states explicitly: 'Again, all the Jews in German lands were burned in the year of Christ MCCCXLVIII and accused of having poisoned wells, to which crime many of them confessed.' Literature: Schramm 1920, XVII, fig.548; *Mon.Jud.Kat.*1963, B.304; Müller 1968, pl. IX; Zafran 1973, I, 181; Kunze 1975, fig. p.375; Rosenfeld 1978, fig.51; Schubert 1979, fig.54; Schild 1980, fig.462; Lohrmann 1982, 322 no.66; Erbstösser 1984, fig.85; Seibt 1987, fig. p.305; Andics 1988, fig. p.180; Deneke 1988, 181; Rücker 1988; Lohrmann 1990, 302f.; Birkhan 1992, 163; Kosch XIV, 1992, 324; *Verfasserlexikon* VIII, 1992, 609–21. Illustration after Liebe 1903, no.16.

3. The Jew Ansteet is hanged upside down with two dogs (on 10 July 1553 in Weissenstein, Swabia; woodcut in the *Swiss Chronicle* of Johann Stumpf, printed in Augsburg, 1586). While this form of execution was not exclusively reserved for Jews, in the fifteenth and sixteenth centuries it was preferred for these offenders as a particularly humiliating and painful form of execution, since the dogs, whom anxiety made particularly aggressive in this situation, tended to bite the Jew, who was fettered and defenceless, and inflict severe wounds on him. 'The dog on the right has already inflicted a powerful bite, while the dog on the left is attacking him with its paws. Under the gallows is the judge on horseback, with a staff; two executioners are busy with nooses, and there is a whole forest of spears' (Fehr 1923, 86). In this particular instance the victim was the Jew Ansteet, who would not accept baptism; finally, when he continued to be stubborn, he was hanged by his feet from the gallows. When even this did not make him willing to be baptized, two dogs were hung next to him; 'they immediately fell on him and bit his ears off, and began to gnaw his elbows as if someone had thrown them a bone. When he now began to cry out wretchedly and the mass priest admonished him that he should save his soul because he could see that his physical and temporal life was over, he still had nothing to say and persisted in his stubbornness' (from a contemporary report, printed in Schreiner 1981). After vain attempts by the (Protestant) pastor of Weissenstein to convert him, Jacob Andreä (Protestant pastor at Göppingen: for him see Stupperich 1984, 27–8) tried his luck with a long conversion sermon, which finally had the desired effect. Ansteed was baptized – still hanging on the gallows – and pardoned by simple hanging with a noose. Literature: Fehr 1923, fig.103; Schreiner 1981; Stupperich 1984, 27f.; Aschoff 1988; cf. *EJ* 1971, XV, 1056, and Güde 1981, 58. Illustration after Schild 1980, no.121.

4. Execution of Lippold, the master minter and court factor of Brandenburg, in Berlin on 28 January 1573. Acting for the Elector Joachim II of Brandenburg, Lippold had similar powers to those of Joseph Süss Oppenheimer at the court of Stuttgart in the eighteenth century. While Joachim had great confidence in Lippold, the latter's reputation in the land was not good, and so his downfall began with the surprising and sudden death of his lord at the beginning of January 1571. He was accused and, after a long imprisonment, tortured, whereupon he confessed to having poisoned the Elector. He was carried on a cart through the city to his execution, tortured with glowing tongs on the way, and then put on the wheel and quartered in the New Market; the four parts of his body and his head were put on public display. Engraving of 1573 from the printing works of Leonhard Thurneisser. Literature: Schuder and Hirsch 1990, 436–43 (with illustrations, 442f.). Illustration after Liebe 1903, no.73.

5. In connection with the social unrest of the so-called Fettmilch riot in Frankfurt (1614), the Jewish quarter there was plundered, the Jewish community was (temporarily) expelled, and finally, when the emperor had restored order by his intervention, in 1616 Fettmilch and his companions were executed. These events are well known from the contemporary publicity, also in the form of pictures, and in a way they are typical of similar events in other cities and at other times. Literature: Hirth 1923, I, pl.325; *Mon.Jud.Kat.*1963, B 378 (fig.B 33); *EJ*, 1971, VII, 472; Brückner 1975, fig.68; Ben-Sasson II, 1979, fig.37; Karasek 1979; Paas I, 1986, 57, 310 (folding pages), 339; II, 1986, 48f., 51f., 54f., 74, 76; Friedrichs 1978; Battenberg I, 1990, 250f.; Nachama 1992 (catalogue), 307f. The three illustrations are after Liebe 1903, no.35 (engraving by Matthew Merian the Older [plundering in the Jewish quarter; the rings on some Jews can be recognized]), no.36 (engraving by Georg Keller [the great crowd by the wall]), no.37 (engraving by Georg Keller [in the foreground, left, the rings on the outer garments of the Jews can be recognized]); cf. Paas II, 1986, 53 and 293 (execution of Vinzenz Fettmilch and his companions; on the left edge of the picture are some members of the community with the Jewish ring).

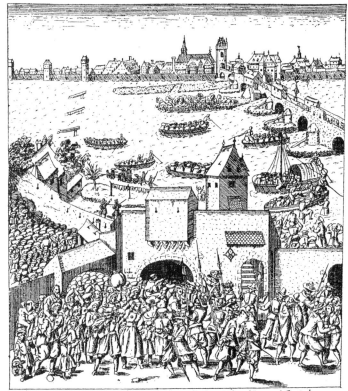

Aufzug der Iuden den 23.Augusti da man ihnen das Fischerfelds Pförtlein eröfnet, vnd sie vff dem Wasser hinauf vnd hirunder abführen lassen, daselbst ihrer 1380. Personen lang vnd. Alt. so zu der Pforten hinaufz gangen, abgezehlet worden

Plünderung der Iudengassen zu Franckfürt am Main den 22.Augusti 1654. Nach Mittag vmb 8 uhr von den Handtwercks gesellen angefangen vnd die gantze Nacht durch Continuirt, da dan ein Bürger vnd 2 Iuden gar todt geschlagen vnd aber beideseits beschedigt worden, bitz sin entlich / als sie bitz in die helft der gassen komen / von der Bürgerschafft gentzlich abge-ruckt worden

Eine sehr denckwürdige Historia/

Von einem getaufften/ doch wider vom Christenthumb abgefallenen Juden/ welcher wegen Diebstal sampt zweyen andern Juden in Wien ergriffen/ vnd *justificirt* worden.

DEn (12) 22 Augusti/1642. Jahrs/hat man in Wien/der Kays. Residentz-Statt drey der vornembsten Juden (darunter einer hiebevor ein sehr berühmter Rabbi vnd Jüdisch Hoher Priester gewesen/ vnd sich vor etlich Jahren zu Rackowitz in Polen tauffen lassen/ vnd Ferdinand Frantz Engelberg genannt worden/ welcher Zeit seines gewehrten falschen Christenthumbs wider die Juden geschrieben/ vnd etlich Bücher in Truck außgehen lassen/ in welchen er alle Juden/ als lebendige Höllenbränd/ dem Teuffel zu eygen übergeben) wegen verübten/ vnd lange Jahr über/ so wol im Christen: als auch im Judenthumb getriebenen Diebstals halben/ zu welchem dann der getauffte Rabbi meisterlich mit Rath vnd That geholffen/ insonderheit aber den andern zweyen Gelegenheit vnd Anschlag an die Hand gegeben/ in Ihrer Hochfürstl. Durchl. Ertz-Hertzog zu Oesterreich Schatzkammer/ vermittels gebrauchter Gewöhnlicher Diebsschlüssel/ vnd anderer dergleichen/ ihnen Juden wolbekannter Instrumenten/ vnd diebischer Handgriff/ einzuschleichen/ wie sie dann solches ein geraume Zeit über practicirt/ vnd etlich viel tausend Thaler werth darauß gestolen: an ihre diebische Hälß hencken sollen. Weiln aber GOtt der Allmächtige nicht zulassen noch verhengen wollen/ daß ein solcher Ertzdieb vnter dem Titul vnd Namen eines Christen sein Gottloses Leben enden solte/ sintemal die andern Juden hetten sagen mögen/ sobald er were ein Christ worden/ were er auch zugleich ein Dieb worden. So hat sichs zugetragen/ als man besagten Freytags selbige drey Juden/ als offentliche Dieb/ vor peinlich Halßgericht gestellt/ dieser getauffte Rabbi vermeynt vnd gehofft gehabt/ man würde seiner/ als eines getaufften Juden vnd Christen/ an dem Leben verschonen/ wie er sich dann andächtig vnd heilig gestellet/ vnd das Crucifix so er in Händen gehabt vielfältig geküsset/ vnd mit grosser Andacht auff die Brust geschlagen/ vnd zum öfftern gesagt: Ach mein lieber HErr Jesu/ sey mir doch auff dißmal gnädig vnd barmhertzig. So ist aber jedoch ein solches seiner Hoffnung vnd Meynung nach nicht erfolgt/ sondern das Vrtheil wider sie alle drey dieses Inhalts eröffnet vnd abgelesen worden: daß sie/ als offentliche Dieb mit dem Strang vom Leben zum Todt gerichtet werden solten. Als solches der Rabbi gehöret/ daß er an den Galgen gehenckt werden vnd sterben solte/ hat er in grossem Grim vnd Zorn das Crucifix zu boden geworffen/ (1) dasselbe angespeyet/ darnach mit beyden Füssen wie ein rasender vnd wütender Hund darauff gesprungen/ geflucht getobt vnd gelästert/ mit vermelden/ weiln er ja sehe/ daß er durch der Christen Vrtheil sterben müste/ so wolte er sterben als ein rechter Jud/ vnd nicht als ein Christ/ vnd solte er gleich lebendig in den vntersten Abgrund der Höllen zu Korah/ Dathan vnd Abiram fahren/ wolte den Christen nicht so viel Ehr anthun/ daß er als ein Christen-Dieb sterben solte/ wie er dann alsobald das Christenthumb/ so er biß dahero in dem schein geführet/ vnd damit zugleich den Christlichen Glauben verläugnet/ demselben offentlich abgesagt/ vnd vnerhörte grausame Lästerung wider GOtt vnd alle getauffte Christen außgegossen.

Ob nun wol der zugegebne *Pater Societatis Jesu*, vnd Herr Statt-Richter jhme beweglich zugesprochen/ was er thäte/ er hette ja allererst den Tag zuvor das hochwürdige Sacrament empfangen/ so hat er trutziglich darauff geantwortet/ Nein/ keines were/ er habe nichts empfangen/ sondern habe das Sacrament wider auß dem Mund in ein Fasenetlein oder Wischtuch gespeyet/ darein gewickelt/ vnd mit Reverentz zu melden/ in ein heimlich Gemach in dem Amptshauß/ wo er gefangen gesessen/ geworffen/ allda solte mans suchen/ so würde mans finden/ wie dann auch geschehen/ vnd die Hostia sampt dem Wischtuch daselbst in dem allerärgsten Vnflat gefunden worden: Vber welcher verteuffelten Gottlosigkeit dieses Juden sich männiglich entsetzet/ der *Pater* Jesuit aber im Grim vnd Eyfer gesagt: Es were kein Wunder/ daß man die Juden alle zu boden schlüg/ vnd mit Füssen trette: Worüber dann sogleich ein grosser Tumult vor dem Rahthauß/ oder der Schrannen entstanden/ vnd viel Juden/ mit rauffen schändlich tractiert/ ja theils gar zu boden geschlagen worden/ daß sie neben den Dieben gelegen/ wie dann auch etlichen jhre Gewölber von dem gemeinen Volck geplündert worden.

Als solches Ihrer Kays. Majest. *notificirt* worden/ haben sich dieselbe sehr darüber alterirt vnd entsetzt/ dabeneben allergnädigst befohlen/ daß man die zween Dieb zwar der Vrtheil gemeß/ hencken (2) den dritten Ertzdieb vnd Bößwicht aber/ als den Gamarlitischen Rabbi wider in das Amptshauß führen solte/ wie dann auch jenes zwar beschehen/ dieses aber wegen deß erzörnten vnd ergrimmten gemeinen Volcks eher nicht als bey eingetrettner Nacht zu Werck gerichtet werden können.

Deß nachfolgenden Sonnabend/ welcher der der Juden heiliger Sabbath war/ wurde der Rabbi widerumb hervor geführt vnd examinirt/ warumb er mit dem Crucifix gestern so erschröcklich vmbgangen/ vnd solche Gotteslästerliche Reden außgegossen/ da er doch zuvor sich zu einem Christen tauffen lassen/ vnd wider das Judenthumb geschrieben hette? Darauff hat er mit trotzigen vnd halßstarrigen Worten geantwortet/ das habe er den Juden zum ewigen Ruhm vnd Preiß/ den Christen aber zu ewigem Spott vnd Schand gethan/ alles theils mit fleiß/ theils nur zum Schein von jhm geschehen/ welches er aber hiermit öffentlich bekannt/ vnd zugleich widersprochen haben wolte/ hette auch in seinem Christenthumb/ das Sacrament nie genossen/ sondern allezeit wider auß dem Mund genommen/ in ein heimlich Gemach geworffen/ vnd seye das Sacrament jederzeit bey jhm vor abschewlicher vnd verdampter/ als bey den Juden das Schweinenfleisch gehalten worden. In Summa/ er hat solche grewliche Gotteslästerung außgegossen/ welche weder außzusprechen/ noch zu beschreiben seyn/ dahero man dann besorgt hat/ es möchte sich die Erde auffthun vnd den Gotteslästerer lebendig verschlingen.

Derhalben ist man mit dem gottlosen vnd verruchten Bößwicht fortgefahren/ denselben wider auff die Schrannen geführt/ eben vmb die Zeit/ da die andere Juden jhre Abgötterey verrichtet/ vnd jhme ein ander Vrtheil vorgelesen/ welches auch alsobald an jhm folgender Gestalt exequirt vnd vollzogen worden.

Erstlich ist er/ als ein offenbarer Gotteslästerer vnd Verletzer der höchsten Göttlichen Majestät auff einem hohen Wagen/ gesetzt/ in solchem Pomp auff alle vier Hauptplätz der Kays. Residentz-Statt Wien/ als erstlich auff den Hohenmarckt/ zum andern auff den Hof/ zum dritten auff den Graben vnd zum vierdten auff den newen Marckt geführet/ vnd auff dem ersten mit glüenden Zangen (3) in die rechte Brust etlichmal gerissen/ auff dem andern ein Riemen (4) vom Halß an/ über den Ruck auß dem Leib geschnitten vnd gerissen/ auff dem dritten/ widerumb mit glüenden Zangen in die lincke Brust etlichmal gezwickt/ auff dem vierdten abermaln ein Riemen auff vorige Manier geschnidten vnd abgezogen/ hernacher von dem hohen Wagen herab genommen/ auff eine Schleiffe gebunden (5) da er grausamlich Zetter vnd Mordio geschryen/ O Gott Adonay/ der du nie geborn bist/ erbarm dich meiner/ etc. vnd biß an die Richtstatt geschleifft/ daselbst jhm die Gotteslästerische Zunge/ (6) welche allbereit kohlschwartz gewesen/ herauß geschnidten/ darauff die rechte Hand (7) jhm/ als einen Tauff- vnd Eydbrüchigen/ mit einem Beihel abgehauen/ hernacher aber als ein Ertzdieb bey den Füssen an Ketten auffgehenckt/ vnd endlich als ein verteuffelter Jud/ vnd abgefallner verlaugneter Christ (8) lebendig gebraten/ vnd mit dem Galgen verbrennt worden/ vnd in seiner vermaledeyten Verstockung also wider alle Vermahnung dahin gefahren.

GOtt wolle sich der Vnglaubigen in Gnaden erbarmen vnd sie alle bekehren/ zu der Warheit/ vmb Christi willen/ Amen.

◀ 6. Execution of Jews. Contemporary single-leaf print with engraving, Vienna 1642. Literature: Liebe 1903, fig.84; *JüdLex* V, 1930, 1423–4; *EJ* 1971, XVI, 129, fig.5; Kunzle 1973, 183, figs. 6–34; Andics 1988, fig. p.188. Illustration after Stock 1939, 82.

7. The so–called Hep–Hep riots of 1819 (in Würzburg, Frankfurt and elsewhere). Engraving by Johann Michael Voltz, Nördlingen 1819. In the late phase of Napoleon's rule (especially after Waterloo, 1815), a German national self-consciousness suddenly developed, which is visible e.g. in the writings of Fichte, Jahn, E.M.Arndt, Fries and Rühs. Jews and Judaism were increasingly regarded as alien, un-German or even inferior. As well as the nationalistic prejudices there were also the old religious prejudices and quite often fear of economic competition from the Jews, who were regarded as shrewd businessmen. So between 1819 and 1822, above all in Franconia and the upper Palatinate, there were anti-Jewish riots, brawls and outcries, which sometimes were only half-heartedly suppressed by the authorites. This engraving clearly shows anti-Jewish elements in the burlesque scene: in the foreground, centre, is an Ahasuerus type, the unsteady Jew without a firm place to stand, and – being forced from his house – the unsympathetic fat 'Jewish usurer'. Literature: *EJ* 1971, VIII, 330–2; Heuberger and Krohn 1988, fig. p.34; Battenberg 1990, II, 123–5; Dittmar 1992, fig. 39; Rohrbacher 1993, 94–156. Illustration after Deneke 1988, 313.

8. Expulsion of the Jews from Frankfurt by King Philip Augustus, 1182. Miniature in a Chronicle of France made after 1321. The illuminator gives the Jews the Jewish ring (*rota*) of his own time without knowing or noticing that this group characteristic is attested only for the time after 1215 (the relevant regulation of the Fourth Lateran Council). Brussels, BR, Ms.5, folio 265. Literature: Revel-Neher 1992, fig.68; cf. Lammers 1982, 32; Blumenkranz 1965, no.15.

4. The Christian view of Jewish religion, customs and life

1. Deuteronomy 16.1ff. (feast of the Passover). Miniature in the Wenzel Bible, c.1390. Vienna, ÖN, Cod.2759–2764, Vol. III, folio 193 recto. Illustration after *Wenzelsbibel* (facsimile edition), III, 1983, 193 recto.

2. Joshua 5.2ff (circumcision of the Hebrews in Gilgal). Miniature in the Wenzel Bible, c.1390. Vienna, ÖN, Cod.2759–2764, Vol. III, folio 217 verso.

3. Prayer of pagans, Jews and Christians. In this comparative view, the sequence of which is probably also chronological and evaluative, the pagans are praying to idols and the Jews are worshipping a Torah scroll. Miniature in a manuscript (fifteenth century) of the *Rationale divinorum officiorum*, a handbook of liturgy composed by William Durandus (1219–1292). Beaune, Bibliothèque municipale, Ms.21, folio 149. Illustration after Rabel 1992, fig.8.

4. Jewish Passover meal and Melchisedek (as the Old Testament prefigurations of Christ's Last Supper). Text: *Judei manducantur agnum paschale: Melchisedeth [sic] optulit panem et vinum*. Miniature in a late medieval block book made betwen 1475 and 1479. Literature: Wilson 1984, pl. p.173. Illustration after Kloss 1925, pl.37.

5. The Jews at the Passover (on Ex.12), a picture with elements of caricature. Woodcut in a *Speculum salvationis* from the workshop of the painter Peter Drach (Speyer 1478). Literature: Kästner 1985, II, fig. 613. Illustration after Schramm 1920, XVI, no.380.

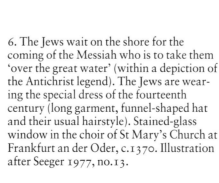

6. The Jews wait on the shore for the coming of the Messiah who is to take them 'over the great water' (within a depiction of the Antichrist legend). The Jews are wearing the special dress of the fourteenth century (long garment, funnel-shaped hat and their usual hairstyle). Stained-glass window in the choir of St Mary's Church at Frankfurt an der Oder, c.1370. Illustration after Seeger 1977, no.13.

7. II Chronicles 35.7–18 (celebration of the Passover). Miniature in the Wenzel Bible, c.1390. Vienna, ÖN, Cod.2759–2764, Vol. III, folio 112 verso. Illustration after *Wenzelsbibel* (facsimile edition), VII, 1987, 112 verso.

Ritus et celebratio phase iu

deoꝝ/cum orationibus eoꝝ/ ʒ benedictionibus menſe ad litterã interꝑtatis/cum omĩ obſeruatione vti ſoliti ſũt ſuũ paſca extra terrã ꝓmiſſionis ſine eſu agni paſcalis celebꝛare ꝑer egregiũ ꝺoctorem. Ⱬhomã murner ex hebꝛeo in latinũ traducta eloquium

8. Woodcut frontispiece of the work *Chukat ha-Pesach. Ritus et celebratio phase iudeorum* of Thomas Murner (died 1537), Frankfurt am Main: Beatus Murner 1512. Christian interest in the religion and customs of the Jews clearly increases after the beginning of the sixteenth century, and Murner's little book (sixteen pages in all) belongs in this context. The two persons in the middle and on the right can be seen to be wearing the Jewish ring on their upper garment, although this was prescribed only for wearing in public. Illustration after Lehmann 1984, II, pl.39. Cf. *Mon.Jud.Kat.* 1963, B 255; for the Christian image of the Jew at this time see R.I.Cohen, *Zion* 57, 1992, 275–340.

9. Jews (in their typical form of dress including Jewish ring) in conversation with one another. Frontispiece of a work by the Jew Antonius Margaritha (died after 1537), who went over to Christianity; it appeared from Steiner in Augsburg in 1530 (in the title of the work *Leser* is printed by mistake for *Le[h]rer*). This picture, too, documents in its way the growing interest in the faith and life of the Jews at this time. Literature: Liebe 1903, fig.53; *Mon.Jud.Kat.* 1963, B.271; *EJ* 1971, XI, 958; Zafran 1973 (I, 264f.); Bienert 1982, fig.34. Illustration after Stock 1939, 34 pl.2.

Der gantz Jüdisch glaub mit sampt ainer gründtlichen vnd warhafften anzaygunge/ Aller Satzungen/ Ceremonien/ Gebetten/Haymliche vnd offentliche Gebreüch /deren sich bye Juden halten/durch das gantz Jar/Mit schönen vnd gegründten Argumenten wyder jren Glauben. Durch Anthonium Margaritham Hebrayschen Leser der Löblichen Statt Augspurg / beschriben vnd an tag gegeben.

M. D. XXX.

10. Jews in conversation. Frontispiece to the 1705 Leipzig edition of the work by Antonius Margaritha mentioned above. Despite the lack of Jewish rings as compared to the Augsburg edition of 1530, the Jews do not make a good impression, and appear to be an alien group on the margin of Christian society. Here the interest in the faith and life of the Jews is focussed on their delight in discussion, but is already becoming almost a caricature: the Jews (with their Jewish hats and beards) seem strange beings – distinct from ordinary Christians – and their behaviour appears remarkable. Illustration after Stock 1939, 36 pl.3.

11. The Passover. Woodcut on Ex.12 in the Cologne Bible of the printer and publisher Heinrich Quentell (Cologne, c.1479). Literature: Kästner 1985, fig. 611. Illustration after Schramm 1920, VIII, no.388.

12. The Passover lamb. Woodcut by Hans Holbein the Younger (Basel 1523). Matthäus Merian copied this picture mirror-fashion in 1630. Literature: Kästner 1985, fig. 610. Illustration after Schmidt 1977, no.89.

13. Discussion between Jews (perhaps over a problem of religious law or the exposition of a biblical passage). The artist notes the proneness of learned Jews to extended discussions. Woodcut by Johann von Armssheim in the collection *Der Seelen Wurzgarten* of examples orientated on salvation history which appeared from Konrad Dinckmut (Ulm 1483). Literature: Weil 1929, 59; Zafran 1973, I, 254. Illustration after Schramm 1920, VI, no.94.

14. The Passover. Woodcut in a German Bible printed by Johann Grüninger, Strasbourg 1485. Illustration after Schramm 1920, XX, no.31.

15. The Passover lamb. Engraving (11 x 16 cm), a mirror copy of the corresponding woodcut by Hans Holbein the Younger. Literature: Köhl 1978, fig. 287; Kästner 1985, fig. 116. Illustration after Schmidt 1977, no.226.

Introduction to the History of
Christian-Jewish Relations

The historical starting point

Historically speaking, Christianity is a daughter religion of Judaism. The most common assumption nowadays is that the processes of the separation of early Christianity from Judaism took place in the first century over a lengthy period and with different degrees of intensity (thus e.g. B.Wander, *Trennungsprozesse zwischen 'Frühem Christentum' und Judentum im 1.Jahrhundert n.Chr.*, Tübingen ²1994). Primitive Christianity initially took shape within Judaism as a group of Jews who believed in Jesus of Nazareth as Messiah (Jewish Christians); soon, however, they were outnumbered by the Gentile Christians, who no longer felt obliged to obey the Jewish law. The New Testament texts with their occasional polemic against the Jews (the majority of whom did not believe in Christ) already reflect the dispute over the question of the Messiah.

Jesus was charged by the Jews for 'reasons of state' (John 11.47–50) with claiming the title 'king of the Jews' and handed over to the Romans – who could pass the death sentence and carry out executions (Wander, 259; cf. ibid.: Jesus was 'regarded as a threat to country, people and temple in leading Jewish circles. So he had to be removed before the feast [Mark 14.2]. Herod Antipas had also taken a similar preventive measure in the case of John the Baptist. The behaviour of the leading groups is not to be seen as pressure on the Jews, but as a measure to protect the population and the pilgrims in particular... The charge of claiming the title of king levelled against Jesus was one that made sense to the Romans').

The traditions underlying the passion narratives in the four Gospels paint roughly the following picture of the 'guilt of the Jews' over the death of Jesus. The high priests (along with the scribes) wanted his death from the beginning, and they used the Roman governor Pilate, whose collaboration they forced by 'street pressure', as an instrument to implement their plan. 'This depiction of events is historically inaccurate. Rather, the earliest portrayal of the person of Jesus which we can still arrive at is governed by a concern to acquit Jesus of any charge that might be relevant on the Roman side and rather to put the real blame for his death on the Jews. The result of this tendency was that in the course of time the Roman involvement in the execution of Jesus was increasingly minimized, while the Jewish involvement was maximized. This tendency already emerges with abundant clarity in the accounts in the canonical Gospels' (W.Reinbold, *Der älteste Bericht über den Tod Jesu*, Berlin and New York 1994, 318). The brief 'redactional scene' in Matt.27.25 ('Then the whole people cried out, "His blood be upon us and upon our children!"', cf. I Thess.2.15, plays a significant role in this connection, in so far as it called to life the pernicious fiction of the collective guilt of the Jewish people and became a main source of an anti-Judaism with a Christian motivation (Reinbold, 319ff.).

In fact the canonical Gospels already indicate a particular combination of ideas: Jesus is innocent – Pilate regards him as innocent but nevertheless has him crucified (i.e. executed with a punishment for crime and sedition which was customary among the Romans for slaves and non-Romans). Now the narrative structure only becomes convincing 'if the responsibility for the death of Jesus is shifted from Pilate to another group which puts Pilate under pressure. As things are, this group can only be Jewish, whether it is made up of the high priests, the Pharisees or the people of Jerusalem. Furthermore, since Jesus' innocence is a fixed axiom, this group must have had base motives and evil intents.' Thus there is much to suggest that the alleged collective guilt of the Jews is a 'theological thesis in historical garb'. 'The tragic and finally pernicious aspect of this historicization is that it conceals the fact that the controversy between Judaism and Christianity is in the first place solely about the question of the significance of the person of Jesus and the correct interpretation of the Holy Scriptures which they share, and not about any historically tangible "guilt". In this way it contributed substantially to the escalation of the conflict between Judaism and Christianity... It is time that Christian theology abandoned the false thesis that the quintessence of Judaism can be seen in its inability to tolerate the presence of Jesus in its midst and therefore its insistence on his removal' (Reinhold, 323–5).

The gradual separation of Christianity from Judaism was encouraged above all by two factors. 1. The Jewish Christians did not take part in the freedom fight of the Jews against Rome (which sometimes had messianic overtones), and from the perspective of the centre of Judaism this, and their belief in Jesus as Messiah, made them a marginal group (and one to be excluded). 2. By observing the Torah, Jewish Christianity became a small minority compared with the far more numerous Gentile Christians, and could no longer play any part in determining the theological way forward. Thus in the time of the church fathers theological positions developed which made the 'parting of the ways' irreversible (e.g. the statement of the Council of Nicaea in 325 that as Son of God Jesus is 'of one substance with the Father' [*homoousios to patri*] and the trinitarian confession).

One stage in this development, and an important one, is the twelfth benediction which was introduced into the so-called Eighteen Benedictions used in synagogue worship around the year 90. The earliest version of it runs: 'For the apostates let there be no hope. Uproot the kingdom of arrogance soon in our day. And the Nazarenes and the Minims shall perish in a moment, they shall be blotted out of the book of life and not be inscribed with the righteous. Blessed are you, Lord, who humbles the arrogant' (J.J.Petuchowski and C.Thoma, *Lexikon der jüdisch-christliche Begegnung*, Freiburg 1989, 204–5; cf. already Justin Martyr, *Dialogue with the Jew Trypho* 16.4). So if the Jewish Christians did not want to curse themselves, from now on they had to keep away from synagogue worship.

In discussing the history of Christian-Jewish relations we should note that Jesus of Nazareth, from whom Christianity derives itself, was a practising Jew all his life and that Judaism is and remains the 'holy root' (Paul, Rom.11.6) of Christianity.

The history of Christian–Jewish relations since the second century

The majority of Christians simply could not understand why even after and despite Golgotha the majority of Jews did not believe in Jesus of Nazareth as Messiah and Son of God. Some theological interpretations and evaluations were developed in order to understand the situation in some way, since the ongoing existence of a vital Jewish religion seemed a thorn in the flesh of Christianity; indeed it seemed to put the Christian religion generally in question. Thus for example John Chrysostom (died 406) judges: 'If the Jewish cult is venerable and significant, ours can only be lies and deception' (*Patrologia Graeca* 48,852).

The interpretations and evaluations include the following views:

1. The Old Testament (i.e. the Jewish Bible) is a Christian book through and through, which (when interpreted typologically and allegorically) points everywhere to Christ, the Christian saving event and the church. The New Testament starting-point for this tradition of interpretation can be found e.g. in I Cor.10.6,11 (cf. II Cor.3.14–16).

2. The Jews do not understand their own scriptures, because they grasp the literal instead of the spiritual sense of the texts. They are blind to Christian truth and hardened, either because of their own wickedness, because they have been led astray by the devil, or because they lack the capacity for thought (*ratio*) of normal (Christian) people. Their religion is in truth unbelief, an aberrant, perverse faith (*perfidia*), and instead of the exalted religion of biblical times they have only superstition (*superstitio*).

3. By their refusal to believe, the Jews are apostates from the Old Testament tradition which issues in Jesus Christ and has been taken up by the church; the church is now the 'true Israel' and the 'new people of God', whereas the Jews have been rejected by God.

4. The rejection and crucifixion of the Messiah continues the persecution and murder of the Old Testament prophets and as ancestral guilt is a burden on the whole Jewish people for ever.

5. The dialectic of the numerous biblical pronunciations of repudiation and promise is regularly resolved by applying God's threats to the Jews and God's promises of salvation to the Christians. By a one-sided choice of appropriate biblical passages it is demonstrated that the Jews are now enemies of God, who no longer hears their prayers.

6. The destruction of Jerusalem in 70 is the just and irreversible divine punishment upon the Jews for their killing of Christ (often seen by Christians as 'the murder of God'). Since then they have become slaves (*servi*) of the Christian Gentile peoples or wander homeless over the earth, burdened with the curse of their deed, until the end of the world. Only conversion to Christ opens up a way of salvation to them.

7. Following the example of Matt.28.19 and Acts 1.8 there is to be a mission among the Jews (if need be using compulsion, in accordance with Luke 14.23: *compelle intrare, ut impleatur domus mea*: 'Compel them to come in, that my house may be full'). If they are not converted, then their conversion (promised in Rom.11.15–16) has to wait for the end of the world. Until then they must survive and may by no means be exterminated (according to Ps.59.12: 'Kill them not... disperse them') so that God's plan of salvation, which also includes them, cannot be put to shame. Accordingly, from the twelfth century on many popes issued bulls protecting the Jews, and after the twelfth century, as 'servants of the chamber' they were collectively under the protection of the worldly ruler. From the start, and for a long time, the apologetic devices used in the course of the mission to the Jews worked with christological biblical exegesis, and from the period of scholasticism (eleventh to thirteenth centuries) also with rational proofs; finally, from the high and late Middle Ages it worked with an approach to the Talmud in which the messianic passages in it were applied to Jesus Christ.

Factors in the historical development

Historians seek causes. The essential factors in the history of Christian-Jewish relations – which has often been full of tension – and thus the subjects to be investigated are:

1. The theological opposition, visible above all in the apologetics and polemics of the extensive Christian *Adversus-Judaeos* literature (treatises *Contra Judaeos* and *Adversus Judaeos*; from the sixteenth century also relevant works of Luther, the Reformers and Pietists).

2. Authoritative and normative texts of councils and popes which regulate Christian-Jewish social life (one theme is that in order to avoid danger to the salvation of Christian souls, the Jews must remain recognizable as Jews among Christians; thus they may not discard their traditional special form of dress with a view to assimila-

tion; they are to live in a ghetto). Here too we must ask how the church's law about the Jews is accompanied by and supported by the local secular laws of the rulers relating to Jews.

3. The attitudes of the Christian majority of Europe towards the Jews as 'aliens' (who have immigrated from the East), which have a basis in social psychology. Such attitudes come into being on the periphery and outside Christianity as anti-Jewish 'group prejudices'. In times of social crisis the xenophobia can increase markedly.

4. The overlapping and mixing of religious and profane prejudices. This particularly favoured the origin of anti-Jewish legends, which in turn often sparked off persecutions amounting to pogroms.

5. On the whole no notice continued to be taken of the fact that Jesus was a practising Jew and that Judaism is the 'holy root' (Rom.11.6) of Christianity.

Stages, fields of events and problem zones as topics in Christian sources, texts and pictures

I. The destruction of Jerusalem in the year 70 CE and the Christian theological doctrine of the everlasting servitude of the Jews *(servitus Judaeorum)* to the Christian peoples.

(a) Argument with the New Testament, e.g. Luke 21.20–24 and Gal.4.23–31 (on Gen.21.10).

(b) Argument with the Old Testament, e.g. Gen.25.23 (the *maior minori serviet* of Jacob and Esau, the twin sons of Isaac and Rebecca): the older (Esau, typologically the Jews), will serve, i.e. be subjected to, the younger (Jacob, typologically the Christians).

(c) The relevant Christian pictorial art and its predecessors *(Judaea capta* coins and the relief on the arch of Titus in Rome).

II. The rise of a Christian anti-Jewish apologetic from the second century CE.

(a) The *Adversus Judaeos* literature.

(b) The typological and allegorical exegesis of the Old Testament in terms of Christ; the OT as a book of the church (or an extension of the NT backwards).

(c) The juxtaposition of the allegorical personifications of Ecclesia and Synagoga in Christian art.

III. Significant religious disputations between Christians and Jews
(a) Paris (1240)

(b) Barcelona (1263)
(c) Tortosa (1413/1414)

IV. The Christian mission to the Jews
(a) Its New Testament basis (Mark 16.15; Matt.28.19; Acts 1.8; Rom.1.16; 11.14).
(b) As a theme of Christian pictorial art (e.g. Jesus and the apostles often no longer appear as Jews among Jews but are already depicted as Christian 'missionaries to the Jews').

V. The predominance of negative theological assessments
(a) From the beginning the Jews are enemies of Christ and the Christians.
(b) They are allied with the devil and have gone to hell.
(c) Emphasis on the opposition between the OT (old covenant) and NT (new covenant) or devaluation of the former.

VI. Laws about the Jews and the protection of Jews
(a) Ecclesiastical (councils, papal texts, various kinds of texts in canon law).
The main purpose is to compel the Jews to behave in a way which cannot endanger the salvation of Christian souls. Thus the motif is 'pastoral care'; among other things the Jews are to keep their traditional (oriental) mode of dress so that they remain recognizable as Jews. This purpose also leads to the introduction of 'new' marks of recognition (e.g. rings) in the thirteenth century.
(b) Secular (Christian rulers)
1. Codex Theodosianus 16, 8, 9 (Emperor Theodosius, 29 September 393): *Iudaeorum sectam nulla lege prohibitam satis constat* (*religio licita* principle).
2. Cod.Theod., Novella 3.1–8 (Theodosius II, 31 January 438): summary of the laws about the Jews applying in his time.
3. Emperor Frederick II (July 1236, renewal of privilege for the Jews of Worms): the Jews of the empire become 'court servants' (*servi camere nostre*, i.e. they are so to speak minors under the supervision of the emperor; they are under protection but lack essential civic freedoms); at the same time the anti-Jewish ritual murder legend is repudiated.
4. The imperial police regulations of the sixteenth century.

VII. The Jews under the special protection of the popes
(a) Gregory the Great takes over and hands on the protection of the Jews laid down in the Codex Theodosianus.
(b) The *Sicut Judaeis* bulls.

VIII. Persecutions of Jews
(a) During the Crusades (from 1096) and during the plague in Europe (1348/1349), when the Jews were accused of having poisoned all the wells.
(b) In connection with anti–Jewish Christian legends:
1. Profanation of images of Christ and Christian saints.
2. Blood–guilt (ritual murder).
3. Profanation of hosts.

IX. Special forms of Christian hostility to Jews (precursors of modern antisemitism)
(a) The 'Judensau' depictions in Christian churches.
(b) The 'Frankfurt Judensau'.
(c) Aggressive texts of very varied kinds e.g. by Conrad Celtis (died 1508) and Hans Folz (died c.1515).

X. Secular and ecclesiastical regulation, hindrances to the professional activity of Jews and discrimination against it
(a) The Jews as doctors, merchants, money-lenders.
(b) Restriction on or prohibition of the inheritance of land: ban on engaging in crafts (membership of guilds was open only to Christians).
(c) Prevention of business activity by different rules of a very varied kind (e.g. standing on the skin of a sow when giving the 'Jewish oath').

Differences between Christianity and Judaism

I. *Jesus as Messiah and Son of God.* Jesus is seen by some Jews as a significant figure of Jewish religious history and faith, and occasionally also as a prophetic figure, but not as Son of God (pre-existent, or of the same substance) or as God. The assumption that the Messiah has a divine quality is incompatible with the Jewish concept of monotheism.

From the Jewish side, in this connection it is occasionally pointed out that Jesus is not yet called 'God' in the synoptic Gospels.

Judaism does not regard typological and allegorical biblical exegesis aimed at demonstrating that Jesus is Messiah and Son of God as valid. From the Jewish side it is emphasized that Jesus Christ was not rejected out of malicious stubbornness, as Christians have often assumed, but because of 'the messianic conception of total redemption, which did not dawn with him' (S.Ben-Chorin, *Jüdische Glaube*, Tübingen 1975, 287).

The twelfth of the thirteen principles of faith in Maimonides, 'The Messiah will come' (i.e. the messianic expectation of the Jews continues despite Jesus and Muhammad [Mishnah commentary on Sanhedrin X,1]), is in line with this view.

Thus the traditional *titulus* on the cross, *Iesus Nazarenus Rex Iudaeorum* (INRI) is not acceptable from a Jewish perspective either.

The christology of Paul is often regarded as an especially divisive factor.

II. *Incarnation*. The incarnation is incompatible with the Jewish notion of God. God is indivisible, and nothing outside God is really holy. While Jews do not doubt the historicity of Jesus of Nazareth, he is regarded only as man *(purus homo)*.

III. *Trinity*. Belief in 'God the Father, God the Son and God the Holy Spirit' is rejected by Judaism as being incompatible with strict biblical monotheism (Deut.6.4). Accordingly the thirteen Jewish 'dogmas' in Maimonides state, among other things, that God alone is creator (i.e. he knows no second person alongside himself); he is one (i.e. an indivisible unity); he is incorporeal; and he alone, no other, is to be worshipped.

However, Christianity and Judaism do share the notion of a Father God in heaven.

IV. *Jesus as mediator between God and humankind*. For Judaism a human being can be a child of God only indirectly. However, before 70 (the destruction of Jerusalem), the high priest represented the whole people before God; in Philo (*De somniis* 2, 188–9) he is even 'a kind of intermediary being between God and man', but not himself divine. The perspective of the letter to the Hebrews is to some degree related: God is the heavenly high priest who becomes the atoning mediator.

V. *The role of the priesthood*. In Christianity (especially in Catholic Christianity), priests administer the sacraments and have the power to bind and loose.

By contrast, the Jewish religion is more of a lay religion without a group distinguished by rank. Members of the community have equal religious rights (only the Torah is binding). Every Jewish father of a family is

so to speak a priest, in accordance with Ex.19.6: the whole people is to be a people of priests and a holy people.

Accordingly, the rabbis usually have no exalted function in synagogue worship. As a kind of theological authority, the rabbi is active above all as a pastor; his study makes him competent in matters of religious matters and he also performs marriages and is present at funerals.

VI. *Worship, religious commandments*. One fundamental difference here is that the Jewish religion knows no veneration of saints, and religious images are not customary (according to Ex.20.4 and Deut.5.8–9 no pictures may be made for cultic purposes), or are regarded as offensive because of the danger of idolatry and a deviation from strict monotheism; from a Jewish perspective the Christian veneration of saints is often seen to be a pagan practice.

Christians transferred the weekly day of celebration from Saturday to Sunday, the first day of the Jewish week. For Christians this is the day of remembrance of the resurrection of the Lord, combined with eucharistic worship (Acts 20.7 and I Cor.16.2 are regarded as New Testament starting points). Easter replaces the Jewish Passover.

The inner room of a synagogue to some degree reflects the lay-out of the temple in Jerusalem: holy of holies, sanctuary, forecourt (forecourt of men, forecourt of women). Here a holy shrine in which the Torah scrolls are kept, set behind a curtain, corresponds to the holy of holies; the women's balcony in synagogues has a forerunner in the 'court of the women'. The perpetual light before the Torah curtain recalls the seven–branched lampstand in the temple.

The physical separation of women from men in synagogues thus has a long tradition. It is also traditional that they do not play an active part in synagogue worship, that they are present only voluntarily, and need observe only some of the religious commandments incumbent upon Jewish men.

VII. *Original sin, sin, ideas of redemption*
(a) *Christian*. Adam's fall made human beings collectively sinful and guilty. Only belief in Jesus Christ and in his atoning death for humankind or the baptism of the new–born brings freedom from sin. Here the doctrine of

grace and the sacraments is particularly significant. According to this, in addition to faith in Jesus and the intercession of the saints (in the Catholic Church) human beings need grace, which is effective above all in connection with the sacraments. With the conviction of the *a priori* sinfulness of human beings goes a strong emphasis on the need for redemption, often combined with a tendency to flee the world or a pessimistic attitude to the things of this world (the earth as a 'vale of tears'). The Christian notion of redemption is more individual and transcendental than that of Judaism.

(b) *In Judaism*. Sin is an individual, voluntary transgression and is not hereditary. In this connection reference is often made to Gen.4.7: human beings are to rule over sin, in other words they are free as far as sin is concerned and can decide freely, even about returning from sin to God (cf. Isa.55.7: 'Let the wicked forsake his way, and the unrighteous man his thoughts; let him return to the Lord, that he may have mercy on him, and to our God, for he will abundantly pardon'). Human beings are not *a priori* sinful. In contrast to the tendency to flee the world which is widespread in Christianity, Judaism affirms the world strongly. Marriage is regarded as a divine commandment, and there is usually little understanding of Christian celibacy. Human redemption in Judaism is seen more in terms of the people and of this world. An indication of this is that in prayer Jews tend to speak of 'our God' whereas Christians speak of 'my God' (Ben Chorin, *Jüdische Glaube*, 75).

VIII. *Faith, action, justification*. Correct belief is more important in Christianity than in Judaism, for which correct action, action in accordance with the Torah, has priority. The person who observes the Torah is righteous and well–pleasing before God. Faith in God must be accompanied by the practice of the Torah, which guarantees salvation. Ethics (which concerns duties towards one's fellow human being) is therefore rated highly, especially in Reform Judaism (since the Enlightenment).

IX. *Tolerance*. In contrast to the church's *extra ecclesiam nulla salus* ('outside the church there is no salvation'), Judaism does not just recognize one exclusive way of salvation through the Torah, but also gives the 'righteous among the nations', above all those non-Jews who observe the Noachide commandments (Gen.9; bSanh 56a–b), a share in the world to come ('*olam ha-ba*, thus first Tosefta Sanhedrin 13.2). So no formal

conversion to Judaism is needed for salvation; a place in the future world (or in 'heaven') awaits pious non-Jews as well. Therefore mission to non-Jews was and is unusual (and not because Jews are arrogant about their salvation, as they are often accused of being). The Christian principle of love of enemy (Matt.5.43ff.; Luke 6.27–29, 35–36; cf. Mark 11.25) goes beyond this. Jesus Sirach 28.1–7 (c.190 BCE) already calls for the forgiveness of enemies.

X. *Love of neighbour and love of enemy*. The commandment to love the neighbour (Lev. 19.18: 'Love your neighbour as yourself', cf. Lev. 19.34: 'You shall love him [i.e. the alien dwelling in Israel] as yourself') is common to Judaism and Christianity (e.g. Matt. 22.39). The Christian principle of love of enemy (Matt. 5.43ff.; Luke 6.27–29, 35–36; cf. Mark 11.25) goes beyond that. But Jesus Sirach 28.1–7 (c. 190 BCE) already requires forgiveness for enemies.

XI. *Binding precepts of faith* (dogmas, dogmatics). In Judaism there are individual 'dogmas', but there are no dogmatics. Not even all the thirteen 'principles of faith' in Maimonides' 'creed' are generally acknowledged and binding. Jews occasionally put this in a pointed way: Judaism knows no pope, and no stake for heretics either. According to the Talmud there are 613 binding commandments and prohibitions (248 commandments and 365 prohibitions), derived from the five books of Moses. In the course of tradition their total number has increased to around 2,000.

XII. *Eschatology, resurrection of the dead*. Christians and Jews have in common the expectation of a final, all-embracing, perfect kingdom of peace brought in by God (Isa.11.1–9), but Christianity usually sees this future realm in transcendent terms. Judaism also envisages a world in the beyond, but usually sees the 'world to come' in immanent terms; here Jerusalem and the land of Israel play a significant role. At all events hope is focussed on a universal time of hope and blessing with absolute peace in the world.

For Christianity, Jesus is the Messiah who brings redemption from sin and death, and the full and final realization of God's kingdom of peace begins with his second coming, the eschatological return.

In contrast to the Christian assumption that there is a partial, provisional time of salvation in connection with the first coming of Christ, Judaism believes that the world is unredeemed: 'The notion of a Messiah who has come without turning the world into the kingdom of God but who will come again to crown his work of redemption in the visible kingdom of past history is alien to the Bible of the Old Testament and thus also to later Judaism' (Ben Chorin, *Jüdischer Glaube*, 287).

From the Christian side, the Jewish messianic hope is often dismissed as 'flat' compared with that of Christianity. However, this comparison is unjust, because pious Jews expect salvation less from the Messiah himself – he is only a human being – than from the state of blessing which he introduces: the return of all the Jews from the dispersion to the promised land, the revival of a flourishing land of Israel in whose capital, Jerusalem, God dwells; a renewal of the biblical priesthood and the worship of the God of Israel by all the peoples of the earth. But the Jewish people is already in a provisional state of salvation, brought about by God's covenant, which has continued since biblical items, and by practising the Torah. Thus the expectation of salvation is structurally different: at the centre of Jewish religion stands the Torah (which according to the conviction of some Jews will also continue to apply in the eschatological realm of peace), while Jesus Christ stands at the centre of Christian faith. Comparisons of the two religions must note the structural difference between them.

The conviction of a resurrection of the dead already begins in isolated instances among the Jews in the biblical period (e.g. Isa.26.19; Deut.12.1), and it is fixed doctrine in the second petition of the Eighteen Benedictions (towards the end of the first century CE: 'Blessed are you, Eternal One, who give life to the dead'). The view of the immortality of the human soul which is shared by most Jews today is to be distinguished from this. The Christians took over both views, but in their religious convictions they are more strongly orientated on the beyond and transcendence than Judaism, whose piety is first and foremost focussed on the here and now of practising the Torah, the liturgy of synagogue worship, and prayer.

Bibliography

I. Christian-Jewish relations, past and present

Rendtorff, R., and Henrix, H.H. (eds.), *Die Kirchen und das Judentum. Dokumente von 1945-1985*, Paderborn: Bonifatius and Munich: Kaiser 1988

Rengstorf, K.H. and Kortzfleisch, S.von (eds.), *Kirche und Synagoge. Handbuch zur Geschichte von Christen und Juden. Darstellung mit Quellen* (2 vols), Munich: DTV 1988 (reprint of 1968–1970 edition)

Petuchowski, J.J., and Thomas, C., *Lexikon der jüdisch-christlichen Begegnung*, Freiburg: Herder 1989

Schreckenberg, H., *Die christlichen Adversus-Iudaeos-Texte* (3 vols), Frankfurt: Peter Lang 1990–1994

II. The depiction of Jews and Judaism in Christian art

Reallexikon zur deutschen Kunstgeschichte, Stuttgart 1937ff., e.g. IV, 1189–1215, 'Ecclesia und Synagoga'

Seiferth, W., *Synagoge und Kirche im Mittelalter*, Munich: Kösel 1964

Blumenkranz, B., *Juden und Judentum in der mittelalterlichen Kunst*, Stuttgart: Kohlhammer 1965

Zafran, E.M., *The Iconography of Antisemitism. A Study of the Representation of the Jews in the Visual Arts of Europe 1400–1600*, Diss.New York University 1973

Schachar, I., *The 'Judensau'. A Medieval Anti-Jewish Motif and its History*, London 1974

Kirschbaum, E. (ed.), *Lexikon der christlichen Ikonographie* (8 vols.), Freiburg 1968–1976, reprinted 1990, e.g. I, 569–78, 'Ecclesia und Synagoge'; II, 449–54, 'Juden, Judentum'

Schiller, G., *Ikonographie der christlichen Kunst* (4 vols), Gütersloh 1966–1980, IV, 45–68, 'Ecclesia und Synagoge'

Kötzsche, L., and Osten-Sacken, P. von der (eds.), *Wenn der Messias kommt. Das jüdisch-christliche Verhältnis im Spiegel mittelalterlicher Kunst*, Berlin 1984

Rohrbacher, S. and Schmidt, M., *Judenbilder. Kulturgeschichte antijüdischer Mythen und antisemitischer Vorurteile*, Reinbek: Rowohlt 1991

III. Reference works on Judaica, history and theology

Germania Judaica, ed.. I.Elbogen et al. (3 vols), Tübingen 1963ff.

Encyclopaedia Judaica (16 vols), Jerusalem 1971

Theologische Realenzyklopädie, Berlin 1977ff. (e.g. 'Antisemitismus', 'Antijüdische Apologetik', 'Judentum und Christentum'

Ben-Sasson, H.H. (ed.), *Geschichte des jüdischen Volkes* (3 vols.), Munich 1978–1980

Lexikon des Mittelalters, Munich and Zurich 1980ff. (e.g. V, 790–2, 'Judenfeindschaft'; V, 792–3, 'Judenrecht')

Poliakov, L., *Geschichte des Antisemitismus* (8 vols), Worms 1977–1988

Battenberg, F., *Das europäische Zeitalter der Juden* (2 vols), Darmstadt 1990

Bibliography

Adhémar, J. (et al.), *Populäre Druckgraphik Europas. Frankreich, vom 15. bis zum 20.Jahrhundert*, Munich 1968

Alexander, J.J.G., *Medieval Illuminators and their Methods of Work*, New Haven 1992

Alexander, D.A. and Strauss, W.L., *The German Single-Leaf Woodcut 1600-1700* (2 vols), New York: Abaris 1977

Amira, K.von, *Die Dresdener Bilderhandschrift des Sachsenspiegels*; I, 1–2 (plates), Leipzig 1902; II, 1–2 (commentary), Leipzig 1925–1926

Andersson, A. (et al.), *Die Glasmalereien des Mittelalters in Skandinavien*, Stockholm 1964

Andics, H., *Die Juden in Wien*, Vienna 1988

Anzelewsky, F., *Toggenburger Weltchronik*, Aachen 1970

Appuhn, H., *Meisterwerke der niedersächsichen Kunst des Mittelalters*, Bad Honnef 1963

– (ed.), *Heilsspiegel. Die Bilder des mittelalterlichen Erbauungsbuches* Speculum humanae salvationis, with postscript and commentary, Dortmund: Harenberg 1981

– (ed.), *Wenzelsbibel* (facsimile edition), with commentary (8 vols), Dortmund 1990

Aronius, J., *Regesten zur Geschichte der Juden*, Berlin 1902

Aschoff, D., 'Eine "Jüdische Hinrichtung" in Westfalen 1486', in *Jüdisches Leben. Katalog zur kulturhistorischen Ausstellung des Mindener Museums*, Gütersloh 1988, 67–78

– , *Juden in Westfalen*, Westfalen im Bild. Wcstfälische Kulturgeschichte 3, Münster 1989, 21f.

– , 'Die Juden in der städtischen Gesellschaft', in *Geschichte der Stadt Münster*, ed. F.J.Jakobi, I, Münster: Aschendorff 1993, 575–93

Ausubel, N., *The Book of Jewish Knowledge*, New York: Crown 1964

Bacher, E., *Die mittelalterlichen Glasgemälde der Steiermark*, I, Graz and Strassengel, Vienna 1979

Baier, G. (et al.), *Kirchen, Klöster und Kunstschätze in der DDR*, Munich 1982

Baldass, L., *Jahrbuch der Preussischen Kunstsammlungen 56*, 1935, 9

Hans Baldung Grien. Prints and Drawings (Catalogue), Washington 1981

Baron, S.W., *A Social and Religious History of the Jews* (18 vols), New York 1952–1984

Barral i Altet, X. (et al.), *Romanische Kunst* (2 vols), Munich: Beck 1983–1984

Battenberg, F., *Das europäische Zeitalter der Juden* (2 vols), Darmstadt 1990

Bauerreis, R., *Pie Jesu. Das Schmerzensmann-Bild und sein Einfluss auf die mittelalterliche Frömmigkeit*, Munich 1931

Baum, E., *Katalog des Museums mittelalterlicher österreichischer Kunst*, Vienna and Munich 1971

Baum, J., *Die Malerei und Plastik des Mittelalters, II. Deutschland, Frankreich und Britannien*, Wildpark–Potsdam 1930

Baumgart, F., *Geschichte der abendländischen Malerei*, Stuttgart 1952

Baumgart, P., 'Joseph Süss Oppenheimer. Das Dilemma eines Hofjuden im absoluten Fürstenstaat', in *Geschichte und Kultur des Judentums*, ed. K.Müller and K.Wittstadt, Würzburg 1988, 91–110

Bayerns Kirche im Mittelalter. Handschriften und Urkunden aus Bayerischem Staatsbesitz, Munich 1960

Becker, K. (et al.), *Die Kunstdenkmäler der Provinz Sachsen I, Die Stadt Erfurt*, Burg 1929

Becker, W., 'Jüdisches in der Bildkunst des 19.Jahrhunderts', in *Judenhass – Schuld der Christen?!*, ed. W.P.Eckert and E.L.Ehrlich, Essen 1964, 257–78

Beckmann, J.H., and Schroth, I. (eds.), *Deutsche Bilderbibel aus dem späten Mittelalter. Handschrift 334 der Universitätsbibliothek Freiburg im Breisgau und M.719–720 der Pierpont Morgan Library New York*, Constance: Jan Thorbecke 1960

Becksmann, R., *Deutsche Glasmalerei des Mittelalters*, Stuttgart 1988

Beenken, H., *Der Meister von Naumburg*, Berlin 1939

Beer, E.J., *Die Glasmalereien der Schweiz aus dem 14. und 15. Jahrhundert*, Basel 1965

– , *Initial und Miniatur. Buchmalerei aus neun Jahrhunderten in Handschriften der Badischen Landesbibliothek*, Basel 1965

– (ed,) et al., *Rudolf von Ems: Weltchronik. Der Stricker: Karl der Grosse. Faksimile-Band der Hs.302 der Kantons-*

bibliothek (Vadiana) St Gallen, with companion volume and commentary, Lucerne: Faksimile Verlag 1982

Behling, L., in *Festschrift W.Braunfels*, Tübingen 1977, 17

Behrens, R (et al.), *Biblia pauperum. Apocalypsis. Die Weimarer Handschrift* (facsimile volume), Frankfurt am Main: Insel 1977

Behrens, E., 'Ein schlesisches Votivbild', *Zeitschrift des deutschen Vereins für Kunstwissenschaft* 8, 1941, 173–8

Bein, A., *Die Judenfrage. Biographie eines Weltproblems* (2 vols.), Stuttgart 1980

Benoschofsky, I. (et al.), *Das jüdische Museum in Budapest*, Wiesbaden 1989

Ben-Sasson, H.H., 'The Reformation in Contemporary Jewish Eyes', *Proceedings of the Israel Academy of Sciences and Humanities* 4, 1969–1970, Jerusalem 1971, 239–326

– (ed.), *Geschichte des jüdischen Volkes* (3 vols.), Munich 1978–80

Berger, N. (ed.), *Wo sich Kulturen begegnen. Die Geschichte der tschechoslowakischen Juden*, Prague 1992

Bergner, H., *Handbuch der kirchlichen Kunstaltertümer*, Leipzig 1905

Berve, M., *Die Armenbibel. Herkunft, Gestalt, Typologie*, Beuron 1989

Bialostocki, J., *Propyläen Kunstgeschichte*, Vol.7, *Spätmittelalter und beginnende Neuzeit*, Berlin 1972

Bienert, W., *Luther und die Juden*, Frankfurt 1982

Bildern sind nicht verboten (exhibition catalogue), Düsseldorf 1982

Bilder und Tänze des Todes in der europäischen Kunst seit dem Mittelalter (exhibition catalogue), Unna 1982

Französische Bilderbogen des 19.Jahrhunderts (Sammlung Sigrid Mettken, Paris), Regensburg 1962

H. Birkhan (ed.), *Die Juden in ihrer mittelalterlichen Umwelt*, Bern 1992 (esp. id., 'Die Juden in der deutschen Literatur des Mittelalters', 143–78)

Bloch, P., 'Eine Dialogdarstellung des frühen 12.Jahrhunderts', in *Festschrift E.Tautscholdt*, Hamburg 1965, 54–62

– (ed), *Reichenauer Evangelistar* (facsimile edition with commentary), Graz: Akademische Druck- und Verlagsanstalt 1972

Blumenkranz, B., 'Das Bilderevangelium des Hasses', in *Judenhass – Schuld der Christen?!*, ed. W.P.Eckert and E.L.Ehrlich, Essen: Hans Driewer 1964, 249–56

–, *Juden und Judentum in der mittelalterlichen Kunst*, Stuttgart: Kohlhammer 1965

– , 'Ecriture et image dans la polémique antijuïve de Matfre Ermengaud', in *Juifs et judaïsme de Languedoc: XIIe siècle*, ed. M.-H.Vicaire (et al.), Toulouse: E.Privat 1977

Blunt, A., *Nicolas Poussin*, London 1967

Bock, E., *Geschichte der graphischen Kunst*, Berlin 1930

Boeckler, A., *Das Stuttgarter Passionale*, Augsburg 1923

–, *Die Regensburg-Prüfeninger Buchmalerei des XI. und XII. Jahrhunderts*, Munich 1924

– , *Deutsche Buchmalerei vorgotischer Zeit*, Königstein im Taunus 1952

Bohatcová, M., 'Die tschechischen Drucke des Nürnberger Druckers Christoph Gutknecht', *Gutenberg-Jahrbuch* 1991, 249–68

Bohatec, M., *Schöne Bücher des Mittelalters aus Böhmen*, Hanau 1970

Boockmann, H., *Die Stadt im späten Mittelalter*, Munich 1986

–, *Stauferzeit und spätes Mittelalter. Deutschland 1125–1517*, Berlin 1987

de Boor, H., 'Skandinavien', in *Handbuch der Kulturgeschichte* 51.8, Potsdam 1934 (and Constance 1964), 203–380

– and R. Newald (eds.), *Geschichte der deutschen Literatur* V, Munich 1967

Börnert, G., et al., *Luther. Dokumente seines Lebens und Wirkens*, Weimar 1983

Borries-Schulten, S.von (ed.), *Die romanischen Handschriften der Württembergischen Landesbibliothek Stuttgart*, Stuttgart 1987

Borst, A., *Lebensformen im Mittelalter*, Frankfurt am Main 1979

Bosbach, F. (ed.), *Feindbilder. Die Darstellung der Gegner in der politischen Publizistik des Mittelalters und der Neuzeit*, Cologne 1992

Bott, G. (et al., eds.), *Martin Luther. Sein Leben in Bildern und Texten*, Frankfurt 1983

Brandis, T, *Die* Codices in scrinio *der Staats- und Universitätsbibliothek Hamburg 1–100*, Hamburg 1973

Brandt, M., 'Schatzkunst aus Hildesheim', *Zeitschrift für Kunstwissenschaft* 42, 1988, 11–38

Braudel, F., *Sozialgeschichte des 15–18 Jahrhunderts. Der Handel*, Munich 1986

Braun, J., *Der christliche Altar in seiner geschichtlichen Entwicklung* (2 vols), Munich 1924

Bredt, E.W., *Katalog der mittelalterlichen Miniaturen des Germanischen Nationalmuseums*, Nuremberg 1903

Bremer, N., *Das Bild der Juden in den Passionsspielen und in der bildenden Kunst des deutschen Mittelalters*, Frankfurt 1986

Brin, H.B., 'A Rare *Judaea Capta* Sestertius', *Israel Numismatic Journal* 8, 1984, 12–13

Browe, P., 'Die Hostienschändungen der Juden im Mittelalter', *Römische Quartalsschrift* 34, 1926, 167–97

Bruck, R., *Die Malereien in den Handschriften des Königreiches Sachsen*, Dresden 1906

Brückner, M. (et al., eds.), *Die Kunstdenkmale der Provinz Sachsen. II 1, Die Stadt Erfurt*, Burg 1931

Brückner, W., *Populäre Druckgraphik Europas in Deutschland, vom 15. bis zum 20.Jahrhundert*, Munich 1975

Buch, W., *Zeitschrift für Kunstgeschichte* 45, 1982, 97–129

Büchler, A., 'Zu den Psalmenillustrationen der Haseloff-Schule', *Zeitschrift für Kunstgeschichte* 52, 1989, 215–38

Deutsche Buchmalerei des Mittelalters. Ausstellung der Bayerischen Staatsbibliothek München, Munich 1938

Büchsel, A., 'Die romanischen Portale im Geiste Clunys', *Städel Jahrbuch* 11, 1987, 7–54

Buck, M.R., *Ulrichs von Richental Chronik des Constanzer Konzils 1414–1418*, Tübingen 1882

Budde, R., 'Zwei vieldeutige Darstellungen der Epiphanie in der Vorhalle des Domes zu Münster?', in *Die Heiligen Drei Könige – Darstellung und Verehrung. Katalog zu Ausstellung des Wallraf-Richartz-Museums in der Josef-Haubrich-Kunsthalle Köln*, Cologne 1982, 131–4

– , *Köln und seine Malerei 1300–1500*, Cologne 1986

Bulard, M., *Le scorpion symbole du peuple juif,* Paris 1936

Bunjes, H. (et al.), *Die kirchlichen Denkmäler der Stadt Trier*, Düsseldorf 1938

Bunte, W., *Juden und Judentum in der mittelniederländischen Literatur (1100–1600)*, Frankfurt 1989

Bur, M., *Suger, Abbé de Saint Denis, régent de France*, Paris 1991

Bürger, Bauer, Edelmann. Berlin im Mittelalter [exhibition catalogue], Berlin 1987

Burger, F., et al., *Die deutsche Malerei vom ausgehenden Mittelalter bis zum Ende der Renaissance* (3 vols), Berlin-Neubabelsberg 1913–1919

Buschhausen, H., *Der Verduner Altar*, Edition Tusch 1980

– , *Die Geschichte der Inschriften auf dem Verduner Altar. Überlegungen zu einer Neudatierung*, Wiener Studien 100, 1987, 265–309

Butsch, A.F., *Die Bücherornamentik der Hoch- und Spätrenaissance*, Leipzig 1891

Butz, A. (ed.), *Die romanischen Handschriften der Württembergischen Landesbibliothek Stuttgart 2*, Stuttgart 1987

Camesina, A. (ed.), *Die Darstellung der* Biblia pauperum *in einer Handschrift des XIV. Jahhunderts, aufbewahrt im Stifte St Florian im Erzherzogthume Österreich ob der Enns*, Vienna 1863

Carli, E., *Pittura medievale Pisana*, Milan 1958

Cerny, P., 'Die romanische Buchmalerei in der Abtei Saint-Sauveur in Anchin', *Nederlands Kunsthistorisch Jaarboek* 36, 1985, 31–70

Champfleury (pseudonym of J.Fleury-Husson), *Histoire de l'imagerie populaire*, Paris 1869

de Chapeaurouge, D., *Einführung in die Geschichte der christlichen Symbole*, Darmstadt 1987

Christoffel, U., 'Einzelstücke der romanischen Plastik Oberitaliens', *Pantheon* 26, 1940, 35–41

Clemen, P., *Die gotischen Monumentalmalereien der Rheinlande* (2 vols), Düsseldorf 1930

The Cleveland Museum of Art. European Paintings Before 1500. Catalogue of Paintings, Part One, Cleveland 1974

Cohen, S.J.D., '"Those Who Say They are Jews and Are Not": How Do You Know a Jew in Antiquity When You See One?', in *Diasporas in Antiquity*, ed. S.J.D Cohen and E.S. Frerichs, Atlanta 1993, 1–45

de Coo, J., *Aachener Kunstblätter* 30, 1965, 71

Cooper, J.C., *Illustriertes Lexikon der traditionellen Symbole*, Leipzig 1986

Cornell, H., *Biblia pauperum*, Stockholm 1925

Coupe, W. A., *The German Illustrated Broadsheet in the Seventeenth Century* (2 vols), Baden-Baden 1966–1967

Craine, R.C., *The 'Heavenly Jerusalem' as an Eschatological Symbol in St Hildegard of Bingen's 'Scivias'*, Diss. Fordham University 1992

C.Csapodi (et al., eds.), *Bibliotheca Corviniana. Die Bibliothek des Königs Matthias Corvinus von Ungarn*, Munich 1969

Davies, H.W., *Bernhard von Breydenbach and His Journey to the Holy Land, 1483–84. A Bibliography*, London 1911

Debus, K. H., in *Geschichte der Juden in Speyer*, Beiträge zu Speyerer Stadtgeschichte, Heft 6, Speyer 1981

H.Deckert (et al., eds.), *Religiöse Kunst aus Hessen und Nassau. Kritischer Gesamtkatalog der Ausstellung Marburg 1928, Tafelband und Textband*, Marburg-Lahn 1932

Dehio, G., *Geschichte der deutschen Kunst* (4 vols), Berlin 1930–1934

Delaisse, L.M.J. (et al.), *Mittelalterliche Miniaturen*, Cologne 1959

Deneke, B., *Geschichte und Kultur der Juden in Bayern* (exhibition catalogue), Nuremberg 1988

Derolez, A. (ed.), *Lamberti S. Audomari canonici 'Liber floridus'. Codex autographus Bibliothecae Universitatis Gandavensis*, Gandavi: Story-Scientia 1968.

Deuchler, F., *Gotik*, Lucerne [nd, 1975?]

– (ed.), *Der Ingeborg-Psalter. Vollständige Faksimile-Ausgabe im Originalformat der Handschrift Ms. olim 1695 aus dem Besitz des Musée Condé-Chantilly,* Graz: Akademische Druck- und Verlagsanstalt 1985

Deutsch, G. N., 'Legends midrashiques dans la peinture de Nicolas Poussin', *Journal of Jewish Art* 9, 1982, 47–53

Diederichs, E. (ed.), *Deutsches Leben der Vergangenheit* (2 vols), Jena 1908

Diemer, D. and P., *Münchner Jahrbuch der Bildenden Kunst* 43, 1992, 33

Dittmar, P., 'Christliche Restauration und Antijudaismus: Aspekte der Kunst der deutschen Romantik', in *Antisemitismus und jüdische Geschichte* (Festschrift H.A. Strauss), Berlin 1987, 329–64

– , in *Wilhelm-Busch-Jahrbuch* 1987, 29–41.

– , '"Die Bekehrung der Juden in Rom" von Hieronymus Hess', *Zeitschrift für Schweizerische Archäologie und Kunstgeschichte* 45, 1988, 117–28

– , *Die Darstellung der Juden in der populären Kunst zur Zeit der Emanzipation*, Munich: Saur 1992

Dobrzeniecki, T., *Catalogue of the Medieval Painting (Gallery of the Medieval Art, Warsaw, National Museum* (exhibition catalogue), Warsaw 1977

Dokumente zur Reformation. Bugenhagen in Braunschweig (exhibition catalogue), Brunswick 1978

Dolfen, C. (ed., on behalf of the Cathedral Chapter of Osnabrück), *Codex Gisle*, Berlin 1926

Drescher, U., *Geistliche Denkformen in den Bilderhandschriften des Sachsenspiegels*, Bern 1989

Duby, G., *Die Kunst des Mittelalters* I, Stuttgart 1984

Duitse tekeningen uit de 18e en 19e eeuw (catalogue), Rotterdam 1964

Dülmen, R. von, *Hexenwelten*, Frankfurt 1987

Dundes, A., 'The Ritual Murder of Blood Libel Legend: A Study of Anti-Semitic Victimization through Projective Inversion', *Temenos* 25, 1989, 7–32

Durliat, M., *Romanische Kunst*, Freiburg: Herder 1983

Dworschak, F. (et al., eds.), *Die Gotik in Niederösterreich*, Vienna 1963

Eckert, W.P., 'Geehrte und geschändete Synagoge. Das kirchliche Mittelalter vor der Judenfrage', in *Christen und Juden*, ed. W.-D.Marsch und K.Thieme, Mainz 1961, 67–114

–, 'Beatus Simoninus – Aus den Akten des Trienter Judenprozesses', in *Judenhass – Schuld der Christen?!*, ed. W.P.Eckert und E.L.Ehrlich, Essen 1964, 329–58

–, 'Thomas von Aquino – Seine Stellung zu Juden und zum Judentum', *Freiburger Rundbrief* 73–76, 1968, 30–1

–, in *Kirche und Synagoge. Handbuch zur Geschichte von Christen und Juden. Darstellung mit Quellen* (2 vols), Stuttgart 1968–1970 (I, 210–306; II, 222–79)

–, 'Antijüdische Motive in der christlichen Kunst und ihre Folgen', *Bibel und Kirche* 44, 1989, 72–89

–, 'Antisemitismus im Mittelalter. Antijudaismus in der christlichen Kunst', in *Antisemitismus. Erscheinungsformen der Judenfeindschaft gestern und heute*, ed. G. B. Ginzel, Cologne 1991, 71–99, 358–88

Eder, M., *Die 'Deggendorfer Gnad'. Entstehung und Entwicklung einer Hostienwallfahrt im Kontext von Theologie und Geschichte*, Passau: Passavia Verlag 1992

Edwards, D. R., 'Religion, Power and Politics: Jewish Defeats by the Romans in Iconography and Josephus', in *Diaspora Jews and Judaism. Essays in Honor of and in Dialogue with A.T. Kraabel*, ed. J. A. Overman and R.S.MacLennan, University of South Florida 1992, 293–310

Ehrenstein, T., *Das Alte Testament im Bilde*, Vienna 1923

Ehrlich, E. L., 'Luther und die Juden', *Judaica* 39, 1983, 131–49

Eichenberger, W. and Wendland, H., *Deutsche Bibeln vor Luther*, Hamburg: F. Wittig 1977

Eichholz, P. (ed.), *Die Kunstdenkmäler von Stadt und Dom Brandenburg*, ed. P. Eichholz, Berlin 1912, pl. 48

Eichler, H., in *Jahrbuch der Arbeitsgemeinschaft der Rheinischen Geschichtsvereine* 2, 1935, 96–105

Eisenstein, J.D. (ed.), *A Collection of Polemics and Disputations*, New York 1928, reprinted Israel 1969

Eltester, W., 'Der Siebenarmige Leuchter und der Titusbogen', in *Judentum, Urchristentum, Kirche* (Festschrift J.Jeremias), ed. W.Eltester, Berlin 1960, 62–76

Encyclopaedia Judaica (10 vols), Berlin 1928–1934; (16 vols), Jerusalem 1971

Endres, J. A., '"Die Verherrlichung des Dominikanerordens" in der Spanischen Kapelle an S. Maria Novella zu Florenz', *Zeitschrift für christliche Kunst* 22, 1909, 323–8

Engelhart, H., *Die Würzburger Buchmälerei im hohen Mittelalter*, Würzburg: F. Schoningh 1987

Erb, R. (ed.), *Die Legende vom Ritualmord*, Berlin 1993

– , and Lichtblau, A., '"Es hat nie einen jüdischen Ritualmord gegeben". Konflikte um die Abschaffung der Verehrung des Andreas von Rinn', *Zeitgeschichte* 17, Vienna 1989, 127–62

Erbstösser, M., *Ketzer im Mittelalter*, Stuttgart 1984

Erlande-Brandenburg, A., *Gotische Kunst*, Freiburg: Herder 1984

– , *Triumph der Gotik, 1260–1380*, Munich 1988

Erler, A., *Das Strassburger Münster im Rechtsleben des Mittelalters*, Frankfurt am Main 1954

Esposito, A., and Quaglioni, D., *Processi contro gli Ebrei di Trento (1475–1478). I, I Processi del 1475*, Padua 1990

Europa und der Orient, 800–1900 (exhibition catalogue), Berlin 1980

Europäische Kunst um 1400 (exhibition catalogue), Vienna 1962

Eydoux, H.-P., *Saint Louis et son temps*, Paris 1971

Farkas, J.von, and Bogyai, T.von, 'Die Kultur der Ungarn', in *Die Kulturen Eurasiens*, Handbuch der Kulturgeschichte 2, 13, Frankfurt am Main 1968

Fäthke, B., in *Aus Hessischen Museen. Band 1*, Hessen 1975, 79–90

Feger, O.(ed.), *Ulrich Richenthal. Chronik des Konstanzer Konzils 1414–1418* (facsimile edition), Constance 1964

Fehr, H., *Das Recht im Bilde*, Erlenbach-Zürich 1923

Feldmann, C., *Hildegard von Bingen. Nonne und Genie*, Freiburg 1991

Feulner, A., and Müller, T., *Geschichte der deutschen Plastik*, München 1953

Field, R.S. (ed.), *The Illustrated Bartsch (Supplement). German Single Leaf Woodcuts before 1500*, Vol. 161, *Anonymous Artists* (Nos. 1–400), New York 1987; Vol. 162 (Nos. 401–735), New York 1989; Vol. 163 (Nos. 736–996), New York 1991

Fillitz, H., and Pippal, M., *Schatzkunst*, Salzburg and Vienna 1987

Fischer, H. (ed.), *Hans Folz. Die Reimpaarsprüche*, Munich 1961

Fischer, O., *Geschichte der deutschen Malerei*, Munich 1942

Flemming, W., *Deutsche Kultur im Zeitalter des Barock*, Handbuch der Kulturgeschichte 1, 6, Graz 1960

Illustrierte Flugblätter aus den Jahrhunderten der Reformation und der Glaubenskämpfe (exhibition catalogue, ed. W. Harms), Coburg 1983

Forberg, G. (ed.), *Gustave Doré. Das graphische Werk* (2 vols), Munich 1975

Forbes Johnson, A. (ed.), *German Renaissance Title-Borders*, Oxford 1929

Fox, M., *Illuminations of Hildegard of Bingen*, Santa Fé 1985

Franconia sacra. Meisterwerke kirchlicher Kunst des Mittelalters in Franken. Jubiläumsausstellung im Mainfränkischen Museum Würzburg, Munich 1952

Francovich, G. de, in *Kunstgeschichtliches Jahrbuch der Bibliotheca Hertziana* 2, 1938, 141–261

Frankenberger, R., and Rupp, P. B. (eds.), *Universitätsbibliothek Augsburg. Wertvolle Handschriften und Einbände aus der ehemaligen Oettingen-Wallensteinschen-Bibliothek*, Wiesbaden 1987

800 Jahre Franz von Assisi. Franziskanische Kunst und Kultur des Mittelalters (exhibition catalogue), Krems 1982

Freiburger Rundbrief, XII. Folge, 1959/60 (Nos. 45/48), 66; XXXVII–XXXVIII. Folge, 1985/1986, 87–9

Frey, W., 'Vom Antijudaismus zum Antisemitismus. Ein antijüdisches Pasquill von 1608 und seine Quellen', *Daphnis* 18,1, 1989, 251–79

– , 'Gottesmörder und Menschenfeinde. Zum Judenbild in der deutschen Literatur des Mittelalters', in *Die Juden in ihrer mittelalterlichen Umwelt*, ed. A. Ebenbauer and K. Zatloukal, Vienna 1991, 35–51

Friedenberg, D. M., *Medieval Jewish Seals from Europe*, Detroit 1987

Friedman, J., 'The Reformation in Alien Eyes: Jewish Perceptions of Christian Troubles', *The Sixteenth Century Journal* 14, 1983, 23–40

Friedman, M., 'The First Printed Picture of a Jew', *Hebrew Union College Annual* XXIII, Part II, 1950–1951, 433–48

Friedrich, M., *Zwischen Abwehr und Bekehrung*, Tübingen 1988

Friedrichs, C. R., 'Politics or Pogrom? The Fettmilch Uprising in Germany and Jewish History', in *Central European History* 19,2, Atlanta 1986, 186–228

Fritz, R., (ed.), *Fresken, Altäre, Skulpturen. Kunstschätze aus dem Kreis Unna*, Cologne 1970

Fritzsche, G., 'Ein Retabelfragment des 14. Jahrhunderts im Schweizerischen Landesmuseum in Zürich', *Zeitschrift für Schweizerische Archäologie und Kunstgeschichte* 38, 1981, 189–201

Frodl, W., *Glasmalereien in Kärnten. 1150–1500*, Klagenfurt 1950

Frodl-Kraft, E., *Die mittelalterlichen Glasgemälde in Wien*, Graz 1950

Fuchs, E., *Die Juden in der Karikatur*, Munich 1921

Füglister, R. L., *Das Lebende Kreuz*, Einsiedeln 1964

Gantner, J., *Konrad Witz*, Vienna 1943

Ganz, P. L., *Konrad Witz von Rottweil*, Bern and Olten 1947

Garber, J., in *Jahrbuch der kunsthistorischen Sammlungen des allerhöchsten Kaiserhauses* 32, 1915, XLV–XLVIII

Gardet, C., *De la peinture du moyen âge en Savoye* (2 vols), Annecy 1965

Gardill, I. and Wolfson, M., 'Überlegungen zu Stil und Ikonographie des Wenninger "Marientodes"', *Niederdeutsche Beiträge zur Kunstgeschichte* 31, 1992, 38–49

Gaspar, C. and Lyna, F., *Les principaux manuscrits à peintures de la Bibliothèque Royale de Belgique* (2 vols.), Brussels 1984

Gaul, O., and Korn, U.D., *Bau- und Kunstdenkmäler von Westfalen, 49.1, Stadt Lemgo*, Münster 1983

Geck, E. (ed.), *Bernhard von Breydenbach. Die Reise ins Heilige Land. Ein Reisebericht aus dem Jahre 1483* (New High German translation with postscript), Wiesbaden 1961

Geiger, L., 'Die Juden und die deutsche Literatur', *Zeitschrift für die Geschichte der Juden in Deutschland* 2, 1888, 297–374

Geiges, F., *Der mittelalterliche Fensterschmuck des Freiburger Münsters*, Freiburg im Breisgau 1931

Geisberg, M. (ed.), *Die deutsche Buchillustration in der ersten Hälfte des XVI. Jahrhunderts* (2 vols), Munich 1930–1932

– , *The German Single-Leaf Woodcut* (English translation of *Der deutsche Einblatt-Holzschnitt*, Munich 1923–1930), rev.and ed. W.L.Strauss (4 vols), New York: Hacker Art Books 1974

Geissler, K., *Die Juden in Deutschland und Bayern bis zur Mitte des vierzehnten Jahrhunderts*, Munich 1976

Gelber, M, and Finkelstein, H., in *Bulletin des Leo Baeck Instituts* 87, 1990, 45–66

Gerber, B., *Jud Süss. Aufstieg und Fall im frühen 18. Jahrhundert. Ein Beitrag zur Historischen Antisemitismus- und Rezeptionsforschung*, Hamburg 1990

Gercke, H. (ed.), *Der Baum*, Heidelberg 1987

Germania Judaica, ed. I.Elbogen et al. (3 vols), Tübingen 1963–1987

Getzener, H. (ed.), *Der mittelrheinische Altar im Erzbischöflichen Diözesanmuseum zu Utrecht*, Stuttgart 1928

Gidal, N. T., *Die Juden in Deutschland von der Romerzeit bis zur Weimarer Republik*, Gütersloh: Bertelsmann Lexikon Verlag GmbH 1988

Giesau, H., *Der Dom zu Magdeburg*, Burg bei Magdeburg 1924

Gillen, O. (ed.), *Herrad von Landsberg, Hortus deliciarum*, Landau: Pfälzische Verlagsanstalt 1979

Ginzel, G. B. (ed.), *Antisemitismus. Erscheinungsformen der Judenfeindschaft gestern und heute*, Cologne 1991

Glöger, B., and Zöllner, W., *Teufelsglaube und Hexenwahn*, Vienna 1985

Goetz, O., *Der Feigenbaum in der religiösen Kunst des Abendlandes*, Berlin 1965

Goldkuhle, F., *Mittelalterliche Wandmalereien in St. Maria Lyskirchen [Köln]*, Düsseldorf 1954.

Goldschmidt, A., *Elfenbeinskulpturen aus der Zeit der karolingischen und sächsischen Kaiser* (4 vols), Berlin 1914–1926

–, *Die deutsche Buchmalerei* (2 vols), Florence and Munich 1928

–, *Die Bronzetüren von Nowgorod und Gnesen*, Vol. 2 of *Die frühmittelalterlichen Bronzetüren*, ed. R. Hamann, Marburg 1926–1932

Gollek-Gretzer, R., in *Niederdeutsche Beiträge zur Kunstgeschichte* 5, 1966, 91–132

Gosebruch, M., *Zeitschrift für Kunstgeschichte* 38, 1975, 118–19

Gow, A.C., *The Red Jews*, Diss. University of Arizona 1993

Graetz, H., *Geschichte der Juden*, Leipzig 1853ff.

Green, R. (et al., eds.), *Herrad of Hohenburg, Hortus deliciarum* (2 vols), Leiden: E.J. Brill 1979

Griessmaier, V., 'Nikolaus von Verdun', *Wienerjahrbuch für Kunstgeschichte* 25, 1972, 29–52

Grimm, Jacob und Wilhelm, *Deutsches Wörterbuch*, IV 2, Leipzig 1877

Grimme, E. G., 'Mittelalterliche Scheiben in einer Aachener Privatsammlung', *Aachener Kunstblätter* 19–20, 1960–61, 25–44

–, *Die Geschichte der abendländischen Buchmalerei*, Cologne 1980

–, *Bronzebildwerke des Mittelalters*, Darmstadt 1985

–, *Das Evangelistar von Gross Sankt Martin*, Freiburg 1989

Grodecki, L., *Romanische Glasmalerei*, Stuttgart 1977

– (et al.), *Les vitraux de centre et de pays de la Loire*, Corpus vitrearum, France. Recensement II, Paris 1981

Grodecki, L., and Brisac, C., *Gothic Stained Glass. 1200–1300*, London 1985

Güde, W., 'Zur rechtlichen Stellung der Juden in der früheren Neuzeit', in *Festgabe zum Schweizerischen Juristentag 1973*, Basel 1973, 1–20

Gümbel, A., in *Mitteilungen des Vereins für Geschichte der Stadt Nürnberg* 26, 1926, 302–4

Gurewich, V., *Journal of the Warburg and Courtauld Institutes* 20, 1957, 358–62

Johannes Gutenberg. 1400–1468. Druckkunst verändert die Welt (exhibition catalogue), Mainz 1968

Haas, W., and Pfistermeister, U., *Romanik in Bayern*, Stuttgart 1985

Hägler, B., *Die Christen und die 'Judenfrage'. Am Beispiel Osianders und Ecks zum Ritualmordvorwurf*, Erlangen 1992

Hahn, J., *Erinnerungen und Zeugnisse jüdischer Geschichte in Baden-Württemberg*, Stuttgart 1988

Hamann, R., *Zeitschrift des deutschen Vereins für Kunstwissenschaft* 1, 1934, 28

Hamp, V. (et al.), *Die Heilige Schrift. Familienbibel. Altes und Neues Testament. Vollstandige Ausgabe nach den Grundtexten übersetzt*, Bonn: Verlag des Borromäusvereins 1966

Haney, K. E., *The Winchester Psalter*, Leicester 1986

Harbison, C., 'Reformation Iconography: Problems and Attitudes', in *Festschrift W. Stechow*, ed. W. L. Strauss, New York 1976, 78ff.

Harms, W. (ed.), *Illustrierte Flugblätter des Barock. Eine Auswahl*, Tübingen 1983

–, see *Flugblätter*

–, (ed.), *Deutsche illustrierte Flugblätter des 16. und 17. Jahrhunderts* (3 vols), Tübingen 1980–1989

Harrsen, M. (ed.), *Central European Manuscripts in the Pierpont Morgan Library*, New York 1958

Hasan-Rokem, G., and Dundes, A., *The Wandering Jew*, Bloomington: Indiana University Press 1986

Hassan, W.O. (ed.), *The Holkham Bible Picture Book* (facsimile), London 1954

Hasse, M., *Niederdeutsche Beiträge zu Kunstgeschichte* 21, 1982, 37

Hauffen, A., *Johann Fischart. Ein Literaturbild aus der Zeit der Gegenreformation* (2 vols), Berlin 1922

Hauke, H., and Kroos, R. (eds.), *Das Matutinalbuch von Scheyern. Die Bildseiten aus dem CLM 17401 der Bayerischen Staatsbibliothek* (facsimile with commentary), Wiesbaden 1980

Hauttmann, M., *Die Kunst des frühen Mittelalters*, Propyläen Kunstgeschichte 6, Berlin 1929

Heimann, H., *The Bible in Art*, London 1956

Heinzer, F., and Stamm, G., *Mittelalterliche Andachtsbücher* (exhibition catalogue), Karlsruhe 1992

Heitz, P., *Hundertfünfzig Einzelbilder des XV. Jahrhunderts*, Strassbourg 1918

–, *Primitive Holzschnitte*, Strasbourg 1919

Hermann, H.J., *Beschreibendes Verzeichnis der illuminierten Handschriften in Österreich*, Leipzig 1926

Hernad, B., *Die Graphiksammlung des Humanisten Hartmann Schedel* (catalogue), Munich 1990

Herzig, A., and Schoeps, J.H., *Reuchlin und die Juden*, Sigmaringen: Thorbecke 1993

Heuberger, R., and Krohn, H., *Hinaus aus dem Ghetto. Juden in Frankfurt am Main 1800–1950. Begleitbuch zur ständigen Ausstellung des jüdischen Museums der Stadt Frankfurt am Main*, Frankfurt: S. Fischer 1988

Heyd, M., *Journal of Jewish Art* 7, 1980, 65

Heyen, F.J., *Kaiser Heinrichs Romfahrt. Die Bilderchronik*

von Kaiser Heinrich VII. und Kurfürst Balduin von Luxemburg (1308–1313), Boppard 1965

Hind, A. M., *An Introduction to a History of Woodcut* (2 vols), London 1935

– , *Early Italian Engraving* (3 vols), New York and London 1938

Hirth, G., *Kulturgeschichtliches Bilderbuch aus vier Jahrhunderten* (2 vols.), Munich 1923–1925

Hoffmann, J., *Zeitschrift für Kunstgeschichte* 44, 1981, 351–3

Hoffmann, W,., *Luther und die Folgen für die Kunst (Ausstellungskatalog der Hamburger Kunsthalle),* Munich: Prestel 1983

– , *Gazette des Beaux-Arts* 107, 1986, 43

Hans Holbein der Ältere und die Kunst der Spatgotik (exhibition catalogue), Augsburg 1965

Holdschmidt, H. C., *Der Jude auf dem Theater des deutschen Mittelalters*, Emsdetten 1935

Hollstein, F. W. H., *German Engravings, Etchings and Woodcuts*, Amsterdam 1954ff.

Hoofacker, G., *Avaritia radix omnium malorum*, Frankfurt 1988

Hootz, R. (ed.), *Deutsche Kunstdenkmäler. Ein Bildhandbuch*: 6, *Hamburg, Schleswig-Holstein*, Darmstadt: Wissenschaftliche Buchgesellschaft 1968; 10, *Thüringen*, Darmstadt 1968; 12, *Sachsen*, Darmstadt 1970; 14, *Mark Brandenburg und Berlin*, Darmstadt 1971

Horn, A., and Meyer, W., *Die Kunstdenkmäler von Schwaben* V, Munich 1958

Hürkey, E., *Das Bild des Gekreuzigten im Mittelalter*, Worms 1983

Hutchinson, J.C., in *Tribute to W. Stechow*, ed. W.L. Strauss, New York 1976

Irtenkauf, W. (ed.), *Zimelien. Württembergische Landesbibliothek. Aus den Schätzen ihrer Handschriftensammlung*, Stuttgart 1985

Irmer, G., *Die Romfahrt Kaiser Heinrichs VII. im Bilderzyklus des Codex Balduini Trevirensis*, Berlin 1881

Jacobi, F., *Die deutsche Buchmalerei*, Munich 1923

Jahn, J., *Introduction to 1472–1533. Lucas Cranach der Ältere,* Munich 1972

Jantzen, H., *Deutsche Bildhauer des dreizehnten Jahrhunderts*, Leipzig 1925

Jászai, G., 'Seltene kunsthistorische Dokumente zum Martinskult in Westfalen', *Unser Bocholt* 28, 1977, Heft 3

– , *Mittelalterliche Glasmalereien*, Münster 1986

– (ed.), *Imagination des Unsichtbaren. 1200 Jahre Bildende Kunst im Bistum Münster* [exhibition catalogue], Münster 1993

Jerchel, H., *Spätmittelalterliche Buchmalereien am Oberlauf des Rheins*, Breslau 1932 (and in *Oberrheinische Kunst* 5, 1932, 17–82)

– , *Zeitschrift für Kunstgeschichte* 2, 1933, 381–98

Jochum, H., *Ecclesia und Synagoga. Das Judentum in der christlichen Kunst* (exhibition catalogue), Ottweiler 1993

Juden in Kassel. Eine Dokumentation anlässlich des 100. Geburtstags von Franz Rosenzweig (exhibition catalogue), Kassel 1986

Juden in Köln von der Römerzeit bis ins 20. Jahrhundert. Foto–Dokumentation (exhibition catalogue), Stadt Köln, Kölnisches Stadtmuseum 1984

Jüdisches Lexikon (5 vols), Berlin 1927–1930

Jung, M., *Die württembergische Kirche und die Juden in der Zeit des Pietismus (1675–1780)*, Berlin 1992

Junghans, H., *Wittenberg als Lutherstadt*, Göttingen 1979

Jungjohann, A., *Zeitschrift des Deutschen Vereins für Kunstwissenschaft* 2, 1935, 253–9

Kaftal, G., *Saints in Italian Art* (3 vols), Florence 1952–1978

Karasek, H., *Der Fedtmilch-Aufstand, oder, wie die Frankfurter 1612/14 ihrem Rat einheizten*, Berlin: Wagenbach 1979

Kashnitz, R., *Zeitschrift für Kunstgeschichte* 51, 1988, 33–125

Kästner, M., *Die Icones Hans Holbeins des Jüngeren* (2 vols), Heidelberg 1985

Kauffmann, C. M., *Romanesque Manuscripts 1066–1199*, London 1975

Kemp, W., *Sermo Corporeus. Die Erzahlung der mittelalterlichen Glasfenster*, München 1987

Kessel, V., 'Ein Antiphonar in Koblenz', *Wallraf-Richartz-Jahrbuch* 53, 1992, 323–33

Kindlers Literatur-Lexikon (12 vols), Zurich 1970–1974

Bayerns Kirche im Mittelalter. Handschriften und Urkunden aus bayerischem Staatsbesitz (exhibition catalogue), Munich 1960

Kirschbaum, E. (ed.), *Lexikon der christlichen Ikonographie* (8 vols), Freiburg 1968–1976

Kirschner, B., *Deutsche Spottmedaillen auf Juden*, Munich: Battenberg 1968

Kisch, G., *Jewry Law in Medieval Germany*, New York 1949

– , *Ausgewählte Schriften* (2 vols), Sigmaringen 1978–1979

Klassert, A., 'Entehrung Mariä durch die Juden. Eine antisemitische Dichtung Thomas Murners', *Jahrbuch für Geschichte, Sprache und Kultur Elsass-Lothringens* 21, 1905, 78–155; 22, 1906, 255–75

Klemm, E., *Ein romanischer Miniaturenzyklus aus dem Maasgebiet*, Vienna 1973

– , *Der Bamberger Psalter*, Wiesbaden 1980

– , *Die romanischen Handschriften der Bayerischen Staatsbibliothek* (2 vols), Wiesbaden 1980–1988

Kloss, E. (ed.), *Speculum Humanae Salvationis*, Munich 1925

– , *Die schlesische Buchmalerei des Mittelalters*, Berlin 1942

Knapinski, R., 'Die romanische Tür von Plock in Nowgorod',

Niederdeutsche Beiträge zur Kunstgeschichte 30, 1991, 29–66

Knoepfli, A., *Kunstgeschichte des Bodenseeraumes* (2 vols), Constance 1961–1969

Köhl, P. H., *Dekorative Graphik*, München 1978

Köllner, H. (ed.), *Die illuminierten Handschriften der Hessischen Landesbibliothek Fulda.Teil I. Handschriften des 6. bis 13. Jahrhunderts* (illustrated volume), Stuttgart 1976

Köln Westfalen 1180–1980 (exhibition catalogue, 2 vols), Münster 1980

Kopp-Schmidt, G., *Das Bild der Gottesmutter in der Buchmalerei*, Freiburg 1992

Körber, R., and Pugel, T. (eds.), *Antisemitismus der Welt in Wort und Bild*, Dresden 1935

Kosch, W. (ed.), *Deutsches Literatur-Lexikon. Biographisch- bibliographisches Handbuch,* Bern and Munich 1968ff.

W.Koschorrek (ed*.), Der Sachsenspiegel in Bildern. Aus der Heidelberger Bilderhandschrift ausgewählt und erläutert*, Frankfurt am Main 1977

Kötzsche, L., 'Das wiedergefundene Hostiengrab im Kloster Heiligengrabe/Prignitz', *Berliner Theologische Zeitschrift* 4, 1987, 19–32

Kretzenbacher, L., *Das verletzte Kultbild*, Munich 1977

Kreytenberg, G., *Andrea Pisano und die toskanische Skulptur des 14.Jahrhunderts*, Munich 1984

Kristeller, P., *Die Strassburger Bücher-Illustration im XV. und im Anfange des XVI. Jahrhunderts*, Leipzig 1888

Kristeller, P., *Early Florentine Woodcuts*, London 1968

Krotzer, G., 'Der Judenmord in Deggendorf und die Deggendorfer "Gnad"', in *Judenhass – Schuld der Christen?!*, ed. W. P. Eckert und E. L. Ehrlich, Essen 1964, 309–27

Krummer-Schroth, I., *Glasmalereien aus dem Freiburger Münster*, Freiburg im Breisgau 1967

Kühnel, H. (ed.), *Alltag im Spatmittelalter*, Graz, Vienna and Cologne: Styria 1985

Der Kunst-Brockhaus (2 vols), Wiesbaden 1983

Künstle, K., *Ikonographie der christlichen Kunst*, Band I, Freiburg 1928

Kunze, H., *Geschichte der Buchillustration in Deutschland. Das 15. Jahrhundert* (2 vols), Leipzig: Insel, 1975; Frankfurt: Insel, 1979

Künzl, H., 'Die Frage der jüdischen Identität in den Werken von E. M. Lilien und anderen jüdischen Künstlern des späten 19. und 20. Jahrhunderts', *Kairos* 30–31, 1988–1989, 188–217

Kunzle, D., *The Early Comic Strip. Narrative Strips and Picture Stories in the European Broadsheet from c. 1450 to 1825*, Berkeley 1973

Kurmann, P., 'Die Pariser Komponenten in der Architektur und Skulptur der Westfassade von Notre Dame zu Reims', *Münchner Jahrbuch der Bildenden Kunst* 35, 1984, 41–82

Laborde, A. de, *La Bible moralisée, conservée à Oxford*, Paris and London (5 vols), Paris 1911–1927

Laib and Schwarz (eds.), *Biblia pauperum. Nach dem Original in der Lyceumsbibliothek zu Constanz,* Zürich 1867

Lammers, J., *Buchmalerei aus Handschriften vom 12. bis zum 16.Jahrhundert*, Münster 1982

Lanc, E., *Die mittelalterlichen Wandmalereien in Wien und Niederösterreich*, Vienna 1983

Laske-Fix, K., *Der Bilderzyklus des Breviari d'amor*, Münich 1973

Lasko, P., *Ars sacra 800–1200*, Harmondsworth 1972

Lauts, I., *Meisterwerke der Staatlichen Kunsthalle Karlsruhe*, Honnef 1957

Lazar, M., 'The Lamb and the Scapegoat: The Dehumanization of the Jews in Medieval Propaganda Imagery', in *Antisemitism in Times of Crisis*, ed. S. L. Gilman and S.T.Katz, New York 1991, 38–80

Vom Leben im späten Mittelalter. Der Hausbuchmeister oder Meister des Amsterdamer Kabinetts (exhibition catalogue), Frankfurt 1985

Legner, A., *Die Parler und der Schöne Stil 1350–1400* (exhibition catalogue, 3 vols.), Cologne 1978

– , *Deutsche Kunst der Romanik*, Munich 1982

Lehmann, K.-D. (ed.), *Bibliotheca publica Francofurtensis* (2 vols), Frankfurt am Main 1984

Lehmann-Haupt, H., *Schwäbische Federzeichnungen. Studien zur Buchillustration Augsburgs im XV.Jahrhundert*, Berlin 1929

Lehrs, M., *Geschichte und kritischer Katalog des deutschen, niederländischen und französischen Kupferstichs im XV.Jahrhundert* (9 vols), Vienna 1908–1934

Leonhard, F., *Deutsche Bibeln vor und nach Luther* [exhibition catalogue], Heidelberg 1982

Leroquais, V., *Les pontificaux manuscrits des bibliothèques publiques de France*, Paris: Planches 1937

– , *Les psautiers manuscrits latins des bibliothèques publiques de France* (3 vols.), Mâcon 1940–1941

Lewis, S., *The Art Bulletin* 68, 1986, 543–66.

– , *The Art of Matthew Paris in the* Chronica Majora, Berkeley 1987

Lexikon des gesamten Buchwesens, ed. S. Corsten et al., Stuttgart 1987ff.

*Lexikon der Kunst (*12 vols), Freiburg 1987–1990

Liebe, G., *Das Judentum in der deutschen Vergangenheit*, Leipzig 1903 (reprinted Jena 1924)

Liebreich, A., 'Der mittelrheinische Altar im erzbischöflichen Museum zu Utrecht*', Wallraf-Richartz Jahrbuch* 3–4, 1926–1927, 130–40

Liliencron, R. von, *Die historischen Volkslieder der Deutschen vom 13. bis 16. Jahrhundert* (5 vols), Leipzig 1865–1869

Lind, K., *Ein Antiphonar mit Bilderschmuck aus der Zeit des XI. und XII. Jahrhunderts, im Stifte St Peter zu Salzburg befindlich*, Vienna 1870

Lippmann, F., *Jahrbuch der Königlich Preussischen Kunst-sammlungen* 5, 1884, 308

–, *The Art of Wood-Engraving in Italy in the Fifteenth Century*, London 1888

List, 'Ein seltener Druck aus der Offizin des Matthias Hüpfuff', *Centralblatt für Bibliothekswesen* 4, 1887, 290–3

Löffler, K., *Schwäbische Buchmalerei in romanischer Zeit*, Augsburg 1928

Lohrmann, K. (ed.), *1000 Jahre österreichisches Judentum* (exhibition catalogue), Eisenstadt: Edition Roetzer, 1982

–, *Judenrecht und Judenpolitik im mittelalterlichen Öster-reich*, Vienna 1990

Lotter, F., 'Hostienfrevelvorwurf und Blutwunderfälschung bei den Judenverfolgungen von 1298 ("Rintfleisch") und 1336–38 ("Armleder")', in *Falschungen im Mittelalter, Teil IV*, Hanover 1988, 533–83

–, *Die Bau- und Kunstdenkmaler von Westfalen: 17. Kreis Bochum-Stadt*, Münster 1906; *34. Altena*, Münster 1906; *Kreis Coesfeld*, Münster 1913

Lülfing, H., and Tietge, H.-E., *Handschriften und alte Drucke. Kostbarkeiten aus Bibliotheken der DDR*, Wiesbaden 1981

Lustiger, A., 'Der Fettmilchaufstand in Frankfurt und die Juden', in *Scheidewege*, ed. G.B. Ginzel und E.Pfisterer, Düsseldorf 1985, 23–31

Luther, J., *Die Titeleinfassungen der Reformationszeit*, Hildes-heim 1973

Martin Luther und die Reformation in Deutschland (exhibi-tion catalogue), Frankfurt 1983

Lutz, E., and Wiegand, E., *Kataloge des Germanischen Nationalmuseums zu Nürnberg. Die Gemälde des 13. bis 16. Jahrhunderts* (2 vols), Leipzig 1937

Mader, F. (ed.), *Die Kunstdenkmaler der Oberpfalz, XXII. Stadt Regensburg* (3 vols), München 1933

Major, I., *Holzschnitte in der offentlichen Kunstsammlung zu Basel*, Strasbourg 1908

Mâle, É., *Die Gotik. Kirchliche Kunst des XIII. Jahrhunderts in Frankreich*, Stuttgart and Zurich 1986

Mälzer, G., *Die Inkunabeln der Universitätsbibliothek Würz-burg*, Würzburg 1986

–, and Thurn, H., *Universitätsbibliothek Würzburg. Kost-bare-Handschriften* (exhibition catalogue), Wiesbaden 1982

Marrow, J. H., *Passion Iconography*, Kortrijk 1979

Marsy, Comte de, 'Excursion en Espagne', *Congrès Archéologique de France* 55, 1888, 121–51

Martin, H., *La miniature française du XIIIe au XVe siècle*, Paris 1924

Martin, H. and Lauer, P., *Les principaux manuscrits à peintures de la Bibliothèque de l'Arsenal, à Paris*, Paris 1929

Matthiesen, W., 'Ulrich Richentals Chronik des Konstanzer Konzils', *Annuarium historiae conciliorum* 17, 1985, 323–455

Mayer, A., 'Die Gründung von St Salvator in Passau – Geschichte und Legende', *Zeitschrift für bayerische Landes-geschichte* 18, 1955, 256–78

Mayer, A., *Das Bild der Kirche*, Regensburg 1962

Mayr-Harting, H., *Ottonische Buchmalerei*, Stuttgart 1991

Mazal, O., *Buchkunst der Gotik*, Graz: Akademische Druck- und Verlagsanstalt 1975

–, *Schatzkammer der Buchkunst*, Graz 1980

–, et al., *Ein Weltgebäude der Gedanken. Die Österreichische Nationalbibliothek*, Graz 1987

–, *Der Baum. Ein Symbol des Lebens in der Buchmalerei*, Graz 1988

Meckseper, C. (ed.), *Stadt im Wandel. Kunst und Literatur des Bürgertums in Norddeutschland 1150-1650* (exhibition catalogue, 4 vols), Stuttgart 1985

Meinardus, O. F., 'Zur Verkündigungsdarstellung der Titelblätter der Luther-Bibeln von 1533 und 1541', *Wolfen-bütteler Notizen zur Buchgeschichte* 16, 1991, 32–40

Meisen, K., *Nikolauskult und Nikolausbrauch im Abend-lande*, Düsseldorf: Schwann 1931

Meiss, M., *French Painting in the Time of Jean de Berry* (2 vols), London 1974

Meister, E. S., *Ein oberrheinischer Kupferstecher der Spätgotik* (exhibition catalogue), Munich 1986

Mellinkoff, R., *The Horned Moses*, Berkeley 1970

–, *Journal of Jewish Art* 1, 1974, 40–2

–, *The Mark of Cain*, Berkeley 1981

–, *Journal of Jewish Art* 9, 1982, 36

–, 'Three Mysterious Ladies Unmasked', *Journal of Jewish Art* 10, 1984, 14–28

Mende, U., *Die Bronzetüren des Mittelalters*, Munich 1983

Meng-Koehler, M., *Die Bilder des Konrad Witz und ihre Quellen*, Basel 1947

Mertens, S. (et al.), *Blockbücher des Mittelalters* (exhibition catalogue), Mainz 1991.

Messerer, W., *Der Bamberger Domschatz*, Munich 1952

Metzger, T. und M., *Jüdisches Leben im Mittelalter, nach illuminierten hebräischen Handschriften vom 13. bis 16. Jahrhundert*, Würzburg 1983

Michel, A. (ed.), *Histoire de l'art* II, 1, Paris 1906

Middeldorf-Kosegarten, A., 'Nicola and Giovanni Pisano 1268-1278', *Jahrbuch der Berliner Museen* 11, 1969, 36–80

Mittler, E., and Werner, W., *Codex Manesse* (exhibition catalogue), Heidelberg 1988

Monumenta Judaica (exhibition catalogue), Cologne: Köln-isches Stadtmuseum 1963

Moriz-Eichborn, K., *Der Skulpturencyklus in der Vorhalle des Freiburger Münsters*, Strasbourg 1899

Müller, A., *Geschichte der Juden in Nürnberg*, Nuremberg 1968

Müller, C., *Jahrbuch der Staatlichen Kunstsammlungen in Baden-Württemberg* 21, 1984, 29

Müller, U. (ed.), *Die grosse Heidelberger "Manessische" Liederhandschrift*, Göppingen 1971

Münzel, G., *Der Skulpturenzyklus in der Vorhalle des Freiburger Münsters*, Freiburg im Breisgau 1959

Musper, H. T., 'Die ältesten Haarlemer Blockbücher', *Pantheon* XI, 21–22, 1938, 382–4

– , *Gotische Malerei nördlich der Alpen*, Cologne 1961

– , *Der Holzschnitt in fünf Jahrhunderten*, Stuttgart 1964

Muther, R., *Die deutsche Buchillustration der Gothik und Frührenaissance (1460–1530)* (2 vols), Munich and Leipzig 1884

Mütherich, F., *Zeitschrift für Kunstgeschichte* 42, 1979, 215–17

Myter (Stockholm, National Museum, exhibition catalogue), Stockholm 1983

Nachama, A. (et al., eds.), *Jüdische Lebenswelten. Katalog und Essays*, Berlin 1992

Nagler, G. K., *Künstler-Lexikon*, Leipzig 1835–1852, 3rd edition (reprint)

Het boek in Nederland in de 16de eeuw (exhibition catalogue), The Hague 1986

Neumeister, I., *Flugblätter der Reformation und des Bauernkrieges*, ed. H.Meucher, Leipzig 1976

Neumüller, W., OSB (ed.), *Speculum Humanae Salvationis. Vollständige Faksimile-Ausgabe des Codex Cremifanensis 243 des Benediktinerstifts Kremsmünster* (with commentary), Graz 1972

Neuss, W., *Das Buch Ezechiel in Theologie und Kunst bis zum Ende des XII.Jahrhunderts*, Münster 1912

Nickel, H. L., *Mittelalterliche Wandmalerei in der DDR*, Leipzig 1979

Nolden, R. (ed.), *Juden in Trier* (exhibition catalogue), Trier 1988

Katalog der im Germanischen Museum vorhandenen zum Abdrucke bestimmten Holzblöcke vom XV. bis zum XVII. Jahrhundert. Erster Teil: XV. und XVI. Jahrhundert, Nuremberg 1892

Nürnberg 1300–1550. Kunst der Gotik und Renaissance (exhibition catalogue), Munich 1986

Oberman, H. A., in *Flugschriften als Massenmedien der Reformationszeit*, ed. H.-J. Kohler, Stuttgart 1981

– , *Wurzeln des Antisemitismus. Christenangst und Judenplage im Zeitalter von Humanismus und Reformation*, Berlin 1981

– , 'Die Juden in Luthers Sicht', in *Die Juden und Martin Luther – Martin Luther und die Juden*, ed. H. Kremers, Neukirchen 1985, 136–62

Oepke, A., *Das neue Gottesvolk*, Gütersloh 1950

Ohly, F., 'Synagoge und Ecclesia. Typologisches in mittelalterlicher Dichtung', in *Judentum im Mittelalter*, ed. P.Wilpert, Berlin 1966, 350–69

– , *Gesetz und Evangelium. Zur Typologie bei Luther und Lucas Cranach*, Münster 1985

Oliver, J., in *Wallraf-Richartz-Jahrbuch* 40, 1978, 32

Olschki, L.S., *Le livre illustré au XVe siècle*, Florence 1926

Osten, G.von der, *Katalog der Bildwerke in der Niedersächsischen Landesgalerie, Hannover*, Munich 1957

Otte, H., *Handbuch der kirchlichen Kunstarchäologie des christlichen Mittelalters* (2 vols), Leipzig 1883–1884

Paas, J. R., *The German Political Broadsheet 1600–1700* (2 vols), Wiesbaden 1985–1986

Pausch, A. and J., *Steuern in der Bibel*, Cologne: Verlag Dr Otto Schmidt KG 1986

Peintner, M., *Kloster Neustift. Neustifter Buchmalerei. Klosterschule und Schreibstube des Augustiner-Chorherrenstiftes*, Bolzano 1984

Petzoldt, L., 'Der ewige Verlierer. Das Bild des Juden in der deutschen Volksliteratur', in *Das Bild des Juden in der Volks- und Jugendliteratur vom 18. Jahrhundert bis 1945*, ed. H. Pleticha, Würzburg 1985, 29–60

Peuckert, W.-E., *Die grosse Wende. Das apokalyptische Saeculum und Luther* (2 vols), Darmstadt 1966

Pfister, K., *Die primitive Holzschnitte*, Munich 1922

Philo-Lexikon. Handbuch jüdischen Wissens, Berlin 1936

Pieper, P., and Müller, I., *Das Paradies des Domes zu Münster in Westfalen*, Münster 1993

Pinder, W., *Die Kunst der deutschen Kaiserzeit bis zum Ende der stauffischen Klassik* (2 vols), Frankfurt 1952

Pinder, W., *Die Kunst der ersten Bürgerzeit bis zur Mitte des 15. Jahrhunderts* (2 vols), Frankfurt 1952–1956

Pleister, W., and Schild, W. (eds.), *Recht und Gerechtigkeit im Spiegel der europäischen Kunst*, Cologne 1988

Pleticha, H. (ed.), *Das Bild des Juden in der Volks- und Jugendliteratur vom 18. Jahrhundert bis 1945*, Würzburg 1985

Plotzek, J.M., and Surmann, U., *Biblioteca Apostolica Vaticana. Liturgie und Andacht im Mittelalter* (exhibition catalogue of the Erzbischöflichen Diözesanmuseum Köln), Stuttgart: Belser 1992

Po-Chia Hsia, R., *The Myth of Ritual Murder. Jews and Magic in Reformation Germany*, New Haven and London: Yale University Press 1988

– , *Trent 1475. Stories of a Ritual Murder Trial*, New Haven and London: Yale University Press 1992

Prache, A. (ed), *Les vitraux de Champagne-Ardenne*, Paris 1992

Preisendanz, K., and Homburger, O., *Das Evangelistar des Speyerer Domes*. Leipzig 1930

Puppi, L., *Les supplices dans l'art*, Paris 1991

Rabel, C., 'L'illustration du "Rational des divins offices" de Guillaume Durand', in *Guillaume Durand, Textes réunis par P.-M. Gy*, Paris 1992, 171–81

Raddatz, A., 'Johannes Ecks Widerlegung der Schrift Osianders gegen die Blutbeschuldigung der Juden', in *Zur Aktualität des Alten Testaments*, ed. S. Kreuzer and K. Lüthi, Frankfurt 1991, 177–86

Rademacher, F., *Die Gustorfer Chorschranken*, Bonn 1975

Rader, Matthäus, SJ, *Bavaria Sancta* (3 vols.), Munich 1615–1627 (^{2}1704), see on Rassler

Rassler, M., *Heiliges Bayer-Land*, Augsburg 1714 (= German language edition of Rader, *Bavaria Sancta*, including copperplate engravings by Raphael Sadeler [died Munich 1632] and Jeremias Kilian [died 1730])

Reallexikon zur deutschen Kunstgeschichte (RDK), Stuttgart 1937ff.

Reber, F., *Die Ruinen Roms*, Leipzig 1877–1879

Reformation in Nürnberg. Umbruch und Bewahrung (exhibition catalogue), Nuremberg 1979

Regensburger Buchmalerei. Von frühkarolingischer Zeit bis zum Ausgang des Mittelalters (exhibition catalogue), Munich: Prestel 1987

Reinach, S., 'L'arc de Titus', *Revue des études juives* 21, 1890, LXVff.

Reinitzer, H., *Biblia deutsch. Luthers Bibelübersetzung und ihre Tradition*, Wolfenbüttel 1983

Die Renaissance im deutschen Südwesten (catalogue), Karlsruhe 1986

Ress, A. (ed.), *Die Kunstdenkmäler von Mittelfranken VII, Stadt Rothenburg o. d. T. Kirchliche Bauten*

Revel-Neher, E., *The Image of the Jew in Byzantine Art*, Oxford: Pergamon Press 1992

Rill, B., *Die Inquisition und ihre Ketzer*, Puchheim: IDEA 1982

Robb, D. M., *The Art of the Illuminated Manuscript*, London 1973

Robert, U., *Les signes d'infamie au moyen Age*, Paris 1891

Roberts, A. M., *Zeitschrift für Kunstgeschichte* 50, 1987, 204

Rohrbacher, S., *Gewalt im Biedermeier*, Frankfurt 1993

– , and Schmidt, M., *Judenbilder. Kulturgeschichte antijüdischer Mythen und antisemitischer Vorurteile*, Reinbek: Rowohlt Taschenbuch Verlag GmbH 1991

Rokeah, Z. E., 'Drawings of Jewish Interest in Some Thirteenth–Century English Public Records', *Scriptorium* 26, 1972, 55–60

Rölle, W., 'Zu den Judeneiden an der Schwelle zur Neuzeit', in *Zur Geschichte der Juden im Deutschland des späten Mittelalters und der frühen Neuzeit*, ed. A. Haverkamp, Stuttgart 1981, 163–203

Rosenfeld, H., *Gutenberg-Jahrbuch* 1974, 35–46

Rosenfeld, H.-F., and Rosenfeld, H., *Deutsche Kultur im Spätmittelalter. 1250–1500*, Handbuch der Kulturgeschichte 1, 4, Wiesbaden 1978

Roth, C., *Essays and Portraits in Anglo-Jewish History*, Philadelphia 1962

Rothe, E., *Buchmalerei aus zwölf Jahrhunderten*, Berlin: Rembrandt-Verlag 1965

Röttgen, H., in *Jahrbuch der kunsthistorischen Sammlungen in Wien* 57, 1961, 48

Rubens, A., *A History of Jewish Costume*, London: Peter Owen Ltd 1967

Rücker, E., *Hartmann Schedels Weltchronik. Das grösste Buchunternehmen der Dürerzeit*, Munich 1988

Rudolph, C., *Artistic Change at S.-Denis. Abbot Suger's Program and the Early XIIth-century Controversy over Art*, Princeton 1990

Run, A. J. van, '"Bene Barbatus". Over de oudste Eeuwige Jood in de beeldende kunst', *Nederlands Kunsthistorisch Jaarboek* 38, 1987, 292–301

Rupprich, H., *Die deutsche Literatur vom späten Mittelalter bis zum Barock*, Geschichte der deutschen Literatur, ed. H. de Boor and R. Newald, IV 1, Munich 1970

Rütz, J., *Text im Bild. Funktion und Bedeutung der Beischriften in den Miniaturen des Uta-Evangelistars*, Frankfurt 1991

Rybár, C., *Das jüdische Prag*, Prague: TV-Spektrum in collaboration with Verlag Akropolis 1991

Sachs, H., *Eygentliche Beschreibung aller Stände auf Erden ... durch den weiterümpten Hans Sachsen Gantz fleissig beschrieben und in Teutsche Reimen gefasset (Holzschnitte von Jost Amman)*, Frankfurt 1568 (reprint)

– (et al.), *Erklärendes Wörterbuch der christlichen Kunst*, Hanau: Werner Dausien [nd]

Sauer, J., *Symbolik des Kirchengebäudes*, Freiburg 1924

Saurma-Jeltsch, L. E., *Wienerjahrbuch für Kunstgeschichte* 41, 1988, 180

Schardt, A. J., *Die Kunst des Mittelalters in Deutschland*, Berlin 1941

Schatzkunst Trier, ed. for the Bischöflichen Generalvikariat Trier, Trier 1984

Schawe, M., 'Zur "Alltagsseite" des Göttinger Barfussaltars von 1424', *Niederdeutsche Beiträge zur Kunstgeschichte* 27, 1988, 63–84

Schedel, H., *Weltchronik*, Nürnberg: Koberger 1493, facsimile edition Leipzig 1933; Dortmund: Harenberg 1978 (pocket book facsimile ed. ^{5}1993)

Scheele, F., '*Di sal man alle radebrechen*'. Todeswürdige Delikte und ihre Bestrafung in Text und Bild der Codices picturati des Sachsenspiegels (2 vols), Oldenburg: Isensee 1991

Scherer, J. E., *Die Rechtsverhältnisse der Juden in den deutsch-österreichischen Landern*, Leipzig 1901

Schiffler, H., and Winkeler, R., *Tausend Jahre Schule*, Stuttgart 1988

Schild, W., *Alte Gerichtsbarkeit*, Munich 1980

Schiller, G., *Ikonographie der christlichen Kunst*, Gütersloh 1966–1980

Diebold Schilling. Berner Chronik (facsimile edition, 4 vols), Bern 1943–1945

Schmid, A.A. (ed.), *Die Luzerner Chronik des Diebold Schilling 1513. Faksimile-Ausgabe der Handschrift S. 23 fol. in der Zentralbibliothek Luzern,* Lucerne: Faksimile-Verlag 1981

– , Beer, E.J. (et al.), Das *Graduale von St Katharinenthal* (facsimile edition with commentary), Lucerne: Facsimile-Verlag 1983

Schmidt, G., *Die Armenbibeln des XIV.Jahrhunderts,* Graz and Cologne 1959

– , and Unterkircher, F., *Krumauer Bildercodex* (facsimile and text), Graz: ADEVA 1967

Schmidt, P., *Die Illustration der Lutherbibel 1522–1700,* Basel: F. Reinhardt, 1962, 1977

Schmidt–Wiegand, R. (ed.), *Untersuchungen zu den Bilderhandschriften des Sachsenspiegels* (2 vols), Münich: W. Fink 1986

Schmitt, F.A., and Beer, E.J. (eds.), *Das Evangelistar aus St Peter. Eine spätromanische Bilderhandschrift der Badischen Landesbibliothek Karlsruhe. Vollfaksimile-Ausgabe,* Basel: Feuermann 1961

Schmitt, O., *Stadel-Jahrbuch* 2, 1922, 109–44

– , *Gotische Skulpturen des Freiburger Münsters* (2 vols), Frankfurt 1926

Schmitz-Cliever, *Aachener Kunstblätter* 34, 1967, 224

Schnee, H., *Die Hoffinanz und der moderne Staat* (6 vols), Berlin 1953–1967

Schneemelcher, W., *New Testament Apocrypha* (2 vols), English version by R.McL.Wilson, Louisville, Ky: Westminster John Knox Press and Cambridge: Lutterworth Press 1991, 1992

Schnitzler, H., *Rheinische Schatzkammer* (2 vols), Düsseldorf: Schwann 1957–1959

Schnur, H. C., *Teuton Tortures. A Pictorial Record of Persecution in Germany,* London [nd, 1939?]

Schoeller, I., *Die Kunst im deutschen Buchdruck* (exhibition catalogue), Weimar 1915

Schoeps, J. H. (ed.), *Neues Lexikon des Judentums,* Gütersloh 1992

Scholem, G., *Sabbatai Zwi. Der mystische Messias,* Frankfurt 1992

Schouwink, W., *Der wilde Eber in Gottes Weinberg. Zur Darstellung des Schweins in Literatur und Kunst des Mittelalters,* Sigmaringen 1985

Schramm, A. (ed.), *Der Bilderschmuck der Frühdrucke,* Leipzig 1920ff.

Schreckenberg, H., *Die christlichen Adversus-Judaeos-Texte* (3 vols), Frankfurt: Peter Lang 1990–1994

Schreiber, W. L., *Handbuch der Holz- und Metallschnitte des XV. Jahrhunderts* (11 vols), Stuttgart 1969–1976 (reprint of 1926 ed.).

Schreiber, W. L., *Der Buchholzschnitt im 15.Jahrhundert in Original-Beispielen,* Munich 1929

Schreiner, S., 'Der Fall des Juden Ansteet – zugleich ein Beispiel protestantischer Inquisition', *Judaica* 37, 1981, 90–102

Schubert, K. (ed.), *Judentum im Mittelalter* (exhibition catalogue), Eisenstadt: Edition Roetzer 1978

Schubert, K., *Die Kultur der Juden* II, Wiesbaden 1979

Schuder, R., and Hirsch, R., *Der gelbe Fleck. Wurzeln und Wirkungen des Judenhasses in der deutschen Geschichte,* Berlin: Rütten and Loening 1990

Schuegraf, J. R., 'Geschichte des Doms von Regensburg, II', *Verhandlungen des Historischen Vereins für Oberpfalz und Regensburg* 12, 1848

Schulz, F.T., *Das Germanische Nationalmuseum von 1902-1927. Festschrift,* Nuremberg 1927

Schwartz, F., *Mainzer Zeitschrift* 83, 1988, 23–45

Seeger, J., 'Die Antichristlegende im Chorfenster der Marienkirche zu Frankfurt an der Oder', *Städel-Jahrbuch* 6, 1977, 265–92

Seibt, F., *Glanz und Elend des Mittelalters,* Berlin 1987

Seiferth, W., *Synagoge und Kirche im Mittelalter,* Munich: Kösel 1964

Shachar, I., *The 'Judensau',* London: The Warburg Institute, University of London 1974

Shestack, A., *Fifteenth Century Engravings of Northern Europe. From the National Gallery of Art, Washington DC* (exhibition catalogue), Washington DC 1967

Siegele-Wenschkewitz, L., 'Josel von Rosheim: Juden und Christen im Zeitalter der Reformation', *Kirche und Israel* 6/1, 1991, 3–16

Sievers, L., *Juden in Deutschland,* Hamburg 1981

Simonsohn, S., *The Apostolic See and the Jews* (8 vols), Toronto 1988–1991

Simson, O. von, *Das Mittelalter Il. Das Hohe Mittelalter,* Propyläen Kunstgeschichte 6, Berlin 1972

– , 'Ecclesia und Synagoga am südlichen Querhausportal des Strassburger Münsters', in *Wenn der Messias kommt,* ed. L. Kötzsche and P.von der Osten–Sacken, Berlin 1984

Skubiszewski, P., 'Eine Gruppe von romanischen Goldschmiedearbeiten in Polen', *Jahrbuch der Berliner Museen* 22, 1980, 35–90

Solms-Laubach, E. Graf zu, 'Der Hausbuchmeister', *Städel-Jahrbuch* 9, 1935, 13–96

Spätgotik in Salzburg. Die Malerei 1400-1530 (exhibition catalogue), Salzburg 1972

Spätrenaissance am Oberrhein. Tobias Stimmer 1539-1584 (exhibition catalogue), Basel 1984

Historisches Museum der Pfalz, Speyer (exhibition catalogue), Speyer 1983

Stamm, L. E., *Die Rüdiger-Schopf-Handschriften,* Frankfurt: Sauerlander 1981

Stange, A., in *Festschrift Heinrich Wölfflin,* Munich 1924, 203

– , *Deutsche Malerei der Gotik (*11 vols.), Berlin (and Munich) 1934–1961

Stanton, A. R., *The 'Queen Mary Psalter': Narrative and Devotion in Gothic England,* Diss. Austin, Texas 1992

The Stavelot Triptych. Mosan Art and the Legend of the True Cross (exhibition catalogue), New York 1980

Steche, B. (ed.), *Beschreibendes Verzeichnis der älteren Bau- und Kunstdenkmäler des Königreichs Sachsen. XIII. Amtshauptmannschaft Glauchau*, Dresden 1890

Stegemann, W., and Eichmann, J. (eds.), *Der Davidstern, Dorsten: Eigenverlag des jüdischen Museums*, Dorsten 1991

Steingräber, E., *Anzeiger des Germanischen Nationalmuseums* 1963, 23

– , *Die neue Pinakothek München*, Munich [nd, c. 1980?]

Stelzer, G. and U. (eds.), *Bildhandbuch der Kunstsammlungen in der DDR*, 1985

Stemberger, G., *2000 Jahre Christentum. Illustrierte Kirchengeschichte in Farbe*, Herrsching: M. Pawlak 1983

– (ed.), *Die Juden. Ein historisches Lesebuch*, Munich 1990

Sterling, C., *La peinture médiévale à Paris, 1300–1500*, I, Paris 1987

Stern, S., *Josel von Rosheim – Befehlshaber der Judenschaft im Heiligen Römichen Reich Deutscher Nation*, Stuttgart 1959

Stock, R. W., *Die Judenfrage*, Nuremberg: Verlag Der Stürmer 1939

Stoffers, W., *Juden und Ghetto in der deutschen Literatur bis zum Ausgang des Weltkrieges*, Nijmegen 1939

Strand, K. A., *German Bibles Before Luther. 14 High-German Editions*, Grand Rapids, Michigan 1966

Strauss, W. L., *Clair-Obscur*, Nuremberg 1973

– , *The German Single-Leaf Woodcut 1550-1600. A Pictorial Catalogue* (2 vols), New York 1975

Stupperich, R., *Reformatorenlexikon*, Gütersloh 1984

Katalog der Staatsgalerie Stuttgart, Stuttgart 1962

Suckale, R., *Städel-Jahrbuch 6*, 1977, 177–208

Sudley. Illustrated Catalogue and History of the House, Liverpool 1971

Suermondt-Ludwig-Museum, Aachen (catalogue), Aachen 1982.

Suevia sacra. Frühe Kunst in Schwaben (exhibition catalogue), Augsburg 1973

Swarzenski, H., *Vorgotische Miniaturen*, Königstein im Taunus and Leipzig 1927

– , *Die lateinischen illuminierten Handschriften des XIII. Jahrhunderts in den Ländern an Rhein, Main und Donau* (2 vols), Berlin 1936

– , *The Berthold Missal* (2 vols), New York 1943

Synagoga. Kultgeräte und Kunstwerke. Von der Zeit der Patriarchen his zur Gegenwart (exhibition catalogue), Recklingshausen: Städtische Kunsthalle 1960

Theologische Realenzyklopädie, Berlin and New York 1977ff.

Thieme, U., and Becker, F. (eds.), *Allgemeines Lexikon der Bildenden Künste* (37 vols.), Leipzig 1907–1950

Thomas, M. (ed.), *Le psautier de Saint Louis. Reproduction des 78 enlumineures à pleine page du manuscrit Latin 10525*

de la Bibliothèque Nationale de Paris, Graz: Akademische Druck- und Verlagsanstalt 1970

– (ed.), *The Rohan Book of Hours. Bibliothèque Nationale, Paris (Ms. latin 9471)*, London 1973

–, and Schmidt, G., *Die Bibel des Königs Wenzel* (with 32 Miniatures), Graz 1989

Thornton, T. C. G., 'The Crucifixion of Haman and the Scandal of the Cross', *Journal of Theological Studies* 37, 1986, 419–26

Thümmler, H. (ed.), *Die Bau- und Kunstdenkmäler von Westfalen, 47.1 Kreis Unna*, Münster 1959

– , *Weserbaukunst im Mittelalter*, Hamelin 1970

Sammlung Thyssen-Bornemisza (catalogue, 2 vols), Lugano 1969

Tietze, H., *Die illuminierten Handschriften der Rossiana in Wien-Lainz*, Leipzig 1911

– (ed.), *Österreichische Kunsttopographie, Band XXIII. Geschichte und Beschreibung des Stephansdoms in Wien*, Vienna 1931

Tissot, J.J., *La vie de nôtre seigneur Jésus Christ* (2 vols), Tours 1896–1897

Trachtenberg, J., *The Devil and the Jews*, Cleveland 1961

Treue, W., 'Schlechte und gute Christen. Zur Rolle von Christen in antijüdischen Ritualmord- und Hostienschändungslegenden', *Aschkenas* 2, 1992, 95–116

Timmermann, W., 'Antisemitismus in spätmittelalterlichen und frühneuzeitlichen Medien', *Wirkendes Wort* 36, 1986, 354–72

Tinkle, T., 'Saturn of the Several Faces. A Survey of the Medieval Mythographic Traditions', *Viator* 18, 1987, 289–307

Troescher, G., *Die burgundische Malerei* (2 vols), Berlin 1966

Twining, L., *Symbols and Emblems of Early and Medieval Christian Art*, London 1852

Ulmer Museum. Bildhauerei und Malerei vom 13. Jahrhundert bis 1600 (catalogue), Ulm 1981

Unger, H. (ed.), *Zwöfjahrhunderte Literatur in Bayern* (exhibition catalogue), Krems 1982

– , *Text und Bild im Mittelalter*, Graz 1986

Unterkircher, F., *König Wenzels Bilderbibel*, Graz 1983

– , and Demus, O. (ed.), *Das Antiphonar von St. Peter. Vollständige Faksimile-Ausgabe im Originalformat des Codex Vindobonensis. Series nova 2700 der Österreichischen Nationalbibliothek* (commentary volume), Graz: Akademische Druck- und Verlagsanstalt 1974

Verdier, P., in *Wallraf-Richartz-Jahrbuch* 43, 1982, 62

Die deutsche Literatur des Mittelalters. Verfasserlexikon, Berlin 1978ff.

Verheyen, E., 'Das Fürstenportal des Bamberger Domes', *Zeitschrift für Kunstwissenschaft* 16, 1962, 1–40

Victoria and Albert Museum 1927. A Pictorial Book of Medieval Enamels (exhibition catalogue), London 1927

Vignau-Wilber, T., *Christoph Murer und die 'XL. Emblemata Miscella Nova'*, Bern 1982

Viollet-le-Duc, E.-E., *Dictionnaire raisonné de l'architecture française du XIe au XVIe siècle* (9 vols), Paris 1867–1875

Vitzthum, G., and Volbach-Berlin, W. F., *Die Malerei und Plastik des Mittelalters in Italien*, Wildpark bei Potsdam 1924

Volz, H. (ed.), *D.Martin Luther. Die gantze Heilige Schrift Deudsch, Wittenberg 1545. Die letzte zu Luthers Lebzeiten erschienene Ausgabe*, München 1972

– , *Martin Luthers deutsche Bibel*, Hamburg: F.Wittig 1978

Vos, D. de, 'Maître de la Légende de sainte Ursule', in *Brugge Musée communaux. Catalogue des tableaux 15e et 16e siècles*, Bruges 1982, 151–4

Wander, K.F W., *Deutsches Sprüchwörter-Lexikon* (5 vols), Leipzig 1867–1880

Warner, G., *Queen Mary's Psalter*, London 1912

Wartmann, W., *Gemälde und Skulpturen 1430–1530. Schweiz und angrenzende Gebiete* (exhibition catalogue), Zürich 1921

Weber, P., *Geistliches Schauspiel und kirchliche Kunst in ihrem Verhältnis erläutert an einer Ikonographie der Kirche und Synagoge*, Stuttgart 1894

Wegener, H. (ed.), *Beschreibendes Verzeichnis der Miniaturen-Handschriften der Preussischen Staatsbibliothek zu Berlin. V. Band. Die deutschen Handschriften bis 1500*, Leipzig 1928

Wehrhahn-Stauch, L., *Zeitschrift des Deutschen Vereins für Kunstwissenschaft* 21, 1967, 119

Weidinger, E. (ed.), *Legenda aurea. Das Leben der Heiligen*, Aschaffenburg 1986

Weigert, H., *Geschichte der deutschen Kunst* I, Frankfurt 1963

Weil, E., 'Zu Petrus Nigri's Judendisputation', *Soncino-Blätter* (Berlin) 1929–1930/1, 57–62 (with illustrations)

Wendland, H., *Die Buchillustration*, Stuttgart 1987

Wenninger, M. J., 'Zum Verhältnis der Kölner Juden zu ihrer Umwelt im Mittelalter', in *Köln und das rheinische Judentum*, Cologne 1984, 17–34

Wentzel, H., *Der Cismarer Altar*, Hamburg 1941

– , *Meisterwerke der Glasmalerei*, Berlin 1951

– , *Die Glasmalereien in Schwaben von 1200–1350*, Berlin 1958

Wenzel, E., 'Zur Judenproblematik bei Hans Folz', *Zeitschrift für deutsche Philologie* 101, 1982, 79–104

– , 'Do worden die Judden alle geschant'. Rolle und Funktion der Juden in spätmittelalterlichen Spielen*, Munich 1992

Wenzelsbibel (facsimile edition), Graz: Akademische Druck- und Verlagsanstalt, 1981ff.

Wescher, P. (ed.), *Beschreibendes Verzeichnis der Miniaturen-Handschriften und Einzelblätter des Kupferstichkabinetts der Staatlichen Museen Berlin*, Leipzig 1931

White, J., *Art and Architecture in Italy 1250 to 1400*, Harmondsworth 1966

Wilkens, L. von, *Anzeiger des Germanischen Nationalmuseums* 1977, 46

Williams, D., *The Illustrations in the 'Liber Floridus'*, Diss. East Anglia University 1992

Wilson, A., and Lancaster Wilson, J., *A Medieval Mirror. Speculum humanae salvationis, 1324–1500*, Berkeley 1984

Winkler, F., *Jahrbuch der Preussischen Kunstsammlungen* 57, 1936, 156

Winter, P. M. de, *The Sacral Treasure of the Guelphs* (exhibition catalogue), Cleveland 1985

Wirth, K.-A., *Münchnerjahrbuch der Bildenden Kunst* 14, 1963, 51–78

– , (ed.), *Die Biblia pauperum im Codex Palatinus latinus 871 der Biblioteca Apostolica Vaticana sowie ihre bebilderten Zusätze* (2 vols.) Stuttgart and Zurich: Belser 1982 (I, facsimile of pictures; II, introduction and facsimile of text)

Wittelsbach und Bayern. I, 2: Von Otto 1. zu Ludwig dem Bayern. Beiträge zur Bayerischen Geschichte und Kunst 1180–1350 (exhibition catalogue), Munich 1980

Woisetschläger-Mayer, I. (ed.), *Österreichische Kunsttopographie, XXXV, Die Kunstdenkmäler des Gerichtsbezirks Murau*, Vienna 1964

Wolfenbütteler Cimelien (exhibition catalogue), Weinheim 1989

Wolfilus, J., *Lectionum memorabilium et reconditorum centenarii XVI* (2 vols), Lauingen 1600

Worringer, W., *Urs Graf. Die Holzschnitte zur Passion*, Munich 1923

Yarden, L., *The Spoils of Jerusalem on the Arch of Titus*, Stockholm 1991

The Year 1200. A Centennial Exhibition at the Metropolitan Museum of Art (3 vols), New York 1970

Zafran E. M., *The Iconography of Antisemitism: A Study of the Representation of the Jews in the Visual Arts of Europe 1400–1600*, Diss. New York University 1973

– , 'An Alleged Case of Image Desecration by the Jews and its Representation in Art: The Virgin of Cambron', *Journal of Jewish Art* 2, 1975, 62–71

– , 'Saturn and the Jews', *Journal of the Warburg and Courtauld Institutes* 42, 1979, 16–27

Zarnecki, G. (et al.), *Romanik, Gotik, Byzanz*, Neue Belser Stilgeschichte 4, Stuttgart 1986

Zeeden, E.W., *Deutsche Kultur in der frühen Neuzeit*, Handbuch der Kulturgeschichte 1a, Frankfurt 1968

Die Zeit der Staufer. Katalog der Ausstellung (2 vols), Stuttgart 1977

Zeller, A., *Die Kunstdenkmale der Stadt Hildesheim. Kirchliche Bauten,* Osnabrück 1979

Zimmermann, E., and Staub, K.H., *Buchkunst des Mittelalters. Zimelien der Hessischen Landes- und Hochschulbibliothek Darmstadt,* Wiesbaden 1980

Zimmermann, M.G., *Oberitalische Plastik im frühen und hohen Mittelalter,* Leipzig 1897

Zimmermann, V., *Die Entwicklung des Judeneides,* Frankfurt 1973

Zimmermann, W., 'Antisemitismus in spätmittelalterlichen und frühneuzeitlichen Medien', *Wirkendes Wort* 36, 1986, 354–72

Die Zisterzienser. Ordensleben zwischen Ideal und Wirklichkeit (exhibition catalogue), Cologne 1980

Kunsthaus Zürich. Aus der Sammlung (catalogue), Zürich 1959

Abbreviations

BA	Bibliothèque de l'Arsenal		*LGB*	*Lexikon des gesamten Buchwesens*
BAV	Bibliot(h)eca Apostolica Vaticana		LM	Landesmuseum
BCE	Before the Common Era		*LMA*	*Lexikon des Mittelalters*
BL	British Library		*LThK*	*Lexikon für Theologie und Kirche*
BM	The British Museum			
BN	Bibliothèque Nationale		MG(SS)	Monumenta Germania Historica
BR	Biblothèque Royale			(Scriptores)
			Mon.Jud.Handb.	*Monumenta Judaica*, Handbuch
CE	Common Era		*Mon.Jud.Kat.*	*Monumenta Judaica* (catalogue)
Cod.	Codex			
			nd	No date of publication given
DMA	*Dictionary of the Middle Ages*		np	No place of publication given
			NT	New Testament
EJ	*Encyclopedia Judaica*			
EWA	*Encyclopedia of World Art*		ÖN	Österrreichische Nationalbibliothek
			OT	Old Testament
GermJud	*Germania Judaica*			
GNM	Germanisches Nationalmuseum		PL	Patrologia Latina
HAB	Herzog August Bibliothek		*RDK*	*Reallexikon zur deutschen Kunstgeschichte*
JüdLex	*Jüdisches Lexikon*		SB	Staatsbibliothek
KML	*Kindlers Malerei Lexikon*		*TRE*	*Theologische Realenzyklopädie*
LB	Landesbibliothek		UB	Universitätsbibliothek

Appendix: Titles of Christian Texts on the Jews

I. Second to eleventh centuries

(a) Theological treatises, religious dialogues and other texts relevant to the theme

Aristo of Pella, *Altercatio Jasonis et Papisci*
Justin, *Dialogue with the Jew Trypho*
Miltiades, *Against the Jews*
Apollinarius of Hierapolis, *Against the Jews*
Melito of Sardis, *Peri Pascha*
Irenaeus of Lyons, *Adversus haereses*
Clement of Alexandria, *Ecclesiastical Canon, or Against the Judaizers*
Tertullian, *Adversus Judaeos*
Hippolytus of Rome, *Demonstratio adversus Judaeos*
Cyprian of Carthage, *Testimoniorum libri adversus Judaeos*; Pseudo-Cyprian, *De montibus Sina et Sion*; *Adversus Judaeos*; *De pascha computus*; *Ad Vigilium episcopum de iudaica incredulitate*
Novatian, *De sabbato*; *De circumcisione*; *De cibis Judaicis*
Lactantius, *Divinae Institutiones*
Eusebius of Caesarea, *Historia ecclesiastica*; *Praeparatio evangelica*; *Demonstratio evangelica*
Aphraates, *Demonstrationes*
Eusebius of Emesa, *Against the Jews, Pagans and Novatians*
Hilary of Poitiers, *De Trinitate*
Zeno of Verona, *Sermons*
Athanasius the Great, *The Incarnation of the Word*; Pseudo-Athanasius, *Historia imaginis Berytensis*; *Dialogue between Athanasius and Zacchaeus*
Diodore of Tarsus, *Against the Jews*
Pseudo-Gregory of Nyssa, *Testimonia adversus Judaeos*
Pseudo-Ambrose, *Mosaicarum et Romanarum legum collatio*; *Apologia David altera*
Epiphanius of Salamis, *Panarion*
John Chrystostom, *Adversus Judaeos*; *Contra Judaeos et Gentiles*; Pseudo-John Chrysostom, *Contra Judaeos et Gentiles et Haereticos*
Antiochus of Ptolemais, *Against the Jews*
[Anonymous,] *Consultationes Zacchaei et Apollonii*

Maximinus, *Contra Judaeos*
Pseudo-Jerome, *Disputatione de solempnitatibus paschae*; *De vera circumcisione*
Severianus of Gabala, *Contra Judaeos in serpentem aeneum*
Augustine, *Adversus Judaeos*; *Ad Asellicum episcopum de cavendo Judaismo*; *De duobus filiis ex Evangelio*; Pseudo-Augustine, *Contra Judaeos, paganos et Arianos*; *Adversus quinque haereses*; *Altercatio Ecclesiae et Synagogae*
Evagrius, *Altercatio Simonis et Theophili*
Cyril of Alexandria, *De Synagogae defectu*
Theodoret of Cyrrhus, *Against the Jews*
Pseudo-Basil of Seleucia, *Argument against the Jews concerning the Advent of the Redeemer*
Pseudo-Isaac of Antioch, *Sermon against the Jews*
[Anonymous,] *Dialogus Christiani et Judaei (Dialogue between Timothy and Aquila)*
Jacob of Serug, *Letter of Consolation to the Himaritic Christians*; *Discourses against the Jews*
Caesarius of Arles, *De comparatione Ecclesiae vel Synagogae*; *De filio prodigo*; *De esca vel potu Judeorum prohibendis*
[Anonymous,] *Doctrine Jacobi nuper baptizati*
Isidore of Seville, *De fide catholica ex veteri et novo testamento contra Judaeos*; *Quaestiones in Vetus Testamentum*; Pseudo-Isidore of Seville, *Liber de variis quaestionibus adversus Judaeos seu ceteros infideles vel plerosque haereticos iudaizantes ex utroque Testamento collectus*
Leontius of Neapolis, *Dialogue against the Jews*
Idelfons of Toledo, *De virginitate perpetua sanctae Mariae adversus tres infideles*
[Anonymous], *Tropaea contra Judaeos*
Julian of Toledo, *De comprobatione aetatis sextae*
Stephanus of Bostra, *Against the Jews*
Anastasios Sinaites, *Against the Jews*; Pseudo-Anastasios, *Disputatio adversus Judaeos*; *Dialogus parvus ad Judaeos*
John of Damascus, *De fide orthodoxa (Against the Jews, On the Sabbath)*; *Responses to the Jews*
Sergius Stylites, *Disputation against a Jew*
Theodorus Abu Qurra, *Dissertatio cum Judaeo*
Agobard of Lyons, *Ad proceres palatii consultatio et supplicatio de baptismo Judaicorum mancipiorum*; *Epistola ad proceres palatii contra praeceptum impium de baptismo*

Judaicorum mancipiorum; De insolentia Judaeorum; De Judaicis superstitionibus; De cavendo convictu et societate Judaica

Walafrid Strabo, *De subversione Jerusalem*

Amolo of Lyons, *Contra Judaeos*

Gregory Asbestas, *Treatise to the Effect that the Hebrews are not to be Baptized Hastily and without a Previous Thorough Testing*

[Anonymous,] *Altercatio Aecclesie contra Synagogam*

Adso, *De ortu et tempore Antichristi*

Gabriel ibn Ubaidallah, *Refutation of the Jews*

Fulbert of Chartres, *Tractatus contra Judaeos*

Elias bar Sinaja, *Proof of the Truth of Faith*

Peter Damian, *Antilogus contra Judaeos; Dialogus inter Judaeum requirentem et Christianum e contrario respondentem*

Nicetas Stethatos, *Treatise against the Jews and Demonstration of the Beginnings of their Disobedience and Unbelief*

(b) Poems and religious dialogues in poetic form, legends and reports with a legendary colouring

Commodian, *Carmen apologeticum*

[Anonymous,] *Silvester Legends*

Sedulius, *Paschale carmen*

Isaac of Antioch, *Poems on the Fast*

[Anonymous,] *Religious Dialogue at the Court of the Sasanids*

Jacob of Serugh, *Poem on the Veil upon the Countenance of Moses; Poem on Synagogue and Church*

[Anonymous,] *Disputation of Gregentius with the Jew Herban*

[Anonymous,] *Antiphon between Church and Synagogue*

Severus of Menorca, *Epistula de virtutibus ad Judaeorum conversionem in Minoricensi insula factis ('Epistola Severi episcopi')*

[Anonymous,] *Vindicta Salvatoris*

[Anonymous,] *Vindicta Poem*

Christophoros Protasekretis, *Exhortatio ad Israel*

[Anonymous,] *Physiologus*

[Anonymous,] *Dialogus Judaei cum Christiano quodam ceco, cui et visus restituitur*

Amarcius, *Sermones (Quod ineluctabilis sit Judaeorum duricia)*

William of Ebersberg, *Exposito in Cantica canticorum*

[Anonymous,] *De Maria et Synagoga*

II. Twelfth-thirteenth centuries

(a) Theological treatises, dialogues on religion and other kindred texts

Anselm of Canterbury, *Monologion; De fide Trinitatis et de incarnatione verbi; Cur deus homo*

Odo of Cambrai, *Disputatio contra Judaeum Leonem nomine de adventu Christi filii dei*

Gilbertus Crispinus, *Disputatio Judei et Christiani*

Euthymios Zigabenos, *Panoplia dogmatike* (Against the Hebrews)

Lambert of St Omer, *Liber floridus (De bona arbore et mala. Arbor bona – Ecclesia fidelium. Arbor mala –Synagoga)*

Petrus Alfonsi, *Dialogus Petri cognomento Alphonsi ex Judaeo Christiani et Moysi Judaei*

Pseudo-William of Champeaux, *Dialogus inter Christianum et Judaeum de fide catholica*

Bruno of Segni, *De sacrificio azymo; De sancta Trinitate*

Guibert of Nogent, *De incarnatione contra Judaeos*

Rupert of Deutz, *Anulus sive dialogus inter Christianum et Judaeum*

Hildebert of Lavardin, *Contra Judaeos de incarnatione*

Honorius Augustodunensis, *Expositio in Cantica canticorum*

Peter Abelard, *Dialogus inter Philosophum, Judaeum et Christianum*

Mari ibn Sulaiman, *Book of the Tower for Viewing and Fighting*

[Anoymous,] *Ysagoge in theologiam*

Peter the Venerable, *Adversus Judaeorum inveteratam duritiem*

Paschalis Romanus, *Disputatio contra Judaeos*

[Anonymous,] *Tractatus adversus Judaeum*

Dionysios bar Salibi, *Against the Jews*

Richard of St Victor, *De Emmanuele*

Hildegard of Bingen, *Liber Scivias; Liber divinorum operum; Visio ad Guibertum missa*

Michael Glykas, *De ratione qua oportet contra Judaeos respondere*

Hermann of Scheda, *Opusculum de conversione sua*

Bartholomew of Exeter, *Dialogus contra Judaeos ad corrigendum et perficiendum destinatus*

Andronikos Komnenos, *Dialogue contra Judaeos Christiani et Judaei*

Martin of Leon, *Sermones*

Balduin of Canterbury, *Liber de commendatione fidei (De Judaeorum excaecatione; De vocatione gentium et idololatriae subversione; De novae legis institutione)*

Herrad of Landsberg, *Hortus deliciarum*

Petrus Cantor, *Summa Abel (Judei)*

[Anonymous,] *Altercatio Synagogae et Ecclesiae (Inter-locutores Gamaliel et Paulus)*

[Anonymous,] *Disputatio contra incredulitatem Judaeorum excerpta ex liberis prophetarum (Arma contra Judaeos)*

Walter of Châtillon, *Tractatus sive dialogus magistri Gualteri Tornacensis et Balduini Valentianensis contra Judaeos*

Joachim of Fiore, *Adversus Judaeos; Concordia novi ac veteris testamenti*

Alanus ab Insulis, *De fide catholica contra haereticos sui temporis (contra Judaeos)*

Peter of Blois, *Contra perfidiam Judaeorum*

Eberhard of Béthune, *Antihaeresis (Disputatio contra Judaeos; Quaestiones ad decipiendum tam haereticos quam Judaeos)*

Adam of Dryburgh, *De fide sanctae Ecclesiae et de vocatione Synagogae ad fidem*

Peter of Cornwall, *Liber disputationum Petri contra Symonem Judeum de confutatione Judeorum*

Adam of Persiegne, *Epistola ad amicum*

William of Bourges, *Liber bellorum domini contra Judeos et Hereticos (Epistula ad Hebreos; Controversie inter Dominum et Judeos; Liber contra Hereticos)*

(b) Poems and religious dialogues in poetic form, legends and reports with a legendary colouring, spiritual plays

Marbod of Rennes, *Historia Theophili metrica*; Pseudo-Marbod of Rennes, *De Judeo in latrinam lapso*

Acardus de Arroasia, *Super templo Salomonis*

Thomas of Monmouth, *De vita et passione sancti Wilhelmi martyris norwicensis*

[Anonymous,] *Adam Play*

[Anonymous,] *Imperial Chronicle*

[Anonymous,] *Ludus de Antichristo*

[Anonymous,] *Alexander Song*

[Anonymous,] *Christianus, Judeus, Sarracenus*

The Wild Man, *Veronica; Vespasian*

[Anonymous,] *Jerusalem, civitas inclita*

[Anonymous,] *La venjance nostre seigneur*

Adgar, *The Little Jewish Boy; The Voice heard above the Altar in a Church in Toledo; Theophilus Legend; The Pawning of a Picture of Mary; The Vengeance of God on the Jews through Titus, Vespasian and the Devil in the Form of Moses; How the Jew at Constantinople Mocks an Image of Mary*

Robert de Boron, *Le Roman de Saint-Graal*

[Anonymous,] *Das Jüdel*

III. Thirteenth to twentieth centuries

(a) Theological treatises and other kindred texts

Ibrahim ibn 'Aun, *Book of the Resolution of Doubt and the Reformation of Hostile Jews*

[Anonymous,] *Treatise against the Jews*

[Anonymous,] *Disputa entre un cristiano y un judío*

Isu'yab ibn Malkun, *Refutation of the Jews and Muslims*

Peter of London, *De adventu Messiae contra Judaeos*

Nektarios of Casole, *Kata Joudaion dialexis*

Theobald de Saxonia, *Extractiones de Talmut*

Ibn at Tayib, *Summa of the Faith of the Christian Confession und Refutation of the Nations of Islam und Judaism by their own Principles and Doctrines*

Paulus ar-Rahib al-Antaki, *A Question about the Abolition of the Law of the Jews*

Robert Grosseteste, *De cessatione legalium*

Raimund Martin, *Capistrum Judaeorum; Pugio fidei*

Inghetto Contardo, *Disputatio contra Judeos (Flagellum Judeorum)*

Guibert of Tournai, *Disputatio Ecclesiae et Synagogae*

Pseudo-Thaddaeus Pelusiotes, *Contra Judaeos*

Petrus Pascual, *Disputa contra los jueus sobre la fe catolica*

Thomas Aquinas, *Epistola ad ducissam Brabantiae (De regimine Judaeorum)*

[Anonymous,] *Pharethra fidei contra Judeos super Talmuth*

Raymond Lull, *Liber de gentili et tribus sapientibus; Liber praedicationis contra Judaeos*

Porchetus de Salvaticis, *Victoria adversus impios Hebraeos*

Ricoldo de Monte Croce, *Contra errores Judaeorum*

Lauterius de Batineis, *Capistrum Judaeorum*

Petrus de Pennis, *Liber contra Judaeos nomine Thalamoth (Dialogus inter Judaeum et clericum)*

Alfonso of Valladolid, *Mostrador de justicia; Concordia de las leyes; Las maldiciones de los Judíos*

Bernhard Oliver, *Contra caecitatem Judaeorum (Contra perfidiam Judaeorum)*

John Bacon, *De Judaeorum perfidia; Rationes contra Judaeos; De adventu Messiae; Concordia Christi et Prophetarum*

Nicholas of Lyra, *Quaestio de quolibet (Contra Judaeos); Responsio ad quendam Judaeum*

[Anonymous,] *Disputacio wider die juden*

Alfonsus Bonihominis, *Epistola ad R.Isaac*

Richard Fitzralph, *De inventionibus Judaeorum*

Johannes of Hildesheim, *Contra Judaeos*

Theophanes of Nicaea, *Against the Jews*

John Kantakuzenos, *Against the Jews*

Hieronymus de Sancta Fide, *Hebraeomastix (Tractatus ad convincendum perfidiam Judaeorum; De Judaicis erroribus ex Talmut)*

Vincent Ferrer, *Tractatus contra Judaeos*

Paul Nicoletti, *Liber contra Judaeos*

Paul of Burgos, *Scrutinium Scripturarum sive Dialogus Sauli et Pauli contra Judaeos*

Johannes de Francfordia, *Concordantiae contra Judaeos (Malleus Judaeorum)*

Stephan Bodecker, *Contra Judaeos*

Antoninus Pierozzi, *Trialogus de duobus discipulis euntibus in Emmaus*

Giannozzo Manetti, *Adversus Judaeos et Gentiles*

Petrus de la Cavallería, *Zelus Christi contra Judaeos, Sarracenos et infideles*

Nicolas of Cusa, *De pace fidei*

[Anonymous,] *Tractatus de Antichristo et discipulis eius*

[Anonymous,] *A Proof that the Jews Err*

Alfons von Oropez, *Lumen ad revelationem gentium et gloriam plebis Israel*

Alfons de Spina, *Fortalicium fidei contra Judeos, Saracenos aliosque Christianae fidei inimicos*

Gennadios of Constantinople, *Elenchos tes ioudaices nyn planes*

Petrus Nigri, *Tractatus contra perfidos Judaeos; Der Stern Meschiach*

Johannes Lopez, *Contra superstitiones Judaeorum (Controversiae contra Judaeos)*

Antonius of Avila, *Censura et confutatio libri Talmut*

Jacob Pérez of Valencia, *Tractatus contra Judaeos*

[Anonymous,] *Phaetra fidei catholice syve ydonea disputatio inter Christianos et Judeos*

[Anonymous,] *Collectanea contra Judaeos*

Bernhardin of Busti, *Contra Hebraeos*

Johannes Baptista Gratia Dei, *Liber de confutatione hebrayce secte*

Victor of Carben, *Opus aureum*

Cyprian Benet, *Aculeus contra Judaeos*

Charles Bouelles, *Dialogi duo de Sancta Trinitate inter Christianum et Judaeum*

Petrus Galatinus, *De arcanis catholicae veritatis contra obstinatissimam Judaeorum nostra tempestatis perfidiam*

Johannes Teuschlein, *Aufflosung ettlicher fragen wider die verstocket plinte Juden*

Joseph Pfefferkorn, *Speculum adhortationis iudaice ad Christum; Judenbeicht; Osterbuch; Der Judenfeind; Handspiegel*

Alfonso of Zamora, *Epistola ad Hebraeos*

Antonius Margaritha, *Der gantz Judisch glaub*

Paulus Staffelsteiner, *Wahrhafftig widerlegung der grossen verfelschung der Judischen Lerer des 22.Psalm; Ein kurtze underrichtung*

Hadrianus Finus, *In Judaeos flagellum*

Juan Luis Vives, *De veritate fidei christianae*

Andreas Osiander, *Ob es war und glaublish sey, dass die Juden der Christen kinder heymlich erwürgen und jr blut gebrauchen*

Johannes Eck, *Ains Judenbüchlins verlegung*

Martin Luther, *Letter to Spalatin; A Sermon on Usury; The Magnificat put into German and Expounded; That Christ was Born a Jew; Against the Sabbaths; The Jews and their Lies; Shem Hamphoras and the Generation of Christ; The Last Words of David; Admonition against the Jews*

Paul Fagius, *Liber fidei sue veritatis*

Sebastian Münster, *Wikuach, Christiani hominis cum Judaeo colloquium*

Francisco de Torres, *De sola lectione legis et prophetarum Judaeis cum Mosaico ritu et cultu permittenda*

Jean Calvin, *Ad quaestiones et obiecta Judaei cuiusdam responsio*

Georg Nigrinus, *Der Jüden Feindt*

Ernst Ferdinand Hess, *Juden-Geissel*

Julius Conrad Otto, *Gali razia, occultorum detectio*

Christian gerson, *Der Jüden Thalmud fürnembster Inhalt und Widerlegung*

Adrian von Emden, *Send und Warnungs-Brieff an alle Hartneckige und Halsstarrige Jüden*

Samuel Friedrich Brenz, *Jüdischer abgestreiffter Schlangen-Balg*

Dietrich Schwab, *Detectum velum Mosaicum Judaeorum nostri temporis*

Kyrilllos Lukaris, *Syntomos pragmateia kata Joudaion*

Johannes Stephan Rittangel, *Veritas religionis christianae*

Johann Müller, *Judaismus oder Jüdenthumb, Das ist Ausführlicher Bericht von des Jüdischen Volckes Unglauben, Blindtheit und Verstockung*

P.H.Friedlieb, *Die denen verstockten Jüden zugedeckte Göttliche Klarheit*

Johannes Buxtorf the Elder, *Juden-Schül (Synagoga Judaica)*

Isaac la Peyrère, *Du rappel des Juifs; Praeadamitae*

Paul Felgenhauer, *Bonum nuncium Israeli*

A.P.Kempe, *Israels erfreuliche Botschaft*

J.C.Wagenseil, *Dissertatio de loco classico Gen.XLIX, 10; Tela ignea Satanae; Belehrung der Jüdisch-Teutschen Red- und Schreibart; Benachrichtungen wegen einiger die Judenschafft angehenden wichtigen Sachen; Benachrichtungen wegen einiger die gemeine Jüdischeit betreffenden Sachen*

J.A.Eisenmenger, *Entdecktes Judenthum*

H. von der Hardt, *Paraenesis ad doctores Judaeos*

E.L.Roblik, *Jüdische Augengläser*

A.Rohling, *Der Talmudjude*

(b) Religious dialogues

Paris (1240)

Barcelona (1263)

Tortosa (1413–1414)

Poppelsdorf (1486)

Amsterdam (1642)
P.van Limborch and Orobio de Castro (1687)
Hanover (1704)
Lavater and Mendelssohn (1769–1770)
E.Rosenstock and Franz Rosenzweig (1913, 1916)
Stuttgart: K.L.Schmidt and M.Buber (January 1933)

(c) Texts by humanists, lawyers, philosophers, Orientalists; social-political and culture-political works

Eike von Repkow, *Sachsenspiegel*
Ulrich Zasius, *Questiones de parvulis Judeorum baptisandis*
Johannes Reuchlin, *Tütsch missive, warumb di Juden so lang im ellend sind; Augenspiegel*
Jean Bodin, *Colloquium heptaplomeres*
Hugo Grotius, *De veritate religionis christianae; De iure belli ac pacis*
Blaise Pascal, *Apologie de la religion chrétienne*
Schudt, *Jüdische Merkwürdigkeiten*
John Toland, *Reasons for Naturalizing the Jews in Great Britain and Ireland*
C.K.W.von Dohm, *Über die bürgerliche Verbesserung der Juden*
H.Gregoire, *Essai sur la régénération physique, morale et politique des Juifs*
Börne, *Für die Juden*
K.Marx, *The Jewish Question*
R.Wagner, *Judaism in Music*
A.de Gobineau, *Essai sur l'inégalité des races humaines*
Langbehn, *Rembrandt als Erzieher*
H.von Treitschke, *Ein Wort über unser Judentum*

(d) Poems, plays, legends, folk–tales and sagas, romances and novels

[Anonymous,] *La deputoison du juyf et du crestien*
Clopin, *La desputoison de la Sinagogue et de sainte Église*
Rutebeuf, *Le miracle de Théophile*
[Anonymous,] *Spiele von Mariae Himmelfahrt*
Barthel Regenbogen, *Die blinden Juden*
Matrfre Ermengaud, *Breviari d'amor*
[Anonymous,] *Spiel von der Zerstörung Jerusalems*
[Anonymous,] *Disputision by–twene a cristenmon and a Jew*

[Anonymous,] *Siege of Jerusalem (Vindicta Salvatoris)*
[Anonymous,] *Titus and Vespasian or the Destruction of Jerusalem*
[Anonymous,] *The Sege of Jerusaleme*
Chaucer, *The Prioress's Tale*
[Anonymous,] *Le Mystère de la Passion Nostre Seigneur (Le Debate entre la Synagogue et la Sainte Église)*
Eustrache Marcadé, *La Vengance de nostre Seigneur Jhesucrist sur les Juifs par Vespasien et Titus*
[Anonymous,] *La vengeance et destruction du Hierusalem par personnages, executée par Vespasien et son filz Titus*
[Anonymous,] *Die Jüdin und der Priester*
[Anonymous,] *Des Teufels Netz*
[Anonymous,] *Des Entchrist Vasnacht*
[Anonymous,] *Kaiser Karls Recht*
Michel Beheim, *Contra-Judaeos-Lieder*
Michel Miller, *Von einem Marienbilde*
Hans Folz, *Die alt und neu ee; Kaiser Constantinus; Christ und Jude; Der falsche Messias; Die Wahrsagebeeren; Ein spil von dem Herzogen von Burgund*
Thomas Murner, *Enderung und schmach der bildung Marie von den juden bewissen*
Marlowe, *The Famous Tragedy of the Rich Jew of Malta*
Shakespeare, *The Most Excellent Historie of the Merchant of Venice*
[Anonymous,] *Kurtze beschreibung und Erzehlung von einem Juden, mit Namen 'Ahasuerus'*
Lope de Vega, *Die Jüdin von Toledo*
K.B.A.Sessa, *Unser Verkehr*
Anonymous folk tales, sagas and legends: *The Jews in the Thornbush; The Eternal Jew on the Matterhorn; The Jew-Stone; The Girl Killed by Jews; The Forbidden Swine's Flesh; The Eternal Jew; Ahasuerus, The Eternal Jew; Execution of the Jew Pfefferkorn; Ritual Murder and Banishment; The Golem; The Jewish Caricature at Frankfurt; The Legend of the Swine's Flesh; Jew Süss; Schinderhannes Scarifies the Jews; The Abolition of the Noose*
Wilhelm Hauff, *Abner, der Jude der nichts gesehen hat; Jud Süss; Unterhaltungen des Satan und des ewigen Juden in Berlin*
A.von Droste-Hülshoff, *Die Judenbuche*
H.Heine, *Der Rabbi von Bacherach; Disputation*
Gustav Freytag, *Soll und Haben*